Europe's Untapped Capital Market

Europe's Untapped Capital Market

Rethinking financial integration after the crisis

Diego Valiante

With contributions from
Cosmina Amariei
and Jan-Martin Frie

Final Report of the
European Capital Markets Expert Group
Chaired by Francesco Papadia

Centre for European Policy Studies
European Capital Markets Institute
Brussels

Published by Rowman & Littlefield International, Ltd.
Unit A, Whitacre Mews, 26-34 Stannary Street, London SE11 4AB
www.rowmaninternational.com

Rowman & Littlefield International Ltd. is an affiliate of Rowman & Littlefield
4501 Forbes Boulevard, Suite 200, Lanham, Maryland 20706, USA
With additional offices in Boulder, New York, Toronto (Canada), and Plymouth (UK)
www.rowman.com

Centre for European Policy Studies
Place du Congrès 1, B-1000 Brussels
Tel: (32.2) 229.39.11
E-mail: info@ceps.eu
Website: http://www.ceps.eu

British Library Cataloguing in Publication Data
A catalogue record for this book is available from the British Library

ISBN: 978-1-78660-044-8

∞™ The paper used in this publication meets the minimum requirements of American National Standard for Information Sciences—Permanence of Paper for Printed Library Materials, ANSI/NISO Z39.48-1992.

Printed in the United States of America

This study is based on discussions held among the members of the European Capital Markets Expert Group (ECMEG), composed of academics and international experts. Additional meetings with the CEPS-ECMI Task Force, composed of experts from the industry, academics and policy-makers, were held to support the work of the ECMEG. Meetings were held on five occasions between December 2014 and May 2015.

The findings presented in this study do not necessarily reflect the views of all the members of ECMEG and the Task Force or the views of their respective companies. However, ECMEG members were involved during the drafting of the final report and provided input to the discussions through presentations and the provision of data and other materials, which have been used in this book. A set of principles has guided the entire drafting process to allow all of the interests represented in the Task Force to be heard.

The author, Diego Valiante, is solely responsible for its content and any errors. Neither the ECMEG members nor the Task Force members (or their respective companies) necessarily endorse the conclusions of this study.

Suggested citation: Diego Valiante (2016), *Europe's Untapped Capital Market: Rethinking financial integration after the crisis,* CEPS Paperback, London: Rowman & Littlefield International.

Table of Contents

List of Figures

List of Tables

List of Boxes

Foreword

The great financial crisis that hit Europe, along with other advanced economies, threw into relief a long-standing structural weakness of the European economy: the overreliance on its banking system. In the aftermath of the crisis, Europe's capital markets emerged even more clearly as underdeveloped compared to the sophistication and maturity of the European economy. This weakness manifested itself in two developments that aggravated the crisis. First, insufficient financial integration severely limited the ability of cross-border financial transactions to mutualise the shocks that, in particular in the euro area, eventually caused a persistent split between the 'core' and the 'periphery'. Second, as the banking system became unable to intermediate an adequate amount of funds at reasonable cost, the European economy encountered serious funding problems, with inevitably deleterious macroeconomic consequences.

The European Commission was thus right in identifying the need to develop a true Capital Market Union (CMU). CMU is an opportunity to relaunch financial integration, on a sounder footing, after the crisis. This project applies to the entire EU, but it assumes a special significance for the euro area. Together with banking union, it is a fundamental step towards building private risk-sharing and towards finishing what the Maastricht Treaty had left incomplete. The difficult experience in building Banking Union (BU), with its three components of single supervision, single resolution and single deposit guarantee, confirms that intellectual and practical difficulties emerge when moving from a general concept to implementation. The task is not made easier in the case of CMU by the fact that it differs from BU in that it takes a 'bottom-up' approach, which does not necessarily require a new institutional architecture.

This study offers a comprehensive overview of financial integration in Europe and a thorough assessment of the barriers that still hinder its realisation. It builds on the material collected in meetings of a dedicated group of experts (the European Capital Markets Expert Group, or ECMEG), which I had the pleasure and honour of chairing. The report also draws from an extensive literature review and data analysis assessing the benefits and risks of advancing a Capital Markets Union to boost a still imperfect single market for goods and services. The premise is that, if properly regulated and supervised, market forces will, in the pursuit of profits, lead to market integration, when the barriers standing in their way are removed, and ultimately to a more-efficient asset allocation, with more economic growth and jobs.

The study then suggests a methodology for identifying barriers and prioritising policy actions. The first differentiation is between 'artificial' and 'structural' barriers. Those of the former type are man-made impediments, such as different laws and regulations, which reduce or altogether eliminate incentives to cross-border financial transactions. Those of the latter type, such as language differences, are more difficult to deal with but are less numerous and do not really pose insuperable obstacles to the achievement of capital markets integration. The second important difference is between those barriers that affect the cost predictability of a financial transaction, and thus have a stronger negative effect, and those that increase the cost of cross-border transactions but in a predictable way. The policy conclusions proposed in the report prioritise actions that remove artificial barriers and generate unpredictable costs.

The sheer number of barriers shows the size and difficulty of achieving a genuine Capital Markets Union. But the more the project shows its complexity, the more crucial it is to address it with an organic and considered approach. This report hopes to contribute to this ambitious and necessary effort.

Francesco Papadia
Chairman of the European Capital Markets Expert Group (ECMEG)

Preface

In December 2014, ECMI and CEPS formed the European Capital Markets Expert Group (ECMEG) with the aim of providing a valuable contribution to the debate on the Capital Markets Union (CMU) project, proposed by the European Commission. Following a year of intensive, research and in-depth discussions with ECMEG members, this book aims to rethink financial integration policies in the European Union and to devise an EU-wide plan to remove the barriers to greater capital markets integration. In the aftermath of the financial crisis, the lack of risk diversification in the European financial system, resulting from limited cross-border banking and capital markets activities, is a key contributor to the retrenchment of capital flows within national boundaries. Europe needs private risk sharing mechanisms to withstand asymmetric shocks, such as the recent financial crisis. EU-wide action to promote competition among national capital markets could free up to €1.8 trillion in cash and deposits to invest cross-border in more profitable and riskier projects to create growth and jobs.

This study offers a methodology to identify and prioritise cross-border barriers to capital markets integration and provides a set of policy recommendations to improve its key components: price discovery, execution and enforcement. In particular, the evidence suggests that data comparability across European financial and non-financial firms, in areas like accounting or conflicts of interest, is very low. Less discretion and greater transparency of internal calculation methodologies for IFRS reporting and a centralised database for company filings and business registries are among its 33 policy recommendations. Tax and authorisation procedures are in some cases unnecessarily cumbersome or even discriminatory for foreign EU firms. Enforcement of rules and contracts is currently the weakest piece of Europe's financial system, as convergence relies on a handful of bodies that have limited powers and on a system of governance that does not protect the 'European interest'. This study calls upon the European Securities and Markets Authority (ESMA) to play a central role in the integration process, equipped with more binding powers to advance convergence in specific areas, such as accounting practices and licensing of UCITS and AIFs. ESMA would still rely on the network of national regulators, but with a more independent management, more shared competences and a specific list of entities under its direct supervision.

I wish to thank the Chairman of the ECMEG, Francesco Papadia, for his valuable input and guidance throughout the drafting of this study and during the meetings of the Group. I am very grateful to Cosmina Amariei and Jan-Martin Frie for their hard work in providing excellent research support, in particular for their extensive data gathering in chapters 3 and 4. I am also grateful to many other people at CEPS, but most importantly to Veselina Georgieva and Karin Lenk for their administrative support, as well as to Lee Gillette for editing the text and to Els Van den Broeck for formatting the manuscript.

This study has greatly benefited from the generous input of the ECMEG members (listed on the following page) and the Task Force members (listed in the annex) through their presentations and comments on earlier drafts. In particular, I would like to acknowledge the valuable comments received from Nicholas Dorn (University of London) Guido Ferrarini (Genoa University), Sam Holland (S&P), Andrei Kirilenko (Imperial College), Niamh Moloney (LSE), Marco Pagano (ESRB and Naples University) and participants at seminars at ESMA, ECB, LUISS University (SEP) and CEPS.

Diego Valiante
Head of Financial Markets and Institutions, CEPS
and Head of Research, ECMI

Members of the European Capital Markets Expert Group

CHAIRMAN

Francesco Papadia, Chairman of the Board, Prime Collateralised Securities (PCS)

RAPPORTEUR

Diego Valiante, Head of Financial Markets and Institutions, CEPS and Head of Research, ECMI

EXPERT GROUP

Franklin Allen, Executive Director, Brevan Howard Centre for Financial Analysis, Imperial College London

Thorsten Beck, Professor of Banking and Finance, Cass Business School in London

Olivier Beroud, Managing Director, Regional Head-EMEA, Moody's

Carmine Di Noia, Deputy Director General, Head of Capital Markets, Assonime

Mark Hemsley, CEO, BATS Chi-X Europe

Marco Lamandini, Professor of Company and Securities Law, University of Bologna

Karel Lannoo, Chief Executive, CEPS and General Manager, ECMI

Christian Leuz, Joseph Sondheimer Professor of International Economics, Finance and Accounting, University of Chicago's Booth School of Business

Florencio Lopez de Silanes, Professor of Finance and Law, EDHEC Business School

Paolo Manasse, Professor of Economics, Università di Bologna

Donato Masciandaro, Professor of Economics, Chair in Economics of Financial Regulation, Head, Department of Economics, Director, Baffi Center on International Markets, Money and Regulation, Bocconi University

Barbara C. Matthews, Managing Director, BCM International Regulatory Analytics LLC

Russell Schofield-Bezer, EMEA Head of Debt Capital Markets and Corporate Treasury Solutions, HSBC Holdings

Nicolas Véron, Senior Fellow, Bruegel and Member of the Scientific Advisory Board, Autorité des Marchés Financiers

Eddy Wymeersch, Emeritus Professor of Commercial Law, University of Ghent, Chairman of the Public Interest Oversight Board, Independent Director at AFME and Euroclear SA

Executive Summary

I. Building Europe's capital market: Guidelines for an action plan

- This report builds upon an intensive year-long research effort, enriched and guided by discussions within a group of experts, the **European Capital Markets Expert Group (ECMEG)**, composed of stakeholders, academics, policy-makers and industry experts. The aim of this report is to contribute to the debate at the EU and international level on what kind of Capital Markets Union (CMU) Europe needs.
- The report offers a **comprehensive overview of the current state of financial integration** in Europe and an assessment of major barriers to further capital market integration.
- **More integrated European capital markets** have been a long-awaited outcome of European policies, to ensure greater financial stability and sufficient funding for EU firms competing in a global economy. Financial integration stimulates further financial development, which can ultimately advance economic development and thus produce more growth and jobs.
- The lack of **cross-sectional risk sharing** in Europe is the main source of the recent retrenchment of capital flows due to the crisis, after flooding with credit southern European countries in past years. Financial fragmentation is now an important contributor to the growing funding gap for companies at an early stage of development that are in need of fast liquidity injections, and for mid-sized fast-growing companies that are looking for cheap and stable (equity or debt) funding opportunities to expand their business activity.
- Improving the quality of the financial integration process is a core aim of the Capital Markets Union project, which should thus promote the removal of legal and economic barriers to the free movement of capital and financial services in order to create a complementary **EU-wide, cross-border private risk sharing mechanism** to support the public ones.
- While **CMU and Banking Union** aim at more private risk sharing, they differ in some respects. In particular, CMU may not necessarily require the creation of new institutions and public risk sharing mechanisms, such as a common fiscal backstop for bank deposits. The CMU plan should entail a set of reforms to reorganise and strengthen the current institutional framework and to remove major **economic and legal barriers,** so to leave to the **single market** the decision if Europe needs 28 equity markets. Unlike Banking Union, there is no emergency in the financial system that

requires an immediate policy answer. CMU can be spread over the years, but with a **detailed and firm timeline, as well as measurable objectives,** to ensure certainty.

Methodology for the barrier removal test

- Due to the nature of a financial claim in a market environment with dispersed monitoring, the **legal system** (calibrated for investor protection) is a cornerstone for public and private remedies to support a solid financial integration process. A weak legal system does not yield deep capital markets.
- Indeed, as **financial sophistication** increases, there is a pressing need for a more effective system of rules and an informational infrastructure (disclosure rules) in order for market mechanisms to complement bank lending and create a financial ecosystem that is conducive to a more diversified resource allocation (private risk sharing).
- Both financial institutions and markets face **specification costs** (ex ante) and **monitoring costs** (ex post), due to the inability to write the 'perfect contract' or to opportunism.
- To deal with information asymmetry, which creates moral hazard and contract incompleteness, financial contracting in market-based systems requires public information collected and re-elaborated by third parties, on top of private information. This can happen alternatively via **contracting or renegotiation**. 'Contracting' is the process leading the investor to enter a financial transaction after using all the information available to price the product and the credit risk of the counterparty (pre-investment). 'Renegotiation' is the process of redefining the terms of a financial contract, via contractual negotiation, or exiting a financial transaction, via a sale in the secondary market, before the end of the contract (post-investment).
- The **financial contracting approach** to identify and classify barriers on the basis of their harm to cross-border trading reduces discretionary actions and increases measurability against well-defined objectives. It also helps to draw a line between measures that require harmonisation and areas that can be left to regulatory competition among member states.
- Contracting and renegotiation take place via three key components: price discovery, execution and enforcement.
    - **Price discovery** is the process of 'discovering' the market price that is the closest approximation to the reserve value of the investor, considering his/her assessment of counterparty risk or of the value of the underlying asset at that moment in time.
    - **Execution** is the set of procedures that are involved in the execution of financial transactions taking place with the contracting or renegotiation phase. This includes market entry and exit requirements.

- **Enforcement** is the process of ensuring the smooth performance or renegotiation of a financial contract, i.e. the enforcement of private contracts, including minority shareholders, retail investors and creditors' rights.

- A **'barrier'** can be defined as any domestic or European rule (law), (market and supervisory) practice or procedure that impedes data comparability (price discovery), fairness of procedures (execution) and legal certainty (enforcement) in the contracting or renegotiation phases of a financial transaction. Barriers can be artificial (exogenous to the transaction) or structural (embedded in the transaction), as well as domestic or cross-border (or both).

Cost predictability in cross-border market-based financial contracting

Functions	Output	Cost predictability
Price discovery	Data	Comparability
Execution	Entry/exit requirements	Fairness
Enforcement	Rules & procedures	Certainty

- Barriers are most harmful when they make the costs of a financial transaction **unpredictable**. The more unpredictable costs become, the more negative the impact will these barriers have on financial contracting. In effect, at the core of every market-based financial transaction is the ability to discount **future cash flows**. The less is the information about direct and indirect costs of the transaction that may affect future cash flows, the lower is the ability to discount future scenarios. Once discounting is impaired, the financial transaction will most likely not take place.

Measurability

- **Measurability of objectives** plays an important role for the success of a financial integration plan like CMU, as it ensures accountability. With no accountability, the political support to achieve the objectives of this complex project would most likely fade away. As a consequence, we can identify three measurable objectives:

  a. Improving **data comparability** about underlying assets and financial instruments;
  b. Reducing discrimination in **market entry and exit**; and
  c. Increasing **legal certainty and accessibility** of public and private **enforcement** mechanisms.

These ideas are further developed in sections 4.3 and 4.4.

Policy recommendations

The **objective of the CMU action plan** should be the gradual removal of economic and legal barriers to the creation of a more diversified financial ecosystem that favours cross-sectional and cross-country risk sharing via capital markets.

This report does not offer an exhaustive list of barriers, but rather offers a selection of them and a methodology with which to identify and prioritise intervention, on the basis of their impact on the cost predictability of a financial transaction.

Working groups of experts at European and domestic level should then work to home in on the identified areas to investigate those barriers and survey the outstanding practices by public or private entities that are most damaging to the single market for capital. The proposed methodology also helps to identify areas in which an immediate 'top-down' policy response is necessary, supporting the 'bottom-up approach' proposed by the European Commission.

The following sections list the **33 policy recommendations** included in the report and the cross-border barriers that the recommendations will try to tackle. In accordance with the summary table at the end, the type of barrier also defines the urgency of the policy interventions that are suggested in the following sections.

Price discovery

Due to a multitude of agents and information asymmetry, market-based mechanisms require information, which is reflected in prices and disclosed by third parties (trading venues, data providers and so on). **Information disclosure** allows ex-ante pricing (contracting) and ex-post renegotiation (exit on secondary markets or via private enforcement mechanisms) by signalling the relevant information to price risk and fill the informational gap between counterparties.

Europe currently lacks **a common informational infrastructure**. Low comparability of company (financial and non-financial) data and credit risk information is a fundamental barrier to the creation of a pan-European price discovery process (and risk evaluation). Internal risk assessment methodologies are currently a source of concern in cross-border transactions for both listed and unlisted companies. Moreover, there is still a lack of data about conflicts of interest, including data on ownership and related-party transactions, especially for unlisted companies. This kind of information is crucial to build assumptions about future cash flows and so allow discounting and efficient pricing of financial instruments.

Information on the underlying asset

1) *IFRS calculation methodology (Barrier 1).* The options available for IFRS **asset evaluation methodologies** should be tightened, with more detailed definitions and a harmonised approach among EU supervisory practices. A 'comply-or-explain' regime could apply to the calculation methodology, in case a tailored approach is necessary to improve accounting quality. In the new IFRS 9, for instance, the loan impairment requirement, dealing with the recognition of lifetime losses on loans in case of a "significant increase in credit risk" since initial recognition, leaves the key terminology undefined.

2) *IFRS reclassification (Barrier 4).* Under IFRS, more discretion can be given to the firm on the **reclassification** of balance sheet items because this option still allows the investor to replicate the reclassification of the items according to established methodologies available to the public (and so make proper use of this information). However, different reclassifications for civil and taxation purposes remains a source of cost and uncertainty, as local fiscal authorities often apply different interpretations. EU institutions should work closer with local fiscal authorities to streamline this process and perhaps define ex ante the classifications under uniform accounting rules to be used for fiscal purposes and allow bilateral case-by-case examination when alternatives can be used. The work of the European Commission on a **Common Consolidated Corporate Tax Base (CCCTB**) can be instrumental to the simplification and alignment of reporting for accounting and fiscal purposes.

3) *Alternative performance measures (Barrier 5).* Allowing **alternative performance measures**, which 'adjust' IFRS figures according to internal models for publication purposes, can create uncertainty or even misleading communication. For instance, 21 companies of the FTSE 100 treated restructuring costs as "exceptional" (for their own adjusted profits), even though they were reported for four consecutive years. Tighter supervision of practices and greater transparency with an explanatory note on how and why the firms use it might be an improvement for data comparability. The inclusion in the financial statements, under audit assurance, might be an easier option.

4) *Off-balance sheet items (Barrier 11).* There should be detailed criteria or full transparency of methodology to define the likelihood of an outflow "probable", with probability above 50%, for **'off-balance sheet' items**, such as contingent liabilities or guarantees. In countries where the regulatory system is stronger and voluntary disclosure higher, there is a general trend to provide more information about these items. Cross-border data comparability of these items is severely impaired.

5) *Listed companies' filings (Barrier 3).* As the US SEC does with EDGAR, ESMA could be also given the role to directly collect **company filings for listed companies** with a standardised format and made easily accessible across Europe via a common

repository. ESMA would also coordinate with member states if there is additional information requested by national laws and try to act to limit this additional flow or to standardise formats and report timing as much as possible.

6) *European business registry (Barrier 7).* There is also no **European registry** to disseminate basic information about private corporations. There are currently 28 national registers, which are often very costly and opaque, charging firms when they deposit information and data users when they collect it, applying different standards and procedures across countries. General information about a company should be easily accessible to the public at a reasonable cost or even for free. National repositories should be linked to each other with common search tools and data standards to reduce problems with data comparability. As a result, the creation of a European business register should be further encouraged and supported at European level. This coordination role could be given either to ESMA or to the European Commission.

7) *Central database (Barriers 3 & 7).* The **centralisation**, under a common database, of official **company filings** for listed companies and information collected by national business **registries about all private companies** could be an important innovation and provide a significant boost to the adoption of common practices for data disclosure and improve cross-border data comparability. The benefits of this simplification would trickle down to investors and in particular companies, both domestic and international, which will deal with one entity only under a transparent and fair procedural framework.

8) *Accounting standards for unlisted companies (Barrier 2).* **Accounting standards for private (unlisted) companies**, including SMEs or subsidiaries of multinational companies, would provide high data comparability and a common set of information to compare firms and sectors across borders. The integration of consolidated and individual annual accounts with the EU Directive 2013/34 is an initial step towards a common set of standards for unlisted companies, which takes into account the size of the firm. Nonetheless, more should be done to align the framework of accounting rules with the IFRS for SMEs and, most important, to reduce the options given to member states and achieve greater convergence of accounting practices. To ensure consistency and proportionality, finally, the application of IFRS standards to listed companies (now used for consolidated accounts) should be expanded to annual accounts.

9) *Credit information (Barrier 8).* As of today, there are no common guidelines for **credit scoring** (including the definition of 'defaulted exposure'), **and credit risk information** is stored in national credit bureaus that are not linked to each other. To promote convergence, an initial step could connect the national credit bureaus in Europe via a network that would facilitate cross-border access to credit scores with a

centralised infrastructure. This first step could benefit from ongoing initiatives, such as the one run by the ECB (Anacredit), under EBA supervision. A second step would promote a gradual convergence of credit score methodologies under the direction of a common body, such as the European Banking Authority, with the support of the European Commission and the ECB.

10) *Related party transactions (Barrier 9).* Rules on **related party transactions** (included in IAS 24) are particularly complex and designed to allow significant flexibility. They apply to all IFRS reporters (listed companies). However, several key definitions are left to the local regulator, such as the definition of "control" or of the person who can have a significant influence on the company. The possibility to use different definitions should be coped with a comply-or-explain regime.

These ideas are further developed in section 4.5.1

Financial Instruments information

11) *Key Information Document (Barrier 15).* The implementation of the **Key Information Document (KID)** for all the other packaged retail and insurance-based investment products (PRIIPs) should be closely monitored to avoid new barriers to data comparability between UCITS issued in different countries or UCITS and non-UCITS PRIIPs. At a minimum, information should be collected and classified in the same way and in same formats. Moreover, KID requirements could be extended to all types of retail investment products (especially long-term ones) offered by pension funds, insurance companies and banks, in order to standardise different disclosure requirements that are applied by domestic authorities (often rather opaque).

12) *Listing authority (Barrier 16).* On top of the monopolistic rent, **national fragmentation of equity markets** inhibits market liquidity because it increases the informational rent of informed investors, who can pay to access multiple exchanges, and prevents investors from benefitting from the positive network effects (market externalities) brought about by each additional market participant. The costs of fragmentation are a barrier to a truly consolidated pre-trade European Best and Bid Offer (EBBO). MiFID II should overcome some format issues via the direct licensing requirements for data providers (including trading venues), but the consolidation of the financial infrastructure depends on multiple factors, including competition policies. AS a consequence, due to this cross-border nature, ESMA could become the listing authority of a basket of the most liquid share (European blue chips), using the network of national supervisors and ensuring that its binding supervision ensures greater convergence of practices. More should be done as well to identify and remove the bias in national laws towards the nationality of the regulated market where listing of the security takes place, which should be extended to any member state of the European Union where the venue has been authorised to operate.

13) *Ongoing performance disclosure (Barrier 12).* **Ongoing performance disclosure** might help to create sectorial performance indicators. Periodic disclosure of performance for investment funds, benchmarking it with the sector, can be a great incentive for investing in cross-border investment products. A standardised template about ongoing performance disclosure during the lifetime of the investment product and disclosure of exit conditions could be proposed. Ongoing contractual information is currently very fragmented, which increases the costs of cross-border investments due to limited comparability. Policy action should also include all products performing similar functions, like life insurance products wrapping collective funding schemes.

These ideas are further developed in section 4.5.2.

Execution

- Cross-border barriers to the **accessibility of financial contracting and renegotiation** are difficult to spot and are often entrenched in the domestic legal system, as well as in the regular practices of local authorities or incumbent market participants (e.g. the static implementation of execution policies).
- Transparency and simplification should be the guiding principle to ensure that entry and exit procedures are fair and do not add unnecessary costs to cross-border transactions.

Entry procedures

14) *NCA's filing procedures and quality standards (Barrier 19 & 21).* There are several differences in the **filing process for UCITS** at national level, including registration fees, which make procedures more burdensome for cross-border service providers. These aspects could be left to regulatory competition in the presence of a uniform regulatory environment for the marketing of investment products that does not leave pockets of uncertainty over costs. A review of registration procedures, nonetheless, may be necessary to understand whether different quality standards for supervision hide behind those differences.

15) *Marketing rules (Barrier 19).* The fragmentation of rules and procedures for the **marketing of investment products** keeps distribution channels fairly different across EU member states. A review of marketing rules to ensure no discrimination between foreign and local distributors, together with rules to improve transparency of products (as discussed above), would provide a tool to open up distribution channels and increase choice and returns for end investors.

16) *Open access (Barrier 19).* There should be constant monitoring of the procedures set up by domestic financial authorities to resolve disputes about the application of **open access requirements** for non-domestic market infrastructures. ESMA might

need more binding powers in the mediation of the implementation of open access requirements locally, if the national authority does not sufficiently justify the decision related to an access request.

17) *Execution policies (Barrier 17).* The static implementation of **execution policies** leaves too much discretion at the intermediary level, as conditions related to costs of execution remain vaguely defined. MiFID II attempts to improve the quality of execution policies, but a more uniform cross-country implementation of current policies is even more important. In particular, execution policies to retail investors should be more dynamic, with a binding annual revision, more specific conditions for the identification of a 'material change' that triggers the revision and the possibility for investors to easily compare policies with the use of standard formats.

18) *Taxation arrangements (Barriers 18 & 23).* There are currently situations in which investment funds are treated differently by fiscal authorities according to their nationality, with the application of different tax rates on dividends (for instance). The European Commission should review all current **taxation arrangements at national level** and monitor their development over time.

These ideas are further developed in section 4.6.1.

Exit procedures

19) *Withholding tax reclaim (Barrier 23).* Procedures for **withholding a tax reclaim** are a significant cost to cross-border trading activities, estimated at roughly €8.4 billion per year. While capped to the value of the tax to be refunded, this is a cost that is simply transferred on to end investors, with limited benefit for integration. Building upon the work of the European Commission and the OECD, policy action should focus on: electronic processing and standardisation of formats; recognition of power of attorney and self-declaration of residence, together with a memorandum of understanding among national fiscal agencies for data sharing on fiscal residence and tax reporting with a common identification system. These actions should ultimately create conditions for **relief-at-source as the default procedure**.

20) *Exit rights disclosure (Barrier 24).* **Availability and disclosure of exit rights** are important aspects for a financial transaction, especially for investment products. There is currently no harmonised regime concerning the disclosure of such information, which is usually left to patchy national requirements.

These ideas are further developed in section 4.6.2.

Enforcement

- **A sound legal architecture and the enforcement infrastructure** are essential for the development of market-based mechanisms in an environment with dispersed agents and dispersed information provided by third parties. The evidence suggests that EU directives produced intended (positive) effects mainly where they were implemented more strictly.

- **Uncertainty of enforcement proceedings**, in effect, may produce a lack of enforcement and impact the cost predictability of a cross-border financial transaction, reducing ex-ante incentives to enter into a contract in the first place. Unclear obligations for the counterparties may signal weak enforcement and can also lead to more misconduct.
- Enforcement includes all public and private measures to ensure a **credible deterrence of misconduct** and so the smooth performance or renegotiation of a financial contract. The ex-ante incentives that a good enforcement mechanism provides are crucial for contracting in a cross-border setting with multiple jurisdictions and legal systems.
- Moreover, public enforcement authorities typically set the legal sanctions via regulation, but private enforcers can actually impose significant direct sanctions via the judicial system, e.g. class litigation, and indirect sanctions by preventing the wrongdoer from raising funds in the future (reputational mechanisms). Comparatively, private remedies are more important for institution-based systems, while public remedies are more effective for market-based systems. This observation points to the importance of two key components: **a punitive system of sanctions and a well-functioning and flexible judicial system**.
- **Public enforcement** encompasses the supervisory architecture (including powers of intervention, governance, information sharing and other regulatory practices), the sanctioning regime and the architecture of the legal system, e.g. securities law and judicial system.
- **Private enforcement** mechanisms include: gatekeepers' supervision (including liability), insolvency proceedings, private settlements, functioning of courts (e.g. choice-of-law regime), and whistle blower programmes and other redress procedures (e.g. class action suits, minority shareholders' rights).

Public enforcement

21) *Breach of EU law and ESMA top management appointment (Barrier 28).* The procedure of Article 17 of the ESMA Regulation on the possibility to act against a **breach of EU law** by a member state has never been used to date because of the conflicts in the governance of the authority between the Board of Supervisors (BoS) and ESMA's top management. ESMA's credibility to tackle national decisions and promote supervisory convergence in a cross-border setting with national gold-plating of EU laws is at stake. A more independent action of ESMA's top management is crucial. Either the approval of the recommendation under Article 17 (to start the

procedure) or directly the **appointment of the top management** (or both) should be given to an external body such as the European Commission or the European Parliament, which could then directly choose ESMA's top management.

22) *Independent components in BoS (Barrier 28).* Overall, there is a need to strengthen the **EU-wide interests** in ESMA's decision-making process. In this respect, it would help to reinforce the management board with additional independent components (nominated by the European Commission), and to give them voting rights in the Board of Supervisors, which would ensure that the EU-wide interest leads the decision-making process.

23) *Direct supervision (shared competences with NCAs; Barriers 1, 2, 3, 4, 7, 14, 16, 21, 22, 28, 29).* Evidence discussed in the report suggests that the enforcement of EU legislation is weak. **ESMA's direct supervision in well-defined areas** to support regulatory and supervisory convergence can be strengthened in different ways. One of the following three options, to be implemented with a 'phased-in' timeline, could be considered:

    a. Make ESMA responsible for the direct supervision of all EU listed companies,
    b. Make ESMA responsible for the direct supervision of all the firms that will be classified as 'cross-border' (either listed-only or both listed and unlisted companies)[1] and
    c. Allow an entity, when applying for an EU passport, to opt into ESMA supervision.

24) *Areas of supervision (Barriers 1, 2, 3, 4, 7, 14, 16, 21, 22, 28, 29).* The **'well-defined areas'** where ESMA will exercise its **direct supervision** will be in reality part of a joint supervisory framework, through colleges of supervisors, with ESMA acting with voting rights and issuing binding decisions for NCAs as part of the ESMA network. ESMA could already take up the role of direct supervisor in the following areas:

    a. Accounting rules and practices for listed companies (IFRS) and for unlisted companies (if common EU principles will be harmonised);
    b. Supervision and collection of listed company filings, with responsibility over the harmonisation of timing and formats;
    c. Coordination of the national business registries;
    d. Listing authority of firms that want to cross-list in an EU country different from where their legal headquarters are located;
    e. Licensing and ongoing supervision of UCITS and AIFs;
    f. Prospectus issuance approval and monitoring; and
    g. Licensing procedures of the EU passport granted by NCAs, and the power to revoke the license.

---

[1] A 'cross-border' firm could be any legal entity with legal headquarters and operations in a different EU country.

ESMA's decision in these areas, with the approval of the Board of Supervisors, would become binding for NCAs and be directly enforced by them, so the new supervisory architecture would still rely heavily on the current network and resources of national authorities. The decision-making arrangements of the main body issuing decisions within the SSM or the new European Deposit Insurance Scheme could offer a good benchmark of governance to start negotiations.

25) *Exclusive competence for selected entities.* Beyond credit rating agencies and trade repositories, the **exclusive competence** of ESMA could be extended to other entities such as data providers (under MiFID II), benchmark providers, trading venues, central securities depositories, auditors (via more binding powers over the committee of national auditing oversight bodies, for instance) and central counterparties (CCPs), which are the backbone of a pan-European market architecture.

26) *Due process (Barrier 30).* Recent jurisprudence, such as SV Capital vs. EBA or Grande Stevens et al. vs. Italy, have emphasised the importance of ensuring an adequate judicial review (**due process**) of the ESAs' decisions in order to strengthen their decision-making power and credibility, and to protect human rights. ESMA's decision should be subject to a fair trial, run by an independent tribunal that has full jurisdiction over the case (and not an internal body of the authority), with the possibility for the defendant to exercise his/her right to be heard in a public hearing.

27) *A pan-European consumer agency (Barrier 29).* A **pan-European consumer agency** that provides unified supervision in matters of consumer protection is one of the missing pieces of the European institutional architecture and is in the spirit of the post-crisis financial reforms. There is no integrated capital market without retail markets integration, and national consumer laws protect the current fragmentation of retail service providers. A dedicated agency would provide support for a more coherent implementation of national consumer laws and limit the proliferation of local supervisory approaches, offering more tools for investor protection with stronger monitoring and easier access to private enforcement tools against harmful practices. This agency could be set up under the management and control of ESMA, falling under its broad mandate of protecting investors and consumers of investment services. Nonetheless, a pan-European consumer agency can only achieve meaningful results if sufficient resources to deal with the cross-border nature of its regulatory and supervisory activities are provided.

28) *Sanctions (Barrier 30).* **Sanctions** are also another area of divergence across member states. Combined with passporting of financial services, the wide variety of sanctioning regimes (going from administrative sanctions to criminal charges) found among member states is a source of significant regulatory and supervisory arbitrage that can discourage cross-border trading activities and service provision. An accurate

separation between criminal and administrative charges should be taken into account when further harmonising sanctioning powers.

29) *Securities law (Barrier 25, 26 & 27).* **Securities law** provides the essential toolkit for public enforcement of a financial contract. It embodies the necessary legal architecture to recognise and apply contractual terms in financial transactions. Uncertainty over the legal terms of a financial transaction creates significant entry barriers in a cross-border setting. Limited recognition, across EU countries, of 'good faith' acquisition can produce cross-border barriers and hamper collateral fungibility. There should be a clear recognition that the registration of the security in the account of the CSD is the decisive moment when the legal transfer takes place. In addition, the conflict-of-laws regime in the FCD (Article 9) could be extended to all other acquisition or disposition of securities.

Private enforcement

30) *Gatekeepers' supervision (Barrier 35).* Divergence of supervisory practices in relation to gatekeepers (entry and ongoing requirements) might result in distrust among supervisors relating to the quality of their information and action, and thus may raise costs for end investors. In this respect, the decision to assign exclusive competence to ESMA for credit rating agencies would be an important precedent for **extending the competence to other gatekeepers,** such as auditors, in line with the objective of strengthening supervisory convergence on accounting standards.

31) *Functioning of courts.* The quality of the judicial system across European countries is on average very low, compared to other advanced economies such as Japan and the United States. Investments might be necessary to improve the functioning of courts across Europe. If cross-countries divergences do not come down, there should be a gradual introduction of a **system of European courts,** with branches in every member state and dedicated to cross-border financial transactions in specific areas to be identified in insolvency proceedings and/or enforcement of private contracts, could be an important step forward. Domestic financial transactions would still be run under local proceedings, with the possibility to opt into the EU system in very specific situations.

32) *Insolvency proceedings (Barriers 31, 32, 33 & 34).* Current insolvency proceedings, even after the recent reform, still create cost unpredictability in a cross-border setting. **Secondary proceedings** are still too cumbersome and leave a great deal of uncertainty, as the court of the country of establishment may tend to be excessively conservative in its attempt to protect local creditors under local laws (as history tells us). Perhaps, as requested for the conflict-of-law in the opening of the main insolvency proceeding, a more neutral venue, such as a European court (with the creation of a dedicated arm), could assess the need to open a secondary proceeding

in the country of establishment. For instance, the situations in which the interests of the local creditor may be affected could be further specified in a positive list (whatever is not in the list shall not be considered a justification for opening the secondary proceeding). Another source of potential uncertainty comes from the use of **stays**. An automatic stay when the proceedings begin, rather than the current patchy framework across Europe, may be preferable. Stays on request could be more clearly regulated with criteria that are as objective as possible. Finally, the standard conflict of law system relies on the principle that the proceeding will be opened in the **Centre of Main Interest (COMI)** of the debtor (*lex concursus*). For individuals, the regulation refers to the 'habitual residence' of the individual without further specifying how 'habitual residence' shall be defined. The uncertainty about the COMI presumption for individuals can still be a source of cross-border litigation in insolvency proceedings, after the new rules enter into force in 2017. It may be preferable to have a centralised European court where such decisions can be subject to appeal. Alternatively, the law could provide for European courts to directly resolve matters of where to open proceedings, with a contractual clause signed ex ante.

33) *European alternative dispute resolution (ADR) system and ombudsman service (Barrier 36).* Access to ADRs is still very cumbersome in some countries and certainly in a cross-border setting. The current FIN-NET solution is inadequate for the proportions and complexity of cross-border capital markets activities. As a consequence, it may be beneficial to strengthen, on the one hand, the quality of ADR procedures across member states, which were first introduced by the Directive 2013/11 on alternative dispute resolution for consumer disputes. On the other hand, a bolder action is required to create an EU-wide 'Financial Ombudsman Service', which could be run by a dedicated infrastructure under the current European Ombudsman Service and Network, acting as a single point of contact for users of financial services. This European Ombudsman, through the use of the Ombudsman network, would collect and run a first screening of the complaints regarding the cross-border provision of financial services, which may involve a local broker and a foreign service provider (FSP). Once the validity of the complaint is confirmed, the EU body would connect the national ombudsmen that are involved and offer mediation in defining which of the two national authorities shall take the initiative first, in relation to whether action will be taken against the local broker or the FSP. The FSP may also provide services directly in the country, in which case the EU 'ombudsman' will directly contact the home authority and make sure that the procedure begins and the results or request for information are communicated to the user.

These policy recommendations are further developed in chapter 4.

II. Financial integration policies: A historical overview

- EU policies aimed at capital markets integration go back more than half a century. Since 1957, these policies have evolved over **three major phases,** each spanning roughly 20 years and driven by major political and economic events.

Building blocks of European policies for financial integration

	Political trigger	Period	Integration process	Legal principles
First wave	Post-World War II reconstruction	Late 1950s – late 1970s	✓ Gradual removal of capital restrictions	Non-discrimination
Second wave	Post-end of Bretton Woods crises and end of the Cold War	Early 1980s – mid-2000s	✓ Policy coordination ✓ Mutual recognition (passporting) ✓ Minimum harmonisation	Equivalence
Third wave	Financial globalisation and EMU incompleteness	Late 2000s – to present	✓ Institutional convergence ✓ Single Rulebook ✓ Removal of cross-border barriers	Enhanced subsidiarity

Source: Author.

- Until the recent financial crisis, **mutual recognition (with home country control)** was the main tool used to promote integration among Europe's capital markets. It was at the core of five key post-EU Single Act Directives, such the Second Banking Directive (SBD) and the Investment Services Directive (ISD), and several other measures under the Financial Services Action Plan (FSAP).

- Nonetheless, the recent financial crisis has exposed important failures of the multilateral model of mutual recognition to amalgamate member states' national interests with the ultimate objective of fostering the European single market. After the de Larosière Report and the Banking Union initiative, in particular, a **strengthened subsidiarity principle** is currently trying to push for more supervisory convergence across Europe.

- New European bodies have been created with stronger legal powers to replace previous committees and to ensure the effective removal of non-tariff barriers to the free movement of capital and services and to secure the stability of the European financial system. However, the role of the **'new' European Supervisory Agencies (ESAs)**, created without a change of the European Treaties, has been focused so far on defining the implementing details (level 2) of EU regulations, but they have produced limited results in the coordination of supervisory practices.

- The Capital Markets Union (CMU) plan combines measures for the **deepening of the single market for capital** with efforts at tackling structural issues in financial markets, such as access by SMEs to market-based finance, suggests that the current CMU plan is a combination of integration, investment and financial stability policies. While it is certainly a commendable objective to act on all these policies, this way of planning may further complicate the implementation process, as the **ability to measure the achievement of objectives (accountability)** is diluted by the fact that these policies may result in conflicting outcomes.

- Hence, the CMU plan should only focus on integration policies and leave investment and financial stability policies to separate policy actions. This plan is an opportunity to **rethink financial integration** in Europe in order to produce a financial ecosystem that balances cross-border traditional banking with capital markets activities and, most notably, produces a pan-European financial architecture to the single market that can stand strong in the global financial system by integrating and putting in competition national markets for the benefit of investors and companies. The convergence of supervisory practices is an important step in this process.

These ideas are further developed in chapter 1.

III. Financial integration, risk sharing and economic growth

- The organisation of the financial system, however, is a complex **interaction of legal norms** (including investor protection) **and economic incentives** that shape the behaviour of institutions and investors. General legal principles, such as the right of establishment and free movement of capital and services, are not sufficient conditions to ensure high-quality financial integration, i.e. sound risk diversification.
- **Financial integration** is the process through which different regions or countries become more financially interconnected, ultimately producing **risk sharing** (cross-border asset holdings) to withstand a shock, like the recent financial crisis. The integration process involves the free circulation of capital and financial services to allow cross-border holdings of assets (private risk sharing), which would determine an increase in capital flows across these regions and a convergence of prices and returns on financial assets and services. Price convergence, without cross-border trading activities and holdings of assets (private risk sharing), is a broken promise of financial integration, leading to fragmentation and capital retrenchment when aggregate risk sharply rise.
- **Financial development** can be defined as the size and sophistication (interconnection) of a given combination of institution-based and market-based intermediation. **Financial structure** is then a given combination of credit and equity (funding types) by intermediaries and markets (funding means). A given **combination of financial structure and development** determines the quality of financial integration, which can produce a more efficient allocation of capital (via private risk sharing) and so unleashes further economic development and ultimately growth.

Financial development and integration channels to economic growth

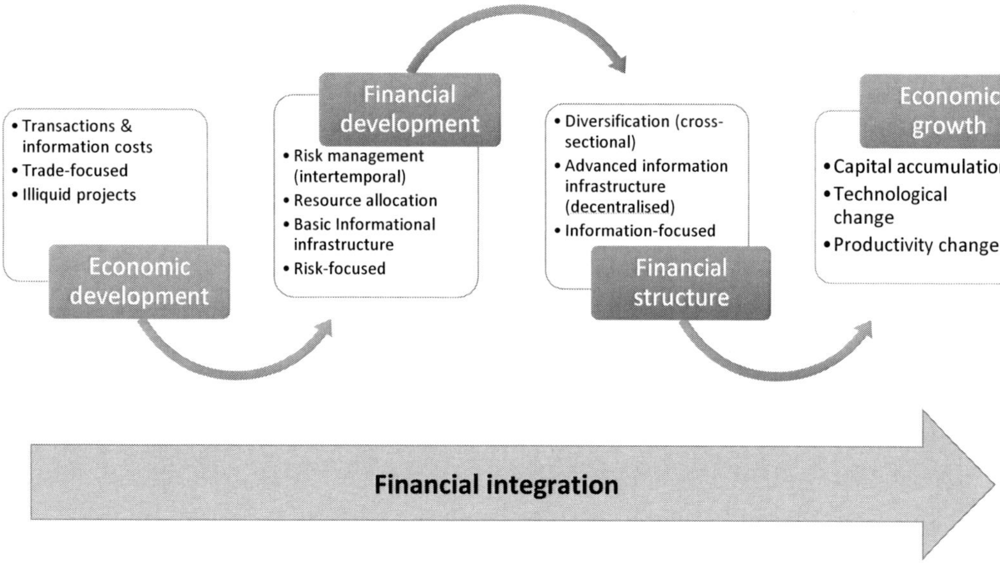

- **Risk diversification** is at the core of any integration process. Relationship-based (or institution-based) finance, e.g. traditional banking, and market-based finance, e.g. capital markets, can improve together the quality of financial integration and can create a **financial ecosystem** that limits the concentration of capital flows and thereby reduces the risks of asset bubbles and a permanent loss of productivity.
- Nonetheless, the growth of the financial sector should be continuously monitored. As the financial sector grows and increase availability of credit, entrepreneurs tend to invest more in low-productivity projects with returns that are relatively easier to pledge. High-productivity projects are typically less tangible and more difficult to pledge. Therefore, beyond a certain threshold, there is a **negative relationship** between the size of the financial sector (and in particular private-debt growth) and **economic growth**. A balanced financial ecosystem would prevent the unsustainable growth of individual pieces of the financial system to drive growth for the entire sector, as the traditional banking sector did in Europe.

These ideas are further developed in chapter 2.

IV. Rationale for more capital markets integration

Risk sharing

- Financial integration, measured as the law of one price (LoP), may only be the result of a temporary convergence in risk. **Private risk sharing,** cross-border holdings of assets, and the **composition of cross-border capital flows** are even more important for financial integration policies. The free movement of capital is beneficial only if the composition of these flows is well balanced. Comparative evidence with other financially integrated regions across the world suggests that Europe needs rebalancing from cross-border (interbank) debt to more **equity and FDI contributions** (with measures like the removal of the debt/equity bias in laws and taxation).

- **Cross-sectional** (horizontal in space, i.e. market-based) **and intertemporal** (vertical in time, i.e. institution-based like traditional banking) **risk sharing** are complementary, as they provide respectively a cushion against both aggregate (permanent shocks, such as the recent financial crisis with widespread failures of financial institutions) and idiosyncratic risk (temporary shocks, such as the failure of one or few financial institutions).

- Strengthening the role of capital markets, nonetheless, would improve financial development, by preventing the financial network from concentrating capital flows (and ownership of foreign assets) in those sectors and areas that generate more positive externalities irrespective of the risk that is being created. In effect, after the initial benefit of cross-border integration, if there were no **private risk sharing**, capital flows would cause risk concentration in good times, with heightened risks of sudden stops and reversals during crises. Risk sharing improves capital allocation, as risk is borne by those who can bear it (whether public or private agents) irrespective of the geographical location, thereby reducing the likelihood of a capital reversal during a financial crisis, as the same risk is shared across areas through their financial integration.
- Overall, evidence shows that **Europe** lacks both cross-sectional and intertemporal risk sharing, i.e. **cross-border capital markets and banking activities**, compared to other regions like the United States. The single currency only limitedly contributed to more risk sharing, exposing the euro area to the build-up of excessive capital inflows in some areas in the pre-crisis period and a significant capital reversal from the beginning of the sovereign crisis.

These ideas are further developed in chapter 2.

Monetary policy transmission

- **Funding concentration** in the financial system, whether debt or equity, can cause asset bubbles and impair the mechanisms of transmission of monetary policy, which can affect information flows and increase interconnection among financial institutions.

- Greater transparency, required by a diversification towards market mechanisms supports the propping up of **financial markets plumbing** by providing accessibility/contestability of established markets, which may ultimately result in greater consolidation at pan-European level and more efficiency (lower costs) due to the network properties of the financial system. This market structure would also reduce **over-reliance on bank-driven reference rates** and improve the overall market pricing.

Access to finance

- The development of a truly European capital market, within a diversified financial ecosystem, would allow easier access to funding, thanks to greater **competition among intermediation channels**, and more specifically among banks and alternative funding sources (see Chapter 3 for data analysis).
- The current financial fragmentation, which hampers access to finance and harms **financial development**. The deepening of capital markets can increase financial development, which usually produces greater positive impact on the small firms that are currently struggling to obtain more credit.
- Ultimately, access to finance also means **greater choice for end investors.** Investors, in effect, often face limited choice and high costs from domestic providers of investment products. More cross-border competition in the provision of investment services and products can abate costs, increase returns and attract more cross-border volumes.

Finance for innovation

- Capital markets-based funding mechanisms are not only beneficial in times of crisis. Our findings suggests that cross-sectional risk dispersion, typical of market mechanisms, is ideal **for funding innovation**, as it provides easier access for high risk-high return projects that are not capital-intensive. Moreover, market mechanisms are preferable for the easier exit options than an institution-based funding relationship, which may be less costly but may not offer easy liquidation.
- Highly innovative projects benefit from **risk dispersion and customisation**, thereby making more 'relationship-based' market mechanisms, such as private equity, venture capital and crowd finance, suitable for high-potential growth firms. By facilitating trading, hedging and pooling of risks, a highly developed financial sector allows investors to fund investment opportunities that would otherwise be forgone.

Bank restructuring

- The **legacy of the recent financial crisis** for European banks is a heavy one. Banks are carrying huge non-performing exposures that they struggle to write off due to the lower margin environment. This situation also affects the ability to signal risk, making banks even less willing to disclose bad exposures for fear of reputational damage.
- Market mechanisms may create an easier exit option for the liquidation of those assets, helping **bank restructuring** and thereby improving the quality of the financial system and rebalancing funding sources.
- Well-functioning capital markets also increase **cross-border contestability of bank ownership**, which can be a great source of diversification and risk sharing, as the experience of Eastern European countries demonstrates.

These ideas are further developed in chapters 2 and 3.

V. Integration and structure of Europe's capital markets

- After the slump caused by the financial and sovereign crises, **financial integration** (measured by price and quantity indicators) has gradually picked up. Quantity indicators have kept converging, but the convergence of price indicators is still well below pre-crisis levels. The countercyclical growth of cross-border equity holdings, compared to the drop in cross-border debt securities holdings, shows the ability of equity flows to withstand asymmetric shocks.
- The **structure of the European financial system** relies heavily on traditional bank intermediation, which is even bigger than the sector in China.

Simplified structure of the financial sector in the EU (% GDP, average 2010-14)

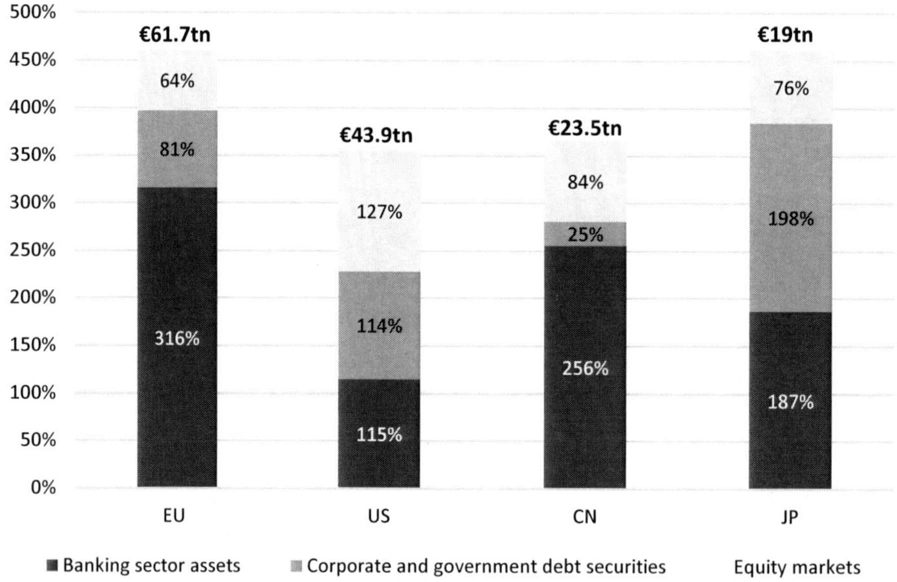

Note: For debt securities, we use outstanding amounts and exclude financial institution debt securities (which are implicitly included in the banking sector assets statistics). For equity, we use domestic market capitalisation. For US bank assets data, we include gross notional value of derivative positions and credit union assets.

Data sources: IMF (GDP), BIS, ECB, US Fed, BoJ, PBoC, WFE, FESE, individual stock exchanges. Eurostat for exchange rates.

- **Europe's capital markets** are on aggregate smaller than markets in the United States and Japan. Equity markets are also smaller than Chinese markets in percentage of GDP. Moreover, issuance of government and financial institutions drives debt markets, while the corporate bond market is just 12% of GDP.

Capital markets structure (value of outstanding securities, excl. derivatives; average 2010-14; % GDP)

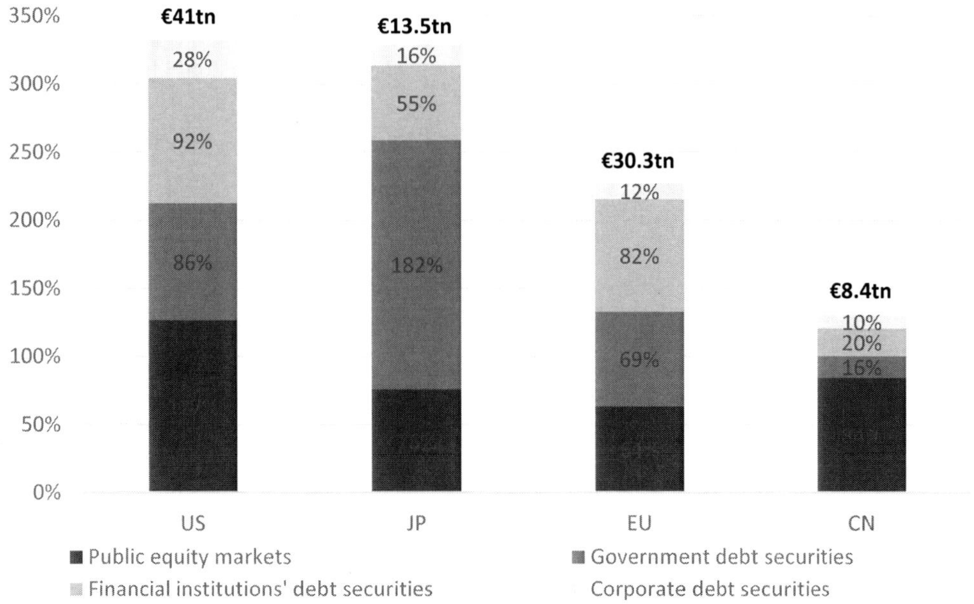

Note: Derivative markets, excluded from this figure, include securitisation, derivative contracts, and indexes (exchange-traded products; see following sections). 'Public equity markets' are equal to domestic market capitalisation.

Data sources: WFE, BIS, individual stock exchanges. Eurostat for exchange rates.

- European **non-financial corporations' (NFCs)** rely heavily on bank loans for funding, which account for 77% of all NFCs debt funding, compared to 40% in the United States. Only 12% of NFC funding is provided by corporate debt issuance, despite the positive net issuance in recent years offset the drop in net lending.
- With highly fragmented markets and high uncertainty in the financial system, **risk aversion** is at historically high levels **among European households**, 31% of their financial assets held in cash or deposits and only 23% in shares and investment funds, compared to 13% and 44%, respectively, in the United States.
- Nonetheless, the **situation varies widely from one country to another**, with some (like UK and the Netherlands) regularly investing in pension funds and shares, while many others (like Greece, Spain or even Austria) have above-average cash and deposits holdings. Taking out all the cash and deposits that go back in the system to fund household or corporate lending (such as consumer credit and mortgage lending to households), we estimate that roughly €1.8 trillion in deposits or cash could be mobilised and invested in more profitable (and riskier) instruments.
- **Households' direct funding of NFCs** (ultimate users of capital) via shares and debt securities instruments is just 16%. **Governments** have significant interference in the EU

economy with direct equity holdings equal to roughly 10% of all NFC equity, compared to 0.8% in the US. Insurance and pension funds are almost one-third and the main vehicle through which households' assets flow into NFCs.

- As a result, the low percentage of listed shares in NFC, the limited participation of households and main institutional investors (insurance and pension funds) and the high government interference in the ownership of companies suggest that a general **lack of risk-taking environment and low contestability of control** in the EU economy. After a significant economic shock, this environment might be unable to attract investments and to create growth and jobs.

Financial industry structure

- The drop in trading volumes, the tightening of capital requirements (especially for those holding large securities inventories) and an environment with very low long-term interest rates have increased the costs of big inventories and pushed **dealer banks** to cease well-established trading activities or restructure their entire business model. In some cases, this entails the adoption of more hybrid models that combine securities dealing and asset management services.

- The evidence about the **impact on liquidity** of dealer banks shrinking their business is mixed, as widening of spreads in some markets is offset by no impact or even improvements in other markets. For instance, despite the move of the US corporate bond market in recent years towards a more agent-based model, liquidity is still resilient. Hence, a well-functioning market can replace some dealer-driven market structures, but the transition to the new model is important and should be closely monitored.

- The **financial sector,** including intermediaries other than banks, is currently at its historical peak with total assets of roughly €100 trillion. While the total size has not declined, despite the crisis, the weight of the different components is changing rapidly.

- The **asset management industry** has grown at an incredible pace in the post-crisis period, doubling its assets under management (from €9.9 trillion to €19.9 trillion) between 2008 and 2014. This situation was supported by the fast retrenchment from direct holdings of market instruments by **insurance companies and pension funds**.

- The high number of funds and small average size keeps a **fragmented and costly market** for investment fund units across member states. At the end of 2010, the total expense ratio (TER) of European funds was 32% higher than the US equivalent. Since then, this gap has widened, as the US TER fees decreased to 120 basis points, while there is limited evidence of the same move in Europe. Fixed charges (subscription and redemption fees) have even increased in recent years and fee structures continue to greatly diverge across countries.

Financial markets structure

- **Primary and secondary equity markets** activity is fragmented and fragile. IPO activity in Europe is not far from that of the largest market (US) in absolute values. Moreover, 73% of newly raised money went to fund already-listed companies in 2014. Despite the liberalisation of trading venues activities, with the abolition of the national concentration rules, and resulting in a structural drop in bid-ask spreads, competition in secondary markets is limited on average to the top 50 most-liquid listed shares in main indexes. The efficiency of secondary trading is still very low, as newcomers struggle to diversify the trading flow with more retail and institutional investors' activities.
- **Cross-border integration** among trading venues thus slowed down and markets still remain fragmented along national borders rather than along specialised segments, such as SMEs or high-tech listings. The low level of participation in equity markets of household and some institutional investors, such as insurance and pension funds, weighs heavily on the integration process.
- European **private equity and venture capital funds** in Europe are far from being systemically relevant, with a combined average amount raised per year in the period 2010-14 equal to €37 billion, compared to €119 billion in the US.
- **Negative net issuance of equity**, driven by buybacks in a very active secondary market, and the 'carried interest' tax mechanism suggest great (ex-post) exit opportunities for equity investors (not necessarily in the market) and thus high ex-ante incentives to inject equity into fast-growing companies and hold for a long time.
- **Crowdfunding** is a new funding model that combines risk dispersion with reputational mechanisms (relationships). It complements private equity and venture capital. Its nature is cross-border and careful minimum regulatory and supervisory design should not hamper their cross-border nature. EU action may actually pre-empt disorderly national actions.
- **Debt securities markets** have shown greater integration over the years, driven by wholesale dealer banks after the monetary union and EU financial reforms, e.g. FSAP. This is particularly true for bonds issued by governments and financial institutions. However, the impact of the financial crisis on wholesale banks produced a reversal of capital flows and that integration process is currently retrogressing.
- For **government and financial institutions,** the market for primary issuance is still fairly fragmented, as country risk (adjustment) leads to different local environments.
- Primary issuance of **corporate debt securities** is developed only in a few countries, such as Portugal, France and Germany. Most notably, issuance of debt securities can also take place in a closed environment (so-called private placement), which today amounts

to roughly €16 billion, compared to €822 billion of corporate debt gross issuance in Europe.

- **Private placement markets** in Europe are fairly local with limited international participation of issuers and investors. The market structure lacks information flow between issuers (mostly unrated companies), and investors may naturally keep this market to a niche compared to public listings or bank lending.
- The high level of outstanding debt securities in Europe creates the conditions for active **secondary markets** in the region. Trading activities today take place mainly over-the-counter via electronic platforms (RFQ) or voice-matching systems. The average size of debt transactions is €70,000 for order books and €8.5 million for negotiated deals matched by exchanges over-the-counter.
- **Participation** is mainly offered to institutional investors or banks, which interpose themselves directly or on behalf of a client. Retail investors' participation only occurs on limit order books available in a few markets, such as Italy. They only represent 3.3% of all secondary bond trading. Matching systems based on voice are mainly used for government bonds trading and represent almost one-third of the total. Electronic platforms are mostly based on a request-for-quote model.
- Overall, by considering the outstanding value of shares (market capitalisation) and outstanding value of debt securities over the related trading turnover, bond and equity markets in Europe show similar levels of activity (one to one), despite their OTC nature. Once again, this points to the poor functioning and **competitiveness of Europe's equity markets** compared to the US, where this ratio is two (turnover) to one (market capitalisation) based on a five-year average.

These ideas are further developed in chapters 2 and 3.

VI. Summary table: Selected cross-border barriers*

Cross-border barrier	Nature	Cost predictability	Policy outcome
PRICE DISCOVERY			
A. INFORMATION ON THE UNDERLYING ASSET			
1. IFRS optionality for discretionary evaluation models, e.g. asset retirement obligations, loan provisions, etc.	Artificial	No	Immediate action
2. Domestic accounting standards for non-listed companies	Artificial	No	Immediate action
3. Reporting formats, e.g. half-yearly reports, etc.	Artificial	Yes	Action needed
4. IFRS optionality for alternative calculation methodologies or definitions, e.g. classification problems, such as pension interest in income statement as interest or operating expense or calculation of debt at amortised cost or fair value	Artificial	Yes	Action needed
5. Alternative performance measures	Artificial	Yes	Action needed
6. Voting share disclosure threshold	Artificial	Yes	Action needed
7. Domestic business registries	Artificial	Yes	Action needed
8. Credit risk scoring and national credit bureaux	Artificial	Yes	Action needed
9. Rules on related-party transactions (definitions)	Artificial	Yes	Action needed
10. Compensation disclosure (methodology)	Artificial	Yes	Action needed
11. Off-balance sheet items	Structural	No	Action needed
B. FINANCIAL INSTRUMENT INFORMATION			
12. Ongoing performance disclosure (domestic market practices)	Artificial	No	Immediate action
13. Exit conditions disclosure (domestic market practices)	Artificial	No	Immediate action
14. Prospectus disclosure requirements	Artificial	Yes	Action needed
15. Calculation methodologies for PRIIPs costs (in KID)	Artificial	Yes	Action needed
16. Market data formats/costs & national bias in securities listing	Artificial	Yes	Action needed
EXECUTION			
A.			
B. ENTRY PROCEDURES			

17. Execution policies	Artificial	No	Immediate action
18. Tax discrimination	Artificial	Yes	Action needed
19. Local facilities, paying agents & other marketing rules	Artificial	Yes	Action needed
20. Corporate action standards	Artificial	Yes	Action needed
21. UCITS filing process	Artificial	Yes	Action needed
22. Passport processing fees	Artificial	Yes	Action needed
C. EXIT PROCEDURES			
23. Withholding tax refund and collection procedure	Artificial	Yes	Action needed
24. Full disclosure of exit charges and conditions	Structural	n/a	Action needed
ENFORCEMENT			
A. PUBLIC ENFORCEMENT			
25. 'Good faith' acquisitions	Artificial	No	Immediate action
26. Acquisition and disposition of securities	Artificial	No	Immediate action
27. Conflict-of-laws regime	Artificial	No	Immediate action
28. Art. 17 Breach of EU law proceedings (ESMA)	Structural	n/a	Action needed
29. Art. 9 consumer protection powers (ESMA)	Structural	n/a	Action needed
30. Sanctioning regimes (illicit profits restitution)	Artificial	Yes	Action needed
B. PRIVATE ENFORCEMENT			
31. Automatic stays	Artificial	No	Immediate action
32. Company's valuation in insolvency (principles)	Artificial	No	Immediate action
33. Secondary proceedings (conditions & deciding court)	Artificial	No	Immediate action
34. **COMI** for legal persons (uncertain presumption) & decentralised appeal	Artificial	No	Immediate Action
35. Gatekeepers' supervision	Structural	n/a	Action needed
36. Cross-border alternative dispute resolution (ADR) mechanism (EU-wide)	Structural	n/a	Action needed

*This list contains a selection of the most harmful barriers and should not be considered exhaustive.

Introduction

This report is the result of a long process of interaction between a dedicated group of experts (the European Capital Markets Expert Group, 'ECMEG') and a group of policy-makers, industry experts and academics. The report offers a comprehensive overview of the status of financial integration in Europe and how EU institutions could contribute to improving financial integration in Europe, via capital markets. Compared to other reports on CMU, this study only focuses on integration policies and it provides the reader with a methodology to identify harmful barriers to capital market integration.

The report offers a methodology to identify and prioritise cross-border barriers to capital market integration and provides a list of policy recommendations to improve its key components: price discovery, execution and enforcement of capital market transactions. As a result, its conclusions rely on three cornerstones: transparency and data comparability, fair access, and legal certainty of enforcement proceedings. It then suggests 33 policy recommendations based on a list of 36 cross-border barriers in the areas of price discovery, execution and enforcement.

The study has the following chapters:

- A brief history of the European Union policies for financial integration;
- A literature review to understand whether Europe needs more capital market integration;
- An empirical analysis of Europe's financial markets structure and integration; and
- An action plan that identifies and prioritises policy actions to overcome barriers to capital markets integration.

1. A brief history of EU policies for financial integration

Three waves of financial integration

Financial integration in the European Union has been a long-term process, begun in 1957, which has involved a complex interaction of economic, social and political factors. Financial integration is the process through which different regions or countries become more financially interconnected, ultimately producing private risk sharing to withstand asymmetric shocks and a convergence of prices and returns for financial assets and services. An increase in cross-border asset holdings would be a proxy of private risk sharing.

The history of EU policies to promote financial integration can perhaps be summarised in three main waves, led by different political and economic events. The first wave was led by the post-world war reconstruction phase. The European stagnation following the two oil crises and the end of the Bretton Woods system led the second wave. The effects of the financial and sovereign crises of 2008 and 2010 currently lead the third wave.

It took on average about 20 years each to complete the first two waves of financial integration and most likely it will take a comparable amount of time to complete the last one. Table 1.1 summarises the key steps of this integration process. The following section will discuss in detail some of these steps to set the stage for the CMU action plan in the European financial integration process.

Table 1.1 Milestones in EU financial integration policies

			FIRST WAVE
i.	**Treaty of Rome**	1957	Capital movement (and controls) to support the single market
ii.	**1st and 2nd Directive on capital movement**	1960-62	Liberalisation of trade-related credits for goods, investment flows and services
iii.	**Segré Report**	1966	State of financial integration and first call for a European market for capital via barrier removal
iv.	**Werner Report**	1970	Realisation of the Economic and Monetary Union in stages, in which goods/services, people and capital move freely
v.	**Commission Memorandum on EMU**	1970	'Stability and growth' Community instruments (incl. a common market for capital) to ensure fiscal coordination to support the economic and monetary union
vi.	**European Monetary System (EMS)**	1979	Exchange rate mechanism (semi-peg) and the European Currency Unit
vii.	**Listing Particulars Directive (80/390/EEC)**	1980	First Directive on listing particulars to be published for the admission of securities to an official stock exchange

			SECOND WAVE
viii.	**EC White Paper on Completing the Internal Market**	1985	Harmonisation of laws via mutual recognition (minimum harmonisation)
ix.	**Single European Act**	1987	Full support to 'mutual recognition' via right of establishment, qualified majority voting in the Council and single market competence (art. 8a)
x.	**Delors Report**	1989	'Three stages' EMU and Institutional framework (e.g. ESCB)
xi.	**EMU – First phase**	1990	No restrictions on capital movements, free use of ECU, more cooperation among CBs
xii.	**Maastricht Treaty**	1992	Coordination and surveillance of economic policies, Protocol on ESCB/ECB/EMI Statute
xiii.	**EMU – Second phase**	1994	EMI and process leading to ECSB/ECB (1998), economic convergence (Stability and Growth Pact), no centralised liquidity management and no monetary policy coordination
xiv.	**Financial Services Action Plan (FSAP)**	1999	Launch of a plan of 42(+3) EU measures to create a truly single market for financial services
xv.	**EMU – Third phase**	1999	Introduction of the euro, ERM II, Stability and Growth Pact, Single Monetary Policy under ESCB
xvi.	**Lamfalussy Report**	2001	New '4 levels' process for legislation and supervision under the single financial market (with level 2 rules under the comitology process)
xvii.	**EC White Paper**	2005	Completing and deepening the single market in financial services (monitoring the FSAP implementation but going beyond its objectives)
			THIRD WAVE
xviii.	**De Larosière Report**	2009	New supervisory architecture with European Supervisory Agencies (ESAs) and the European Systemic Risk Board (ESRB) to develop and implement a Single Rulebook
xix.	**Treaty of Lisbon**	2009	Subsidiarity protocol and rule-making delegation
xx.	**'Four Presidents' Reports**	2012	Banking Union (SSM & SRM)
xxi.	**Green Paper & 'Five Presidents' Report**	2015	*Capital Markets Union*

Source: Author from various websites and reports.

1.1 The first wave of financial integration

Treaty of Rome and Capital Directives

The history of European financial integration goes back to the founding Treaty of the European Communities in 1957.[2] Article 67 established the free movement of capital, but only when necessary to the functioning of the single market. The subordination of capital liberalisation to what was needed for the single market did not allow direct application of this article, but it nonetheless helped to approve two Capital Directives in 1960 and

[2] Treaty Establishing the European Economic Community, 25 March 1957, 298 U.N.T.S. 3, 4 Eur.

1963, which opened up the common market for capital around trade-related credits.[3] It was a great advance, but it was still limited to some banking transactions and ignored capital markets in the broad sense (including securities). Capital markets integration was described not much later on as a pre-condition for the monetary union by the Segré Report (CEEC, 1966).

Segré Report

Taking stock of fragmented capital markets at that stage, the Segré Report reviewed the status quo and proposed a list of areas to which to direct more attention, such as regulation of the financial sector and market funding for public authorities. Most importantly, the report dwelled for the first time on the role of a more integrated securities market as a source of funding for firms and a way to better allocate savings and argued that:

"[...]there can be no monetary union in the Community without such a market" (CEEC, 1966, p. 15).[4]

The report also stated that focusing only on primary markets is insufficient. The efficiency of secondary markets is as important for price discovery. Equity/debt tax bias (CEEC, 1966, p. 214), double taxation and discrimination against host service providers, fragmentation of the investment management industry (i.e. the absence of a pan-European pool of institutional investors) were crucial issues already at that time. Insufficient information flow was instead crucial for secondary markets, which were much smaller in the 1960s.

"Lack of information by which the comparative merits of different types of investment can be assessed, especially from the point of view of their yield and soundness, induces savers to stick to the simplest forms, like sight deposits and savings deposits, because they are not in a position to assess the advantages of other forms of investment, such as securities" (CEEC, 1966, p. 226, para. 5).

Ongoing mandatory corporate disclosure and other company information, which can promote more equity investments and cross-border listings, were missing at that time and their implementation under EU rules is still today a source of concern on a pan-European scale (see Chapter 4 for more details). The report also called for more cross-border trading in bonds for savers to reap the benefits of risk diversification.

---

[3] Council Directive 63/21 of 18 December 1962 (J.O. p. 62/1963), amending the first capital Directive of 11 May 1960 (J.O. p. 921/1960).

[4] The report refers to "European capital markets" in their broadest meaning, which include all sorts of capital movements (including securities markets, to which the report dedicates one chapter).

Werner Report and Commission Memorandum

The gradual collapse of the Bretton Woods system, between 1968 and 1973 (see, among others, Garber, 1993), raised concerns about the stability of the European internal market as currency volatility rose across Europe. To ensure the stability required for the a development of the internal market, in 1969, heads of state or government gave a mandate to a group of experts,[5] chaired by Pierre Werner, to explore the idea of an economic and monetary union (EMU) in the European Community (Council and Commission of the European Communities, 1970). Due to unfavourable market conditions and political pressures, however, the report postponed a strict timetable and focused instead on cooperative systems to ensure irreversible convertibility of exchange rates. This work also led to a memorandum of the European Commission (CEC, 1970), calling for greater coordination of economic policies and putting a common capital market on the same level of the common market for goods. It also proposed the completion of the economic and monetary union by 1976-78, but this attempt also failed, as market conditions did not favour member states' political support to give up control over foreign exchange policies.

1.2 The second wave of financial integration

Post-oil shocks environment

Despite the spectacular failure of the Werner Report and of the Commission memorandum, these reports sowed the seeds for the European Monetary System (EMS) in 1979, in a highly volatile post-Bretton Woods monetary system. The EMS was an exchange rate mechanism through which currencies were semi-pegged to the European Currency Unit (ECU), i.e. a basket of European currencies weighted by a pre-determined value that later became what we call today the euro currency. Not much more than that concretely happened in the field of financial integration since the second capital directive was approved in 1963. The *Casati* case[6] in 1980 confirmed the non-direct applicability and subordination to the single market of the freedom of movement of capital enshrined in Article 67.1 of the Treaty of Rome (see Louis, 1982). Nonetheless, the instability of the global financial system and important political events, after the end of Bretton Woods, led to two major financial crises in 1973 and 1979 (also called the 'oil shocks' because they were triggered by a sudden and sharp rise in oil prices). The slow recovery from the shocks raised concerns that the gradual elimination of tariff barriers and the stabilisation of the exchange rates in the area were insufficient to bring Europe back to growth and

[5] Communiqué from The Hague of December 1969.

[6] Case 203/80, Casati [1981 E.C.R. 2595].

unleash the single market (Key, 1989). Non-tariff barriers, together with the complete removal of capital controls,[7] then came to the attention of European policy-makers as the next step for the financial integration process. Financial integration was again considered (as the Segré Report had done) as a tool to support the exchange rate stabilisation.

Completing the internal market

At the beginning of the 1980s, as the European economy was struggling compared to that of the United States and Japan, integration policies for the single market were seen as a key driver for the economic and political stabilisation of the area. The important *Cassis de Dijon* ruling of the European Court of Justice in 1979[8] established the equivalence of home-country standards applied to goods in a host member state. The principle of the ruling was somehow confirmed by the 'insurance undertakings' case (European Commission v. Germany, Case C-205/84), in which the ECJ denied Germany the possibility of obliging foreign insurance companies to be permanently established and authorised by the German state. Building on these two important rulings, the European Commission released the 1985 White Paper on completing the internal market by 1992 (also called the Single Market Programme), which argued for the first time that the establishment of a single financial market would require both free movement of capital and free movement of financial services (CEC, 1985, p. 6). Financial integration would thus be based on a combination of right of establishment, i.e. the ability of a financial institution to set up a permanent activity in any member state, free movement of capital and free movement of services across the European Union. It *de facto* put goods, services and capital on the same level, thus leaving legal space for the use of the *Cassis de Dijon* ('mutual recognition' for goods) also in the area of cross-border provision of financial services. Mutual recognition would then be combined with a minimum set of European rules (minimum harmonisation) to be more effective and create a minimum level of trust among member states.

Mutual recognition

Mutual recognition was a great legal innovation, which ultimately pushed the single market project forward, after full harmonisation attempts never really gained momentum. The 1985 White Paper, therefore, called for a renewed commitment to the complete the internal market via the removal of physical, technical and fiscal barriers by 1992 (*"The time for talk has now passed. The time for action has come"*, CEC, 1985, p. 7; see also Oliver & Baché, 1989, and Key, 1989). The Single European Act, which entered into

---

[7] This finally came in 1988 with the Directive 88/361.

[8] Rewe-Zentral AG v. Bundesmonopolverwaltung für Branntwein (Cassis de Dijon), Case 120/78, 1979, Eur. Ct. Rpts. 649, 1979 Common Mkt. L. Rpts. 494.

force in 1987,[9] reiterated the importance of completing the single market by the end of 1992 (Article 8a). Most important, though, it indirectly enshrined the mutual recognition principle in the Treaty (to support the ECJ ruling) via the strengthening of the right of establishment (Article 52), which limited local additional restrictions on top of the home-country regime (Article 53) and imposed a principle of equality between foreigners and nationals (Article 58). Most notably, the Single European Act also removed unanimity in the Council for single market matters in financial regulation, introducing the qualified majority voting, which facilitated the approval of key financial reforms over the years.

Delors Report and EMU

At the end of the 1980s, closer European integration was indeed the main political project emerging from the ashes of the Cold War, even before the Berlin Wall collapsed in 1989. This macro-political momentum building around the Single European Act of 1987,[10] together with a renewed attempt to stabilise exchange rates for good this time, led the European Council in 1988[11] to restate the *"objective of progressive realisation of economic and monetary union"*, which originally came out in the Werner Report but had not found enough political support (Council and Commission of the European Communities, 1970). A Committee, chaired by the European Commission President Jacques Delors, was entrusted the task of *"studying and proposing concrete stages leading towards this union."* The report stated (CSEMU, 1989, pp. 14-15) that there were:

"three necessary conditions for a monetary Union:

- *The assurance of total and irreversible convertibility of currencies;*
- *The complete liberalization of capital transactions and full integration of banking and other financial markets; and*
- *The elimination of margins of fluctuation and the irrevocable locking of exchange rate parities."*

The introduction of the single currency, therefore, was only part of the economic and monetary union project, including the "full integration of banking and other financial markets", which we call today banking and

[9] Single European Act, OJ L 169 of 29.6.1987.

[10] Article 8a of the Single European Act states: *"The Community shall adopt measures with the aim of progressively establishing the internal market over a period expiring on 31 December 1992 [...]. The internal market shall comprise an area without internal frontiers in which the free movement of goods, persons, services and capital it ensured in accordance with the provisions of this Treaty."*

[11] European Council in Hannover, 27 and 28 June 1988, Conclusions of the Presidency, SN 2683/4/88, available at www.europarl.europa.eu/summits/hannover/ha_en.pdf.

capital markets (or financial) unions. The EMU plan was then partially enacted in three phases:

1. From 1 July 1990, complete freedom of capital transactions, free use of the ECU and greater coordination among central banks and among governments;
2. From 1 January 1994, greater convergence of economic policies[12] and launch of the European Monetary Institute (predecessor of the European Central Bank, ECB);
3. From 1 January 1999, introduction of the euro and single monetary policy via the European System of Central Banks (ESCB) led by the ECB and entry into force of the Stability and Growth Pact.

From 1989 to 1999, most EU countries decided to undertake a fundamental project of financial integration that was a catalyst for other reforms and further financial integration beyond the EMU boundaries.

Five 'key' Directives

The Single Market Programme (SMP) discussed above and the acceleration of political momentum, led by the phasing-in of the EMU, were able to reinvigorate the financial integration process for the whole European Union with concrete actions, especially in the market for services (CEC, 1994, 1996; Allen et al., 1998). The implementation of the SMP led to at least five key directives in financial services, which are still today (in their revised version) milestones of the liberalisation and integration process of financial services in Europe. These five directives are: the Second Banking Directive,[13] the Undertakings for Collective Investments in Transferable Securities (hereinafter "UCITS"),[14] the Investment Services Directive (hereinafter

[12] First, this was enshrined in the Maastricht Treaty, most notably, in Articles 3a, 102a, 103 and 130b, European Union, *Treaty on European Union (Consolidated Version), Treaty of Maastricht*, 7 February 1992, Official Journal of the European Communities C 325/5). Second, this phase led to the establishment of the Stability and Growth Pact, which is an agreement to create a set of rules that would promote coordination of economic policies. It was first announced in the Resolution of the European Council on the Stability and Growth Pact Amsterdam, 17 June 1997 Official Journal C 236, 02/08/1997 P. 0001 – 0002. Today, it has become a complex set of governance and budget rules for coordination of fiscal policies; see the European Commission's website at http://ec.europa.eu/economy_finance/economic_governance/sgp/index_en.htm.

[13] Second Council Directive 89/646 of 15 December 1989 on the Coordination of Laws, Regulations and Administrative Provisions Relating to the Taking Up and Pursuit of the Business of Credit Institutions and Amending Directive 77/780/EEC, 1989 O.J. (L 386) 1. It entered into force on 1 January 1993.

[14] The first UCITS Directive, which has been reviewed five times since then (the last in 2014), is dated 20 December 1985; see Directive 85/611/EEC. It entered into force on 1 October 1989.

"ISD"),[15] the Life and Non-Life Insurance Directives.[16] The Second Banking Directive is by far the most important because it was the first real application of mutual recognition to financial service provision, also in relation to the large size of Europe's banking systems (Zavvos, 1990). These legislative acts altogether created the regulatory framework for the introduction of a European passport, based on home country authorisation and the application of home state rules based on minimum standards harmonisation, for the provision of services across Europe respectively in banking, the marketing of open-end funds and trusts, investment services and insurance services via the mutual recognition tool. From 1985 to 1995, with most of it approved by 1992 as originally planned, mutual recognition was fully in place for the provision of most financial services. More recent evidence also shows how the opening up of services (via mutual recognition) partially helped to boost integration through legislative convergence (Kalemli-Ozcan et al., 2010).

The Financial Services Action Plan (FSAP) and Lamfalussy

Mutual recognition, free movement of capital and the introduction of the euro were, nonetheless, insufficient to ensure a complete integration of banking and capital markets in Europe and thus the movement of services to stabilise capital flows and support the completion of the EMU. The host state continued to dominate and the harmonisation process was often patchy. As a result, the European Council in 1998, immediately followed by a Communication of the European Commission, called for the creation of a "single market for financial services".[17] The so-called 'Financial Services Action Plan' (hereinafter, FSAP) was then launched in 1999 (European Commission, 1999). The FSAP was the most comprehensive intervention in financial services regulation (Moloney, 2006), which laid the foundations for a more coherent regulatory and supervisory framework in the provision of financial services across the European Union. The plan aimed at:

---

[15] Directive 93/22/EEC. The first proposal was put forward in 1988. It entered into force on 1 July 1995.

[16] Council Directive 90/619/EEC (life) of 8 November 1990 on the coordination of laws, regulations and administrative provisions relating to direct life assurance, laying down provisions to facilitate the effective exercise of freedom to provide services and amending Directive 79/267/EEC. Second Council Directive 88/357/EEC (non-life) of 22 June 1988 on the coordination of laws, regulations and administrative provisions relating to direct insurance other than life assurance and laying down provisions to facilitate the effective exercise of freedom to provide services and amending Directive 73/239/EEC.

[17] See European Council, "Presidency Conclusions", 15-16 June 1998, Cardiff, available at www.consilium.europa.eu/ueDocs/cms_Data/docs/pressData/en/ec/54315.pdf; European Commission, "Financial Services: Building a Framework for Action", *COM 625,* 28 October 1998, p. 3, available at www.europa.eu.

- developing a Single Market for wholesale financial services;
- improving an open and integrated market for retail financial services;
- ensuring better prudential regulation and supervision;
- eliminating tax obstacles to financial market integration and creating a more efficient and transparent corporate governance.

The plan included 45 measures (of which 29 directives)[18] with a level of priority and a timetable for each measure. By 2007, almost all the measures entered into force across the European Union.[19] Among other important measures, for instance, the plan took stock of the liberalisation (demutualisation) process of stock exchanges, with the removal of the concentration rules and the opening up of national markets to competing trading platforms. For the first time, the plan introduced European rules for market abuse and transparency of financial instruments. These rules have played an important role to promote greater capital flows and, with them, financial integration.

The introduction of the euro, right before key measures of the FSAP were introduced, and the crisis, right after some important directives were transposed, do not allow for a proper counterfactual, i.e. to measure the impact of the FSAP. Still, the minimum harmonisation approach to regulation with the extensive use of directives, combined with a weak supervisory mechanism (due in particular to a lack of supervisory coordination among national competent authorities and the absence of a macroprudential framework (de Larosière Group, 2009)), has most likely softened the impact of the FSAP on financial markets integration. Some studies argued that the effects of the FSAP on integration were either weak or difficult to quantify due to the use of directives and their inconsistent implementation in an ever-changing market environment (Kalemli-Ozcan, Papaioannou & Peydró, 2010; Grossman and Leblond, 2011). Nonetheless, with these new rules, there was a tangible reduction of the explicit costs of capital markets transactions (CRA, 2009; Valiante, 2011), Most recently, new evidence shows that EU directives did produce positive effects where enforcement was more effective (Christensen et al., 2015).

---

[18] Originally the measures were 42. Then the Commission proposed an amendment to the 14th Company Law Directive (which was blocked), a Communication on clearing and settlement (COM 312, 2004) and a regulation on cross-border payments (Reg. 2560/2001).

[19] See timetable with the entry into force of the FSAP measures on the European Commission's website at http://ec.europa.eu/internal_market/finances/docs/actionplan/index/070124_annex_a_en.pdf.

During the implementation process of the plan, the Lamfalussy Report (Committee of the Wise Men, 2001) offered an innovation in the legislative process that speeded up the procedures for the approval of new laws.[20] Moreover, it created two levels of legislation: a first level which deals with the principles of the regulatory action; and a second level which involves technical committees in the drafting of detailed rules implementing those principles. Hence, this procedure involved the creation of consultative bodies (comitology) that prepared the proposals for the technical implementing measures, which were adopted by committees composed of member state representatives.[21] These committees have become today three European Supervisory Agencies (ESAs) with powers conferred by the European Commission within the boundaries of the Meroni jurisprudence (for more details, see section 4.7.1).

The 'weak link'

The assumption behind this plan and the Lamfalussy process was that further regulatory convergence would have also boosted supervisory convergence (Ferran, 2004). However, the Lamfalussy process and the regulatory actions supporting its implementation were unable to converge supervisory practices. In particular, the overreliance on non-binding interpretations and the lack of legal powers for the 'level 3 committees' was not able to push convergence and foster greater trust among supervisors (de Larosière Group, 2009). This would be true, however, only if there was an institutional framework at supranational level able to enforce regulatory convergence in a multilateral model of mutual recognition (Verdier, 2011). In the end, the recent financial crisis exposed the 'weak link' between regulatory and supervisory convergence.

1.3 The third wave of financial integration

Post-2008 crisis environment

The 2007-08 financial crisis combined with the sovereign crisis that began in 2010 to produce the worst overall crisis in the European Union's history. The crisis exposed important regulatory loopholes and fragile governance mechanisms, which resulted in a massive financial retrenchment especially

---

[20] This 'special' procedure is now adopted for all key securities regulations and, at that time, for the Markets in Financial Instruments Directive (MiFID) 2004/39, the Market Abuse Directive (MAD)MAD 2004/72, the Prospectus Directive 2003/71 and the Transparency Directive 2004/109.

[21] The three committees were: the Committee of European Securities Regulators (CESR) set up by Commission Decision 2001/527/EC of 06.01.2001; the Committee of European Banking Supervisor (CEBS) set up by Commission Decision 2004/5/EC of 05.11.2003, and the Committee of European Insurance and Occupational Pensions Supervisors (CEIOPS) set up by Commission Decision 2004/6/EC of 05.11.2003.

within the eurozone (ECB, 2015). A new wave of legislative and regulatory action to promote financial integration at European level thus began, with particular focus on the completion of the single rulebook and the supervisory architecture (de Larosière Group, 2009), as well as greater rule harmonisation (which was also led by global initiatives at G-20 level) via wider use of (directly applicable) regulations. The recent experience with the Banking Union shows the determination to create a sound institutional architecture, coupled with the necessary harmonised rules, a genuine economic and monetary union (European Council, 2012a, 2012b) and single financial market. The spillover effects of these actions have important repercussions and certainly strengthen the process of financial integration for the whole European Union. Together with the ESAs and the single rulebook, the Banking Union is a fundamental institutional innovation that creates new European institutions, such as the Single Supervisor Mechanism (SSM), and is producing more effective regulatory and supervisory convergence.

Capital markets union

With this renewed spirit to create a genuine economic and monetary union and to deepen the financial ecosystem, the president of the European Commission called for a "capital markets union" (Juncker, 2014), which would include further development and integration in capital markets across the European Union. In the wake of the historic development of the Banking Union, the European Commission then published in February 2015 a Green Paper aimed at creating a capital markets union via greater accessibility, more funding sources and a sound investment infrastructure by 2019 (European Commission, 2015a). European capital markets should be able to attract institutional, retail and international investors alike (European Commission, 2015a).

Following the Green Paper consultation, a European Commission Communication fleshed out additional details about an action plan to deliver a capital market union, accompanied by an economic analysis (European Commission, 2015b, 2015c). The plan relies on a list of 'early' and medium-term actions (see Figure 1.1). The plan combines actions for investment policies and financial stability objectives with actions for the single market integration and to tackle cross-border barriers.

Figure 1.1 The CMU Action Plan

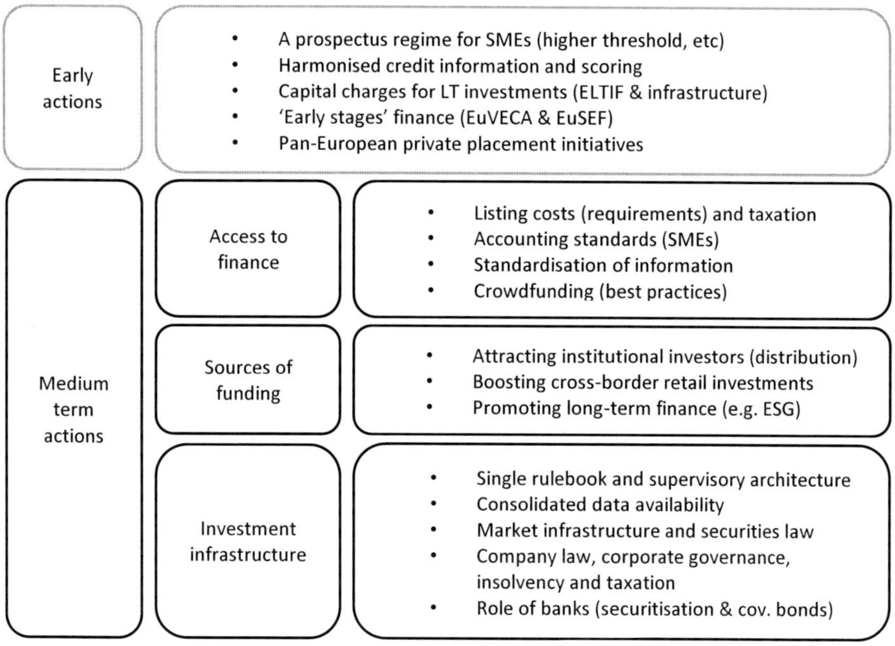

Note: For a more detailed overview of the proposed measures, see Annex.

Source: Author's elaboration from European Commission, 2015a, 2015b.

Short-term actions include, *inter alia*, relaxed capital charges for certain investments (e.g. infrastructure), a new prospectus regime for small and medium-sized enterprises (SMEs) and a new regulatory framework for securitisation. These actions also include initiatives left over by the previous Commission, while medium-term actions aimed at tackling more fundamental issues such as information flows and harmonisation of legal underpinnings of financial markets are mostly a revamp of policy actions that have not really advanced in recent years. The combination of important measures for the deepening of the single market for capital with measures tackling structural issues in financial markets (such as SME access to market-based finance) shows how the CMU, in the eyes of the European Commission, is more than a step towards greater European capital markets integration. While it is certainly a commendable objective to act on all these areas, this way of planning may further complicate the implementation process, as the measurability of its objectives (accountability) is diluted by the fact that investment and integration policy objectives might not be necessarily aligned and may end up with conflicting outcomes. For instance, relaxing capital requirements for insurance companies to stimulate the purchase of securitised products might be a valid investment policy, but may have limited or counterproductive effects on pan-European capital market integration. Most notably, by relaxing those capital charges, there would be a positive economic impact on those markets in which, for historical reasons (such as operating under favourable national laws), a strong insurance sector has developed. If the sector is inefficient, it may be unable to promote cross-border integration and, at the same time, be an obstacle for truly cross-border service providers. The final result might be paradoxically a further widening of divergences among member states and an impediment to the development of a pan-European industry, which may not then emerge as a result of cross-border competition. Investment and financial stability policies may clash with integration policies and dilute their impact. Hence, there should be a clear distinction between actions for integration, investment and financial stability objectives. The action plan requires strong political support, which may fade away if not fed with measurable milestones, i.e. a list of concrete policy action priorities and measurable objectives.[22] There will be a measurability issue if objectives are conflicting.

The 'Five Presidents' Report

In this respect, the 'Five Presidents' Report returned attention to advancing the financial integration process in the region as a key driver for the deepening of the single market for capital (and financial services). The report therefore proposed a more detailed timeline, including the launch of the capital markets union plan by 2017, i.e. to lead to a more binding convergence process, because "the world's second largest economy cannot be managed through rule-based cooperation alone" (European Commission, 2015b, p. 5). Most notably, this statement recognised the role that Europe should play in a globalised financial system and confirmed the new 'post-crisis trend' at European level to improve the multilateral model of mutual recognition (Verdier, 2011) at the centre of the second financial integration wave during the 1980s and 1990s. It thus reaffirmed the importance of a renewed European institutional framework as a way to strengthen the cooperation-based model, by coupling the creation of a sound "macro-prudential toolkit" with a "Single European capital markets supervisor" (European Commission, 2015b, p. 12).

1.4 EU financial integration policies: a recap

Principles of financial

Financial markets integration in the European Union has been shaped by three important 'waves' of EU policies in the last half century (see Table 1.2). The first wave of financial integration began with the 1957 Treaty of Rome,

---

[22] We discuss a methodology to prioritise action and present a list of measurable objectives and selected actions in Chapter 4.

integration and CMU

which established the free movement of capital subordinated to the single market, and continued through the 1970s, when greater convergence of exchange policies was achieved with the European Monetary System (EMS). In this period, the integration process was essentially driven by a negative definition of integration, i.e. member states were not allowed to restrict capital movements that could affect the functioning of the single market, but all other capital movements were essentially allowed. This principle of non-discrimination (equality) between foreign and domestic residents, which basically forced the application of national treatment to both domestic and foreign residents (Key, 1989), led to the gradual removal of capital restrictions that were originally allowed to preserve national sovereignty on foreign exchange policies. This principle, however, was unable to remove all the capital restrictions, as it remained subordinated to the functioning of the single market, i.e. capital movement did not stand alone, but had to support the single market for goods (Usher, 2007).

With the second wave of integration, the principle of non-discrimination evolved into a full-fledged principle of equivalence of the home-state rules with the host-state country rules (mutual recognition). The integration process gradually moved from a negative to a positive definition of integration, i.e. the European institutions were gradually allowed to carry on all the necessary measures to promote the development of the single market. The key policy toolkit included: greater policy coordination, passporting of financial services (mutual recognition) and a minimum harmonisation approach to provide the necessary set of common standards for mutual recognition to thrive across the European Union.

Table 1.2 Building blocks of European policies for financial integration

	Political trigger	Period	Integration process	Legal principles
First wave	Post-World War II reconstruction	Late 1950s Late 1970s	✓ Gradual removal of capital restrictions	Non-discrimination
Second wave	Post-end of Bretton Woods and end of the Cold War	Early 1980s mid-2000s	✓ Policy coordination ✓ Mutual recognition (passporting) ✓ Minimum harmonisation	Equivalence
Third wave	Financial globalisation and EMU incompleteness	Late 2000s to present	✓ Institutional convergence ✓ Single Rulebook ✓ Removal of cross-border barriers	Enhanced subsidiarity

Source: Author.

The inability of the second wave of integration to complete the EMU and the complexity of a more globalised financial system led most recently to a third wave of financial integration. The mutual recognition approach on its own has been unable to remove all the key barriers to free movement of capital and financial services via market pressures, especially because of the weakness of current supranational institutions to police mutual recognition against barriers raised by host-countries to protect national interests. The Protocol 2 in the Treaty of Lisbon,[23] on the application of the principles of subsidiarity and proportionality, gave more legal certainty to the legislative procedure of EU institutions, ensuring constant supervision of the action of the European Commission. As a result, the protocol did not create a straightjacket for EU institutions but rather provided a solid legal tool for driving single market actions in several areas of financial services (including prudential rules), where member states had lagged over the years.

Enhanced subsidiarity

Once the crisis exposed the regulatory and supervisory loopholes of mutual recognition, the principle of equivalence was increasingly coupled with a 'strengthened' subsidiarity principle to support the stability of the European financial system, which took the form of a Single Rulebook to be implemented by the ESAs (de Larosière Group, 2009).[24] This 'new' integration wave fits well in the global harmonisation process led by the G-20 and is thus leading to more 'institutional' convergence with the creation of new European bodies with stronger legal powers to ensure the effective removal of barriers to the free movement of capital and services. For instance, banking union is a set of institutional and regulatory reforms to promote convergence of those rules and supervisory practices that, together with the disorderly fiscal policy actions of member states, have exacerbated financial fragmentation and caused additional instability in Europe.[25] Hence, member states' inability to coordinate fiscal policies to ensure the stability of the European financial system has caused additional damage to the single

---

[23] See Protocol 2, Consolidated version of the Treaty on European Union and the Treaty on the Functioning of the European Union, Official Journal of the European Union, C 83/3, 30 March 2010 (Treaty of Lisbon 2009).

[24] "ESMA can adopt measures under the provision in question only if such measures address a threat to the financial markets or the stability of the EU's financial system and there are cross-border implications. Moreover, all ESMA measures are subject to the condition that no competent national authority has taken measures to address the threat or one or more of those authorities have taken measures which have proven not to address the threat adequately." See Court of Justice of the European Union (2014), Press Release, n. 7/14, Judgment n Case C-270/12 United Kingdom v Parliament and Council, 22 January.

[25] See, for instance, Valiante (2015) on the link between the absence of a common fiscal backstop, the disorderly action of member states and financial fragmentation in the euro area.

market. The CMU should thus support the removal of legal and economic barriers to the free movement of capital and financial services to create a complementary cross-border private risk sharing mechanism to support national public interventions (for more details, please see section 2.1). The challenge is to define the border between harmonisation and regulatory competition in order to achieve this balance. The last chapter of this report proposes a methodology that may help in this endeavour.

Investment vs integration policies

Finally, it is important to distinguish integration policies, such as those discussed in this report, from investment and financial stability policies. Mixing up multiple (sometimes, conflicting) objectives may affect the impact and measurability of policy interventions in this area. For instance, relaxing capital requirements for insurance companies to stimulate the purchase of securitised products might be a valid investment policy, but has limited effect on pan-European capital market integration. Most notably, by relaxing those capital charges, there would be more beneficial economic impact in those markets in which, for historical reasons (such as operating under favourable national laws), a strong but inefficient insurance sector has developed. As a consequence, this sector may be unable to promote cross-border integration and, at the same time, be an obstacle for cross-border service providers. The final result might be a further widening of divergences among member states and an impediment to the development of a pan-European industry that may not then emerge as a result of cross-border competition. Investment and financial stability policies may clash with integration policies and dilute their impact. Hence, there should be a clear distinction between actions for integration, investment and financial stability policies. As discussed above, market developments in recent years suggest that the Capital Markets Union project is and should remain an effort to improve the quality of financial integration and to create a pan-European market architecture that is able to stand strong in a global financial system for the benefit of European savers and the prosperity of European economies.

Key findings #1.

- EU capital markets integration policies go back more than half a century. They developed in three major phases of roughly 20 years each, driven by major political and economic events.
- Mutual recognition was the main tool to boost integration in capital markets, mainly via the ISD (then MiFID) and several measures under the FSAP. The role of the 'new' ESAs has been mainly focused on setting the implementing details (level 2) of those regulations, but they offered limited action to ensure an effective coordination tool for supervisory practices. The single currency had limited effects on capital market integration as a whole, but had more impact on some areas of the wholesale market (such as interbank markets and dealer activities in some liquid bond markets).
- The recent financial crisis has exposed important failures of the multilateral model of mutual recognition to limit member states' national interests. A strengthened subsidiarity principal is leading to more regulatory and supervisory convergence across Europe.
- The creation of supranational institutions with more powers to improve coordination and the removal of non-tariff barriers is an inevitable step to ensure stability of the European financial system.
- Further institutional and regulatory reforms for capital markets shall avoid an unbalanced financial integration process that is driven only by developments in the banking system. The recent crisis taught us that an uneven integration process can cause serious damage to the single market.
- A capital markets union cannot be a mere list of regulatory actions but should entail a comprehensive horizontal plan for barrier removal across all the areas that can potentially affect a cross-border financial transaction.
- The action plan should set a detailed timeline and measurable objectives for the identification of cross-border barriers to capital markets integration and for the institutional reforms to support greater coordination between European and national competent authorities.
- The combination of investment, financial stability and integration policy objectives may result in a dilution of political support for the CMU project.

2. Does Europe need more capital market integration?

Introduction

This section builds upon part of the extensive literature on financial integration and development to better understand the evolution of the European financial system and the implications for its structure. It provides some answers to important questions such as what is a diversified financial ecosystem and what is the role that market mechanisms, with current conditions of financial development, can play in stabilising the financial system and making it more accessible to firms and investors. The first part addresses how risk sharing works and how effective it was in the euro area. It also reviews how capital market integration can improve risk-sharing mechanisms via its risk absorption capacity. The second part provides a comprehensive assessment of legal and economic determinants of financial structure and development, with particular emphasis on the role of market pricing mechanisms. The third part takes a closer look at the long-standing debate on financial development and how it affects economic growth. This sub-section also extends current theories to offer a view on the interaction between financial integration, structure and development and how it channels economic development into economic growth. Finally, the last part of this section provides a summary of macroeconomic and microeconomic rationales for more capital market integration in Europe, while elaborating on previous financial contracting literature to offer a framework to describe the market organisation of the financial system and how (old and new) market pricing mechanisms fit into it.

2.1 Financial integration and risk sharing

Financial integration

Financial integration is the process through which different regions or countries become more financially interconnected, ultimately producing private risk sharing (cross-border asset holdings) and a convergence of price and returns. This process involves the free circulation of capital and financial services among those areas. It usually determines an increase in capital flows across these regions and a convergence of prices and returns for financial assets and services.

As discussed in section 1, financial integration in Europe builds upon three principles:

a. Right of establishment (a financial institution can set up permanently in any EU country).

b. Free movement of services (cross-border provision by a firm located in another country through the use of a passport).

c. Free movement of capital (a transfer of assets from one country to an individual or legal entity in another country).

Despite the effort, the financial integration process in Europe is still a work in progress and has recently taken as many steps forward as backward across the different regions. For instance, the introduction of the euro has accelerated the process of integration in those countries adopting the single currency (see section 3.2 for more details), but the quality of the integration process is questionable (see Box 2.1). The expected effects of financial integration are certainly greater capital flows across the areas that are financially integrating and a gradual convergence of interest rates as the costs of arbitrage among those regions go down (the so-called 'law of the one price'). If there are no frictions, this process of integration would direct capital where it can be best allocated. Financial integration can also create a better environment for more stable direct investments (FDI),[26] which offer more resistance to capital reversals (sudden stops) in the case of shocks (Lipsey, 2001; Albuquerque, 2003) and also some absorption capacity (Sorensen et al., 2007). Overall, financial integration produces 'collateral benefits' that improve the financial and economic environment, but the same integration might be difficult to disentangle in the event of collateral damage (Kose et al., 2006).

Self-fulfilling prophecies & bank runs

Nonetheless, financial integration can also produce negative side effects. It makes the involved regions more financially interconnected, which can lead to gradual or sudden capital movements of great magnitude. Financial integration can thus more easily spread contagion in case of a financial crisis if it is not well engineered. Policy and regulatory interventions should ensure an effective removal of barriers to the cross-border circulation of capital and

---

[26] According to the new OECD benchmark definition, foreign direct investment (FDI) "is a category of investment that reflects the objective of establishing a lasting interest by a resident enterprise in one economy (direct investor) in an enterprise (direct investment enterprise) that is resident in an economy other than that of the direct investor...The direct or indirect ownership of 10% or more of the voting power of an enterprise resident in one economy by an investor resident in another economy is evidence of such a (lasting) relationship." See OECD FDI Glossary, p. 7, available at www.oecd.org/daf/inv/investmentfordevelopment/2487495.pdf. The use of a 10% threshold is questionable, as in economies with more concentrated ownership this may be too low to exercise any relevant power, while in economies with dispersed ownership control can be acquired with much less than 10%.

services in order to allow the spread of diversified foreign asset holdings across the integrated area.[27] Private mechanisms of market surveillance and information flows are important to dealing with capital imbalances in the financial system. But the presence of private agents is not a sufficient condition for managing risk in financial markets. Depending on the level of financial integration, both markets and financial institutions can be subject to crisis sparked either by self-fulfilling prophecies (Diamond & Dybvig, 1983; Allen & Gale, 1998), which can be triggered by the acceleration of capital movements that a temporary downward business cycle or the failure of a major financial institution or corporation can cause (sunspot events), or by aggregate risk with a deterioration of fundamentals and failures of non-financial firms (Gorton, 1988). For banks, this fragility comes from the intrinsic asset/liability mismatch in the nature of banking activities (Diamond & Rajan, 2001), which create a first-come-first-served rule for bank repurchases of deposits (Gorton, 1988). This means that, even if the bank may undergo a temporary liquidity crisis, the risk that this liquidity issue will affect the solvency of the bank increases self-reinforcing expectations that the bank may be insolvent, thus causing a bank run, i.e. a self-fulfilling prophecy. With some caveats, this also applies to financial markets. In the case of markets, the sector specialisation creates the liquidity mismatch with the immediate liquidation attempt that occurs in a liquidity shock. When expectations about market illiquidity are high, i.e. temporary inability to find a market-clearing price that is in line with the fundamental demand for that financial instrument, the lack of participation will exacerbate illiquidity and drive prices away from fundamentals. Liquidity begets liquidity (Admati & Pfleiderer, 1988; Pagano, 1989; Foucault et al., 2013) in the same way 'illiquidity begets illiquidity'. Network effects play a key role in building up self-fulfilling prophecies. According to the type and intensity of the shock, the run on market liquidity may also take the form of an asset fire sale (Shleifer & Vishny, 1992, 2011; Allen & Gale, 1994).

Ultimately, there might also be direct links between liquidity shocks in the banking system and shocks in financial markets. Traders use capital, and any problem in raising funding can actually exacerbate market illiquidity and vice versa. Market and funding illiquidity can mutually reinforce each other (Brunnermeier & Pedersen, 2008). As a consequence, both markets and intermediaries have to deal with the risk of self-fulfilling prophecies. A fiscal backstop, a lender of last resort and a sound legal system are key safeguards

---

[27] For a review of the capital account liberalisation process, see Eichengreen (2001).

to protect this delicate equilibrium based on trust and thus the system from a 'bad prophecy'.

Risk sharing

To limit negative effects, financial integration can notably produce mechanisms of risk sharing (Obstfeld, 1994; Obstfeld & Rogoff, 1996; Asdrubali et al., 1996; Sorensen & Yosha, 1998), i.e. financial integration is a pre-condition for the development of some risk sharing mechanisms with no reverse causality (Rangvid et al., 2014). Risk sharing improves capital allocation, thus risk is borne by those that can bear it the most and improves asset allocation. In other words, risk sharing reduces the likelihood of a capital reversal during financial crises, as risk is shared across the areas that are financially integrated. The eurozone, for instance, is an example of financial integration with limited risk sharing, which exposed the area to a significant capital reversal from the beginning of the sovereign crisis onwards.

Risk sharing takes place via greater risk diversification, including risk arising from country-specific shocks (Kose et al., 2006; Jappelli & Pagano, 2008). According to Allen & Gale (1995, 1997), risk sharing can take place via cross-sectional and intertemporal risk smoothing. As evidence on capital flows in bank-based economies suggests (Milesi-Ferretti & Tille 2011), a combination of risk sharing types determine the quality of financial integration and thus the stability of capital flows during permanent asymmetric shocks.

Cross-sectional

Cross-sectional risk sharing occurs mainly through market mechanisms, which allow the distribution of risk among different agents at a specific point in time. This risk sharing mechanism allows an easy liquidation (exit right) but less stability over time, as agents are less resilient to cyclical factors. Cross-border equity ownership (non-controlling holding) is an example of cross-sectional risk sharing. This mechanism works better in case of permanent income or consumption shocks. It also allows more diversification of country-specific shocks or shocks coming from a specific entity or geographical area. Nonetheless, cross-sectional risk sharing may promote specialisation by channelling capital flows towards sectors that have a comparative advantage, ultimately creating exposure to industry-specific shocks (Kose et al., 2004, 2006).

Figure 2.1 Risk sharing types

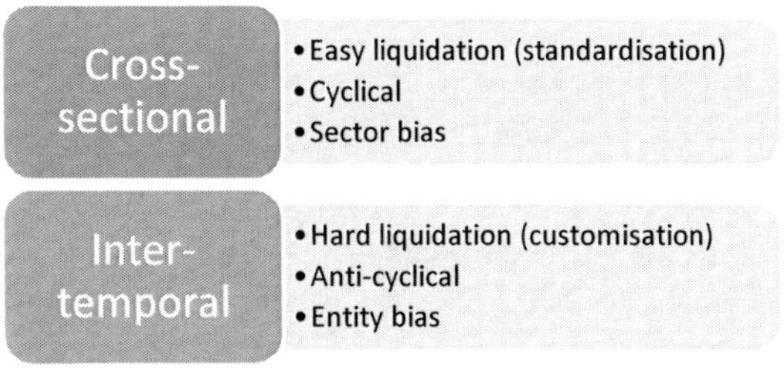

Inter-temporal

Credit institutions, i.e. entities that offer liquidity and maturity transformation services, mainly perform intertemporal risk smoothing of consumption for households and expenditures for firms, typically via accumulation of safe assets. For instance, loan or insurance products respectively provide intertemporal consumption and income smoothing. This risk sharing type is particularly effective for temporary shocks, thus ensuring more stability with funding that is less cyclical. Markets can also provide intertemporal risk sharing, but secondary market activities and mark-to-market accounting limit the intertemporal function. An intertemporal risk sharing mechanism may also be more subject to entity-based shocks, as it is mostly provided by intermediaries that can be more geographically concentrated and subject to home bias. If shocks are permanent, home bias can lead to lower risk sharing (Sorensen et al., 2007).

Intermediary or market-based

Risk sharing channels can be either institution-based, e.g. based on a financial institution or government, or market-based. Markets and institutions, therefore, determine the set of assets that individual/entities accumulate in the economy (Allen & Gale, 1995, 2000a). Institution-based risk sharing provides more customisation for the individual entity seeking a risk smoothing mechanism, while market-based mechanisms offer easier liquidation driven by the standardisation of risk sharing tools. This makes the former often relationship-based and thus a more stable funding mechanism, which is more effective for intertemporal risk smoothing. Market-based risk sharing offers easier accessibility and liquidation due to highly standardised financial contracting, which makes it more suitable for cross-sectional risk sharing. Markets and institution-based intermediation are therefore complementary for the healthy functioning of the financial system. Markets are thus more resilient to permanent shocks, while intermediaries provide a better buffer for (frequent) temporary ones (Bolton et al., 2013).

Risk sharing tools

There is mixed evidence about whether financial integration always leads to proper risk sharing (Kose et al., 2009). Nonetheless, risk sharing in an international environment occurs via the following tools (also based on Asdrubali et al., 1996; Kalemli-Ozcan et al., 2004):

- Foreign direct investments (hereinafter, 'FDI') and equity portfolio investments
- Other portfolio investments (including credit and debt securities)
- Capital gains
- Fiscal transfers
- Labour mobility

Figure 2.2 Cross-border risk sharing tools

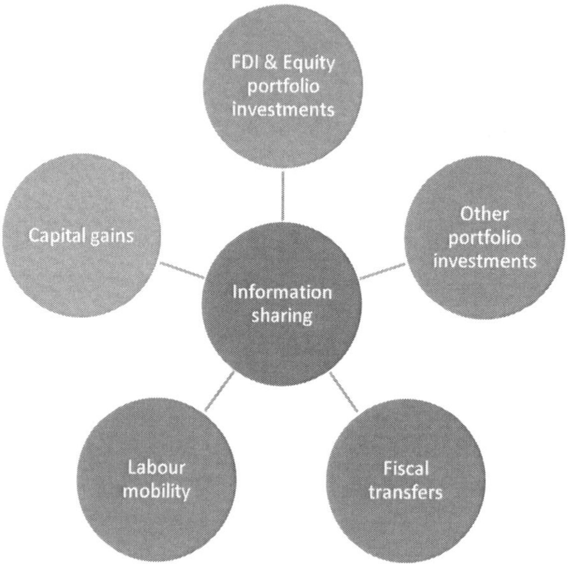

Source: Author.

Capital components

Financial integration mostly involves the first three channels of cross-border risk sharing, i.e. the capital components. FDI are lasting investment flows into the equity of firms located outside the investors' country of residence,[28] while equity portfolio investments are all other types of equity investments that do not entail a lasting interest (below 10% of total voting power). Other types of portfolio investment flows are typically debt securities, interbank loans and, less often, cross-border corporate and retail loans, in particular in Europe (Freixas et al., 2004; European Commission, 2007; Lane, 2008; Jappelli & Pistaferri, 2011; see also Box 2.1). Interbank loans may be the form of risk sharing that works well for temporary shocks (idiosyncratic risk), but not for permanent ones (aggregate risk). In effect, an interbank loan run (with sudden

[28] See footnote 26.

withdrawals) may just occur when banks with excess liquid assets cannot get enough returns from banks in other regions, compared to an insolvency situation (asset/liability mismatches), which is the typical trigger of a retail bank run. This is due mainly to the seniority and the short-term maturity of these loans. Most notably, when a permanent shock hits, the interbank market may be subject to coordination failures, even if most of the banks are solvent, because interbank credit lines provide implicit guarantees of the good banks to those with lower credit quality (Freixas et al., 2000). When the quality of the borrowing bank cannot be properly established due to an external shock, such as the fall in asset value in a country where a bubble bursts, a strong adverse selection mechanism can freeze the market as the short-term liquid and senior claim can be quickly withdrawn. This situation causes immediate contagion across the market and prolonged instability (Allen & Gale, 2000b). As seen during the recent financial crisis, only the intervention of the central bank, interposing itself to smooth counterparty risk, can help to restart the liquidity flows among banks. Moreover, risk sharing can also take place through the income smoothing effect of capital gains on holdings of cross-border assets. This is more difficult to measure and it is not usually captured by standard measures of risk sharing (Balli et al., 2012; see also Box 2.1).

Other components

Furthermore, risk sharing may take place via fiscal transfers, if there is a common institution that uses a common budget or common fiscal policy coordination to offset the impact of capital outflows on consumption and income in a particular area. In effect, the use of local fiscal capacity to offset capital outflows is offset by the reputational impact that may potentially trigger an even bigger outflow (a self-fulfilling prophecy). The labour mobility component refers to the flow of income generated by moving in another country to compensate for the unemployment caused by the shock. Income smoothing comes in the form of remittances and saved unemployment subsidies. Whatever income shock is not smoothed by the mechanisms listed above, it will be then smoothed either by private savings or by lower consumption.

Finally, information is key for the effective functioning of risk sharing mechanisms. For instance, sharing of financial information (such as risk profiles in credit registries or financial information via common accounting standards) improves the joint monitoring of the governance of private entities (corporate governance) and the quality of public institutions and their enforcement mechanisms, thus stimulating more cross-border dealing and sharing of risk. Hence, foreign investors have sufficient information to reduce agency costs, thus allowing greater monitoring of managers by current and perspective shareholders and reducing the cost of outside finance (Stulz, 2005).

Debt & equity

For financial integration, the most relevant risk sharing tools are the three capital components, which are altogether necessary for the effective functioning of an integrated financial system. FDI and equity portfolio investments are the most stable forms of risk sharing, helping in particular to smooth idiosyncratic country risk and guard against sudden reversals in capital flows (Wei, 2001). FDI is a more hybrid form of risk sharing, as it relies less on the interaction of a multitude of agents, such as equity investments (that are mostly market-based). However, they are both more volatile during temporary shocks (before the end of a business cycle) compared to debt flows, which may put the economy under unnecessary financial strain in the short term. Kose et al. (2006) argue that equity flows also bring indirect benefits, such as transfers of managerial and technological expertise, and warn about the risk of excessive debt flows for international risk sharing. In effect, non-equity portfolio investments (debt securities, loans, insurance products, among others) provide more stable funding over time, but they are more prone to sudden reversal if the shock is permanent (e.g., at the end of a long positive business cycle like the recent financial crisis; see Box 2.1). For instance, after the Asian crisis in 1998, the World Bank (2000) argued that short-term bank loans to developing countries were procyclical, as they tend to increase during booms and rapidly decrease during economic slowdowns. The relationship-specific investment in information related to debt requires more long-term commitment, which fails to be present with a permanent shock and low expectations of repayment.

Box 2.1 Risk sharing in the European Union: The case of the euro area

The boom and bust of capital flows within the euro area explains well the consequences of poor risk sharing mechanisms. Indeed, the area suffered a sudden reversal in capital flows in 2009-12 (Merler & Pisani-Ferry, 2012; Lane, 2013), due to the combined shock of the legacy losses of the financial crisis for the banking system and the sovereign debt crisis caused by the cost of fiscal intervention and the drop in fiscal revenues with the fall of aggregate demand. This permanent shock was offset to a limited extent by cross-border equity investments (Alcidi & Gros, 2013), as financial integration in the area was perhaps too reliant on interbank (credit) markets (Hartmann et al., 2003; Lane, 2008; Sapir & Wolff, 2013). In addition, interbank claims were not equally distributed and inflows were mainly concentrated in peripheral countries, which made the market more fragile and subject to asset price bubbles (Lane, 2013). Interestingly, Eastern European countries fared well in recovering from the crisis, as the high foreign ownership of the local banking system provided a buffer with good risk absorption capacity. As a result, those countries underwent a sharp but short-term adjustment, while peripheral countries in the euro area are still undergoing a less steep but much slower adjustment process (Alcidi & Gros, 2013), with perhaps relevant implications for total factor productivity (TFP) and thus long-term economic growth.

The effectiveness of the risk sharing in the euro area, and to some extent in the European Union, is lower than that in a similar federation such as the United States (Furceri & Zdzienicka, 2013; IMF, 2013; Asdrubali et al., 1996). Using data from three different time periods, Figure 2.3 suggests that the ability of the euro area (and the EU) to smooth asymmetric shocks is as low as 26% of the shock. The same ability in the US, in the period 1963-90, was as high as 75%.[29] The international factor income flows include capital market activities and foreign direct investments (FDI), as well as intertemporal risk sharing, i.e. cross-border banking activities via credit. Cross-border cross-sectional and inter-temporal risk sharing absorb close to zero (or are even negative at the EU level), while in the US it is almost 40%. Data for Canada and Germany also show levels of domestic risk sharing that are much higher than what is available in the European financial system (IMF, 2013). Nonetheless, after the introduction of the euro, there has been more risk sharing from international factor income, compared to the EU as a whole. The single currency has stimulated more cross-border activities, especially in interbank markets and holdings of government bonds. Balli et al. (2012) estimate a larger contribution of the international factor income in the euro area vis-à-vis the EU, which they mainly attribute to the introduction of the single currency.

Figure 2.3 Channels of output smoothing in Europe and US

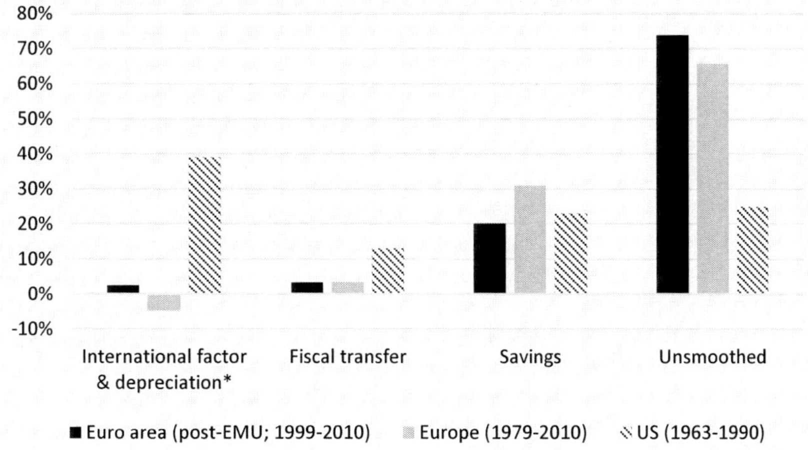

[29] We are not aware of more recent estimates on risk sharing in the United States, but it is fair to assume that there might have been limited changes in the contribution of the different components both before and after the recent financial crisis. In any case, any changes would not be significant enough to undermine this analysis.

*This includes factor income flows and capital depreciation output produced in part by international financial flows (including capital markets, credit markets and FDI). It is the difference between gross domestic product (GDP) and gross national product (GNP), minus the difference between GNP and Net Income (NI). This number may, however, underestimate the contribution of capital markets (including secondary trading activities), which also contribute to the GNP.

Sources: Based on Furceri & Zdzienicka (2013) and Asdrubali et al. (1996).

Nevertheless, the above estimates fail to account for risk sharing produced by capital gains that cross-border holdings of assets located in another country generate. In this respect, Balli et al. (2012) estimated the contribution of capital gains being more than half the contribution produced by the international factor income. They are also stable over time and across countries, which is similar to the risk sharing capacity of equity flows.

Kalemli-Ozcan et al. (2012) assessed the risk sharing components for eurozone distressed and non-distressed countries and compared them before and after the crisis. The international factor income did not provide any contribution, but it was on the contrary negative (especially in distressed countries). In the countries where there have been more cross-border capital inflows in relative terms (distressed countries), the contribution of FDI, credit and capital markets is lower than for non-distressed countries post-crisis, a sign that financial retrenchment was stronger in countries that attracted more capital flows in previous years. This evidence points to poor financial integration even after the introduction of the single currency.

Assessing the international factor income (credit, FDI and capital markets)

Let us understand a bit more the three key components of the international factor income: FDI, credit and capital markets. For what concerns cross-sectional risk sharing, i.e. capital markets and FDI, as explained above, the risk absorption capacity is also related to the composition of international capital flows. Equity portfolio investments (and cross-border equity holdings) are perhaps the first containment barrier to absorb shocks in a country, while FDI (due to the large long-term information component) and debt (due to the nature of protected financial claim) are much costlier to liquidate and more sensitive to information related to the specific project (Daude & Fratzscher, 2008). Figure 2.4 shows how equity, debt and FDI flows absorb differently a structural asymmetric shock. During the peak of the financial (2008) and sovereign (2011) crises, equity reacted much faster as a risk absorber. These flows then gradually recovered in the two to three years after the shock. Debt flows instead reacted with much weaker intensity and their movements appear unrelated to the cycle, while FDI appears to be somewhere in the middle (as they are a combination of equity and debt investments). Hence, debt works better for absorption of temporal asymmetric shocks as its flows are more stable because its value varies with less volatility in these types of shocks and debt is often held to maturity. In structural shocks, such as the recent crises, the slow reaction of debt investments dilutes the absorption of the shock over time, carrying losses and reducing space for new potential investments. It also results in a gradual reduction over time of the cross-border holdings (following the slow reaction of flows), as losses are passed on to investors (see section 3.4.2). Equity, on the contrary, is a good structural shock absorber, as it takes the hit in terms of flows and adjusts quickly to the new income structure. Effectively, Sorensen et al. (2007) found that equity and FDI flows are more suitable risk-sharing mechanisms for structural income shocks. In effect, cross-border holdings of equity have been stable since the crisis or even higher (see section 3.4.1), showing their greater ability to withstand structural asymmetric shocks, perhaps due to the sudden drop in value that makes it convenient for new flows to replace the old ones and for investors to bet on the recovery after the structural downward shift.

Figure 2.4 Debt and equity portfolio investments and FDI positions (% annual change)

Equity investment in	2007	2008	2009	2010	2011	2012	2013	2014
Euro area	18%	-43%	31%	4%	-11%	22%	29%	11%
European Union	15%	-44%	34%	7%	-9%	20%	28%	9%
Australia	28%	-48%	81%	14%	-15%	12%	1%	9%
Canada	26%	-49%	66%	35%	-12%	3%	4%	15%
China (incl. HK)	50%	-47%	63%	15%	-14%	32%	-1%	-2%
Japan	-6%	-38%	9%	15%	-14%	11%	42%	10%
Switzerland	8%	-31%	38%	-1%	-5%	14%	33%	5%
United States	5%	-37%	32%	15%	0%	14%	26%	11%
other	40%	-51%	58%	27%	-3%	17%	10%	23%
Debt investment in	2007	2008	2009	2010	2011	2012	2013	2014
Euro area	14%	-6%	18%	-10%	-5%	11%	7%	2%
European Union	15%	-7%	19%	-8%	-4%	10%	6%	2%
Australia	14%	-10%	57%	15%	10%	5%	-8%	0%
Canada	15%	-2%	22%	12%	20%	13%	2%	4%
China (incl. HK)	24%	4%	8%	142%	50%	26%	83%	11%
Japan	38%	16%	-25%	23%	44%	-7%	-9%	-27%
Switzerland	55%	-19%	18%	-25%	113%	-9%	9%	30%
United States	9%	-6%	14%	8%	0%	-3%	-1%	-3%
other	20%	-15%	8%	28%	-5%	15%	-2%	-3%

FDI position in	2007	2008	2009	2010	2011	2012	2013
Austria	43%	-9%	17%	-7%	-5%	6%	13%
Belgium	68%	5%	13%	-10%	8%	-3%	1%
Denmark	22%	-5%	2%	-8%	0%	4%	6%
Finland	30%	-9%	2%	2%	3%	8%	5%
France	13%	-27%	15%	-5%	-2%	6%	5%
Germany	18%	-4%	5%	2%	3%	7%	8%
Ireland	30%	-8%	33%	14%	2%	17%	11%
Italy	20%	-13%	11%	-10%	8%	2%	11%
Netherlands	39%	-16%	0%	-9%	4%	3%	7%
Poland	42%	-8%	13%	16%	-6%	16%	7%
Portugal	30%	-13%	15%	-3%	0%	7%	7%
Spain	27%	1%	7%	-1%	0%	3%	11%
Sweden	29%	-5%	19%	5%	0%	5%	4%
United Kingdom	9%	-22%	15%	3%	4%	25%	8%

Notes: Portfolio investment data are up to June 2014. 'Selected EU' countries include Germany, France, Italy, Spain, The Netherlands, United Kingdom, Sweden, and Poland. The origin for portfolio investments include Germany, France, Italy, Spain, The Netherlands, Poland, Sweden, United Kingdom, United States, Japan, Australian, Canada, Hong Kong and Switzerland.

Source: Author's elaboration from CPIS-IMF and UNCTAD.

Figure 2.5 shows the composition of the total portfolio investment in different countries and regions of the world, i.e. the cross-border debt and equity investments in these countries that are not FDI, and also within the euro area. Japan and Europe have the greatest concentration of debt portfolio investments, which has a very limited risk absorption capacity in the case of structural income shocks.

As showed in Figure 2.3, this unbalanced portfolio composition of debt and equity yields a contribution of the international factors (including capital flows) to risk absorption at a level close to or even below zero. Any future financial integration process may be an opportunity to rethink the mechanisms of incentives behind the current financial structure to equip Europe with a better infrastructure that is able to attract more diversified capital flows to withstand permanent asymmetric shocks.

Figure 2.5 Total debt & equity portfolio investment (average 2001-14; % total)

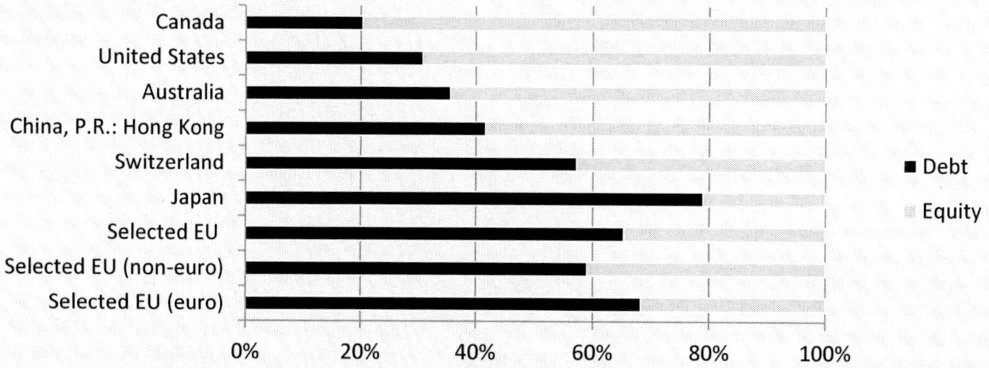

Notes: 'Selected EU' countries include Germany, France, Italy, Spain, The Netherlands, United Kingdom, Sweden and Poland. No 2014 data for Sweden and Australia. 'Euro' means cross-border flows towards euro area countries. 'Non-euro' means cross-border flows towards non-euro area countries (including flows from the rest of the world).

Source: Author's elaboration from CPIS-IMF.

The euro area (and, more broadly, the European Union) also lacks pure intertemporal private risk sharing, as cross-border banking activities are very limited. Of the 129 banking groups under the SSM, only 24% have foreign branches or subsidiaries. Within this 24%, 11% have only one foreign subsidiary and/or one foreign branch. Less than 12% have more than three foreign subsidiaries and/or foreign branches (for more details, Lannoo, 2014; 2014 data). If we look at financial activities in recent years, cross-border banking activities shrunk with the financial retrenchment to pre-sovereign crisis levels and then just stabilised in 2014 (see Figure 2.6).

Figure 2.6 Non-domestic euro area bank affiliates

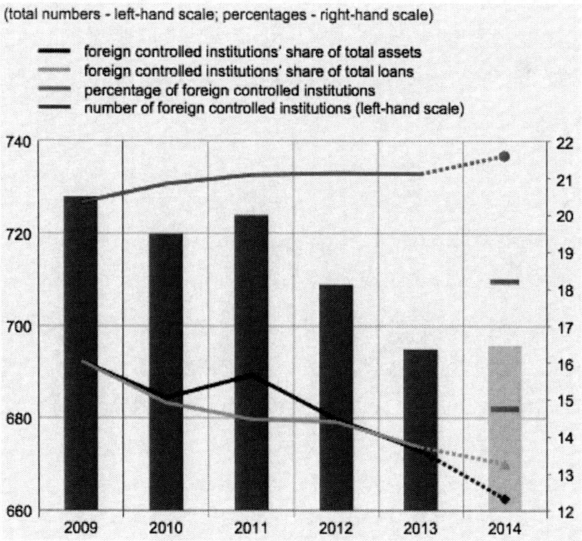

Source: ECB Financial Integration Report (2015).

As suggested in Figure 2.7, most cross-border banking activities are interbank in nature, while direct lending to corporates and individuals is stable over time at less than 10% of all cross-border flows.

Figure 2.7 Cross-border loans in the euro area

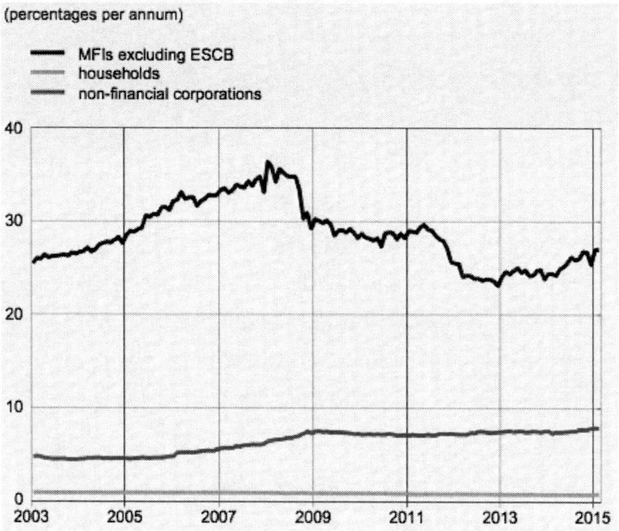

Notes: Cross-border loans include loans to other euro area member states for all maturities and currencies. Interbank loans do not include central bank loans.

Source: ECB Financial Integration Report (2015).

As a result, the euro area lacks both cross-sectional and intertemporal risk sharing. Evidence on cross-sectional risk sharing also denotes a limited equity component, compared to debt flows and holdings. Intertemporal risk sharing continues to rely on interbank markets and only limitedly on corporate and retail credit activities.

Key findings #2.

- General legal principles, such as the right of establishment and free movement of capital and services, are not sufficient conditions to ensure a good quality financial integration, i.e. a good quality composition of the investment portfolio.
- Financial integration is a necessary but not sufficient condition for more private risk sharing. Risk sharing improves capital allocation, so risk is borne by those that can bear it the most and thus improves asset allocation. It also reduces the likelihood of a capital reversal during financial crises, as risk is shared across the areas that are financially integrated. The eurozone, for instance, is an example of financial integration with limited risk sharing, which exposed the area to a significant capital reversal from the beginning of the sovereign crisis onwards.
- Cross-sectional (horizontal in space, i.e. market-based) and intertemporal (vertical in time, i.e. institution-based) risk sharing are complementary and should both have a place in the financial system.
- Evidence shows that Europe lacks both cross-sectional and intertemporal risk sharing, as suggested by a low or negative international factor income. The single currency contributed to more risk sharing in the European Union, but it is by far lower than in the United States (close to zero).
- Intertemporal risk sharing has mainly developed at the domestic level, as cross-border banking activities are only limited to interbank loans and, in just a few instances, to corporate and retail credit activities. Integration via cross-border interbank debt flows is a weak form of risk sharing for the absorption of aggregate risk (permanent shocks), making the system more vulnerable to instability, while it works well for idiosyncratic risk (temporary shocks). If it is not well-engineered, financial integration can thus more easily spread contagion in case of a financial crisis.
- Cross-sectional risk sharing in Europe is weak both at domestic and cross-border levels. More cross-border equity and foreign direct investments would re-establish a balance between the two mechanisms and overcome costly fragmentation. More reliance on cross-sectional risk sharing, via cross-border equity and foreign direct investments (e.g. with measures like the removal of the debt/equity bias in laws and taxation), would re-establish a balance between the two mechanisms. The capital markets union project offers a great opportunity to redesign the financial integration process in Europe to create the conditions for more cross-sectional risk sharing.

2.2 Determinants of financial structure and development

Financial structure & develop-ment

In a process of financial integration, there are multiple determinants that shape the structure of the financial system and its development. Financial structure is thus the combination of institution-based and market-based intermediation (funding means) at the macroeconomic level and debt and equity (funding types) at capital structure level (micro). Financial development can be defined as the size and level of sophistication (interconnection) of those funding means and types. The financial structure influences the level of financial development through the competitive forces of multiple funding sources. Vice versa, the size and sophistication of those sources (financial development) affects the structure of the financial system, i.e. the use of different funding means and types by entities and individuals to fund their economic activities. Financial integration is a process for achieving a combination of financial structure and development to produce a more efficient allocation of capital (via risk sharing) that can unleash further economic development and, ultimately, growth (see Figure 2.8).

Figure 2.8 The financial integration process

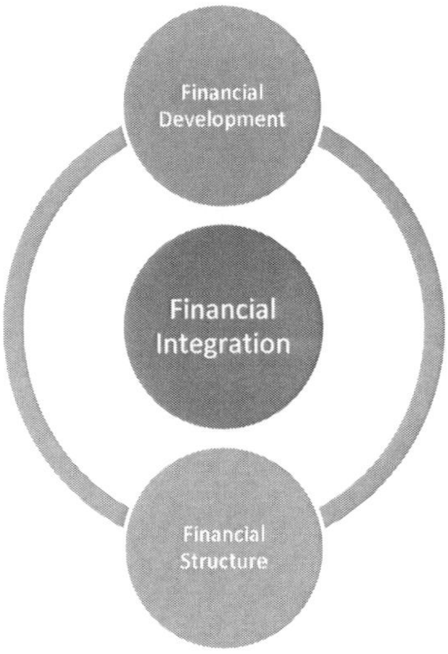

Information & market organisation

According to Boot & Thakor (1997), a financial system is mainly bank-dominated in its infancy, while it becomes more market-dominated when its level of sophistication (and the quality of the borrowers) grows. In effect, financial development is crucial to economic development (Goldsmith, 1969), which ultimately improves borrowers' quality and so can lead to more financial market development. This could prompt a virtuous cycle in which financial structure and development reinforce each other.[30]

Contract incompleteness & opportunism

The development of the financial system is thus strictly linked to its ability to deal with contract incompleteness and to offer decentralised information sources (informational infrastructure; Acemoglu & Zilibotti, 1998) that can smooth the impact of information asymmetry (contract incompleteness) and opportunism (also more generally defined as 'transaction costs'). These costs ultimately determine the organisational structure of economic (and financial) activities (Coase, 1937; Williamson, 1979). Informational problems in financial contracting may arise for two main reasons (Boot & Thakor, 1997; Hermalin et al., 2007):

a. Specification costs (adverse selection)
b. Monitoring costs (moral hazard)

Specification costs, i.e. the inability to foresee in a contractual negotiation all potential contingencies related to a future project (uncertainty), may increase the costs of entering into a transaction. In other words, the inability to signal the actual risk of a borrower or issuer ex ante can set the price for lending or issuance at a level that would only leave bad-quality borrowers or issuers in the market and thus freeze market activity (the so-called 'adverse selection problem'; Akerlof, 1970; Stiglitz & Weiss, 1981). In addition, firms (fund seekers) typically have better information than investors (providers of funds) about the value of business investments, which they may tend to overstate. There is, therefore, a wide information gap between investors and issuers, which requires mechanisms to improve the information flow (typically disclosure rules).

Monitoring costs, i.e. the ability to monitor ex post that a counterparty fulfils his/her contractual obligations, may be affected by asset substitution determined by the 'credence' nature of financial products.[31] Monitoring costs thus lead to opportunism and moral hazard, i.e. to 'free-riding' on the counterparty's inability to verify the behaviour of the other party in a principal-agent relationship (Ross, 1973; Holmstrom, 1979; Milgrom & Roberts, 1992), such as between investors and an issuer. For instance, a state guarantee on deposits (a key liability for banks) can exacerbate risk-taking

---

[30] We review the evidence on the impact of financial (market) development on economic growth in section 2.3.

[31] Financial products (whether a mortgage or a debt security) can be defined as 'credence goods' (see Darby & Karni, 1973), i.e. products for which the quality cannot be fully established even after consumption, because benchmarking cannot be properly performed against an infinite set of potential scenarios.

behaviour of banks if there is no way the state can monitor how the banks use this 'protected' (and thus stable) funding over time. The introduction of capital requirements, such as the 'skin-in-the-game' rules for securitised products, should mainly address a moral hazard problem. Likewise, the dispersed nature of market funding leaves the issuer of a security with the possibility to free-ride the lack of monitoring by a multitude of investors (see e.g. Grossman & Hart, 1980). While residual rights over a firm (ownership) can be selectively allocated, the incentives for opportunism and distortionary behaviour by the management (or by majority versus minority shareholders) will remain and somehow affect the ex-post return and thus the incentive to invest (Grossman & Hart, 1986). Evidence shows the costs of tunnelling or self-dealing by either controlling shareholders or managers, depending on the ownership structure (Johnson et al., 2000; Djankov et al., 2008).

Legal systems

The legal system matters. A minimum level of legal protection for shareholders can reduce costs and thus is a determinant of ownership structure (La Porta et al., 1996). In effect, dispersed control structures are unstable when investors can concentrate control without fully paying for it (Bebchuk, 1999; La Porta et al., 1996). Empirical evidence suggests that companies with an ownership structure that does not protect private benefit of control tend to list in countries where those benefits are not protected (Doidge et al., 2004, 2009). A series of seminal empirical studies confirmed that ownership tends to be more concentrated in jurisdictions with weaker legal systems, and that deeper capital markets are associated with higher levels of legal protection for investors, which include (minority) shareholder protection, disclosure of conflicts of interest, anti-dealing rules and so on (La Porta et al., 1996, 1997, 2000). Investor protection is thus a necessary (but not sufficient) condition for financial development. The US is the epitome of a country that has introduced legal protections (such as disclosure rules) and strengthened enforcement of financial laws once the financial system had become more sophisticated and the failures discussed above were a potential or actual cause of market disruption.

Remedies

As a result of these failures, institution- and market-based financial systems use different mechanisms to ensure pre-contractual commitment and ex-post enforcement, but both rely on collection (disclosure) of information to overcome misspecification and game repetition, and ensure that relationship-specific investments (such as reputation or capital) provide enough incentives for counterparties not to free-ride (implicit contract). The establishment of this relationship would provide an effective tool for dealing with the inability to monitor. Both institution- and market-based systems also rely on two sets of remedies: private and public.

Private remedies

Banks (institution-based relationships) can first exploit internal diversification (Diamond, 1984) to collect a minimum level of information, plus the informational advantage that arises when lending becomes a relationship through duration and multiple product access to internalise costs (Sharpe, 1990; Petersen & Rajan, 1994). This outcome may ultimately create 'hold-up' problems for the costs that the borrower has to encounter to signal his/her good quality and switch to another provider (Hart, 1995). Nonetheless, banks' threats are also less credible, since they face sunk costs if the borrower fails to repay (Allen & Gale, 2000a). Hence, this creates space for renegotiation, as an alternative to the mere enforcement of the financial claim, which may balance out the issues with the hold-up problem. Relationship lending, in effect, can create an 'implicit contract' with enough pre-contractual commitment on both lender and borrower sides, through renegotiation clauses to promote reputational mechanisms and collateral to reveal additional information about the borrower's quality (for a literature review on relationship lending, see Boot, 2000).[32] As a result, the main private remedies in an institution-based system are:

a. Bilateral screening and collateral to deal with specification costs.
b. Renegotiation and bilateral monitoring to deal with moral hazard.

Figure 2.9 Failures and private/public remedies

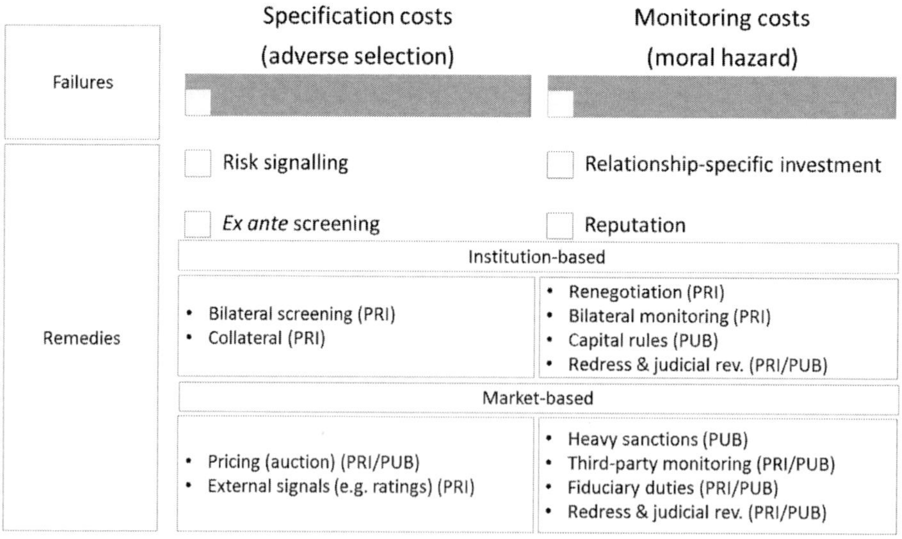

Note: 'PUB' stands for 'public'; 'PRI' stands for 'private'.

[32] There is conflicting evidence on whether collateralised lending reveals good quality or bad quality borrowers. Among others, Berger & Udell (1990) suggest that, despite the theoretical findings, collateral may be more often associated with riskier borrowers and lower quality loans.

Markets, instead, have to face potentially higher monitoring costs due to the dispersed nature of funding. However, markets can combine bilateral monitoring with third-party mechanisms of risk signalling (such as credit ratings or brokers) to address those problems. The ability to trade information, and thus incorporate it into market prices, provides a powerful private means to monitor capital seekers by aggregating the information that traders with different levels of information might have (Gilson & Kraakman, 1983, 2003). Holmstrom & Tirole (1993) argue that stock markets can control managerial performance; stock prices include performance information that cannot be gathered via current future balance sheet data. This information is useful in structuring managerial incentives.

As the acquisition of information is costly, this mechanism may be, nonetheless, very fragile if these market frictions (costs) shift the balance between uninformed and informed traders and thus the incentives for informed traders to stay in the market, i.e. the possibility to free-ride uninformed traders, which may ultimately affect market efficiency (Grossman & Stiglitz, 1980). Informational efficiency relies on liquid secondary markets, which ensure that prices incorporate information. In effect, markets typically become much more heavily intermediated by dealer banks with increasing market-making activities when the liquidity of the instruments drop, thus ensuring a sufficient informational flow and the availability of a price even with less efficient market mechanisms.

The presence of third parties is an important aspect for financial markets compared to relationship-based activities (banking). Market intermediaries, like rating agencies, brokers or auditors, provide risk-signalling mechanisms that can help to reduce ex ante specification costs. Market infrastructures, such as exchanges, provide a platform linking buying and selling interests, thus ultimately helping to minimise those transaction costs. These infrastructures reduce the likelihood that the 'credence' nature of financial instruments would lead to adverse selection and market breakdown. Market frictions (costs) also affect ex post monitoring and require effective third-party enforcement mechanisms, e.g. auditors. While excessive creditor protection in bank lending can also lower the incentives for greater project screening and thus the efficiency of credit markets (Manove et al., 2001), third-party enforcement mechanisms, such as auditing and sanctions, play a crucial role in ensuring the effective functioning of financial markets. Private renegotiation in market-based systems is more difficult as securities are widely held and investors tend to hold out to extract as much as possible (Dewatripont & Maskin, 1995). As a result, relationships in financial markets are not as important as for bank lending. Nonetheless, private enforcement mechanisms (redress procedures) can sometimes be as effective as public enforcement (see section 4.7.2).

Public remedies

While private remedies are important for both institution- and market-based systems, public remedies are very important for market-based systems. As discussed, the transaction costs to privately enforce a financial claim that arises in a setting with a multitude of agents are so high that public remedies inevitably play a role. Public remedies (see Figure 2.9) are typically the following:

i. Disclosure.
ii. Fiduciary duties.
iii. Enforcement (sanctions and judicial review).

These tools are embedded in the legal system and often calibrated to take into account the nature of the counterparties and their ability to use these public or private remedies, according to investor protection policies.

Disclosure rules support the price discovery process, which reveals information about the riskiness of the transaction. These rules concern different elements of the financial transaction, such as the transaction price, the conflicts of interest, the nature of the counterparties and so on.

A fiduciary duty,[33] a legal principle recognised by regulation, also ensures that the counterparty with a stronger informational position provides a sufficient information flow to investors to stimulate access to market mechanisms.

Enforcement

Finally, public enforcement is a key aspect of more efficient markets and lower cost capital (Coffee, 2007). Enforcement is mainly addressed via ex post monitoring by supervisors with strong sanctioning powers and other investors by putting downward and upward pressures on prices. Enforcement of rules, on the one hand, can work as a renegotiation tool driven by public intervention, such as in the case of insolvency, to avoid a disorderly wind-up of a company or a bank. The enforcement of these rules de facto results in a renegotiation of the financial claim based on the new financial situation of one of the two counterparties. On the other hand, in normal times, enforcement of the financial claim is a fundamental piece of the infrastructure in a dispersed agent environment (such as market-based

---

[33] 'Fiduciary duty' here refers to all the obligations imposed on the counterparty that, due to the credence nature of the instrument or the principal-agent relationship, is in a position to exploit a superior contractual power. For instance, these duties may apply to majority shareholders that attempt to concentrate power without paying for it or imposing undue costs on minorities, as well as duties that protect retail investors in transactions with financial intermediaries that can exploit their contractual power or investors' cognitive biases to impose unfair terms.

systems), as it keeps together a widespread set of interests that would otherwise disappear should their financial claim not receive any protection. Enforcement has two main components: sanctions and judicial review. Heavy sanctions are a good deterrent for potential wrongdoing, which has low probability of being detected and high profitability in a dispersed agent environment (see also section 0). The judicial system also plays an important role not only for its ability to enforce sanctions, but also for its flexibility in balancing the impact of bad rules with arbitration tools (Posner, 1998; Ergungor, 2004).

Key findings #3.

- Financial structure is thus the combination of institution-based and market-based intermediation (funding means) at macroeconomic level and debt and equity (funding types) at capital structure level (micro). Financial development can be defined as the size and level of sophistication (interconnection) of these funding means and types. Through competitive forces, financial structure and development influence each other.
- Financial integration is a process to achieve a combination of financial structure and development that produces a more efficient allocation of capital (via private risk sharing) that can unleash further economic development and ultimately growth.
- Both banks and markets face specification costs (ex ante) and monitoring costs (ex post), due to the inability to write the 'perfect contract' or to opportunism.
- Due to the inner nature of a financial claim in a market environment (dispersed monitoring), the legal system (calibrated for investor protection) is a cornerstone for public and private remedies to support a solid financial integration process. A weak legal system does not yield deep capital markets.
- Both private and public remedies are important for institution- and market-based systems, i.e. banks and capital markets. Comparatively, private remedies are more important for institution-based systems, while public remedies are more effective for market-based ones.
- Private remedies for market failures are relatively more important for banks, because they systematically use their contractual power to collect information upfront and make use of tools such as collateral. Private remedies, such as contractual renegotiation, also work better for banks in an ex post environment. In effect, excessive creditor legal protection may even damage credit quality, as it reduces the bank's incentive to assess credit risk independently.

- Enforcement does not only mean sanctioning powers, but evidence suggests that a flexible judicial system with alternative litigation tools, such as common arbitration rules across Europe, can foster further capital market development.
- In market-based systems, enforcement is not only about public intervention, but also private remedies such as third-party monitoring and private enforcement. For instance, the role of rating agencies to signal risk quality or the ex post control of auditing companies is essential to market pricing mechanisms. Policy-makers should monitor their action and hold them accountable, rather than substitute third-party monitoring with more invasive regulation and licensing requirements, which are a static monitoring activity.
- Financial integration that would produce private cross-sectional and intertemporal risk sharing needs to consider the characteristics of a legal system and the calibration of policies for investor protection, finding the right balance between private and public remedies for institution- and market-based systems.

2.3 Financial development and economic growth

Financial development theories

The development of the financial system occurs in different stages. In its infancy, it is mostly bank-dominated (Boot & Thakor, 1997; Boyd & Smith, 1998; Levine, 2002). This is also consistent with the idea that developing economies have lower governance quality and less transparency, which makes banks (relationship-based funding) better placed to deal with frictions that will not be manageable in a dispersed agent environment (such as market-based systems). Banks have better instruments to deal with the agency costs and moral hazard (post-contractual) amplified by a more primitive and opaque market structure. As financial sophistication increases, and increased borrower quality follows, bank lending becomes less important and gives markets more space to flourish as the economy develops infrastructure for decentralised information (Acemoglu & Zilibotti, 1998; Demigurc-Kunt et al., 2011). As discussed above, financial development is a combination of legal and economic factors, which define the size and sophistication of a given combination of funding means and types.

Development & networks

Intermediaries and financial markets are networks (Economides, 1993), i.e. webs of financial contracts (e.g. payments, loans, derivatives contracts) that connect different nodes (mainly financial institutions, firms and individuals). They benefit from direct and indirect production and consumption externalities (Katz & Shapiro, 1985) that can emerge at production (e.g. information sources or a new node that adds new potential goods to the offer), distribution (e.g. ATMs network) and consumption level (e.g.

agglomeration effects for liquidity if there are more investors accessing the platform, as explained by Pagano, 1989). These aspects lead to a list of potential trade-offs between competition and concentration of banks and markets in terms of efficiency gains (Allen & Gale, 2000a; Claessens, 2009). Some level of concentration rather than perfect competition can increase the number of available products with direct positive externalities (Economides, 1993). Interconnection can instead boost indirect consumption externalities and increase the value of the network by just adding more customers, with no more new services or goods. Banks and financial markets also exhibit a 'multi-sided' nature, due to the non-neutral pricing structure (Rochet & Tirole, 2003), with different levels of interactions between the users of the platform, whether it is a banking services or securities treading platform (see Valiante & Lannoo, 2011, chapter 5 for a review of these network characteristics). Banking or trading services are usually less costly (often free) for bank depositors or some categories of traders (liquidity makers)[34] that provide stable liquidity respectively to financial institutions and trading activities on electronic platforms.

Development & integration

Financial integration influences financial development. However, financial integration can increase private risk sharing and competition among funding sources, depending on the aggregate level of development of the financial system. A different degree of development can result in financial integration being the source of global imbalances, i.e. excessive accumulation of foreign liabilities only by advanced economies (Mendoza et al., 2007). The financial integration process, whether global or regional, may thus require preliminary and ongoing policy interventions to support as much as possible the development of the financial system that is part of the integration process. This may include providing these systems with the legal architecture, interconnection and economic incentives for banks and intermediaries to increase size and sophistication (interconnection) to an optimal point. These actions would be mainly directed to less developed systems to catch up with more advanced ones. Numerous initiatives at European level to create common market infrastructure (such as TARGET 2 for payments and TARGET 2 Securities for securities settlement) are among the policy options to help increase the sophistication (specialisation) of the financial system in order to reap the benefits of greater financial integration.

[34] Interest rates on deposits or liquidity provision fees are not part of these considerations as remuneration for the provision of a service, respectively very short-term lending (deposits) and market-making services (liquidity provision).

Improving financial development, such as strengthening the role of capital markets, would limit the collateral damage of a financial integration process led so far by network effects. Without policy intervention to redress imbalances, network externalities will concentrate capital flows (and ownership of foreign assets) where the financial system generates more positive externalities. After the initial benefit of cross-border integration, risk sharing would become risk concentration, which would be potentially subject to sudden stops and reversal during crises, when it would be most needed. Several emerging markets have removed most of their capital controls and have seen capital flows coming in, but most of these flows tend to be pro-cyclical with very limited international risk sharing (Kose et al., 2009). This sequence of events does not exclude financial integration from leading the financial system's development up to a point where it can influence the speed (slowdown) of financial integration, if it changes the composition of the capital flows. A recent 'U-turn' on capital controls by the IMF is indeed the 'smoking gun' (IMF, 2012). If financial integration determines an unbalanced financial structure (a combination of credit and equity funding by banks and markets), there might be detrimental effects on the development of the financial system in the area that suffers the capital flow shock.

Figure 2.10 Financial development and integration channels to economic growth

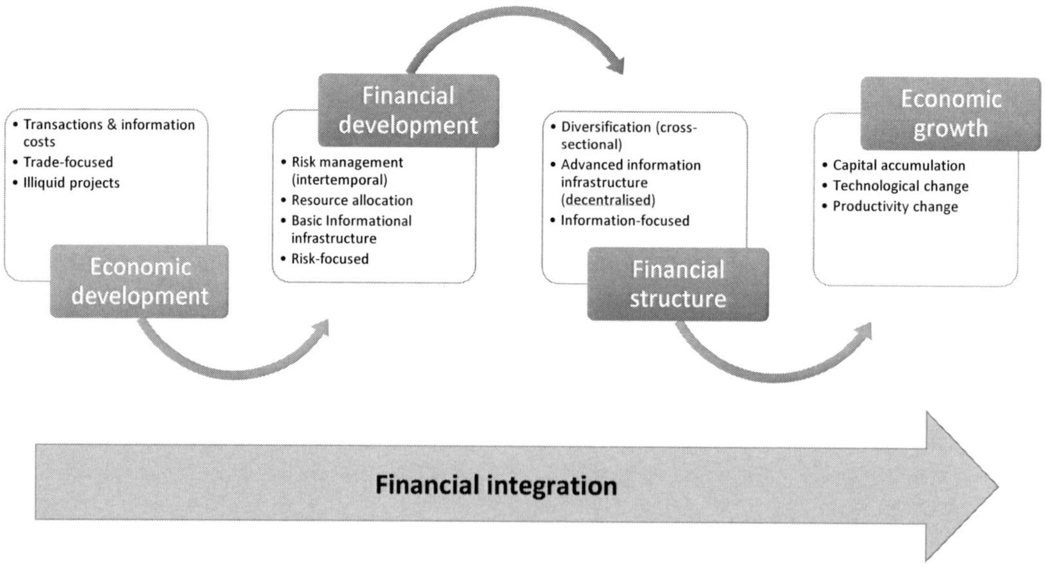

Integration & growth

`Despite the instability of capital flows and the uncertainty on the causality direction (at all times) between financial integration and development, financial integration does produce effects on economic growth. When measured via the capital accounts liberalisation and the total external position (foreign assets and liabilities) of the country, evidence suggests that integration may produce an impact on economic growth via productivity enhancements (Bonfiglioli, 2008). Most likely, this impact on growth takes place via the improvement of financial development that greater integration brings in. The impact of integration on growth may occur via:

i. Greater risk diversification that lowers costs of capital.
ii. Greater competition from external funding sources that lowers transaction costs and increases efficiency.
iii. Greater cross-sectional risk-sharing ability, as the market develops, that increases specialisation with a potential impact on productivity.

Some evidence points to the 'lower cost of capital' channel having a stronger impact on growth for emerging markets, while the 'cross-sectional risk-sharing ability' channel has more impact on growth for advanced economies (for a review, see Papaioannou, 2007). As expectations of financial development shape up, financial integration also influences the financial structure, i.e. the equilibrium of banks and markets, as more players anticipate the development of capital markets.

As they are best placed for cross-sectional risk sharing, capital markets thus are not just a sufficient but also a necessary condition to generate further development and economic growth in advanced economies.

Development & growth

Financial integration is perhaps the main but not the only factor influencing financial development. The impact of financial development on growth shall thus be assessed separately from the integration process. Financial development is indeed important for economic development (McKinnon, 1973) and can have an impact on economic growth. Over the years, there have been many attempts to identify how financial development impacts economic growth and whether there is an optimal level of development after which further expansion and interconnection between banks and markets in the financial system would be detrimental for growth prospects. The contribution of financial development to economic growth can occur via different channels, mainly banking, insurance, and securities markets. The balance between these different channels creates an optimal financial ecosystem for economic growth.

The 'neutrality view'

Neither banks nor markets are individually superior means to achieve economic growth (the 'neutrality' view). While bank and market funding might contribute to economic development in different ways at different stages of development, empirical evidence is neutral about one of the two prevailing in their contribution to economic growth (Levine, 2002; Beck & Levine, 2002). But financial development, via the impact of cross-section risk diversification (mainly delivered by capital markets) on technological development, can indeed impact long-run economic growth (King & Levine, 1993; Levine, 1997). While neglecting country fixed effects (a key factor to track differences in financial development) in their empirical model, Levine & Zervos (1998) provide a first set of evidence of how financial development (both banks and markets, thus credit and securities markets) can impact economic growth via capital accumulation and productivity improvements. Industries that use more external finance tend to grow faster in countries with higher financial development, i.e. in markets with a high degree of both bank and market funding penetration (Rajan & Zingales, 1998a; Beck & Levine, 2002).[35] These firms also tend to grow more in an environment with better financial markets (Kumar et al., 1999). The main channel through which financial development (in this case only assessed for credit markets) spurs growth is productivity (Beck et al., 2000). This is particularly true for R&D-intensive firms, such as high-tech fast-growing firms, based on the greater ability of cross-sectional risk sharing to deal with illiquid short-term projects that can boost total factor productivity (Giordano & Guagliano, 2014).

There have also been attempts to assess if financial development benefits economic growth in every circumstance. The recent financial and economic crisis, led by significant asset bubbles both in the US and Europe, has left the world with several unanswered questions about when and how finance can actually lead to resource misallocation (Pagano, 2012). As mentioned, financial development implies a growth in size and interconnection of the financial system. This process of growth of the financial system may be beneficial up to the point that it becomes detrimental to productivity growth (a 'parabolic' relationship, as defined by Cecchetti & Kharroubi, 2012; Manganelli & Popov, 2013). The growth of the banking system in Europe due to the high leveraging rate during the long boom period is now challenging the 'neutrality' view of Levine (2002), i.e. that banks and markets do not prevail in their individual contribution to growth. In effect, Pagano et al. (2014) show first that the banking system in Europe in the last decade has overgrown with a potential negative impact on growth, and, second, that the same measure of financial structure used by Levine, i.e. value of share traded over private bank credit (both over GDP), is now significant and positive (more equity markets activity may imply more economic growth). If we consider these two findings together, this recent research does not really challenge the 'neutrality' view, but rather reaffirms it by confirming its main implication.

[35] In their cross-country and cross-industry analysis, Beck & Levine (2002) use different measures of financial development, including the value of credits by financial intermediaries (bank and non-banks) to the private sector divided by GDP, the value of total shares traded on the stock market divided by GDP, the logarithm of the sum of private credit and stock market capitalisation.

When the financial system becomes too unbalanced, i.e. credit or equity overgrow, a detrimental impact on economic growth occurs. Whether led by banks or markets, it is thus the imbalance determined by excessive growth of credit over equity markets that undermines economic growth. With a dataset covering 1989-2011, Langfield & Pagano (2015) extend the previous analysis by using a market structure indicator that is less biased towards the 'credit market overgrowth' argument. They use a ratio of total bank assets to stock and private bond market capitalisation. In this way, they in practice measure the impact of the intensity of intertemporal vis-à-vis cross-sectional risk sharing on economic growth. Even including the issuance of financial institution debt securities, until the early 2000s, private bond market volumes in Europe are almost insignificant compared to credit flows. This may also justify the much lower coefficient compared to the previous study.

Debt overhang

The negative connotation of excessive private debt growth would be consistent with the other side of the coin represented by the recent research on the impact of excessive public debt on growth (Reinhart & Rogoff, 2010). Indeed, it may be the overhanging public and private debt to burden economic growth. Bank and market channels shall coexist to make sure that there is a balanced proportion of debt and equity in the economy. Credit booms can harm the total productivity factor by hurting R&D-intensive firms that rely on highly illiquid projects (Cecchetti & Kharroubi, 2015). The interesting argument is that, as the financial sector grows and hires more skilled workers to increase even more the availability of credit, entrepreneurs may be more willing to invest in low productivity projects with returns relatively easier to pledge (high productivity projects are typically less tangible and more difficult to pledge).[36] This conclusion might be consistent with the growth in recent years of collateralised financing activities but also, and most important, with the argument that financial integration and development should take into account the diversification of the financial structure, i.e. the funding sources of the economy.

Key findings #4.

- An underdeveloped financial system that relies on banks and markets does not exist. As financial sophistication increases, there is a pressing need for a more effective system of rules and an informational infrastructure (disclosure rules) in order for market mechanisms to complement bank lending and create a financial ecosystem

---

[36] The model uses cross-industry data and does not take into account cross-country differences, which can be an important factor.

conducive to a more efficient resource allocation (private risk sharing) and ultimately to an ideal environment for economic development and growth.

- Rethinking of financial integration policies means greater focus on the removal of barriers to cross-border financial activity, with the support of stronger institutions that can effectively monitor the process.
- Financial integration can increase private risk sharing and competition among funding sources, depending on the level of development of the financial system. Low financial development can result in financial integration being a source of global imbalances, driven by the network externalities of the financial system.
- Improving financial development, such as strengthening the role of capital markets, would prevent the financial network from concentrating capital flows (and ownership of foreign assets) where they generate more positive externalities irrespective of the risk that is being created. After the initial benefit of cross-border integration, if there is no private risk sharing, capital flows would cause risk concentration, with heightened risks of sudden stops and reversals during crises. Without a policy intervention to develop more cross-sectional market-based private risk-sharing mechanisms (capital markets) to support the intertemporal one, current financial integration will continue to regularly create instability in the financial system.
- Financial integration can produce different outcomes in terms of economic growth if the playing field (financial development) is impaired. Institutions are necessary to balance financial development (funding means; balance of intermediaries and markets) and for financial structure (funding types; balance of equity and debt) to support economic development and thus growth.
- Unleashing competition among funding sources via the single market may provide a tool to even the playing field in financial development. As a stronger pan-European industry and financial infrastructure spreads across Europe, a plan of barrier removal that looks at all the unnecessary impediments to direct cross-border financial activity can accelerate this process and speed up financial development.
- The cross-sectional risk dispersion capacity of capital markets complements the intertemporal nature of relationship-based funding, making it best suited to financing innovation and thus economic growth in advanced economies. Most important, private equity, venture capital and crowdfunding appear most suited to financing fast-growing innovative projects. But their effective functioning is guaranteed only by a proper exit option for investors, which is an efficient open market pricing mechanism (such as stock exchanges).
- The risk of uneven financial development can also take the form of an overgrown bank-lending activity with a debt overhang that harms economic growth, such as recently witnessed in Europe. In effect, overreliance on credit flows can create excessive investments in projects with returns that are easier to pledge. These projects are typically not innovative. As financial development produces an impact on growth via productivity improvements, more market intermediation yields more financial development and so greater ability to fund projects with higher productivity gains.

3. European financial market structure and integration in the CMU era

Introduction

Financial integration in Europe is a complex process, which relies on the behaviours of multiple private agents, investors, issuers, intermediaries, market infrastructures, as well as public policies, such as those designed to remove the weight of national markets and practices on the single market (see chapter 1). Chapter 2 discussed the rationale for greater capital market integration and the ideal design; this chapter reviews the current status of European financial market structure and integration. It examines markets and segments of the financial system in order to identify key critical areas of action for a plan that could revive integration. The first part will review the structure of the European financial system and compare it to other global financial areas. The second part will discuss the overall degree of financial integration in the euro area and discuss the lessons for Europe as a whole. The third and fourth parts will collect updated information about the development of integration in individual market segments and intermediation channels of European financial markets.

3.1 Europe's financial structure: The international and regional dimension

A bank-based financial system

The European financial system relies heavily on traditional bank intermediation. Bank assets are roughly three times the size of the nominal Gross Domestic Product (GDP), which is even bigger than the banking sector in China (see Figure 3.1). It is even bigger than the combined size of equity, government and corporate debt securities markets. This situation has recently led the scientific advisory body of the European Systemic Risk Board (ESRB), which supports the macroprudential oversight of central banks in the European Union, to argue in favour of actions to shrink an 'overbanked' financial system (Pagano et al., 2014). As deleveraging proceeds at a slow pace, securities markets could develop further to attain a size comparable to other regions of the world and reduce the relative weight of the banking sector.

Figure 3.1 Financial sector simplified structure (% GDP, average 2010-2014)

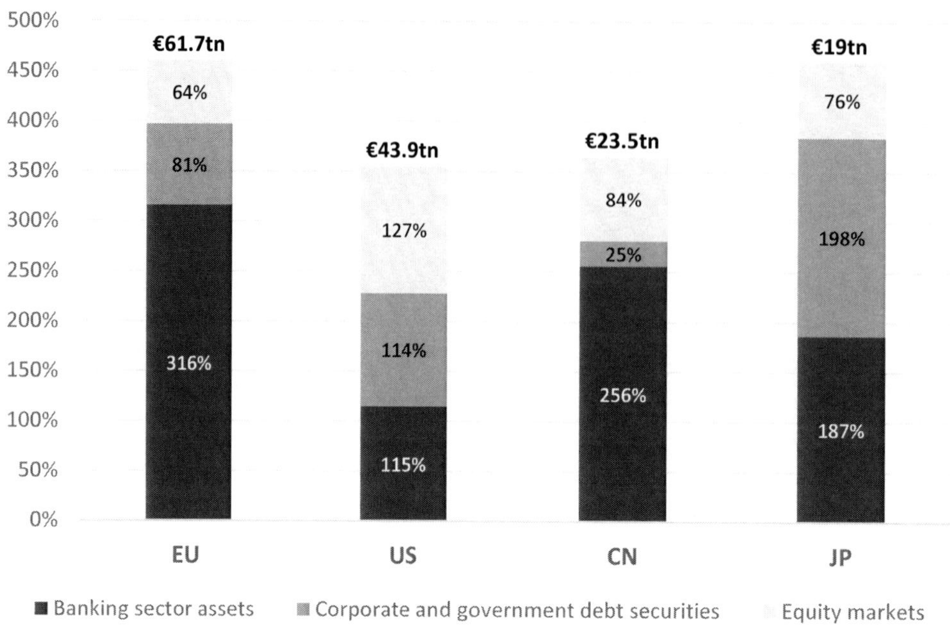

Notes: For debt securities, we use outstanding amounts and exclude financial institution debt securities (which are implicitly included in the banking sector assets statistics). For equity, we use domestic market capitalisation. For US bank assets data, we include gross notional value of derivative positions and credit union assets.

Data Sources: IMF (GDP), BIS, ECB, US Fed, BoJ, PBoC, WFE, FESE, individual stock exchanges. Eurostat for exchange rates.

Corporate bond and equity markets, in particular, remain small vis-à-vis the same markets in other big economies (see Figure 3.2). These data are additional evidence of a poor cross-sectional risk sharing mechanism in the European Union, as market debt and equity instruments are key to sharing risk across national markets (see Box 3.1).

Figure 3.2 Capital market structure (value of outstanding securities, excl. derivatives; average 2010-14; % GDP)

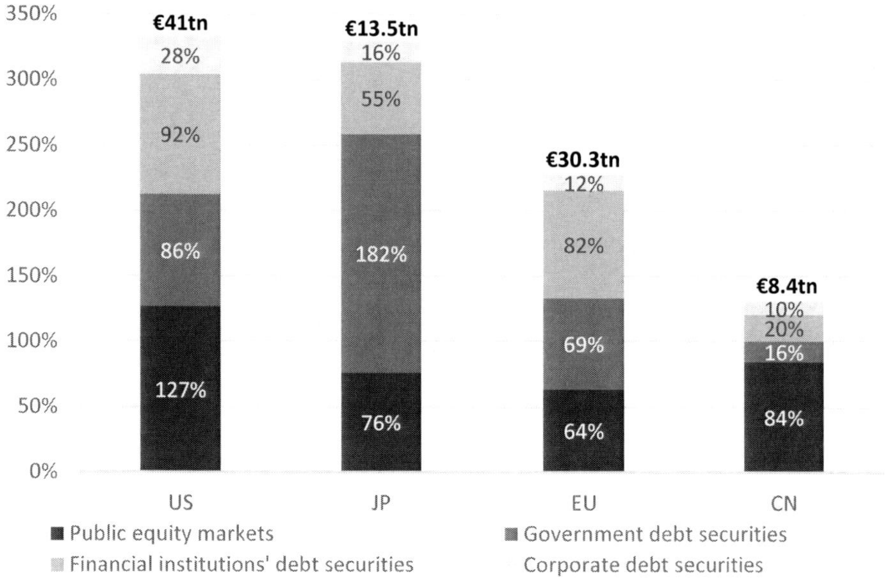

Notes: Derivative markets, excluded from this chart, include securitisation, derivative contracts, and indexes (exchange-traded products; see following sections). 'Public equity markets' are equal to domestic market capitalisation.

Data Sources: BIS, ECB, WFE, FESE, individual stock exchanges. Eurostat for exchange rates.

Regional fragmentation

There is also a strong regional fragmentation of debt and securities markets, with very limited pan-European activity. Every country has local equity and debt securities markets, which go from almost four times the national GDP in the Netherlands to less than 100% in other countries, like Poland (see Figure 3.3). Overall, equity markets play a less relevant role than debt markets. Debt markets are bigger due to the dominant role of financial institutions and government debt securities. This confirms the above-mentioned limited risk sharing in the area due to the portfolio composition of holdings and the fragmentation of the market structure.

Figure 3.3 Stock market capitalisation and outstanding debt securities, selected EU countries (end 2014, % GDP)

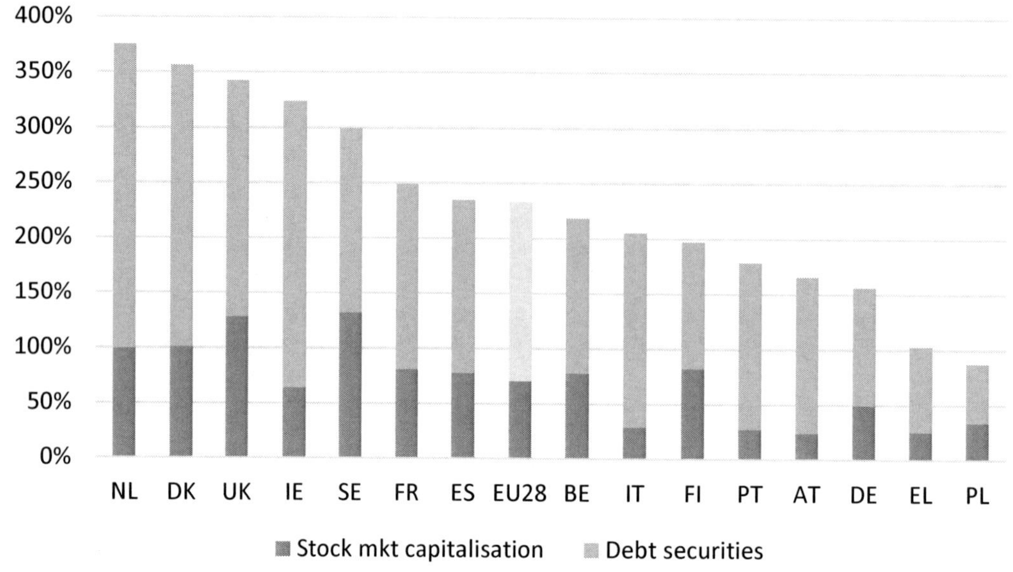

Note: 'Debt securities' includes government, financial institutions and corporate debt securities.

Data Sources: WFE, FESE, individual stock exchanges and ECB.

Most interestingly, countries whose financial markets are larger than their domestic economies are not necessarily those that have small banking sectors. Big banking systems can coexist with more active financial markets. However, the lack of cross-border integration in the banking sector (described in Box 2.1) may encourage current market fragmentation and entrench domestic banking sectors' inability to restructure and reduce their size, reducing space for capital markets to spontaneously develop. In effect, despite both a financial and a sovereign crisis, the aggregate size of the European banking sector (mainly dealers, credit institutions and other lending organisations) is still larger than the non-financial sector. That is, after reaching its historical peak, it is still larger than the combined size of households, non-financial corporations and government's financial assets (see Figure 3.4). In the United States, the opposite holds, with households, non-financial corporations and government assets more than double the size of the domestic traditional banking sector.

There is thus more balance among funding means (bank and intermediaries) and types (equity and debt), which (as suggested by the events in the aftermath of the financial crisis) has made the US financial system more resilient to permanent shocks (aggregate systemic risk).

Figure 3.4 Total financial assets/liabilities of financial intermediaries (including dealers and other lending organisations) vs households, NFCs, government (2004-14; €mn)

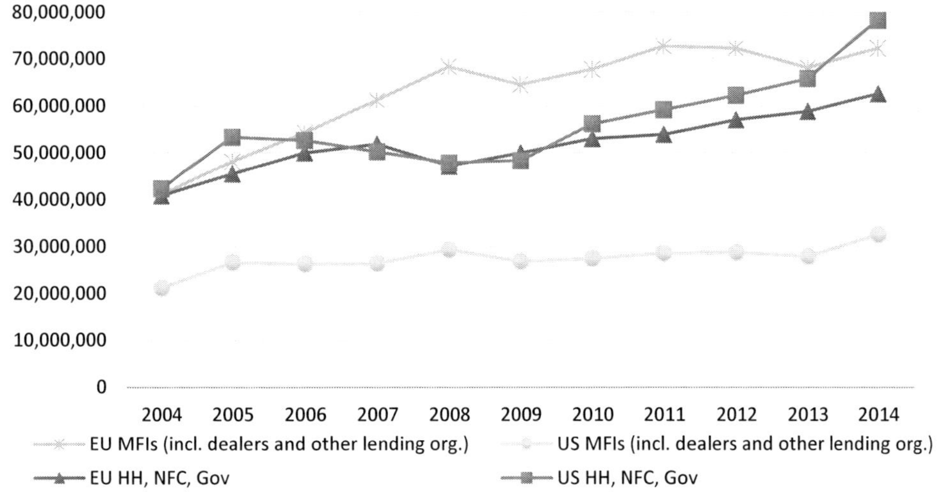

Data Sources: Eurostat and the US Federal Reserve. Eurostat for exchange rates.

Furthermore, the financial asset structure of all financial corporations (including investment funds) has also been growing substantially in recent years, reaching almost €100 trillion, compared to €60 trillion for the non-financial sector. Other financial institutions, such as securities and derivative dealers, and the investment fund industry, have been key drivers of growth, which has not slowed down despite a major financial crisis (see Figure 3.5). *Financial asset structure*

Figure 3.5 Total financial assets by type of entity in Europe (€mn)

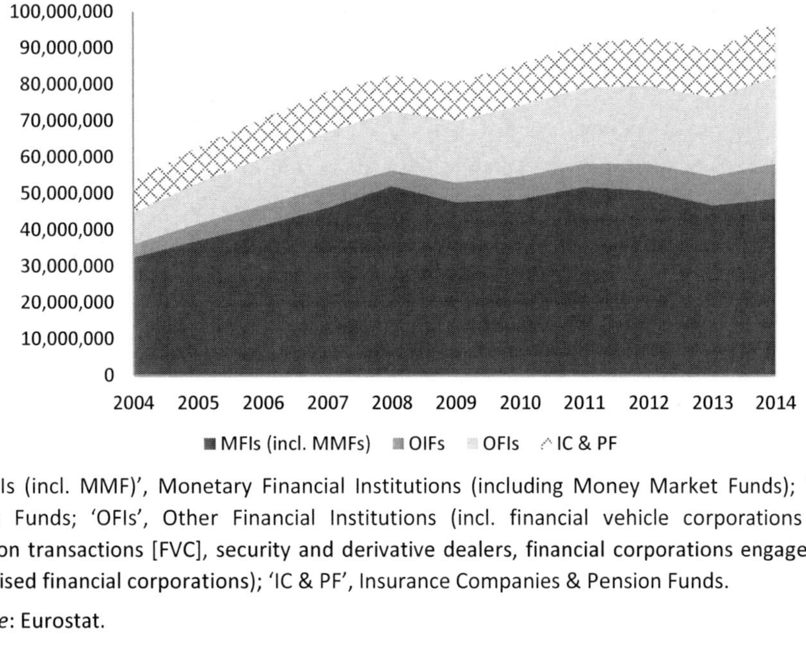

Notes: 'MFIs (incl. MMF)', Monetary Financial Institutions (including Money Market Funds); 'OIFs', Other Investment Funds; 'OFIs', Other Financial Institutions (incl. financial vehicle corporations engaged in securitisation transactions [FVC], security and derivative dealers, financial corporations engaged in lending, and specialised financial corporations); 'IC & PF', Insurance Companies & Pension Funds.

Data Source: Eurostat.

The situation is fairly different across member states. The size of the financial sector vis-à-vis the nominal GDP of the country can go from well below 100% to 180 times its value, such as for Luxembourg (see Figure 3.6). In member states such as Ireland and Luxembourg, the size of the sector is mostly driven by the investment fund industry; other institutions, such as broker-dealers, have boosted the size of small financial centres such as Cyprus and Malta. The United Kingdom is the country with the largest banking sector, i.e. roughly €14 trillion or six times the national GDP.

Figure 3.6 The size of the financial sector by country (over nominal GDP; end 2014)

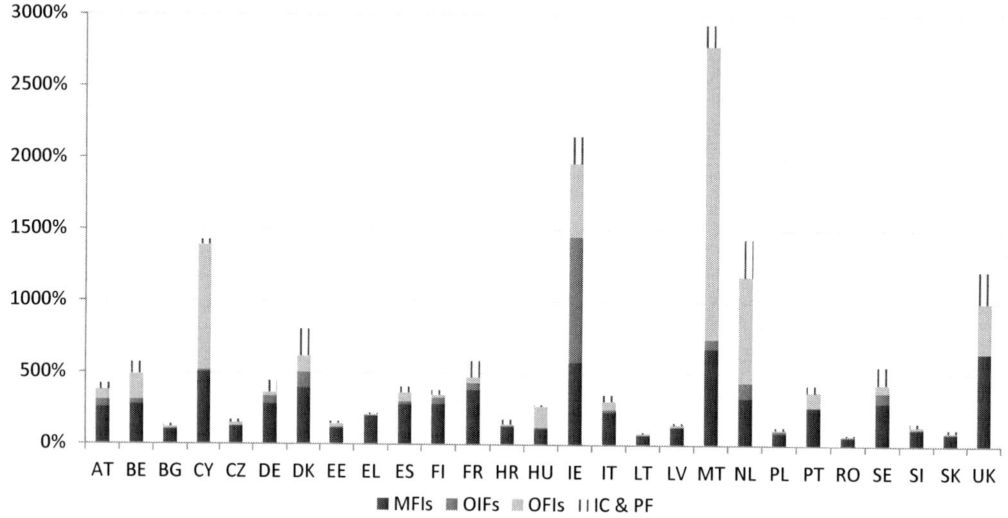

Note: For illustrative purposes, the bar graph does not include Luxembourg, which is around 18,000%, i.e. 180 times national GDP.

Data Source: Eurostat.

Financial assets breakdown

If we look at the composition of those financial assets for the whole financial sector, there are some important differences with the US. First, there is a significant amount of currency and deposits held by financial intermediaries in Europe (17% or roughly €17 trillion), compared to only 4% in the US (see Figure 3.7). This shows perhaps room for improvement in asset allocation of financial intermediaries, which often have to hold high liquidity buffers to match the high deposit holdings of households and NFCs (see sections 3.1.1, 3.1.2). The European financial sector also holds much less equity than US peers, showing the limited activism of financial intermediaries in cross-border or national equity markets. Moreover, issued loans and debt securities holdings also have greater weight in the US than in the EU financial sector.

Figure 3.7 Financial structure of financial intermediation (% total assets; end 2014)

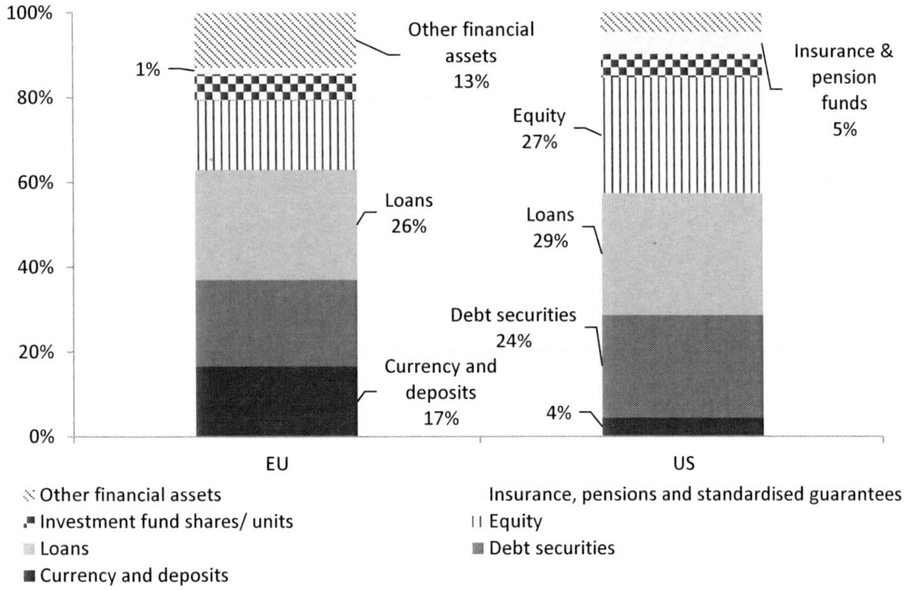

Data Sources: Eurostat and US Fed Reserve. Eurostat for exchange rates.

Interestingly, insurance and pension funds also carry greater weight in the US financial system compared to Europe. In effect, the activism of these players is higher overseas, as suggested by their equity asset holdings, mainly in listed shares for US peers.

Figure 3.8 Investments in equity of insurance and pension funds (end 2014; €mn)

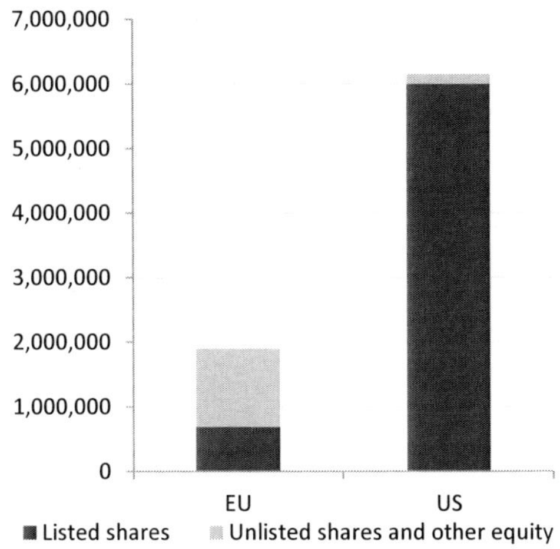

Data Sources: Eurostat and US Federal Reserve. Eurostat for exchange rates.

European insurance companies and pension funds had a similar equity portfolio distribution until the 2008 financial crisis, when this relationship reverted as holdings of listed shares dropped across the board while unlisted shareholdings remained stable. Despite the recovery of equity prices since then, assets are still less than half their 2007 value, as insurance and pension funds are being held back from listed equity, most likely due to expectations about future capital charges on equity (Solvency II for insurance and companies and other prudential requirements for pension funds) and fragmentation (and cost) of local equity markets.

Box 3.1 Central government financial assets: a quick overview

Another element that adds complexity to the financial ecosystem is the role of central governments in asset allocation. The size of the balance sheet of European governments has constantly increased in the last 10 years, from roughly €3.5 trillion to almost €7 trillion (see Figure 3.9), as public intervention has been increasingly needed to support demand after the crisis and public interventions in the financial system.

Figure 3.9 Total financial assets/liabilities of the US and EU-28 central governments (€bn; 2004-14)

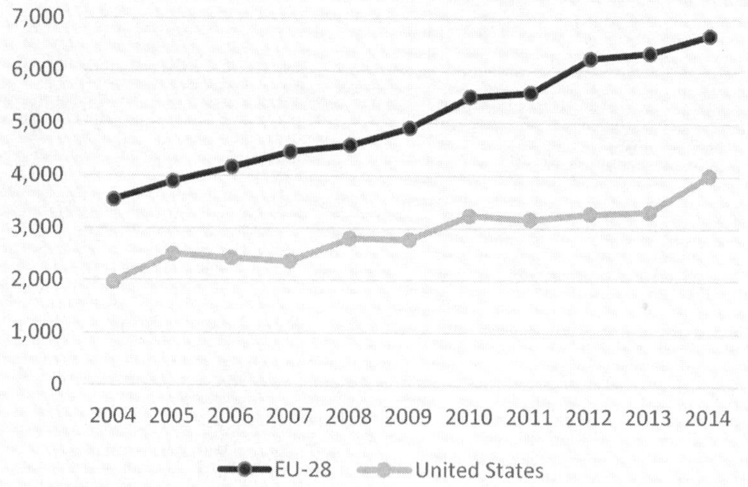

Data Sources: Eurostat and US Federal Reserve. Eurostat for exchange rates.

There are a few interesting differences in the composition of the financial asset structure for the US and European governments. In particular, European governments are historically more interventionist, with large holdings of equity in several companies in their domestic markets. Equity holdings account for 31% (€2.1 tn) of total financial assets, compared to only 6% in the US (€228 bn). EU governments also hold much less in debt securities, perhaps also due to the limited corporate bond issuance of local firms compared to overseas markets.

Figure 3.10 EU & US central government financial asset structure (end 2014; €mn)

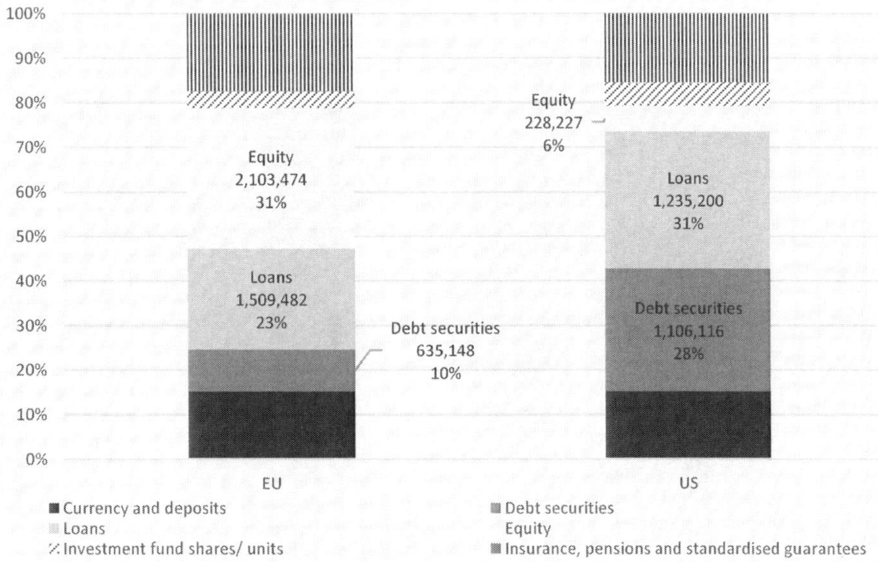

Sources: Eurostat and US Federal Reserve. Eurostat for exchange rates.

The role of government direct intervention in the economy (including the financial system) has expanded in recent years in response to the financial and economic crises. Its influence over asset allocation has also grown: its balance sheet size is now almost 7% of the whole financial sector. In the coming years, when the financial sector will most likely reduce its burden on the economy, governments may be tempted to take a more direct role in influencing asset allocation and market structure in the financial system with direct market interventions to shape incentives, e.g. financial repression, and take care of market failures. But would this be the best possible use of taxpayer money? Would a reduction in equity holdings, accompanied by sound integration policies, better support the development of a more active European capital market?

3.1.1 Funding structure of non-financial corporations

Financial intermedia tion for NFC

A similar view to the one sketched out for the overall structure of Europe's financial system emerges when examining the funding intermediation for non-financial corporations (NFC). In Europe, total NFC funding intermediation (excluding cash and deposits), in the form of bank loans, is equivalent to 44% of GDP, compared to roughly 18% in the US (see Figure 3.11). Overall, the funding to NFC is just above 100% of GDP, as a sign that the corporate sector may be even underleveraged. Corporate debt securities are equivalent to a fourth of bank lending activities. NFC bank lending is at least twice bigger than in the US.

Figure 3.11 NFC bank and market intermediation (% GDP, average 2010-14)

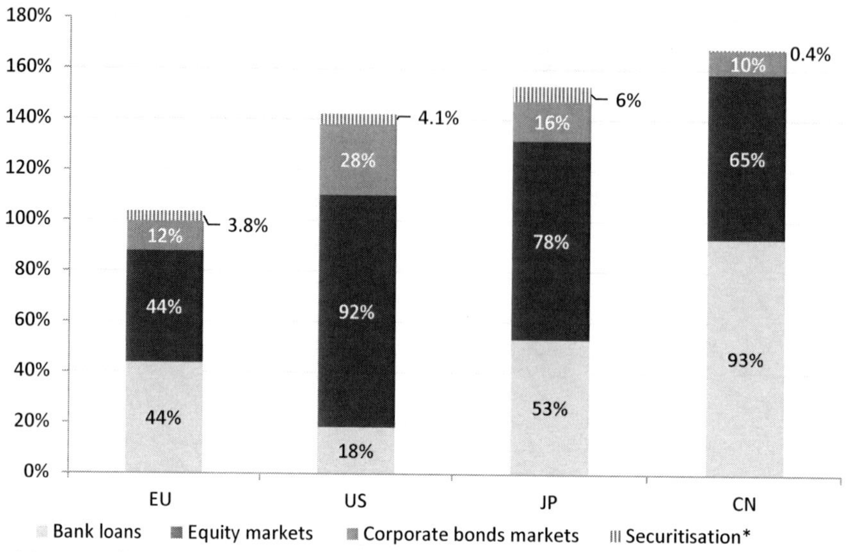

Note: Securitisation refers to the non-financial corporate sector both in the US (CMBS) and the EU (CDO/CLO, CMBS, SME, WBS/PFI), while it includes total outstanding securitised products in JP and CN.

Data sources: IMF, Eurostat, BIS, ECB, US Federal Reserve, BoJ, PBoC, WFE, FESE, individual stock exchanges, AFME, SIFMA, CICC Research. Eurostat for exchange rates.

Excluding equity market capitalisation, which is not necessarily an indicator of ongoing funding availability but rather a measure of market value, Cour-Thimann & Winkler (2013) estimated an 80% bank-based NFC debt financing in Europe, versus 20% in the US. Our updated estimates on bank loans and debt securities financing (see Figure 3.12), over the period 2010-14, show that bank funding grew to 40% of total NFC debt in the US, while in Europe it was a stable 79%. Overall, while the capital market contribution in the US has decreased (in relative terms), NFC market funding in Europe remains far lower and among the lowest worldwide.

NFC issuance

For instance, if we look at the net issuance of loans, debt securities and equity before the crisis in the euro area, non-financial firms were mainly raising money through bank loans (see Figure 3.13). Since the beginning of the financial crisis, which has severely hit the European banking system, the level of net issuance of loans has dramatically dropped. The net issuance of loans, debt and equity altogether went from almost €700 billion in 2007 to less than €100 billion in a few years. Despite that, non-financial corporations (mainly large corporations) have been able to offset the drop in net bank lending into negative territory with higher corporate debt issuance. The net issuance of equity (either negative or positive) is almost irrelevant over time, which shows the lack of importance of equity markets to fund most euro area non-financial corporations (as buybacks are a limited number). Overall, market funding for NFC was a good risk absorber, as it did not disappear during the crisis, but the level of activities remains at such a low level that macroeconomic gains are almost negligible

Figure 3.12 Market vs bank-based NFC debt funding (€bn; average 2010-14)

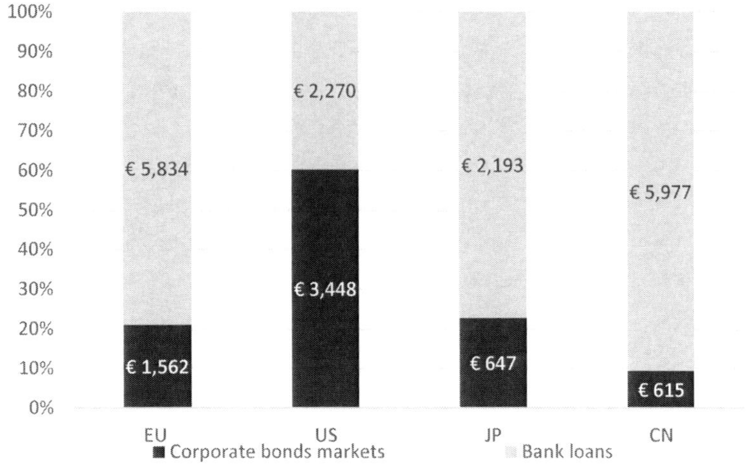

Note: For the US we use the dataset of commercial banks released by the FED, instead of the broader category of depository institutions.

Data Sources: IMF, BIS, ECB, US Fed, BoJ, PBoC, WFE, FESE and individual stock exchanges. Eurostat for exchange rates.

Figure 3.13 Net issuance of loans, debt securities and equity (2000-14; €bn)

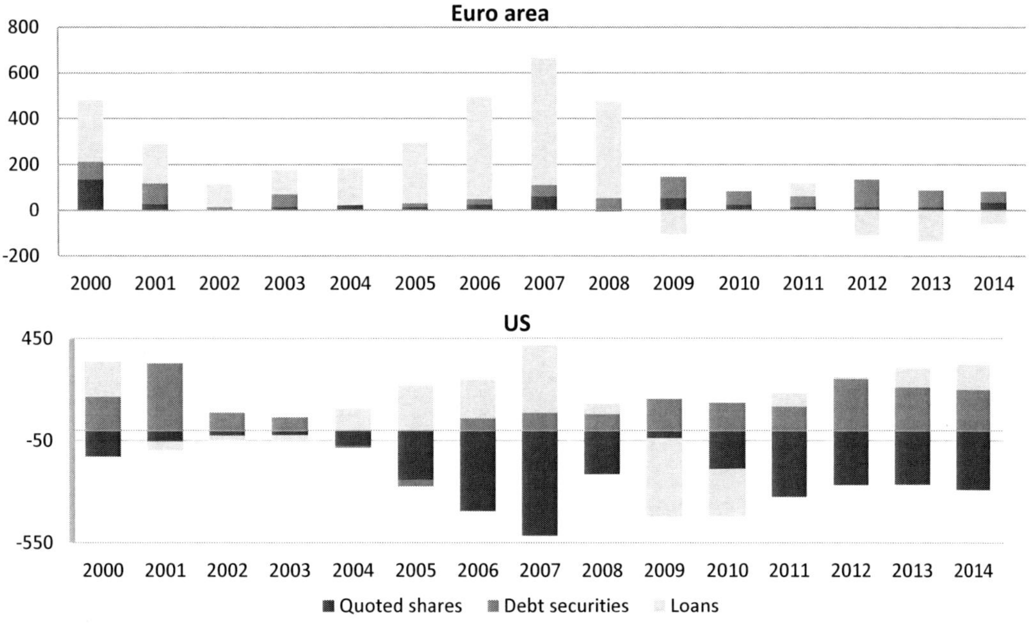

Data Sources: ECB and US Federal Reserve. Eurostat for exchange rates.

In the US, the financial crisis has for the most part reduced net issuance of bank loans, but it did not really affect the growth of corporate debt net issuance, which has almost offset the long-time negative net issuance of equity. Overall the absolute value of net issuance, e.g. new issuance and buybacks, is more than €500 billion in the US, compared to less than €100 billion in the euro area. Gross issuance is also roughly double that of the euro area (Van Rixtel & Villegas, 2015). Most notably, the negative net issuance of equity is not necessarily a bad development. In effect, this means that firms are buying back equity to repay investments of shareholders as an alternative to dividends. Therefore, there is an active use of underlying equity markets to shape incentives in equity investments by providing shareholders with a constant payout, which suggests a very active secondary market and an easy exit for private equity funds or venture capitalists. In effect, share buybacks have currently overtaken the aggregate value of dividend issuances (Van Rixtel & Villegas, 2015). Questions may arise about alternative uses of firm revenues for firm long-term development, instead of taking out equity, but this would be another story.

Funding for SMEs

While the financial situation of large European corporations is almost unscathed, it is more problematic for small and medium firms to access equity and debt securities markets, due to either their small size or the small size of (and costly access to) local markets.[37] Costs can be estimated to a one-off cost of €80,000-100,000 and annual costs of €100,000-120,000, which mainly includes costs for advisory services related to the listing on a public venue (Wyman, 2014; European IPO Task Force, 2015).

As the net issuance of loans stays negative (a supply cut), the cost of new short-term loans below €1 million has significantly increased, as well as its difference with the cost of loans above €1 million. SME liabilities are usually composed of short-term bank funding or bank loans that are facing the sharp upward trend in interest rates (see Figure 3.14).

[37] There is currently no cross-border activity in equity or debt issuance for small and medium-sized enterprises (SMEs). The definition of an SME is set in a Communication of the European Commission (2003/361/EC). Art. 2: "The category of micro, small and medium-sized enterprises (SMEs) is made up of enterprises which employ fewer than 250 persons and which have an annual turnover not exceeding EUR 50 million, and/or an annual balance sheet total not exceeding EUR 43 million. Within the SME category, a small enterprise is defined as an enterprise which employs fewer than 50 persons and whose annual turnover and/or annual balance sheet total does not exceed EUR 10 million. Within the SME category, a microenterprise is defined as an enterprise which employs fewer than 10 persons and whose annual turnover and/or annual balance sheet total does not exceed EUR 2 million." See also Infelise & Valiante (2013) on the discussion around the EU definition of SMEs.

Figure 3.14 Spread between loans below and above €1mn by maturity (% points) and SME liabilities

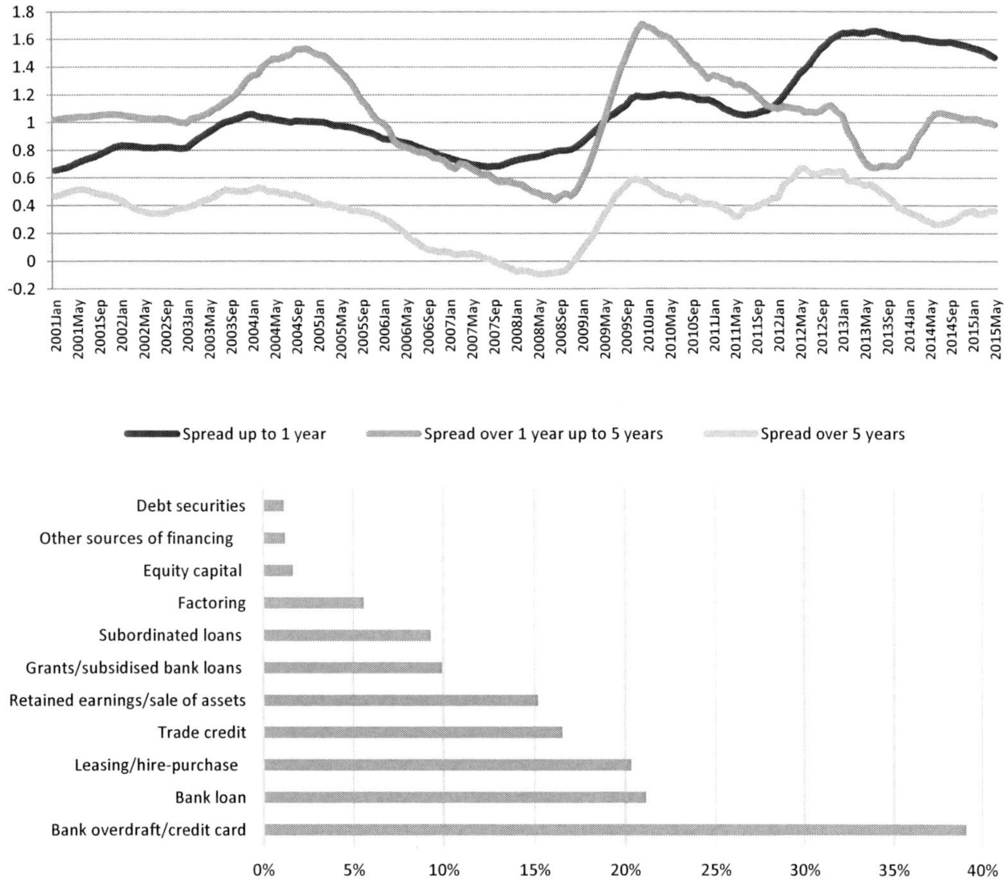

Note: Data coverage (second chart): euro area SMEs, October 2014–March 2015.

Data Sources: ECB Data Warehouse & SAFE, 2015, survey published by the ECB in June 2015.

NFC liabilities

A much closer look at the composition of NFC liabilities (see Figure 3.15) confirms, as hinted at above, the reliance of EU firms on bank financing (28%) and a much less significant role for corporate debt securities (5%). Listed shares in European NFC are roughly 18% of the total liabilities and account for 33% of total equity. In the US, these percentages go up respectively to 33% and 54%.

Figure 3.15 Financial liabilities of EU and US non-financial corporations (€bn, end 2014)

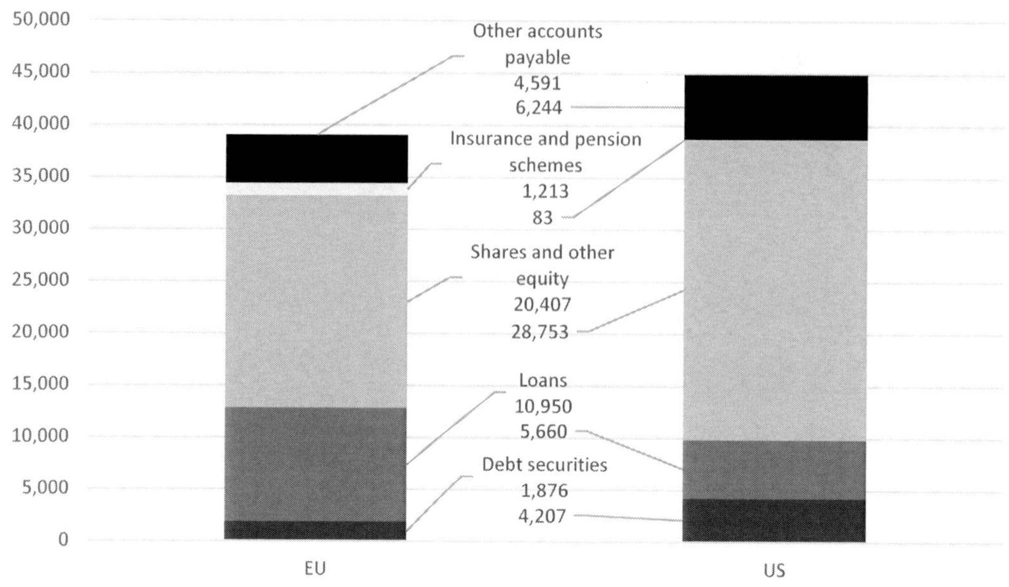

Data Sources: Eurostat and US Federal Reserve. Eurostat for exchange rates.

Yet there is a lot of diversification across the European Union regarding the relative importance of debt securities in NFC liabilities, with countries like the UK and France well above the European average and countries like Greece and Cyprus that issue almost no corporate debt securities. The European average (17%) is anyway well below that of the US where corporate debt securities are instead 75% of all corporate loans (see Figure 3.16). This national diversification reflects the funding structure of local NFCs, suggesting market segmentation along national borders.

Figure 3.16 Corporate debt securities over corporate loans (%; end 2014)

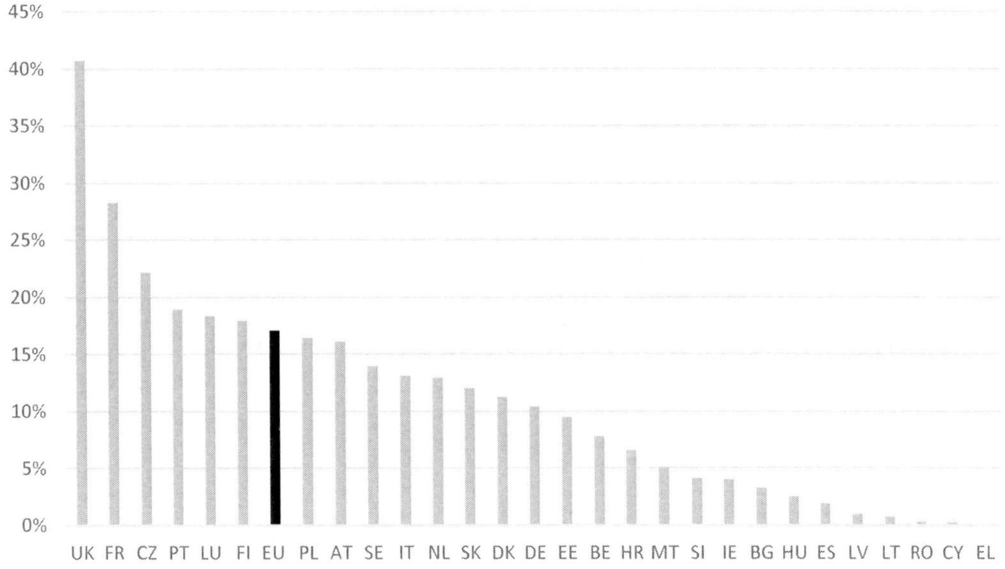

Data Sources: ECB and Eurostat.

The recent financial crisis has taught us that diversification of financial liabilities is a crucial factor in withstanding prolonged economic downturns. NFCs in Europe continue to be too exposed to bank loans, with limited cross-border equity ownership and contestability of control.

3.1.2 Households' financial assets structure

Households' assets

A small part of European households' financial assets has been traditionally directly invested in capital markets (holdings of equity or debt securities), compared to other regions of the world. Cash and deposit holdings, together with greater investments in pension funds and insurance, have driven growth of households' financial assets in recent years to its historical peak (see Figure 3.17). A low long-term interest rate environment reduces risk aversion and accelerates the 'search for yield' and the need for financial protection, especially for households and their pension liabilities.

Figure 3.17 EU households' financial assets (€bn; 2000-14)

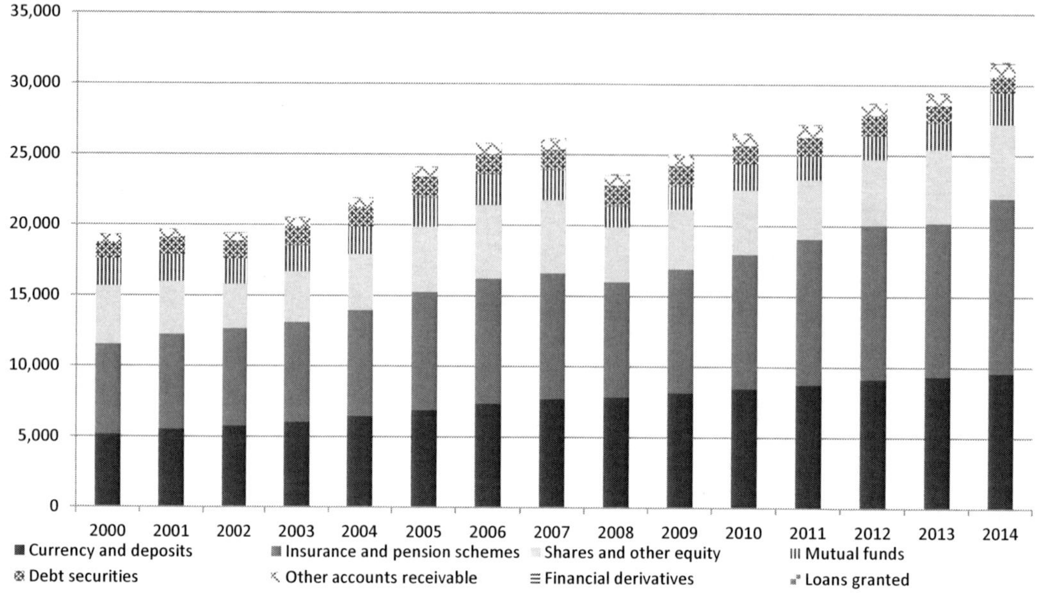

Data Sources: ECB and Eurostat.

EU vs US

The financial assets of households in Europe and the US have a different structure, especially for what concerns cash/deposits and holdings of shares and investment fund units. Cash and deposits are much more important in Europe, which are more than 30% of total assets, compared to 13% in the US. Holdings of shares and debt securities in Europe are only 21%, compared to 39% in the US, which is consistent with smaller, less active and more fragmented financial markets. In particular, investments in listed shares and debt securities are only 8% (4% each) of the total financial assets of European households. Other types of unlisted equity account for 13% of total assets. The size of investments in funds and pension schemes is also different, reflecting divergences in the organisation of the mutual funds industry between the two regions (see section 3.3.2).

Figure 3.18 Households' financial assets in Europe and the US (% total assets; average 2007-14)

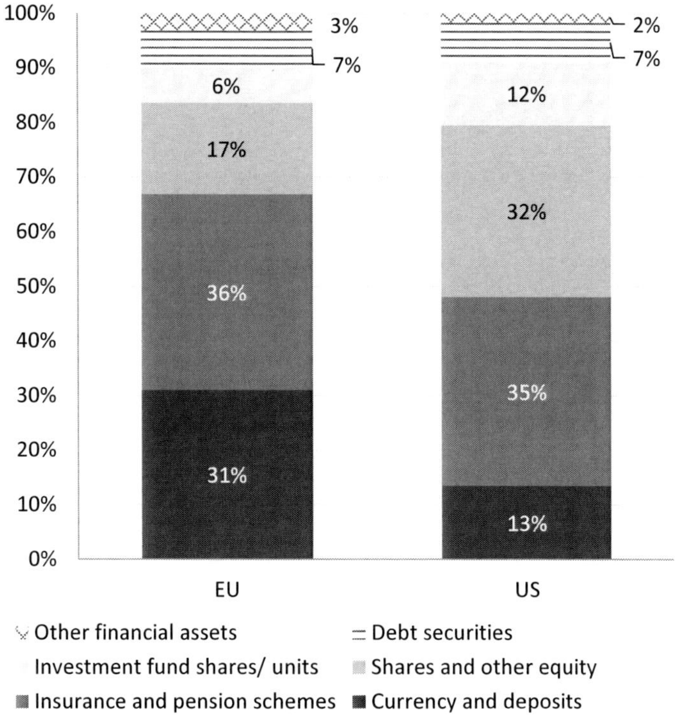

Data Sources: ECB, Eurostat and US Federal Reserve. Eurostat for exchange rates.

EU vs other regions

On a cross-regional level, in systems based on bank intermediation, such as in Europe and Japan, currency and deposits provide the largest contribution. The US has the highest level of financial assets, with pension funds (as in Australia) and shares (as in Canada) playing a key role.

Figure 3.19 Households' financial assets selected OECD countries (% of GDP and €bn; end 2012)

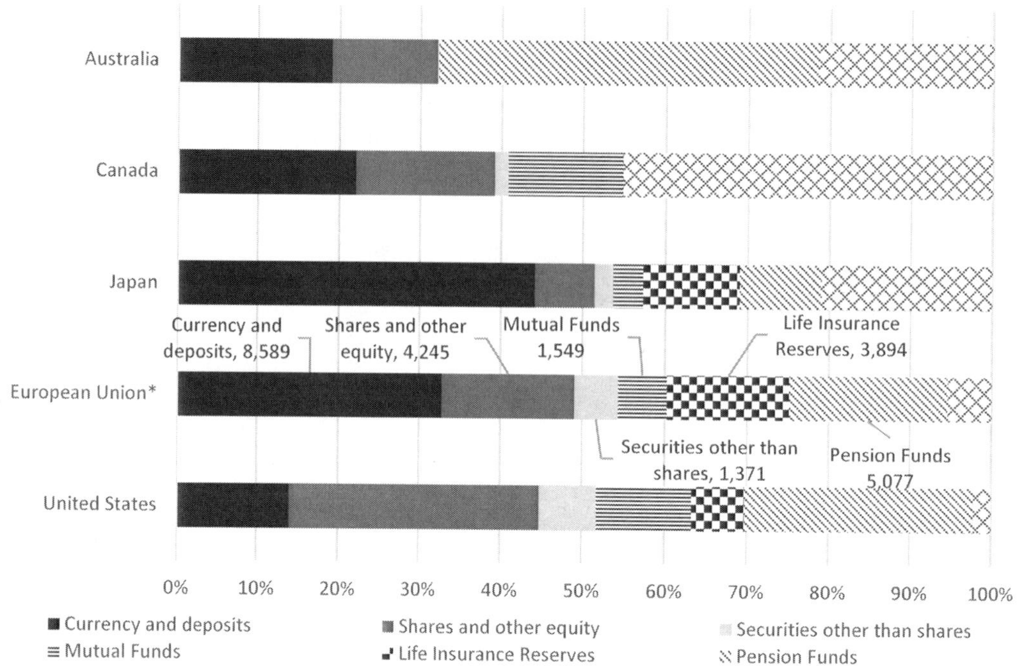

Note: No data available for Bulgaria, Cyprus, Croatia, Lithuania, Latvia, Malta or Romania.

Data Sources: OECD and World Bank. Eurostat for exchange rates.

Cross-country view

The composition of households' financial assets varies greatly across the European Union (see Figure 3.20). Twenty out of 28 European countries have a level of cash and deposits above the European average, with peaks in the crisis countries of Cyprus (64%) and Greece (65%) and lows in Sweden (14%) and Denmark (16%). Large countries, such as Germany, Italy and Spain, are also above the European average. Furthermore, countries that have less cash and deposits tend to invest more in pension schemes and insurance. These countries are typically those that have a strong domestic asset management/pension fund industry supported by domestic laws, e.g. mandatory contribution, and taxation. This shows somehow a substitution effect between cash and investments if there is an infrastructure that can provide access to more investments, whether local or cross-border. The potential for deposits to move into domestic or cross-border investment activities is thus very high for Europe. Nineteen out of 28 countries have households' holdings of shares (listed and non-listed) above the average. Direct participation in equity markets is also very limited in countries, such as the UK and the Netherlands, where financial markets are most developed in Europe, on top of other important countries such as Germany. Direct access to markets is usually less frequent if there is a competitive financial industry that can manage households' assets in an efficient and cost-effective way.

Figure 3.20 EU households' financial assets composition by country (% of total assets; average 2007-14)

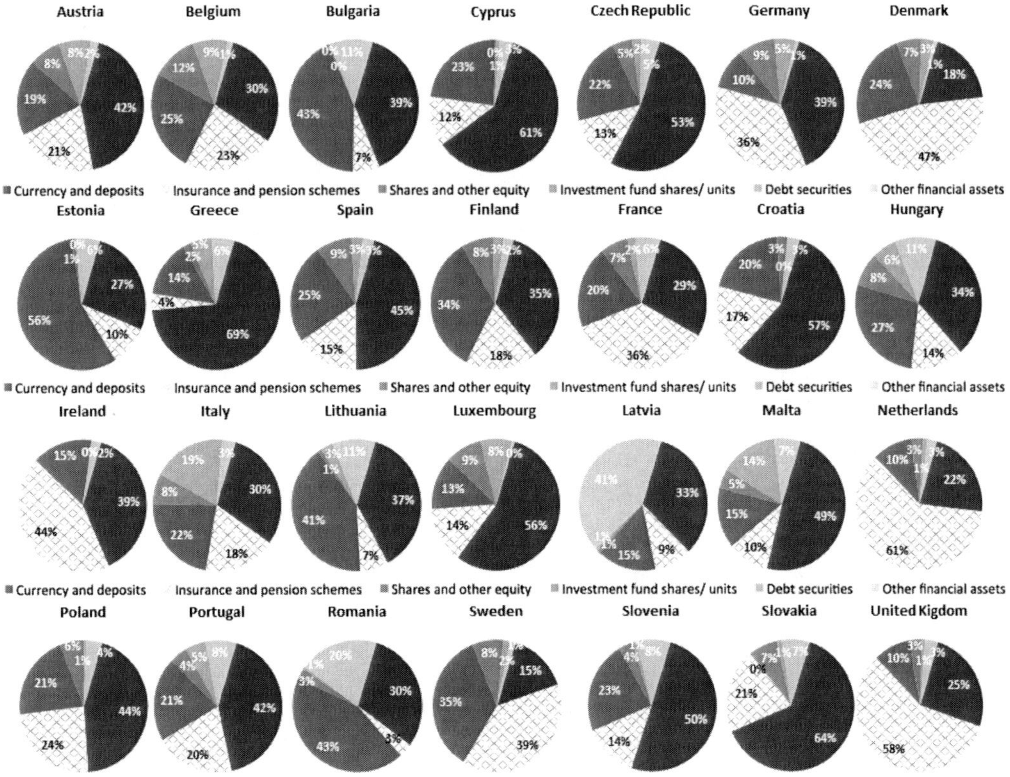

Data Source: Eurostat.

Most important, EU households hold a small amount of investment fund units (7%), with peaks in countries with limited investments in pension funds and higher levels of deposits. This situation makes households either more vulnerable to market volatility (if they hold directly the asset) or to resource misallocation (if they hold their assets in cash-like instruments). As a result, there is a need for an efficient and cost-effective asset management industry, especially in countries where there are limited or costly alternatives and wealth is eaten up by negative real interest rates on deposits.

3.1.3 Matching households' assets and NFC liabilities

Funding the EU economy

Households' assets usually fund an economy. The financial services industry acts as an intermediary that takes resources from households and gives them to firms in the economy in order to produce private goods and services (asset allocation). Governments, instead, take part of the income from households and firms (before it accrues on their accounts) for the provision of public goods, in the form of fiscal revenues and expenditures that are then redistributed according to the public good. By placing households and governments' gross financial assets on the liabilities side and NFC liabilities on the assets side, Figure 3.21 visualises the balance sheet of the financial economy. Real assets (including real estate or net imports/exports) are indirectly captured at their nominal (historical) value, as they can be seen as the purchase of a durable good, which will be equivalent to an increase in financial assets (seller) for some and a decrease for others (buyer). On top of the domestic financial assets of households, there is also the external position, i.e. assets coming from or going abroad in the form of foreign direct investments (FDI) and net portfolio investments (NPI).[38] However, the net position of FDI and NPI is negative, i.e. there are more holdings of foreign assets than holdings of domestic assets by foreign investors. Therefore, the net value of these amounts is already implicitly included in the households' financial assets above. The role of government is important, with roughly 18% of the total liabilities of the EU economy. Another 31% comes from insurance and pension funds. Investment fund units, listed equity holdings and debt securities holdings play a limited role, with respectively 6% (€2.3 trillion), 3% (€1.3 trillion) and 2.8% (€1.1 trillion) of the total funding. Cash and deposits are a significant part of total funding (24%), but most of it is reinvested in households' non-financial investments, such as mortgages and consumer credit.

[38] Foreign Direct Investment (FDI) is an investment by a foreign investor that results in a 'lasting interest' in a domestic company. The OECD qualifies 'lasting interest' as: "The direct or indirect ownership of 10% or more of the voting power of an enterprise resident in one economy"; see OECD FDI Glossary, p. 7, (www.oecd.org/daf/inv/investment-policy/2487495.pdf). Net Portfolio Investments (NPI) are "cross border transactions and positions involving debt or equity securities, other than those included in direct investment or reserve assets" (IMF CPIS Definitions, http://datahelp.imf.org/knowledgebase/articles/505731-how-is-portfolio-investment-defined-in-the-coordin). In other words, NPI include all the positions that are not FDI or reserve assets.

Figure 3.21 Matching households & governments' assets and NFC liabilities: the balance sheet of the (financial) economy (€bn; end of 2014)

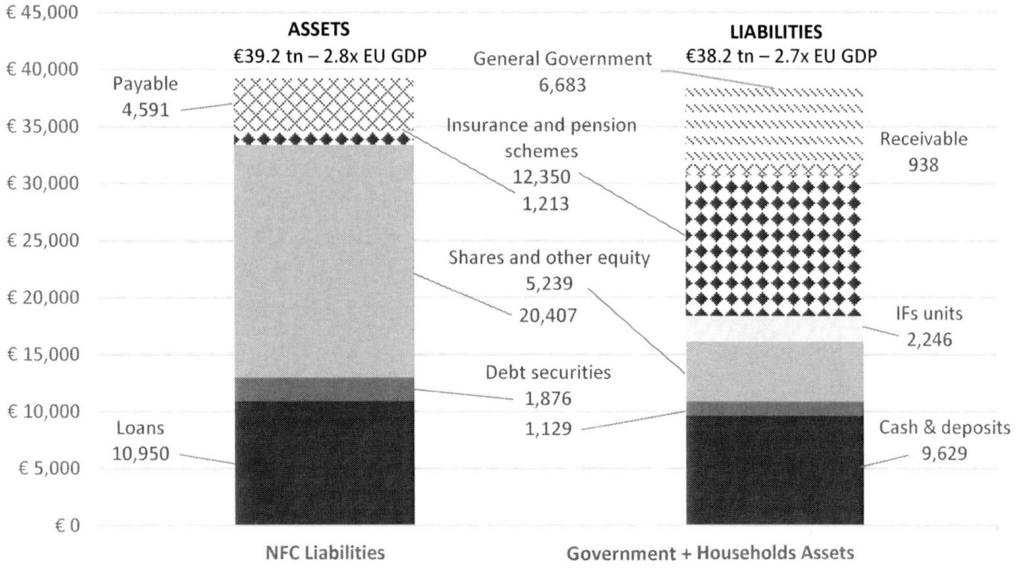

Data Sources: ECB and Eurostat. Eurostat for exchange rates.

As a consequence, numbers on the liability side (HH assets) could be further netted by removing those liabilities that go back to finance households' non-financial assets, such as mortgages (about €6.2 trillion), consumer credit (€0.9 trillion) and cash position (currency, €0.7 trillion). Likewise, numbers on the asset side (NFC liabilities) could be further netted by removing those assets funded by corporate deposits (€2.9 trillion) and cross-firm, bank and government holdings of corporate equity (not quantifiable). This leaves at least €1.8 trillion in deposits that are stable funding to banks at a low or negative interest rate and that could be allocated to more profitable capital markets activities, on top of another €6.2 trillion managed by insurance and pension funds that are only partially allocated to equity instruments (see section 3.4.1).

Key findings #5.

- The financial system in Europe is bank-dominated on both the funding and intermediation/distribution sides. The banking system is larger than the combined size of equity, government and corporate debt securities markets.
- Access to capital markets funding and investments is thus fairly limited, which is additional evidence of a poor risk-sharing mechanism among European countries.
- Bank loans are almost 40% of NFC funding, which are 77% of total debt financing.

- While in Europe the drop in net lending to NFC has been offset by higher corporate debt and equity net issuance, the absolute level of net issuance is still five times smaller than the net issuance in the US, as accessibility is mostly limited to large corporations.
- Over-reliance by European SMEs on short-term bank funding exposed them to a sharp increase in interest rates (relative to cost of funding for larger loans), compared to pre-crisis levels. Debt or equity securities are well below 5% of total liabilities.
- Direct market funding for SMEs might thus not attain a size that can make a significant difference, also considering that funding via markets concentrates where there is more information and SMEs only disclose limited information. Considering on top of this that the costs of listing are fairly high due mainly to advisory services, there is currently almost no room to increase direct access for SMEs to financial markets. Private equity, venture capital and crowdfunding could potentially achieve more in this area.
- Financial diversification of NFC liabilities is a crucial aspect to ensure the sustainability of their capital structure. Corporate debt securities are only 17% of total bank loans issued.
- Households have rapidly increased their cash and deposits position over the years, which is now 30% of all financial assets, compared to 13% in the US. This situation exposes European households to misallocation of resources due to negative interest rates.
- However, there is high variance across countries. In particular, cash and deposits holdings are lower in countries with an active asset management industry or capital markets, which show that there is a need and a demand for more efficient asset management across the European Union. There is up to €1.8 trillion in cash and deposits that could be mobilised and partially replaced by capital markets funding.
- Units of investment funds are still a small fraction of financial assets of households, which are often induced by local laws or fiscal advantages to invest in 'more static' pension funds and insurance products.
- Matching NFC liabilities with households' and governments' assets shows the lack of contribution of listed equity and debt securities, i.e. capital markets, to the funding of corporations (especially cross-border). In addition, expectations of more funding for SMEs via capital markets may be not met, at least until the system is able to minimise the structural informational problem that prevents lenders or investors from providing money, especially on a cross-border basis.

3.2 Financial integration in Europe: evidence from the euro area

The old paradigm

Several events have affected the European financial integration process in the last two decades. Among these, the 'mutual recognition' reforms, the FSAP package, the introduction of the euro and the recent financial crisis are important milestones. Most recently, the financial crisis has changed the old paradigm of financial integration, i.e. financial markets are integrated when the law of the one price holds, so arbitrage mechanisms work (Jappelli et al., 2002). This is not true in all circumstances. In reality, however, the functioning of the arbitrage mechanism may face economic, legal and political impediments, e.g. end of implicit guarantees among member states or liquidity ring-fencing. Therefore, we learned from the euro area crisis that integration might merely reflect a temporary convergence of risk. As a consequence, the degree of financial integration will depend on the number of circumstances in which the law of the one price will hold. The composition of cross-border capital flows (and the ability to absorb shocks) thus plays a crucial role in financial integration (see definition in section 2.1).

Evidence so far

The introduction of the euro is the key focus of most of the recent empirical literature on European financial integration. Some evidence shows that, before the introduction of the euro, country effects dominated equity returns, while after the introduction of the euro industry effects were stronger, especially for countries that had fewer economic linkages with neighbouring countries (Eiling et al., 2012). The elimination of currency risk and, partially, the greater regulatory convergence post-FSAP are the main channels through which the euro impacted financial integration (Kalemli-Ozcan et al., 2010). This process has also led to a reduction of the cost of capital (Freixas et al., 2004; Lane, 2008), mainly via bond markets (see following sections).

According to Spiegel (2009), the euro has basically evened up the creditworthiness of banks among the countries joining the monetary union, thus increasing cross-border interbank lending, while cash securities markets were only slightly affected (Lane, 2008). As a result, financial integration in Europe, and in the euro area in particular, has been mainly driven by the unsecured interbank market and not so much by widespread cross-border financial transactions in financial instruments or even integration in the underlying credit markets.[39] In effect, the introduction of the single currency has facilitated the circulation of capital among banks, in particular via a common payment infrastructure (so-called 'Trans-European Automated Real-

[39] See Jappelli & Pistaferri (2011) for evidence regarding the Italian market.

time Gross Settlement Express Transfer', or TARGET) and the unification of monetary policies (and thus liquidity provisions; Hartmann et al., 2003). Loans to non-domestic monetary financial institutions (MFIs) grew steadily especially after the introduction of the single currency, from over 30% in 1999 to roughly 45% in 2007, before dropping again after the 2008 crisis (see Figure 3.22). In effect, as discussed in chapter 2, interbank liquidity tends to fragment rather quickly during times of systemic stress, as it did in the recent financial and sovereign crises (Garcia de Andoain et al., 2014).

Figure 3.22 Loans to MFIs by residency of the counterparty (% tot.; 1997-2014)

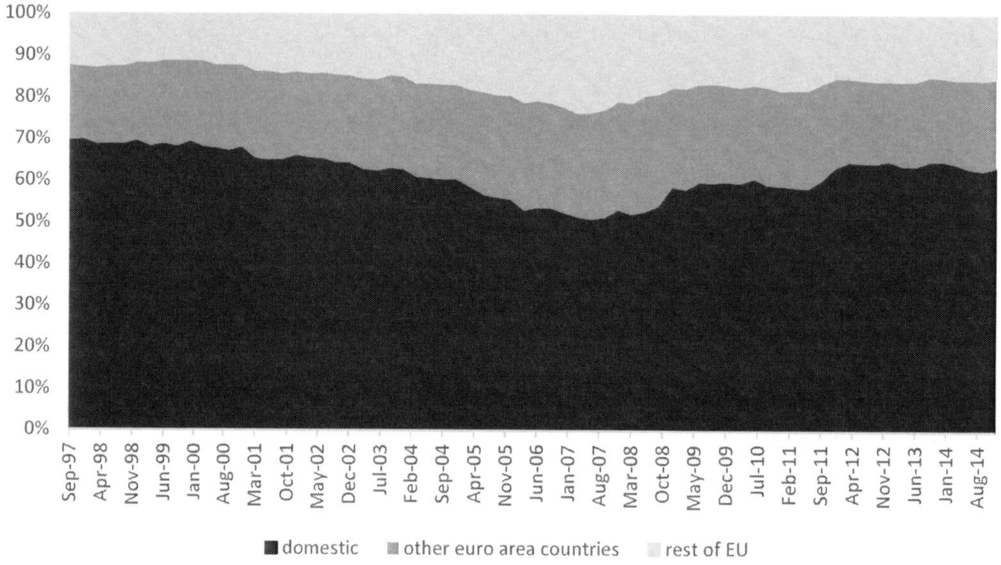

Note: Euro area MFIs.

Data Source: ECB.

Overall financial integration

After the post-financial (2007) and sovereign crises (2010) intervention to prop up the financial system (including a banking union), however, this financial fragmentation process has stabilised. Most notably, financial integration has been gradually on the rise both in terms of price convergence and quantity (see Figure 3.23).[40] Prices are still not close to pre-crisis levels,

[40] This indicator, developed by the ECB, is a selection of price-based and quantity-based indicators of four market segments (money, bond, equity and banking). The indicator is bound between zero and one, but it is not an indicator of absolute financial integration, rather it captures the degree of financial integration achieved during the period of observation. It should not be interpreted as an indicator of absolute financial integration. For instance, as the price-based indicator has now reached 1999 levels, it cannot be interpreted as the level of financial integration being at the same level as in 1999, but rather as the intensity of price convergence. For more details, please see Statistical Annex of ECB (2015).

but quantity indicators show a gradual improvement, even though the following sections show, in absolute terms, how the volume of cross-border flows is still very limited across several asset classes.

Figure 3.23 Price-based and quantity-based FINTEC (1995-2015)

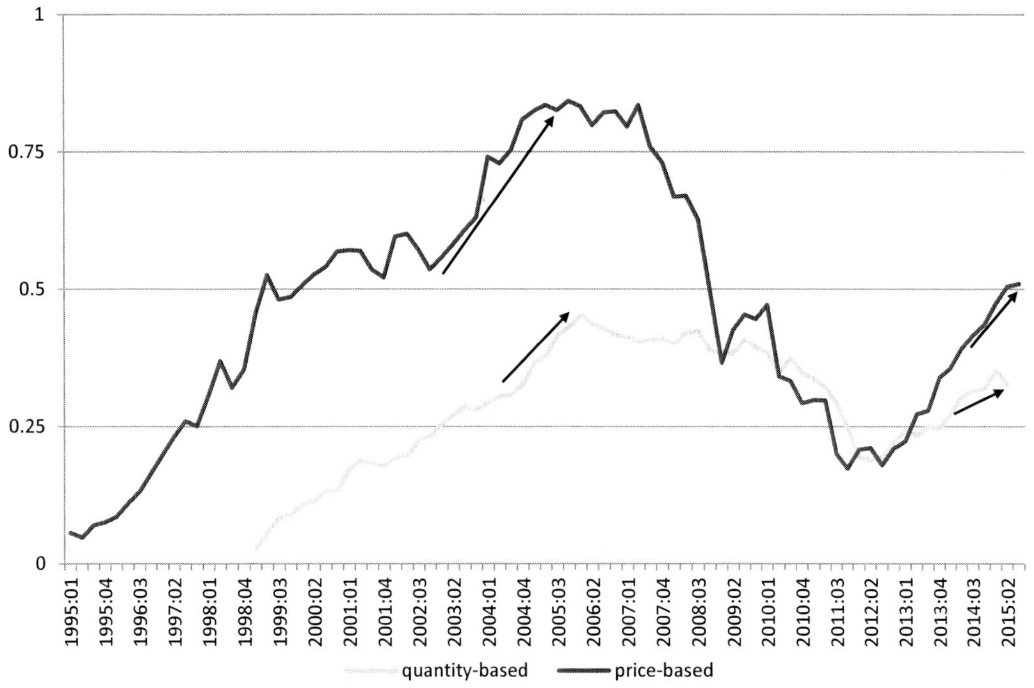

Data Source: ECB.

Nonetheless, Figure 3.23 suggests that price and quantity convergence indicators maybe again on a diverging rate of growth. Price convergence that is not followed by greater cross-border trading activities and holdings of assets (private risk sharing) may have higher chances to create regional bubbles that will burst when systemic risk rise above a certain level.

Investment portfolio

Looking at investment portfolio data, i.e. equity and debt financial flows that are not FDI or reserves, flows among selected European countries have restarted, but the composition is still debt-dominated (see Figure 3.24), which may keep financial integration fragile in case of a permanent asymmetric shock. Most notably, the debt component is larger for investment flows towards euro area countries, in line with previous findings about the fragility of financial integration in the region.

Figure 3.24 Equity and debt investment portfolio of selected EU countries ($mn) and flow composition by countries (% total; average 2001-14)

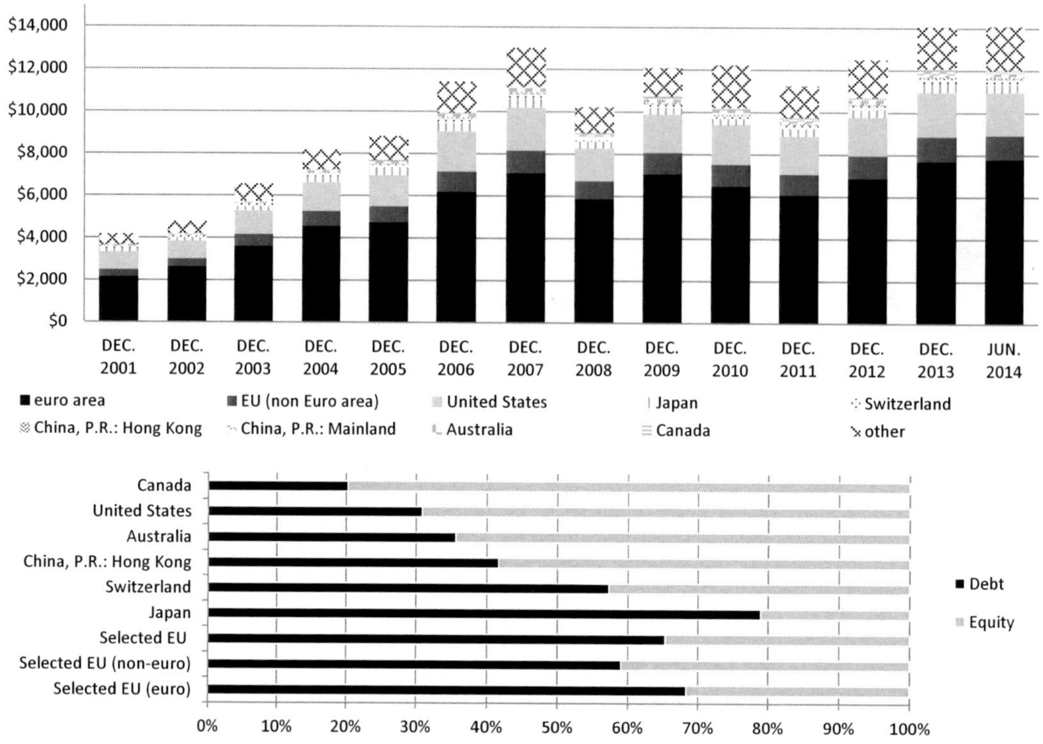

Note: Selected countries in the first chart are Germany, Italy, France, Netherlands, Spain, UK, Sweden and Poland.

Data Source: IMF CPIS.

Goods and services

There is, however, broad consensus that the euro has had very limited impact on the single market for goods and services. While the financial integration process (led by the EU membership) in general might have had some impact (mostly post-accession), home bias has barely changed in recent years (Balta & Delgado, 2009; Pacchioli, 2011). EU membership might have boosted both trade and financial integration, according to stock market valuation analysis, e.g. absolute differences of earnings yields and the inverse of price/earnings ratios, of industry portfolios in different countries (Bekaert et al., 2013). The general view, before the introduction of the euro, that financial integration would be instrumental to the completion of the single market for goods and services is still to be verified. It is hard to establish how much financial integration and trade integration are interdependent, and, most important, whether the depth and quality of financial integration is sufficient to produce long-term effects on the single market.

Key findings #6.

- Financial integration, measured as the law of the one price, may only be the result of a temporary convergence in risk. The composition of cross-border capital flow is even more important in financial integration policies.
- The euro has produced a major impact on risk convergence, by evening out (in good times) the creditworthiness of banks (via a common payment and liquidity infrastructure, and a common monetary policy).
- As a result, integration mainly took place via (unsecured interbank) credit markets and only slightly via cash securities markets, which still remain fragmented at national level. Interbank markets are structurally unstable during times of stress and the worst absorber mechanism for aggregate risk.
- Financial integration is gradually recovering after the financial crisis, but its quality is still limited. On the one hand, the composition of cross-border financial flows is still poor and dominated by debt instruments. On the other hand, markets are still fairly fragmented and cross-border financial flows are small in absolute value (see following sections).

3.3 Capital market-based intermediation in Europe

Before describing developments in the different asset classes that define a financial market, this section reviews the current status of integration in the intermediation channels that provide liquidity to financial markets. The first section looks at developments in dealer banks' activities and the implications for wholesale financial markets. The second section reviews the status of the asset management industry and its complementary (or supplementary) activity to those of dealers in financial markets.

3.3.1 The structure of the dealer bank industry

Dealing activities

Dealer banks are important actors in financial markets. They provide liquidity for financial instruments by charging a spread and ensuring a continuous (or quasi) trading activity through the use of inventories. These banks are usually very active in fixed income and derivatives markets, where liquidity is scarce, i.e. the ability to sell/buy a financial instrument very quickly, with limited price impact and at low cost. They are involved in key capital markets activities to support this liquidity, including:

- Securities borrowing/lending.
- Securities purchase/sale (at discount, i.e. repo).
- Securities trading.

All these activities may or may not appear on the balance sheet, depending on the tools and types of resources committed by the dealer. Securities trading can be split in proprietary trading (trading on behalf of the bank with own capital), principal trading (trading securities or over-the-counter derivatives to earn a spread),[41] and agency trading (trading on behalf of a client without interposing itself in the transaction). These are the core activities of a dealer bank, which typically stands between a buyer and a seller of financial instruments. It can operate by putting at risk own capital or with matched books using principle transactions. Dealer banks can be also part of important banking groups that provide other services, like commercial banking, asset management and investment banking (such as underwriting, etc.). In effect, the dealer banking business requires significant capital and cash, which can be easier to find when putting together different banking activities.

Top 26 dealers

This section analyses the current status of the dealing industry in Europe (including Switzerland) and the US via a dataset collected from the top 26 dealer banks,[42] which account for the vast majority of dealer banking activities in the two regions. Due to the high cost of running such a business, the industry is fairly concentrated.

The US (plus one non-US) dealer banks are: J.P. Morgan, Goldman Sachs, Citigroup, Morgan Stanley, Bank of America Merrill Lynch (BoA ML), Jefferies, Nomura (Japan). The European (and Swiss) dealer banks are: Barclays, Credit Suisse, BNP Paribas, Société Générale, HSBC, UBS, Crédit Agricole, Deutsche Bank, Natixis, ING, Santander, Bank of Nova Scotia, Unicredit, Commerzbank, Royal Bank of Scotland (RBS), ABN AMRO, Unicredit, BBVA, Banca IMI.

Post-crisis financials

The financial crisis originally hit dealer banks in several ways. Among others, the drop in trading volumes, the tightening of capital requirements, especially for those holding large securities inventories, and an environment with very low long-term interest rates and stricter capital requirements have increased the capital costs of inventories (balance sheet space) and pushed some banks to cease well-established trading activities or even restructure the entire business model towards more hybrid models, e.g. a combination of securities dealing, trading and asset management services. Combined with

---

[41] This can also come in more complex market-making agreements in continuous trading environments, where the dealer banks provide liquidity to the market (a bid and ask) in exchange for a spread.

[42] Dealer banks were selected in part from the AFME list of primary dealers and, for non-European banks, from other sources. From the data collected and matched with aggregate market numbers, the coverage of dealer banking activities shall be very close to 90% of the market.

accommodative monetary policies, which allow banks to access cheap liquidity, it did not necessarily result in lower costs of trading activities in markets with significant dealer presence, but spreads widened and market-makers are willing to provide liquidity for shorter time periods (PWC, 2015). More volatile pricing may ultimately become an embedded feature of the new financial market structure. Nonetheless, the US corporate bond market has in recent years moved towards a more agent-based model with limited impact on liquidity (Adrian et al., 2015).

Trading activities

In line with this background, while total revenues are stable and assets have even increased (from €22 trillion to €26 trillion), trading-related revenues and assets have dramatically gone down compared to pre-crisis levels (see Figure 3.25).

Figure 3.25 Revenues (lhs) and trading assets/liabilities (rhs; €bn; 2006 vs 2014)

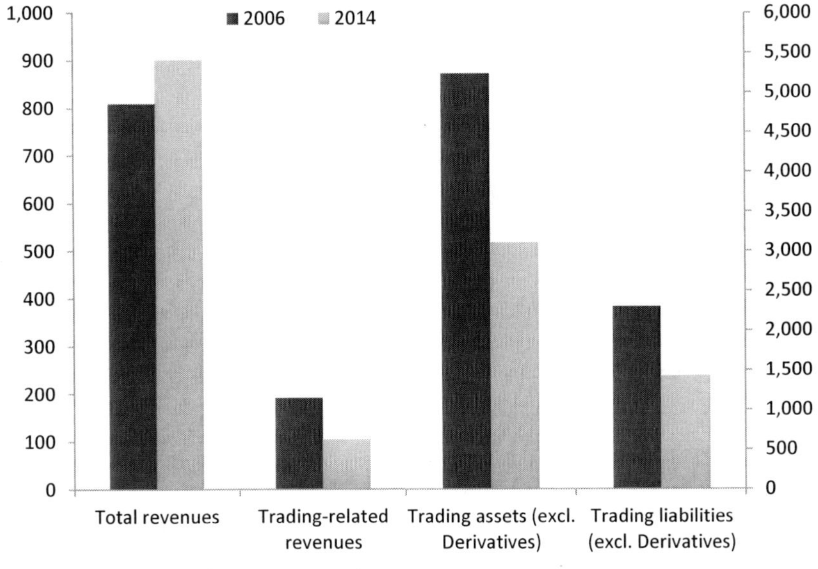

Source: Annual reports. Eurostat (exchange rates).

This is particularly the case for European banks, which have seen a drop in trading assets as many of them ceased or scaled down capital intensive activities (see Figure 3.26), such as fixed income, due either to a restructuring forced by losses (as in the case of RBS) or to a voluntary restructuring towards a lighter capital structure and business model (UBS and Credit Suisse).

Figure 3.26 Trading assets by dealer (€bn, 2006 vs 2014)

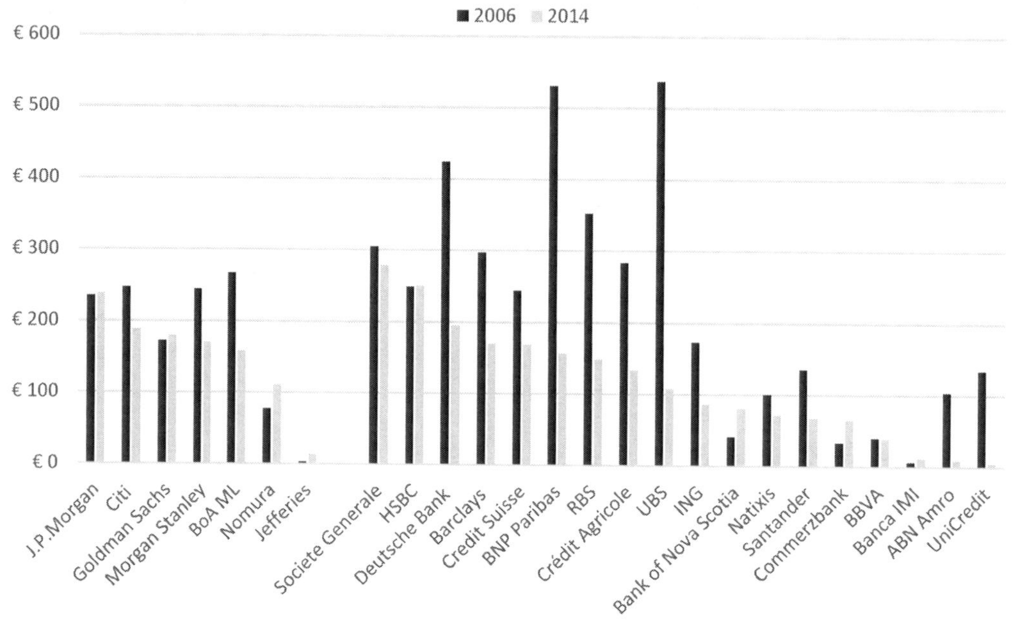

Source: Annual Reports. Eurostat for exchange rates.

Collateral dealing

Another important activity for financial markets is the management of collateral, which is usually performed by dealer banks. They can manage collateral for their own risk, i.e. collateralisation of an OTC derivative transaction, or for a third-party transaction such as repurchase agreements or securities lending/borrowing. The collateral dealing activity continued to drop in 2014, compared to recent years, which is consistent with the reduced involvement of banks in wholesale financial markets activities (see Figure 3.27). The reuse rate of collateral of selected banks has also gone down since 2006, but the drop has been partially recovered as banks improve their financial health and can redistribute more collateral to the system.

Figure 3.27 Total collateral received and repledged (€bn, 2010 vs 2014)

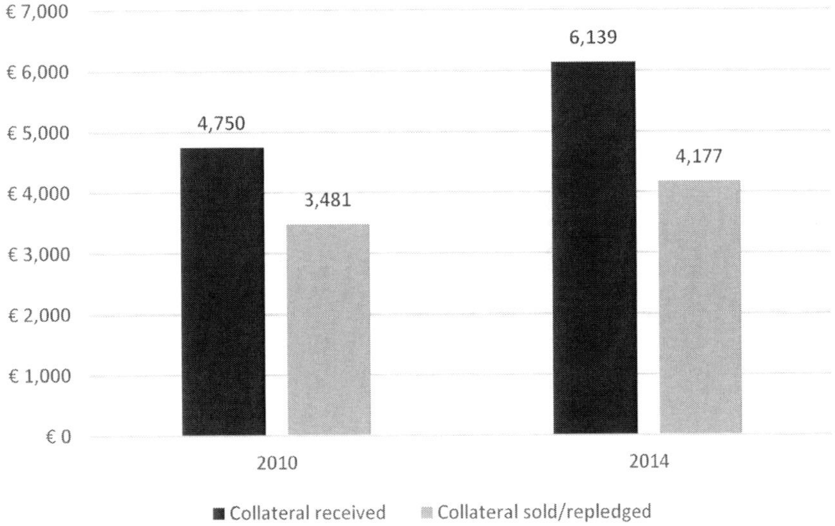

Note: No data for Banca IMI.

Source: Annual Reports. Eurostat for exchange rates.

Figure 3.28 Reuse ratios, selected banks (collateral received over collateral sold/repledged; %)

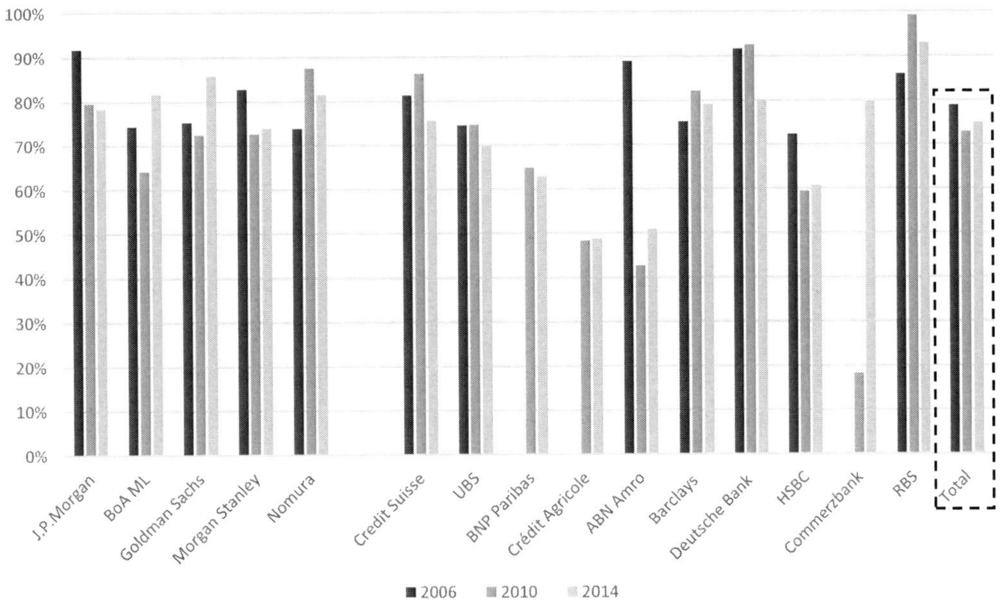

Source: Annual reports. Eurostat for exchange rates.

Moreover, Figure 3.29 suggests that the drop is consistent across all dealer banks in the sample, as their market activity in this business shrinks.

Figure 3.29 Collateral received and repledged by dealer bank (€bn, end of 2014)

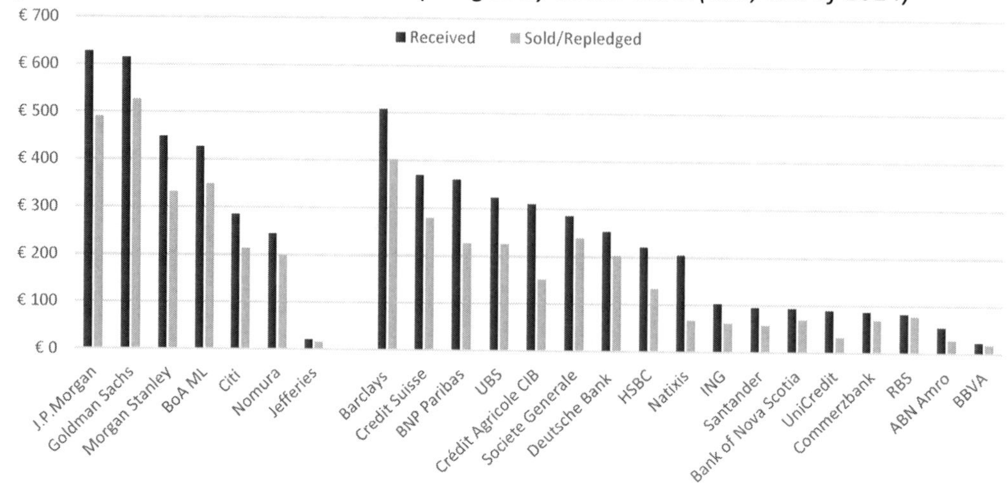

Notes: No data for Banca IMI. For 2010 missing data for BBVA, Unicredit, Jefferies. Citigroup data are estimates.

Source: Annual reports. Eurostat (exchange rates).

Repo and RRP

Evidence on the development in the repo and reverse repo (RRP) markets is mixed. Repo and RRP are important funding tools for asset managers, both for funding (repo) and returns purposes (RRP). Banks that had large repo or RRP exposures have reduced their activities, compared to other banks in 2006 (see Figure 3.30). This happened in favour of greater redistribution of the business across the industry (see Table 3.1), with many banks that have seen a slight increase since 2006. Nonetheless, the repo market has shrunk by roughly €1 trillion since 2006 (ICMA, 2015) to its current level of €2.7 trillion (gross). For our sample, repo activities lost as well almost €1 trillion, currently at €2.1 trillion (net),[43] while the reverse repo market went down by roughly €500 billion, currently at €2.09 trillion (net).[44]

Table 3.1 Repo and reverse repo, net amounts (€bn, 2006-14)

	REPO		RRP	
	2006	**2014**	**2006**	**2014**
Top 5 US	994	596	683	619
	32%	28%	26%	30%
Top 5 EU	1,248	815	1,102	738
	40%	38%	43%	35%
Total repo top 25 dealers (net)	3,121	2,125	2,588	2,090

Source: Annual reports.

[43] The gross amount for the sample can be estimated at around €3.2 trillion.

[44] The gross amount for the sample can be estimated at around €3.05 trillion.

Figure 3.30 Repo & RRP (net amounts, €bn, 2006 vs 2014)

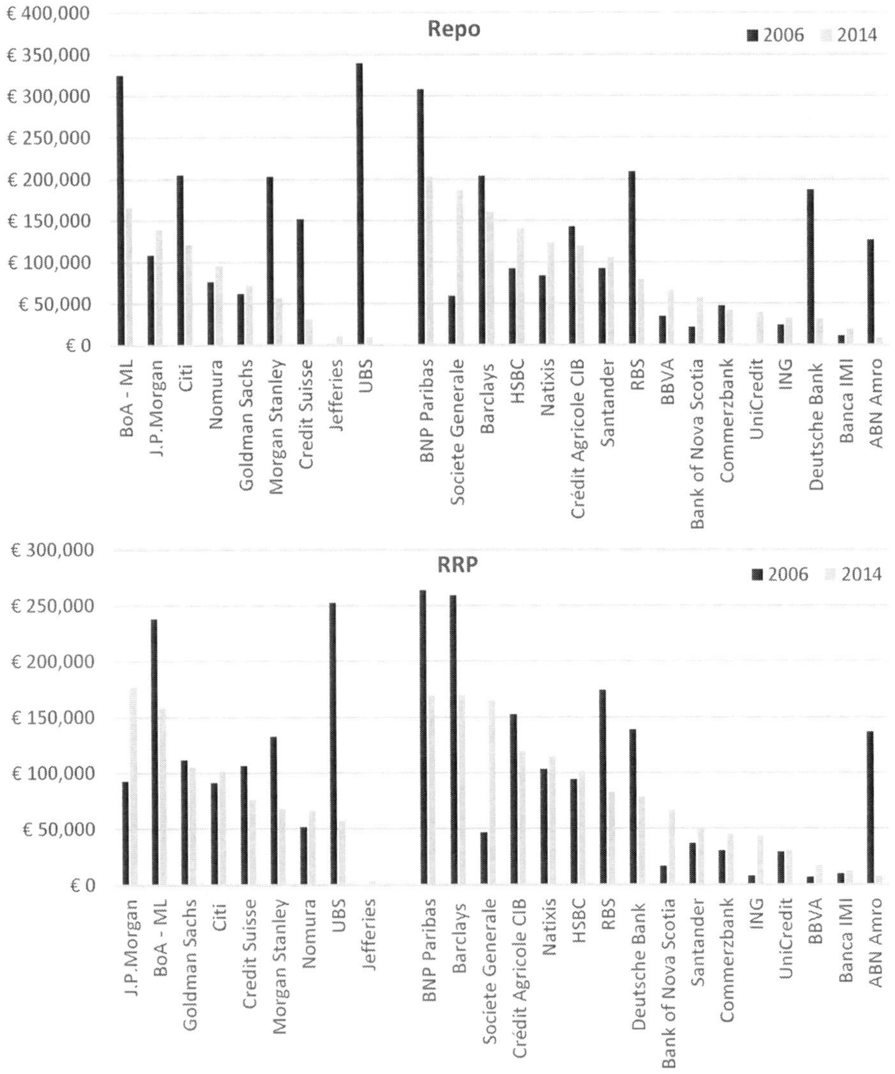

Source: Annual reports.

OTC derivatives

Last but not least, dealer banks are key players in the market for over-the-counter derivatives, which are important tools for risk management of firms and investment funds. The dealer bank often offers these contracts because of its possibility to stand on the other side of the transaction, with a hedged exposure via internal risk management operations. The market is highly concentrated, with the top 10 dealers controlling more than 80% of the market (see Figure 3.31).

Figure 3.31 Top dealers' positions in OTC derivatives (notional amounts, €bn, end of 2014)

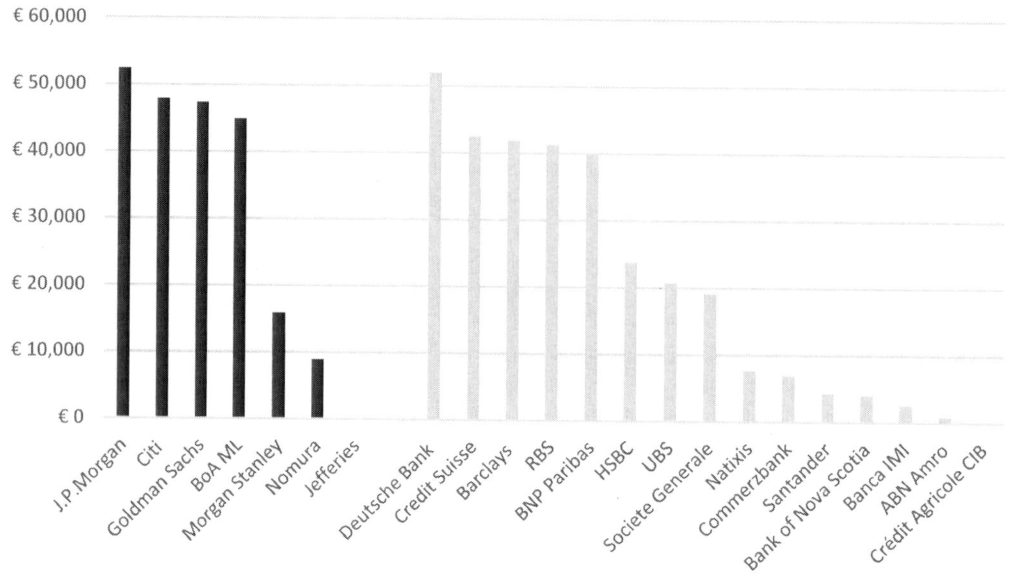

Note: No data for ING, BBVA or Unicredit.

Source: Annual reports.

The US market is more concentrated, while European banks have a bigger market share (59%). Nevertheless, OTC derivatives transactions are international in nature and so the location of the bank does not say much about market integration.

Section 3.4.3 will review the overall market for OTC derivatives at European and global levels.

3.3.2 *Asset management in Europe*

An astonishing growth

The asset management industry is an important segment of financial markets, as it provides investors with the opportunity to meet specific investment goals by putting money in the hands of a specialised investment firm. In an environment where returns are scarce, the role of managers in ensuring the achievement of investment objectives is key. With the retrenchment of investment banks and commercial banks in capital markets, the asset management industry is coming out of the crisis as strong as ever. It is increasingly capturing bank business coming, among others, from private investors, insurance companies and pension funds.

Both investment funds and discretionary mandates have enjoyed strong growth in Europe since 2008, by almost doubling the total assets under management (AuM), which stabilised in 2014 to around €19 trillion (from €9.9 trillion in 2008). Assets managed under discretionary mandates are on average 6% larger than assets in investment funds, while in 2007 it was the opposite (see Figure 3.32).

Figure 3.32 Total assets under management (AuM) of European asset managers and investment funds (€tn)

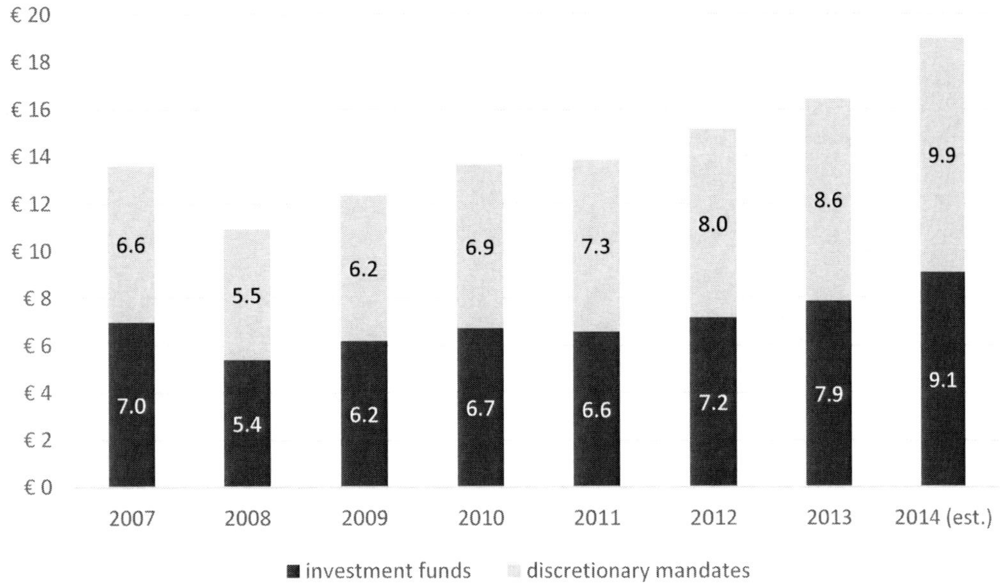

Source: 2015 EFAMA Fact Book.

Asset allocation

In terms of asset allocation, discretionary mandates invest much more in bonds (55% of their portfolio; see Figure 3.33) and tend to be more risk adverse, since they manage money mainly from large institutional investors such as insurers, large corporations and pension funds. Investment funds have a more balanced portfolio, as they serve a more widespread set of investment objectives.

Figure 3.33 Asset allocation in Europe (discretionary vs funds)

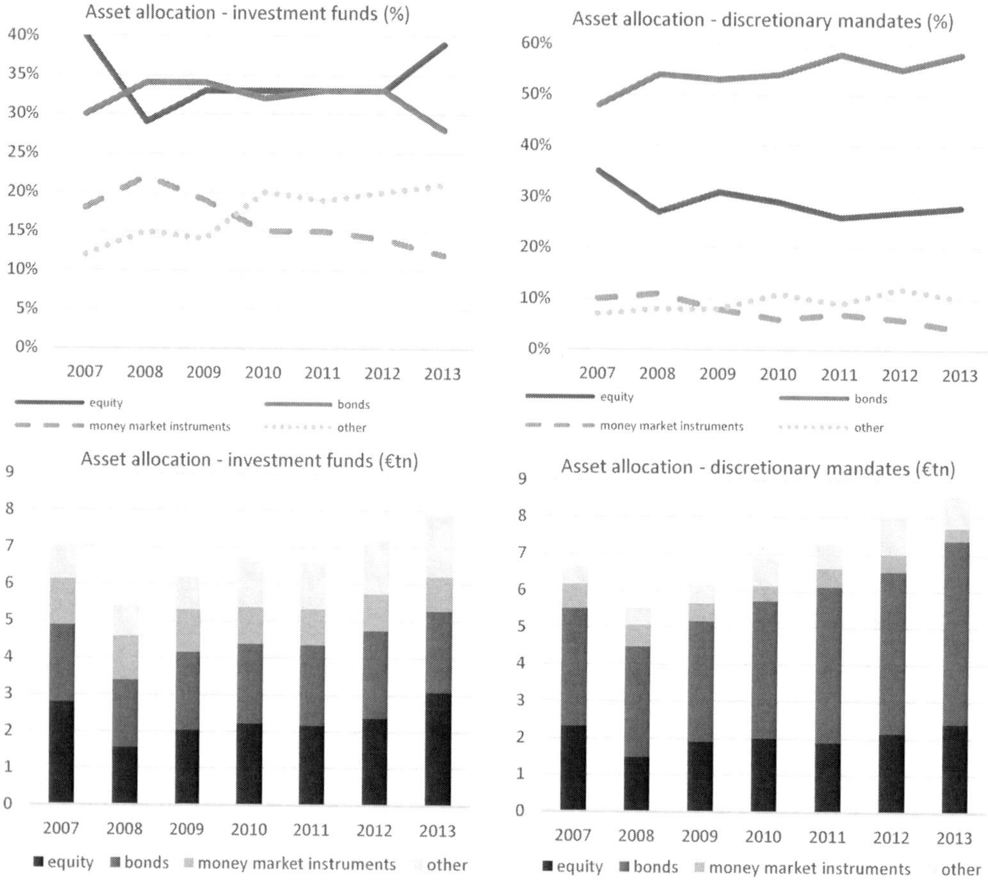

Source: EFAMA.

Other regions

The European asset management industry is also significant compared to other regions of the world. Total net AuM of investment funds grew everywhere worldwide after the financial crisis. In the US, the industry went from roughly 56% of GDP in 2003 to 94% in 2014, with almost 51% of all total global net assets, while in Europe the size is 60% of GDP today compared to 36% in 2003 (see Figure 3.34). China is still a small player, as marketing of funds remains limited to some trading in investment funds going in and out through Hong Kong, but it is already a more significant player than Japan (in GDP terms).

Figure 3.34 Worldwide total net assets of open-end funds by region (€bn)

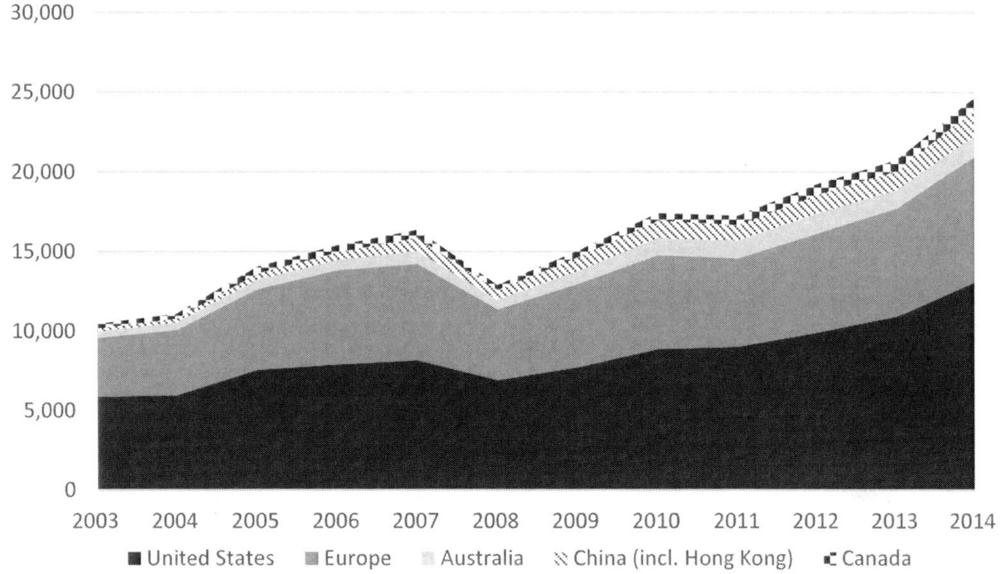

Source: International Investment Funds Association.

UCITS & non-UCITS

The composition of the assets under management in Europe includes two broad categories of products. Undertakings for Collective Investments in are investment funds directly regulated under EU law, for what concerns the manufacturing of the fund unit and the portfolio composition. Non-UCITS are other types of investment funds, such as real estate funds, which target more professional investors. UCITS have gained over the years a market share of roughly 70% (including money market funds, which are mostly designed as UCITS).

Figure 3.35 Net assets of UCITS and non-UCITS (€bn)

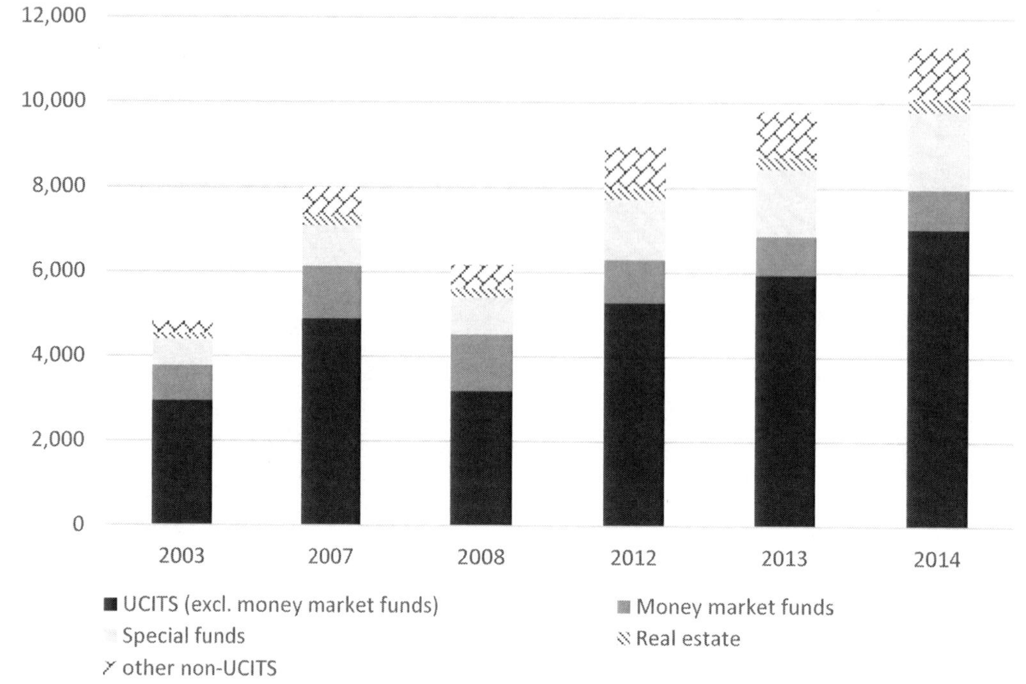

Source: EFAMA Fact Book 2015. Note: Special funds (Spezialfonds) are a separate category of funds marketed in Germany for professional or semi-professional investors (see following box).

The regulatory framework around UCITS investment products has been updated over time with five directives and today is one of the most advanced frameworks for funds regulation. Its simple structure and compliance with international regulatory standards have made this product successful in the investment fund industry, particularly among fund providers and institutional clients. The widespread diffusion of the product in other regions of the world, particularly in Asia, is evidence of its industrial success.

3.3.2.1 *Industry structure and efficiency*

Fragmentation

The structure of the European asset management industry is of particular interest and complexity. While the overall size (and growth rate) is somehow comparable to other regions and larger compared to Japan and China, at regional level the industry is very much fragmented along national borders. As a consequence, the average size of EU funds is below €200 million, which is smaller than that of China, and it has been stable over the years. In the US, the average size of funds increased by 60% since 2007 (to around €1.3 billion). Europe also has by far the highest number of funds (32,868), available across European countries (see Figure 3.36).

Figure 3.36 Average size (€mn) and number of open-end (mutual) funds (average 2010-14)

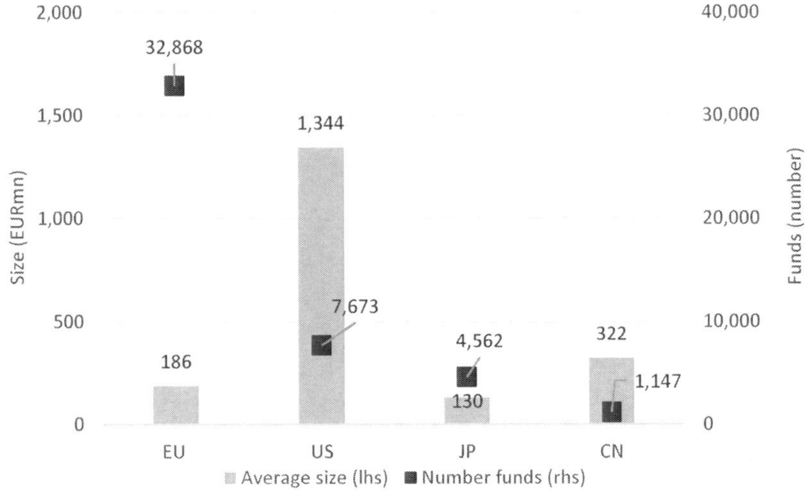

Notes: China includes Hong Kong. Mutual funds include equity, bond, balanced/mixed, money market, and other funds. Funds of funds are not included, except for FR, DE, IT, LU. No data available for Cyprus, Estonia, Lithuania and Latvia.

Source: EFAMA International Quarterly Statistical Releases, 2015 ICI Investment Company Institute Fact Book.

Cost efficiency

The fragmentation of the industry is also reflected in limited cost efficiency. Figure 3.37 shows the total expense ratios of European versus US funds. At the end of 2010, European equity funds on average were more expensive, by 42 basis points. Since then, costs of US funds dropped to 1.2% in 2014. Evidence for European funds is less clear, as fees tend to be 'stickier' with strong differences across countries. Europe also has a different market structure, with roughly 50% of the management fee retroceded to distributors. In the US, 50% of actively managed funds go through an open platform, which creates two distinct markets for fund manufacturing and distribution. With the Retail Distribution Review in the UK and the Markets in Financial Instruments Directive (MiFID), Europe is set to follow a similar path towards a more active role for open platforms, with a more competitive distribution channel and manufacturing industry.

Figure 3.37 Total expense ratios for equity funds – US vs EU (end of 2010)

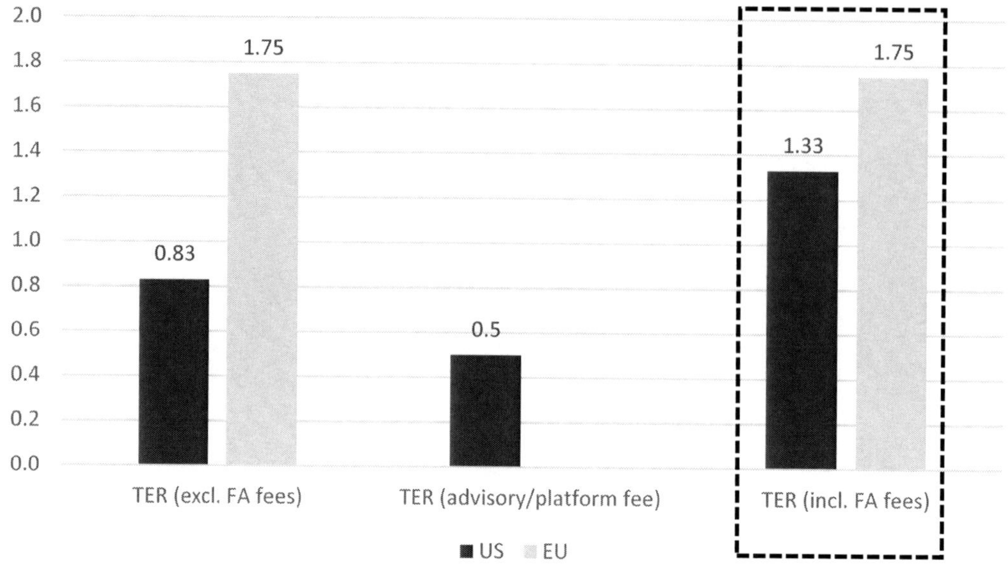

Note: The advisory/platform fee component for Europe is negligible (at least at the end of 2010).
Source: SI (2011), 2015 ICI Investment Company Fact Book.

Active funds

The cost picture is different if we discern actively and passively managed funds. Fees for actively managed funds have been quite stable on average over time or have even increased, in terms of subscription and redemption fees (see Figure 3.38). These fixed charges are also very different across countries, which (together with the increase) may signal a lack of convergence, with limited cross-border integration and thus competition. Overall, fixed charges tend to be very high (over 6%), which per se may be a sign of limited integration and lack of competition.

Figure 3.38 Management, subscription and redemption fees – Active fund management (%; 2002 vs 2012)

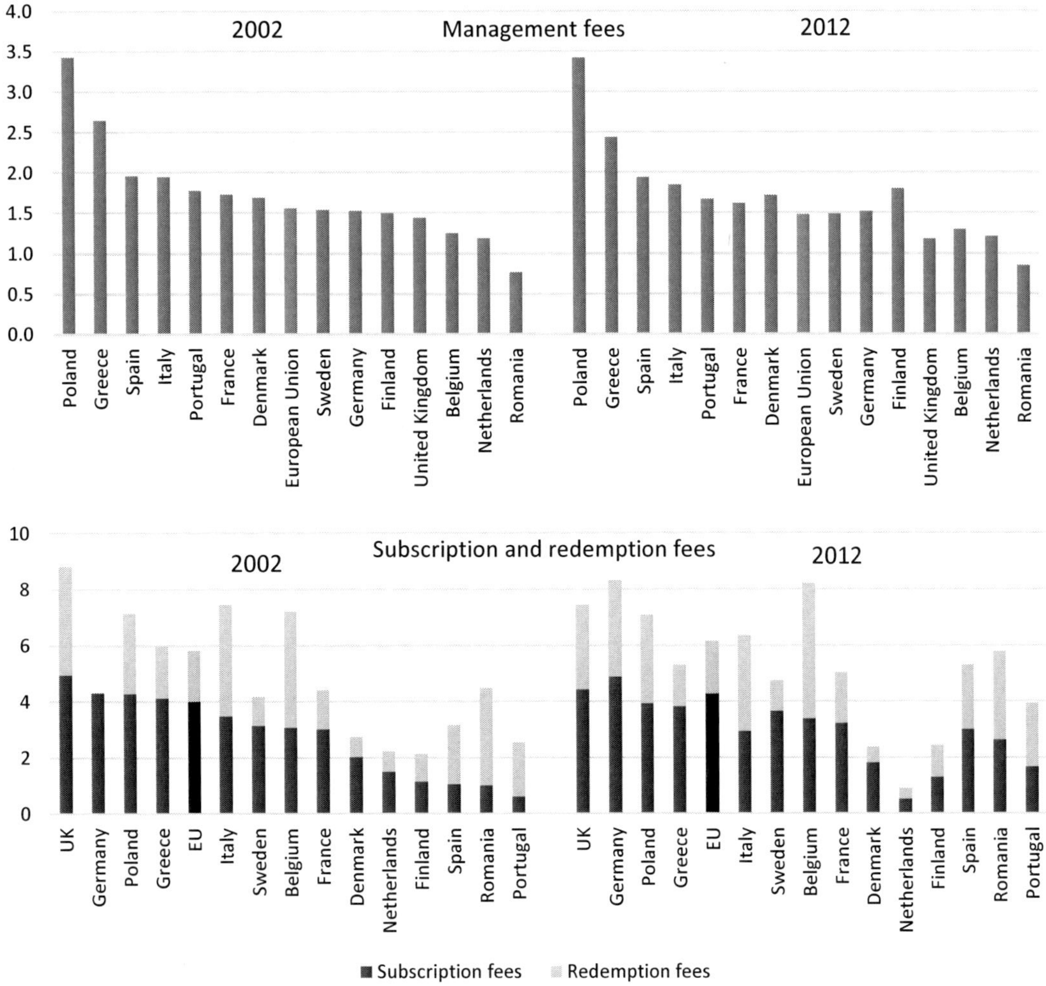

Source: IODS (2014).

Data on passive funds show that management fees have gone down dramatically in recent years (almost halved from 2002 to 2012). This development matches a trend of more widespread diffusion of passive investments, through more standardised products sold also on exchanges. The high standardisation of the product makes manufacturing of funds fairly competitive and this may explain the drop in management fees. Nonetheless, the drop in management fees was partially offset by an increase in subscription and redemption fees in most countries, which (together with the high variability) show how the distribution channels across Europe are not very integrated or competitive. *Passive funds*

Figure 3.39 Management, subscription and redemption fees – Passive fund management (%; 2002 vs 2012).

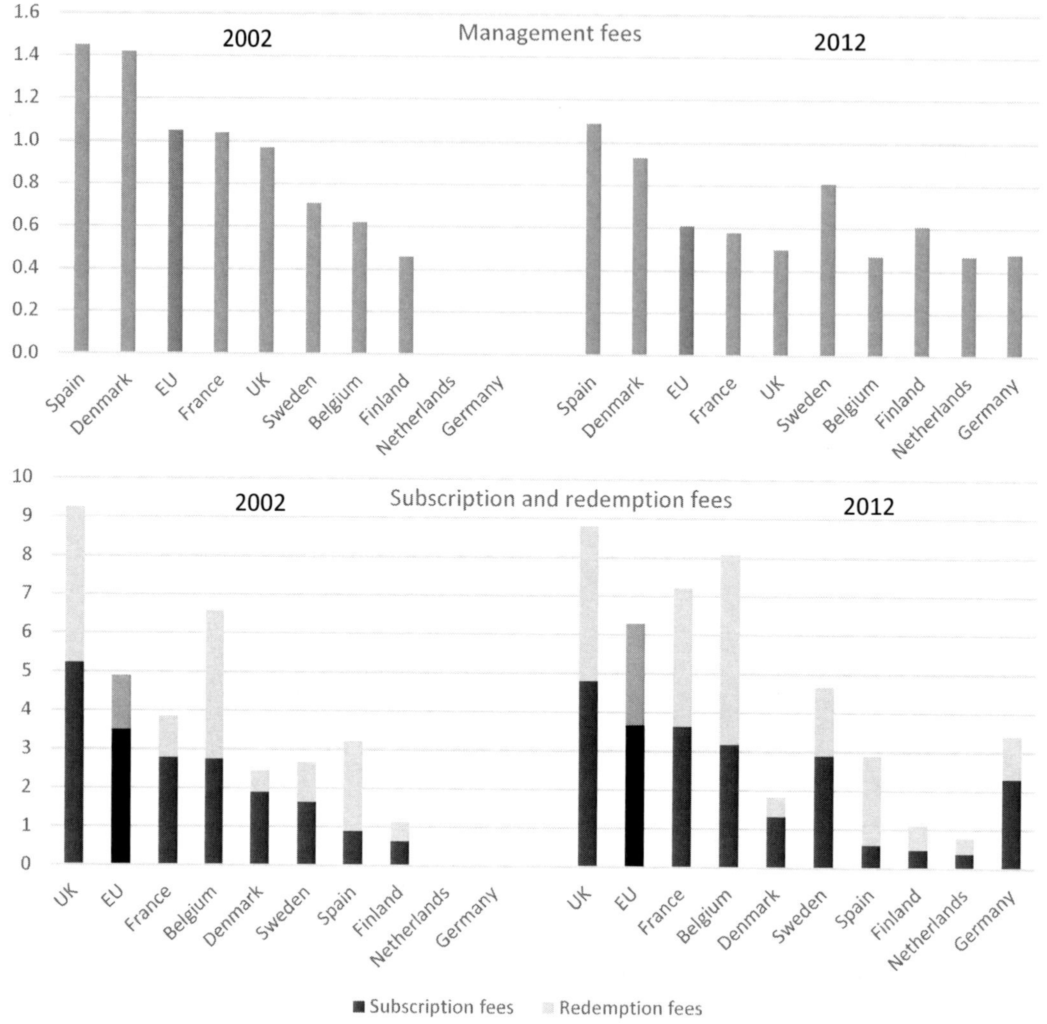

Source: IODS (2014).

Concentration ratios

Industry concentration (CR5) has also gone up, peaking at 90% in Germany and bottoming out at around 30% in the UK, where there has been traditionally a fairly competitive asset management industry. High concentration ratios at national level, however, might not necessarily mean a lack of competition at European level. In effect, greater concentration might be necessary to build capacity and be able to compete at European level. Concentration shall be coupled with easier accessibility to distribution channels of fund units across countries.

Figure 3.40 Concentration of the top five asset managers (end of the year)

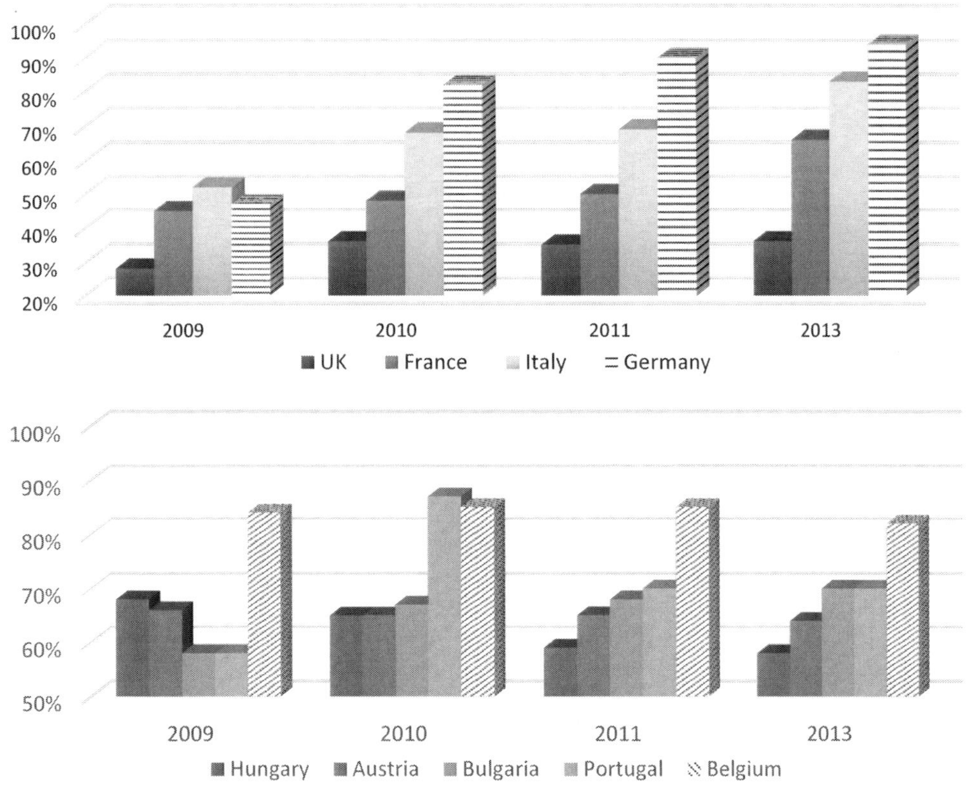

Note: For Italy only discretionary mandate.

Source: 2011, 2012, 2013, 2015 EFAMA Asset Management Report.

Private and retail banks are the largest distribution channels in Europe, with a total share estimated at 75% of total European fund distribution (PWC, 2012). Banks can still fairly easily interpose themselves to the fund sale and buy fund units on behalf of clients, typically in exchange for a retrocession fee. This situation creates an advantage for the fund provider, who will have to deal with one or few counterparties. Nonetheless, investors will have to monitor the ability of the bank to offer a suitable mix of products that are not necessarily produced 'in-house'. In effect, banks with an investment management arm may tend to move towards in-house products, especially in times of poor performance. MiFID II rules implementation shall ensure accessibility and choice for European investors.

Only the UK and in part Sweden have so far managed to develop open platforms for funds,[45] while Germany, France, the Netherlands and Austria are still at an early stage. As a result, most European countries do not have access to independent fund platforms. The main chunk of distribution takes place via banks and insurance products with retrocession fees. The new MiFID II rules will play a key role in encouraging the development of such platforms by limiting inducements (including retrocession fees) to non-independent advice, thus creating a market for the creation of independent fund platforms.

Client base

By assessing the client base and the geographical reach of the sale, i.e. in this case, the cross-border scale of the channel, it is also possible to review the key characteristics of the distribution channel. Despite its success among manufacturers of fund units in Europe and across the world, UCITS was designed as an 'EU-labelled' product in order to become a retail product with cross-border penetration. Even though UCITS account for around 75% of all collective investments by 'small investors' in Europe,[46] European retail investors only hold 7% of their financial assets in investment fund units. As a result of this and limited accessibility, the actual retail and 'true' cross-border penetration is still limited. Considering non-UCITS funds are mainly marketed to professional investors, retail penetration can be proxied by data on client distribution of AuM in Europe. The market share of fund units directly owned by retail clients actually went down from 31% in 2007 to 26% today.

---

[45] Open platforms have no ties with fund distributors or manufacturers and are available to list funds from all competing manufacturers, and they provide access to all competing distributors that meet some minimum non-discriminatory criteria.

[46] See http://ec.europa.eu/finance/investment/ucits-directive/index_en.htm.

Figure 3.41 Total AuM of the European asset management industry, by client type (€tn)

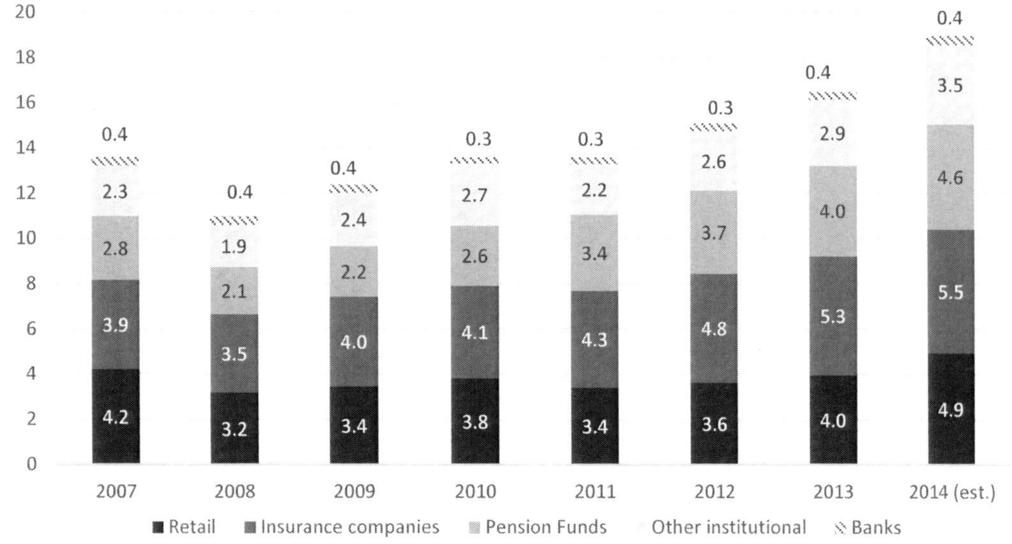

Source: 2015 EFAMA Fact Book.

On the cross-border dimension, Figure 3.42 shows the growth of Ireland and Luxembourg as European investment fund centres, as they are home to half of the net assets of open-end funds. This development does not imply that 50% of mutual funds is cross-border in nature. In effect, funds set up in those countries may have just relocated there for legal or fiscal reasons and offer the fund units only in their country (round-trip fund).

Cross-border dimension

Figure 3.42 Total net assets of mutual funds in Europe (2003-14)

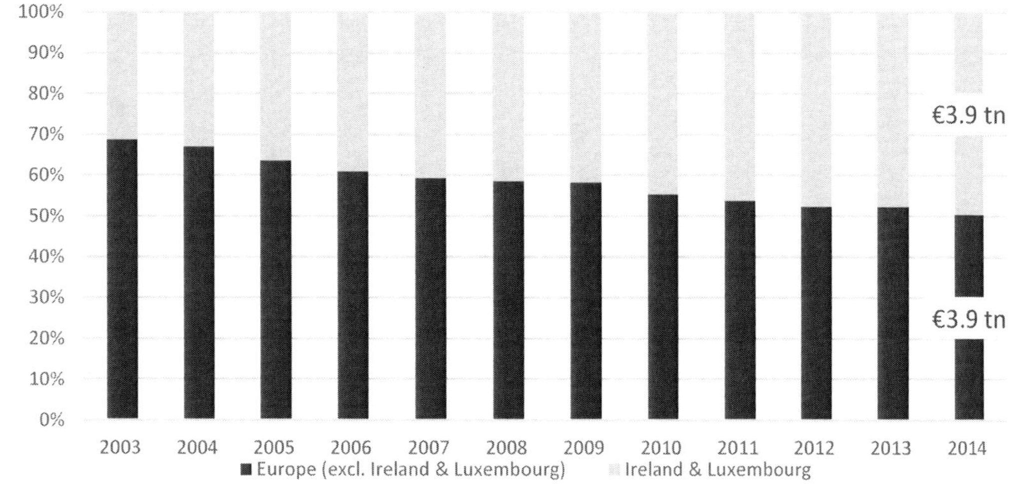

Source: International Investment Funds Association.

According to EFAMA, by excluding round-trip funds in Ireland and Luxembourg, 31% of UCITS and non-UCITS funds (see Figure 3.43) are 'cross-border', i.e. funds sold by the fund provider outside their home country (including funds selling outside the EU). The penetration of these funds in the different countries is, however, uneven due to the marketing rules that apply on top of already applicable EU legislation. Openness of distribution channels

Figure 3.43 Asset under management of cross-border UCITS and non-UCITS funds (€bn; 2002-14)

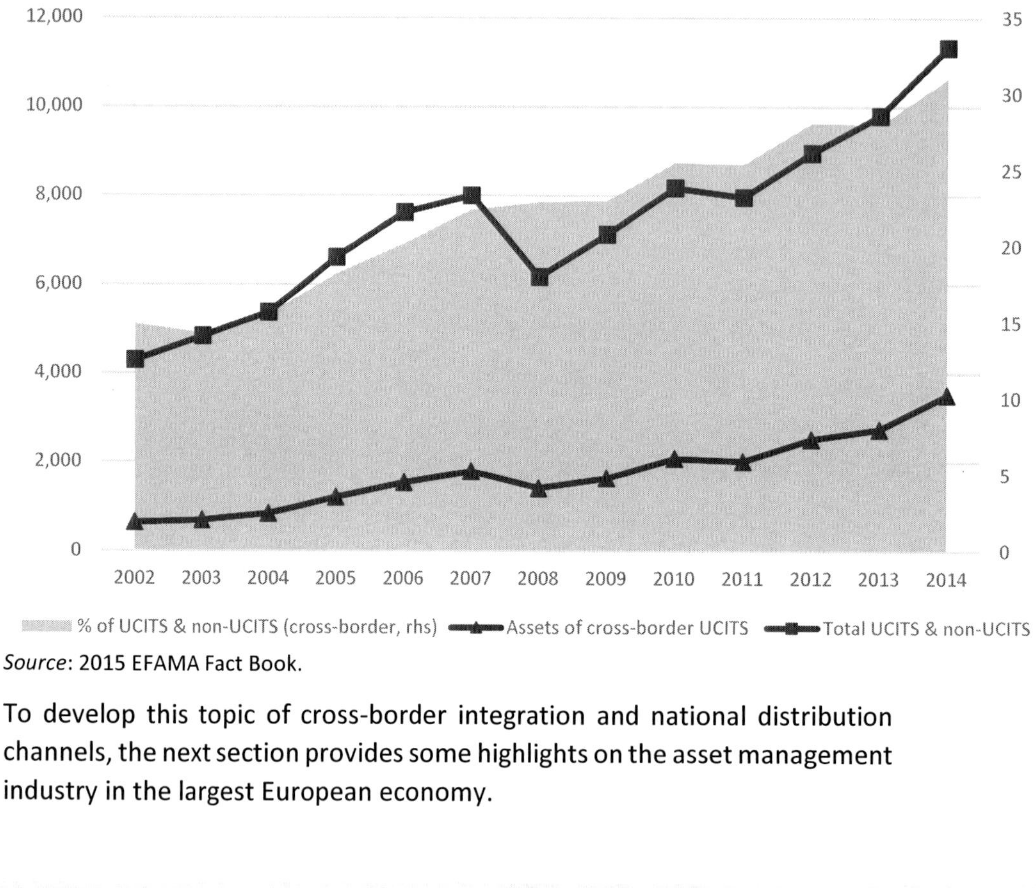

Source: 2015 EFAMA Fact Book.

To develop this topic of cross-border integration and national distribution channels, the next section provides some highlights on the asset management industry in the largest European economy.

Box 3.2 Cross-border asset management: The German Case

The market for investment funds in Germany has been growing rapidly in recent years. From 2010 to 2014, net assets sold have grown by one-third from roughly €1.5 trillion to more than €2 trillion and account for roughly 18% of the European market at the end of 2014 (see Figure 3.44).

Figure 3.44 Net assets sold (€bn)

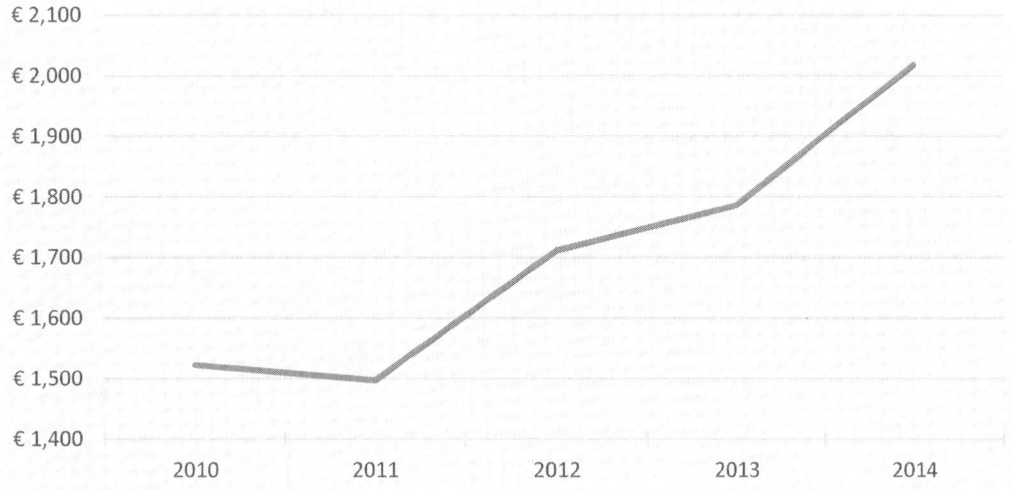

Source: BVI.

The largest part of this increase is due to inflows into so-called 'Spezialfonds' (investment funds only accessible to professional or semi-professional investors), accounting for 80% (€400 billion) of the positive net inflows over the period. This development was mainly driven by the institutional sector, including insurance companies and large private investors. As a result, Spezialfonds are 65% of total net assets sold in Germany (see Figure 3.45).

Figure 3.45 Retail (public funds) vs Spezialfonds (€bn; 2010-14)

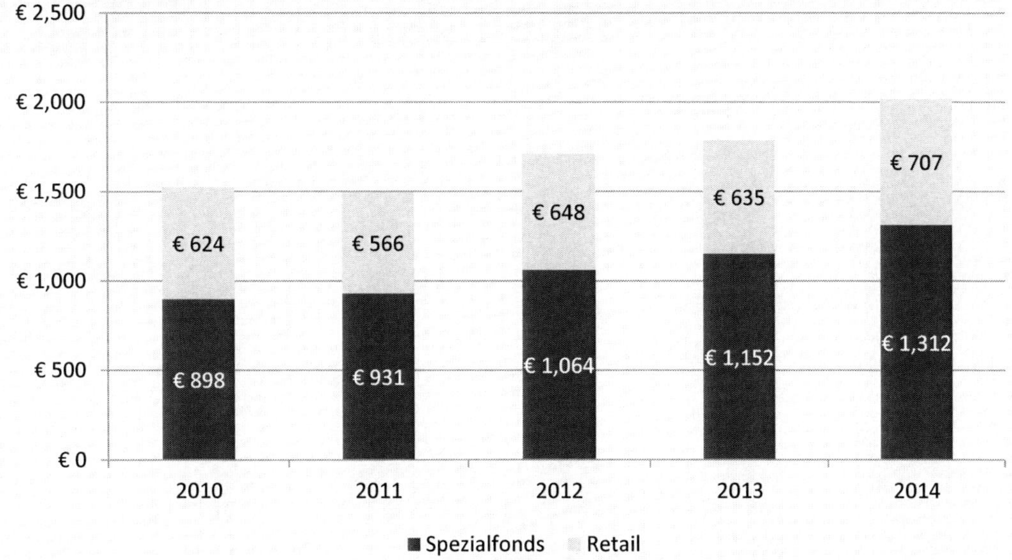

Source: BVI.

Over the same period, the concentration ratio of the top five asset managers in the market increased from 82% in 2010 to 94% in 2013 (EFAMA Asset Management Report). The main distribution channels are retail banks (over 40%), especially cooperative and savings banks, but there is a growing number of independent platforms at an early stage of development (PWC, 2012). The high concentration level may be due to the complex legal system surrounding the distribution of funds in the country, especially if the fund is not domiciled in Germany or sold through a German subsidiary. National requirements, such as the local paying/redemption agent, fund unit owner shareholder registration or the need for a transfer agent for every customer order (unless dealing with a bank-run platform), may create barriers to entry for foreign fund managers.

As a result, the share of cross-border funds active in the country is fairly low. 'Pure cross-border' foreign firms with foreign domiciled funds have only 4% of the market. An additional 14% includes foreign firms with domestically domiciled funds, which are only marketed in Germany. Domestic firms, with funds domiciled abroad, may be either cross-border or round-trip (selling back in their home country only). This is an additional 31%. The presence of the domestic fund industry is strong, with a combined market share of almost 50%. This makes the largest European economy a fairly closed market, where the European passport is occasionally used to compete cross-border but more often to benefit from legal and fiscal advantages by moving domicile to Luxembourg or Ireland. Overall, with current data, it is not possible to clearly establish the cross-border nature of foreign-domiciled funds run by domestic firms.

Figure 3.46 Net assets of funds sold in Germany by nationality of the parent company and country of domicile of the fund as the share of total

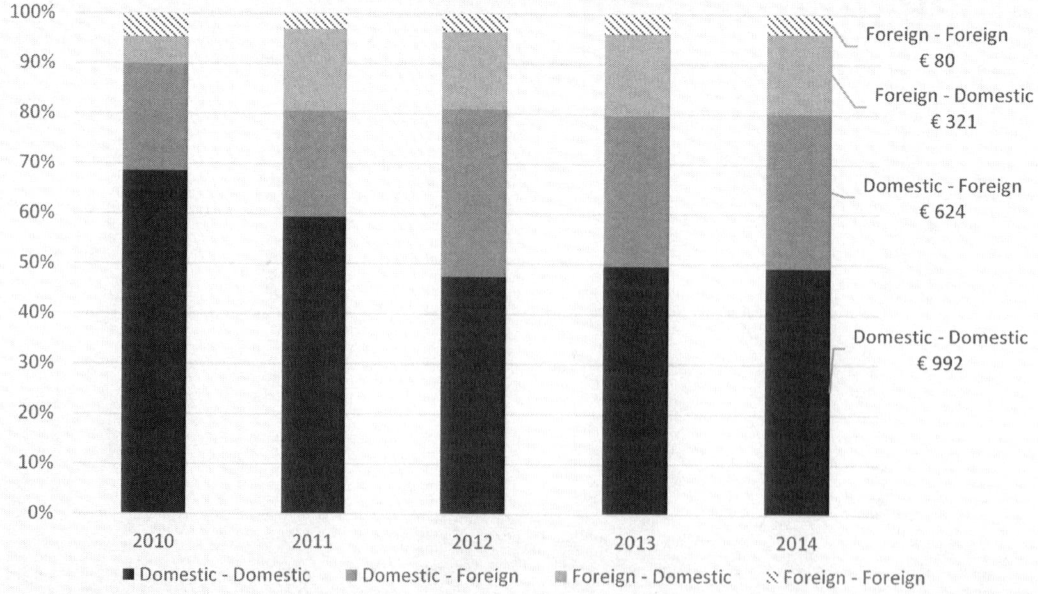

Source: Author's elaboration from BVI.

The average size of the funds changes greatly according to the domicile of the fund. Domestically domiciled funds tend to be larger, especially if run by foreign firms. They mainly serve the institutional market. Pure cross-border funds are very small in size (below €30 million).

Figure 3.47 All funds sold – average size (€mn; 2010-14)

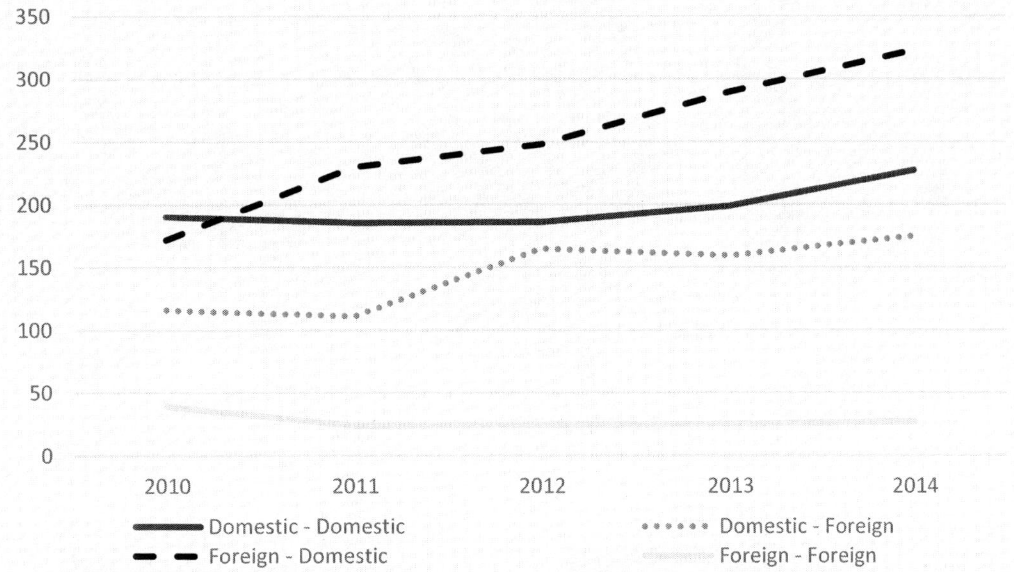

Source: Author's elaboration from BVI.

Average size of funds also changes with the type of investment fund. Spezialfonds are typically larger on average and run via domestic entities, which account for the vast majority of these funds. Public (retail) funds are instead sold mainly via foreign-domiciled funds run by foreign firms (37%) and foreign-domiciled funds run by domestic firms (including round-trip funds, 39%), which are higher than European averages (see Figure 3.48). The foreign component, however, is limited for Spezialfonds, which are essentially domestic funds run by German firms. Cross-border integration in this market, which accounts for two-thirds of the investment fund unit sales in Germany, is thus non-existent.

Figure 3.48 Number of funds sold – Public (Retail) vs Spezialfonds

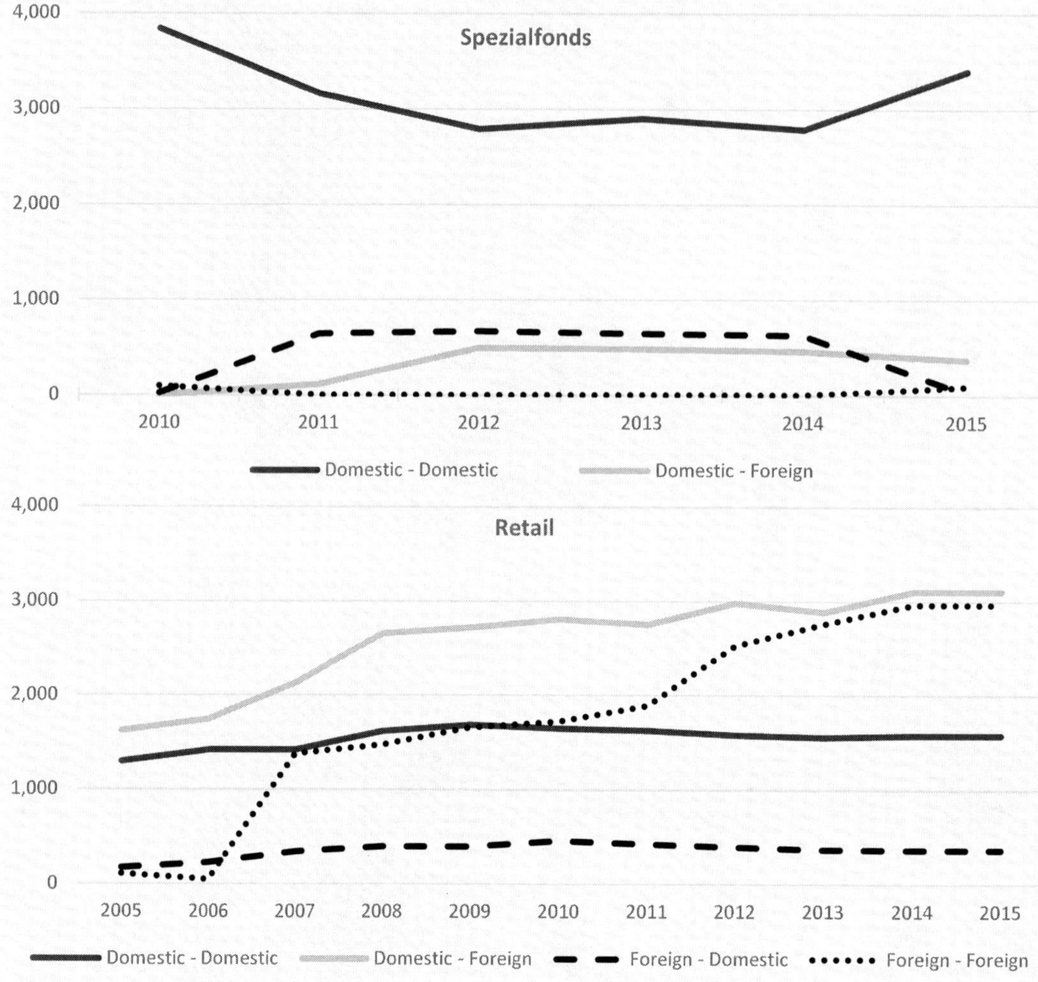

Source: Author's elaboration from BVI. Note: 2015 data are estimates from end of May 2015 data.

Finally, the rapid growth of the German market for fund units provides early signs of cross-border integration in the retail sector in particular. However, further commitment may be required to bring the institutional market into a more competitive cross-border dimension, by removing national rules that can become an obstacle for the entry of foreign funds.

3.3.2.2 Private equity and venture capital developments

The transatlantic funding gap

Private equity and venture capital are two forms of early-stage equity financing that are very important for firms with high growth potential. Its development may be an important driver of innovation and long-term growth for Europe. However, there is currently a big funding gap between the US and the European industry. In the period 2010-14, US private equity and venture capital funds invested on average €119 billion per year, compared to €37 billion in Europe (roughly 31%; see Figure 3.49).

Figure 3.49 Average amount raised in the period 2010-14 (€bn)

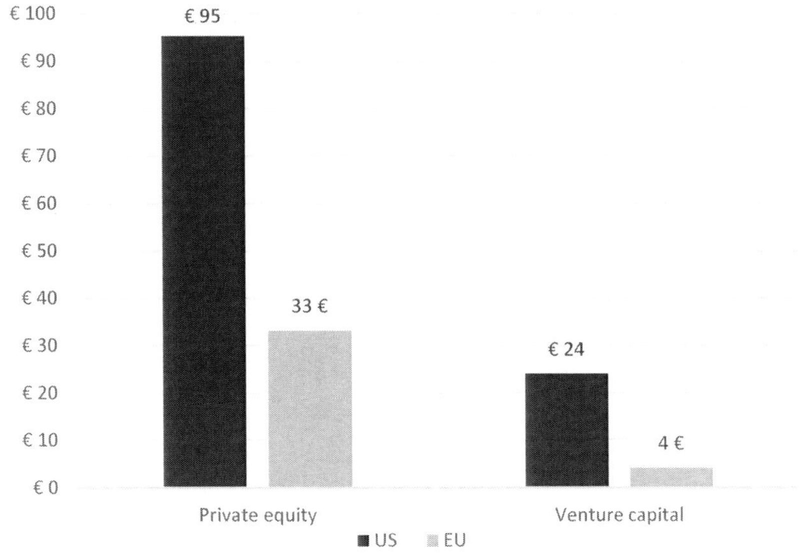

Source: 2015 NCVA Yearbook, Private Equity Growth Capital Council, EVCA.

Foreign contribution

After the financial crisis, volumes have picked up, but they are not at pre-crisis level. Most notably, 35% of funds come from non-European investors (see Figure 3.50), which shows how the market is still in the phase of creating stable pan-European funding for private equity and venture capital. This is also true if we consider that private equity and venture capital are only developed in a few European countries, with a lot of cross-country differences.

Figure 3.50 EU private equity and venture capital funds raised by geographic location (€bn)

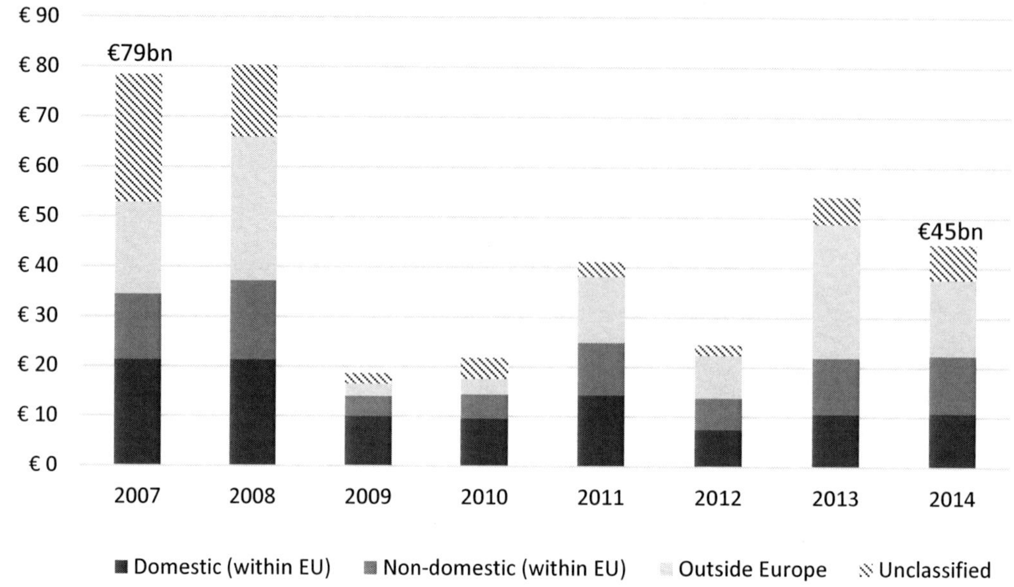

Source: EVCA.

Two key reasons

There are two main reasons for the limited development of this funding infrastructure in Europe: exit opportunities and taxation. US equity markets provided an exit amount equivalent almost to 150% of the equity fundraising in 2014 (compared to 114% in the EU). This means that there is an equity market in the US that is able to provide market-based incentives for private equity funds and venture capitalists to invest in high-growth potential companies. Finally, tax advantages, with the carried interest mechanism,[47] play a key role in the US. Recent developments in the UK, with the Seed Enterprise Investment Scheme (SEIS), are also an example of how tax mechanisms can create incentives for more equity financing, especially for start-ups with high innovation potential.

Box 3.3 The crowdfunding industry: is it here to stay?

The development of new technologies has led to greater integration between social networks and financial services. In recent years, hundreds of platforms have been created to offer access to small firms and start-ups (or simply individuals with a good idea) to finance provided by thousands of individuals who are willing to invest in a business idea.

[47] The carried interest is part of the profits realised by the exit of the private equity fund on the market. It is treated as a capital gain under US tax law, providing a fiscal and economic advantage compared to regular income. For more details see www.pegcc.org/news-and-policy/articles/carried-interest/.

Four models of crowdfunding have emerged: donation, reward, debt and equity. Models based on donation or rewards do not involve financial flows and so do not really compete with other forms of financial funding (banks or markets). Peer-to-peer lending and equity funding platforms are growing at a very quick pace. In 2014, global crowdfunding raised roughly €12.2 billion and for 2015 it is forecasted to grow to more than €31 billion (Massolution, 2015). The European share of this market is still tiny, with €2.5 billion in 2014, compared to €2.6 billion and €7.1 billion respectively in Asia and North America.

Crowdfunding platforms have introduced a new funding model which provides risk dispersion (and thus more financial and governance independence) and a high level of customisation based on a peer-reviewed and feedback-based enforcement mechanism. This helps to establish reputational capital, which is an essential feature of a more relationship-based funding model. As a result, crowdfunding is combining risk dispersion with relationship lending models, thus filling a gap in finance, which was only partially covered by private equity funds and venture capitalists (for start-ups). It has the potential to become a funding source for well-established and start-up firms (small and medium) alike. Hence, this funding model is here to stay, but policy-makers will have to ensure that a minimum set of rules and supervisory guidance is in place to minimise information asymmetries that can destabilise a reputation-based mechanism.

Key findings #7.

- The drop in trading volumes, tightening of capital requirements (especially for those holding large securities inventories), and an environment with very low long-term interest rates (and limited interest carry trade with central bank liquidity) have increased costs of big inventories and pushed some banks to cease well-established trading activities or even restructure the entire business model towards more hybrid models, i.e. a combination of securities dealing, trading and asset management services.
- Trading assets shrank as banks scaled down activities in capital-intensive businesses, e.g. fixed income.
- Collateral reuse decreased, as more of it remains encumbered on the balance sheet of banks for own risk management services. These developments also produced an impact on repo activities, which have lost absolute value because top players reduced their activities.
- The asset management industry has grown at an incredible pace post-crisis, doubling its assets under management (from €9.9 trillion to €19.9 trillion) between 2008 and 2014.
- The high number of funds and the small average size keeps a fragmented and costly market for investment fund units across member states.

- The success of UCITS rules in the fund industry at manufacturing level has not been matched by the same success in the integration of the distribution system, which in many countries still relies on a closed bank distribution channel with retrocession fees.
- The level of retail and cross-border penetration for UCITS is also only partially satisfactory. The retail client base is stable at 26% of total AuM (it was 31% in 2007). The cross-border penetration of UCITS (excluding round-trip funds) is estimated at 31%. Nonetheless, data about the German market put this estimate potentially anywhere between 4% and 35%.
- At the end of 2010, total expense ratio (TER) of European funds was 32% higher than the US equivalent. Since then, this gap has widened, as the US TER fees decreased to 120 basis points, while there is limited evidence of the same move in Europe. Fixed charges (subscription and redemption fees) have even increased in recent years and fee structures continue to greatly diverge across countries. As a result, these developments may suggest that the level of cross-border integration and competition in this market is still fairly limited.
- Private equity and venture capital funds in Europe are far from being systemically relevant, with a combined raised average amount per year in the period 2010-14 equal to €37 billion, compared to €119 billion in the US.
- Negative net issuance of equity, e.g. buybacks, and the 'carried interest' tax mechanism suggest respectively great (ex post) exit opportunities for equity investments and thus high ex ante incentives to inject equity into fast growing companies.
- Crowdfunding is a new funding model that combines risk dispersion with reputational mechanisms (relationships). It complements private equity and venture capital. Its nature is cross-border and careful minimum regulatory and supervisory design should not hamper their cross-border nature. EU action can actually pre-empt disorderly national action.

3.4 Integration in Europe's financial markets

Asset classes

The following section reviews the status of integration of key asset classes in financial markets, splitting where possible between primary and secondary market activities. There is currently mixed evidence about the depth of European integration of the different financial markets, which are still more driven by global trends than regional ones.

3.4.1 *Equity markets*

Mixed evidence

Evidence on equity market integration is not straightforward. In terms of capital flows, there is some evidence that countries where financial reforms were implemented attracted more FDI and equity portfolio investments (Faria et al., 2007).[48] Lane & Milesi-Ferretti (2007) also find that the membership of the euro has had a beneficial impact on cross-border equity holdings. Convergence in equity premia is also a sign that country factors are less important. This development is explained by the introduction of the euro (Adjaouté & Danthine, 2004). The euro also explains most of the stock market integration at least until 2006 (Hardouvelis et al., 2006). Moreover, Cappiello, Kadareja & Manganelli (2010) find that equity return co-movements between EU member states increased after 1998, especially for country-pairs that have adopted the euro. Finally, Bartram & Wang (2011) find more stock market dependence among countries that adopted the euro. The euro also increased the global integration of our financial markets, as global factors are increasingly more important in determining equity returns (Baele & Inghelbrecht, 2008).

However, there is also disagreement about the euro's role in leading to more equity markets integration. Aggarwal et al. (2010) argue that equity markets responded only to the Delors Report (1989) and the Strasbourg Declaration (1989) – which forecast the European Economic Community moving towards European Monetary Union – but not to subsequent developments pertaining to the European Monetary Union. This finding would be consistent with the idea that equity market integration is driven by market forces but constrained by regulatory barriers and informational frictions (Portes & Rey, 2005). The level of integration is thus neither uniform across market segments nor across time. Consequently, increasing equity market interdependency is found to be consistent with (although neither necessary to nor sufficient to bring about) increasing equity market integration. There is some additional evidence that the monetary union has caused the apparent segmentation between bond and stock markets within but not outside Europe, due to flight-to-quality issues related to the (incomplete) nature of the monetary union with a common monetary policy (Kim et al., 2006).

---

[48] In particular, Faria et al. (2007) exploit a database constructed by Detragiache, Abiad & Tressel (see reference in the paper), which tracks financial reforms in seven areas and provides indices of reforms in each area: credit controls, interest rate controls, entry barriers, bank regulations, privatisation, capital account and securities markets. They use data on equity liabilities for the period 1996 to 2004, extracted from a worldwide database developed by Lane & Milesi-Ferretti (2006).

Equity holdings

If we look at the static view, holdings of equity across the euro area have doubled since the introduction of the euro, both in distressed and non-distressed countries. Holdings also show strong resilience to the financial and sovereign crises. Nonetheless, total equity holdings are still small compared to other financial instruments and next sections illustrate the level of activity in primary and secondary markets for listed equity instruments.

Figure 3.51 Cross-border equity holdings issued by euro area residents (% total holdings)

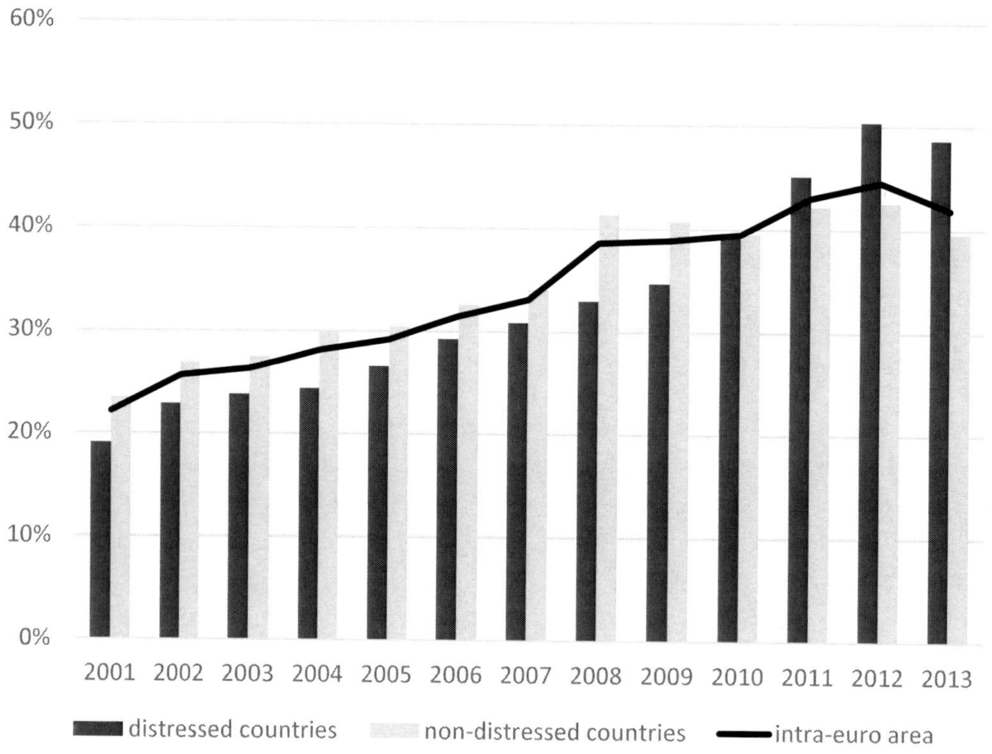

Note: Non-distressed countries are Germany, the Netherlands, France, Austria and Finland. Distressed countries are Italy, Spain, Portugal, Greece and Ireland.

Data Source: ECB.

Holdings

The breakdown of equity holdings shows the dominance of non-financial corporations in holdings and other financial intermediaries on the European scene (see Figure 3.52). However, for NFCs and OFIs, only 12% and 14% respectively are holdings of listed shares. Investment funds (other than MMFs) hold almost all their portfolio in listed shares both in Europe and the US, while other financial intermediaries mainly hold unlisted shares (especially in the US, with 97% of the equity holdings). Low amounts of listed shares holdings accrue to households (23%) and insurance and pension funds (36%), compared to the US, where over 90% of the portfolio is invested in listed shares for the same two funds. Moreover, households play a key role as direct holders of equity for almost half of all listed shares.

Figure 3.52 Equity holdings by type of holder (€mn; average 2010-14)

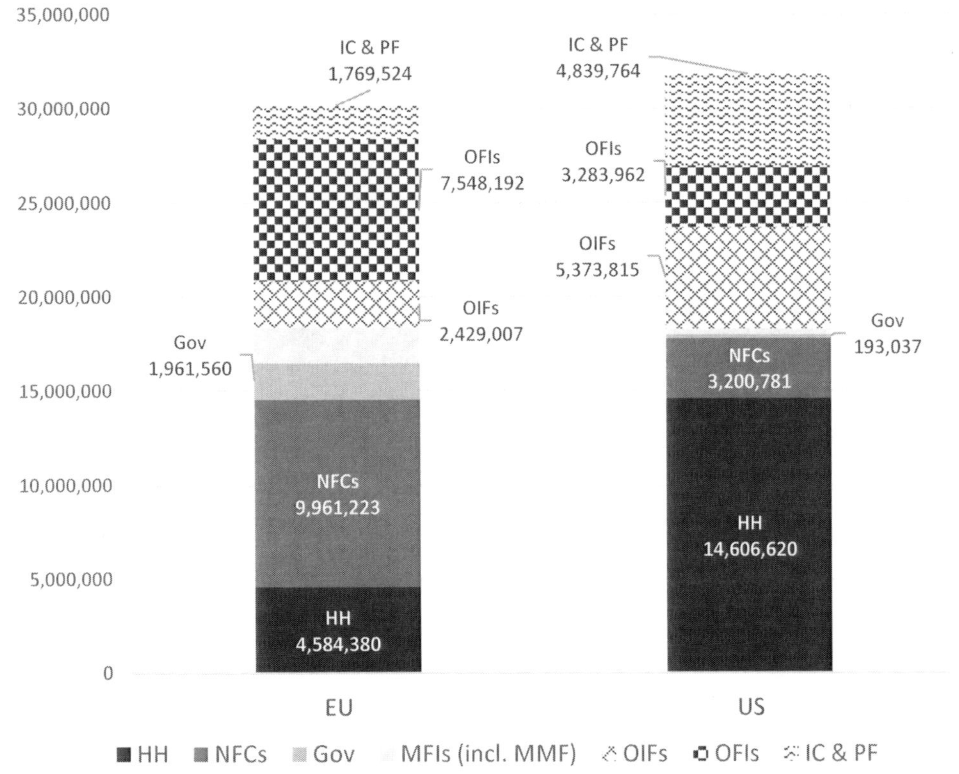

Note: 'HH', Households; 'NFCs', Non-Financial Corporations; 'Gov', General Government; 'MFIs (incl. MMF)', Monetary Financial Institutions (including Money Market Funds); 'OIFs', Other Investment Funds; 'OFIs', Other Financial Institutions; 'IC & PF', Insurance Companies and Pension Funds.

Data Sources: Eurostat and US Fed. Eurostat (exchange rate).

The allocation of equity in the economy significantly changes between the US and Europe, where households have a less active role in equity markets for reasons that will be discussed in the following sections.

3.4.1.1 Primary markets

IPOs

The primary market for listed equity instruments is the key source of long-term funding for the economy, in particular large corporations. The number of Initial Public Offerings (IPOs) has partially picked up post-crisis, but there is a lot of instability in Europe and China, as financial conditions are still unstable. The trend in the US, which is the biggest IPO market, seems steadily positive over time.

Figure 3.53 IPO activity by regions (value and number of trades; 2008-14)

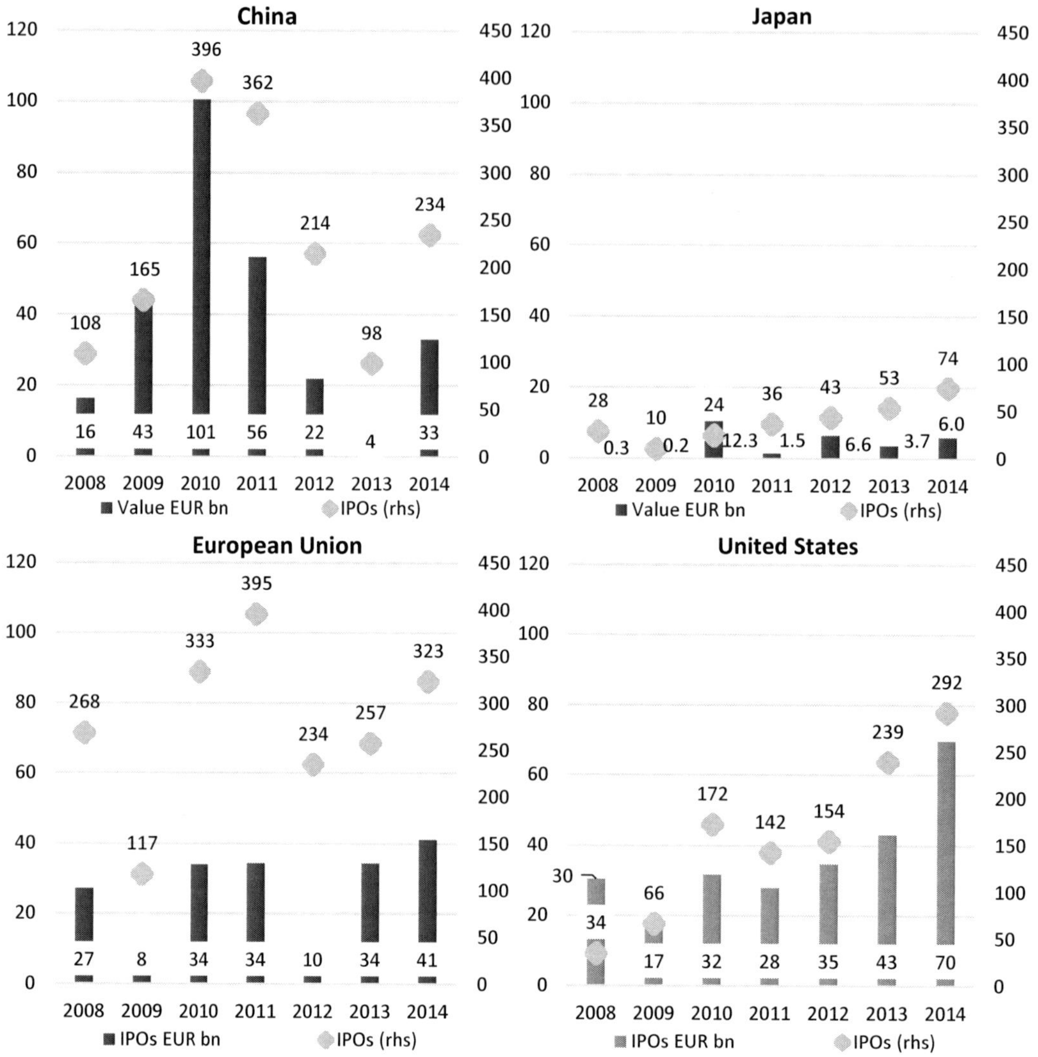

Data Sources: FESE, WFE, individual stock exchanges, PwC IPO Watch.

Equity flows

The composition of newly raised equity paints a different picture. While firms have raised more equity, most of these equity inflows go to already listed companies (76%), in line with other regions of the world. Going to markets to raise additional money could also be a sign of financial difficulties for the company. Relative to GDP, the size of equity flows for newly listed companies in Europe is much lower than in China and the US. The average size of issuance is also bigger than the average size in Europe, which has 7,599 listed companies (3,246 in the euro area) vis-à-vis 5,248 in the US (see Figure 3.54). Most notably, in the US, there are historically many fewer listed companies now than a few decades ago, as a result of an international consolidation process due to factors such as international trade (Doidge et al., 2015), but the overall IPO flow is still fairly high compared to past years and is recovering quickly after the financial crisis.

Figure 3.54 Equity flows into newly and already listed companies by region (€bn; end of 2014)

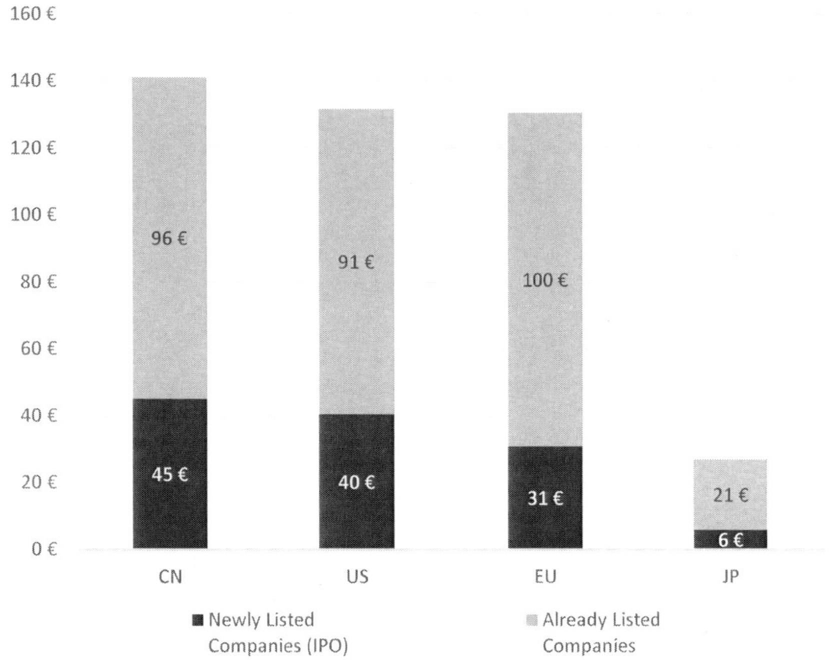

Data Sources: FESE, WFE, individual stock exchanges.

Figures change greatly across countries, with the London Stock Exchange Group (LSEG; grouping the UK and Italian markets) being the largest market for equity issued by newly listed companies (€21 billion) and Euronext (grouping the French, Dutch, Belgian and Portuguese markets) being the largest one for equity issued by already listed companies (see Figure 3.55).

Figure 3.55 Equity flows into newly and already listed companies by selected EU countries (€bn; end of 2014)

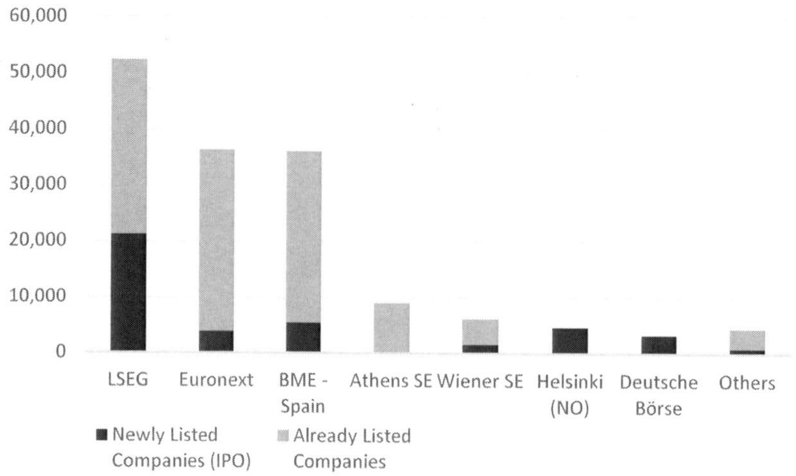

Note: LSEG includes both UK and Italian markets. No data on already listed companies on Nasdaq OMX Helsinki, Deutsche Boerse, Prague, and other NASDAQ OMX Nordics and Baltics.

Data Sources: FESE, WFE, individual stock exchanges.

Foreign listing is also more diffused in the US, with roughly 20% of firms being foreign companies. Only the LSEG has reached a similar share in Europe (30%), while all the others are well below 20% (including firms from other EU countries). In effect, the split of issuance along geographical markets and the limited size of foreign listings suggest that primary issuance is still very much a national matter, which is inconsistent with the creation of a pan-European market. Opening up listings across Europe may require a harmonised regime for the legal enforcement of corporate actions, among other things. In any case, primary issuance markets can be considered integrated when issuance is no longer driven by geographical factors but by the specialisation of the market, irrespective of where it is located in the EU.

Market capitalisation

The ability to attract new funding via equity markets is also related to the market's ability to increase the value of companies' net worth. Domestic market capitalisation has been steadily growing post-crisis, but the divergence between Europe and the US has been widening. The US has reached a historical peak, with almost €22 trillion in capitalisation and an average of €4 billion per firm, while Europe has yet to top pre-crisis levels (see Figure 3.56).

Figure 3.56 Domestic market capitalisation (€bn; 1995-2014)

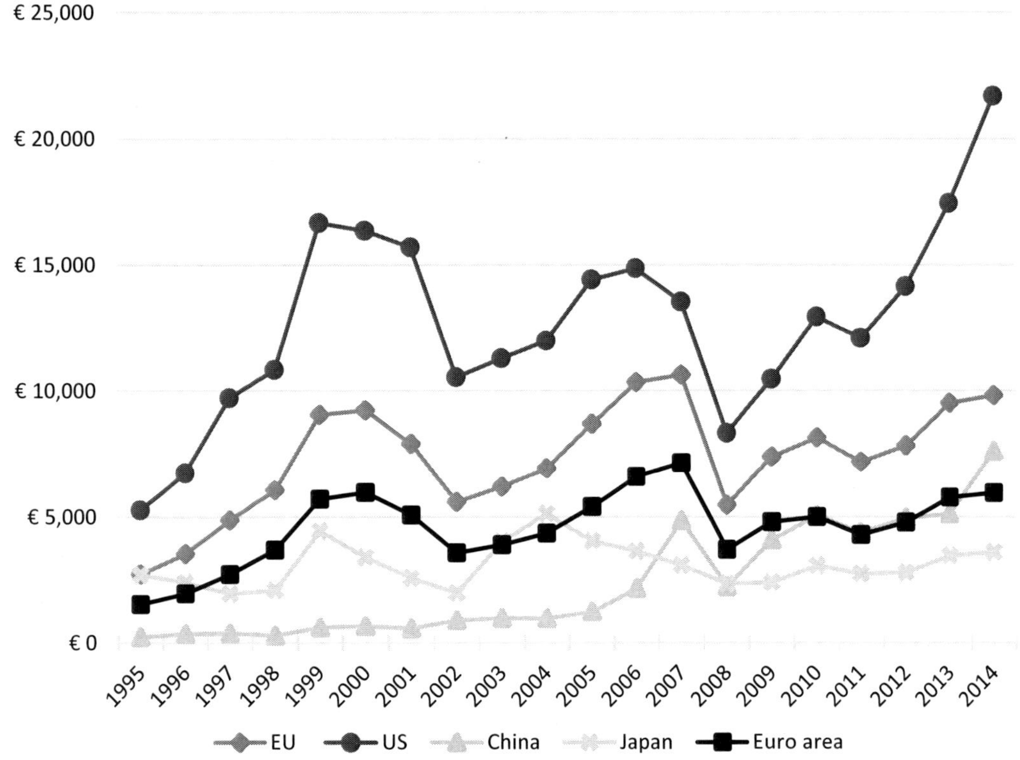

Data Source: WFE.

Fragmentation is thus hitting the ability of European markets to generate value over time if reasons to issue on a venue are independent from the efficient functioning of that venue. There are also additional differences within the EU. Euro area equity markets are more concentrated than the European average, with a higher average market capitalisation per listed company (€1.8 billion) vis-à-vis the European average (€1.2 billion). Since the introduction of the euro, the number of listed companies decreased constantly to a low in 2014. This may be a signal that the market is increasingly concentrating, thus providing support to big corporations that have perhaps a greater cross-border dimension and scale to access fragmented equity markets. These developments are not necessarily a sign of fragmentation across markets. Many trading venues have already consolidated order books of national stock exchanges that have merged over time with other groups across Europe. This process will most likely continue, as the process of consolidation among exchanges is not finished and may produce important synergies for the integration process.

3.4.1.2 Secondary markets

MiFID and secondary markets

Secondary equity markets have undergone many changes in recent years, thanks to the gradual integration of European rules on transparency and market structure. Under the umbrella of the FSAP, the Markets in Financial Instruments Directive (or MiFID; 2004/39) opened up the market for investment services, in particular in the area of secondary market activities run by alternative trading venues.[49] By removing the concentration rule, growing pan-European secondary market activities emerged. Other measures, such as the Market Abuse Directive (MAD; 2004/72), the Prospectus Directive (2003/71), and the Transparency Directive (2004/109), helped to overcome some informational frictions that impeded cross-border secondary market trading, even though there is more to be done to overcome member states' gold plating. These regulatory developments came in an environment that was already moving towards consolidation, as technology allows the separation between the physical location of trading and the act of executing a trade, thus also reducing financial stability concerns (Aggarwal & Dahiya, 2006; for a review, see Valiante, 2011, Chapter 5).

While market capitalisation is close to or has already reached pre-crisis levels, the value of share traded (see Figure 3.57) and the total turnover (see Figure 3.58) are only slowly growing. China showed a different trend, which reached a historical peak in 2014, but it might have slipped back below this level with the collapse of stock markets around mid-2015.

[49] For a review of the market structure developments, before and after MiFID, see Valiante (2011).

Figure 3.57 Value of share traded (€bn; 1995-2014)

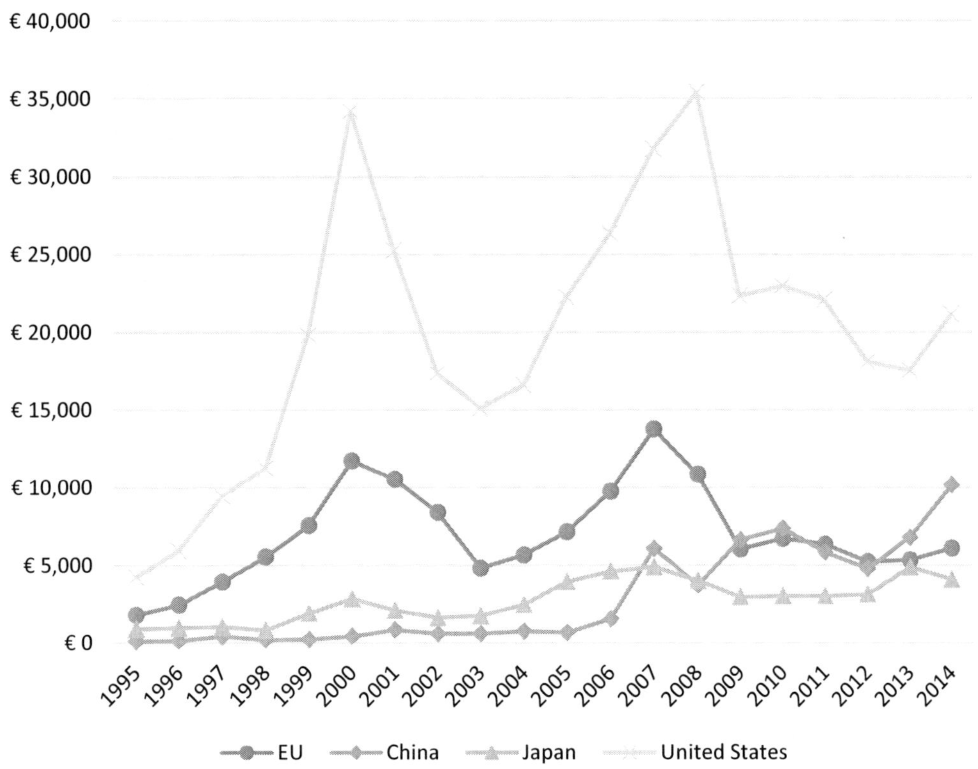

Data Source: WFE.

Turnover

The slowdown in the value of share traded could be, on the one hand, only temporary and a normal development after a major financial crisis, which has imposed huge losses on the financial system that is now healing. On the other hand, the financial system could also be entering a new stable equilibrium caused by a combination of market developments and regulatory actions, which are putting liquidity in global financial markets under severe strain (PWC, 2015).

Turnover is also slowly recovering, but the gap between Europe and the US is not shrinking. US secondary equity market activities are roughly five times greater in scale than those of European markets (see Figure 3.58). Greater liquidity can thus support corporations with cheap funding and, most notably, provide 'easy' exit for private equity and venture capital investments.

Figure 3.58 Total turnover of European and US exchanges (€bn; 2009-14)

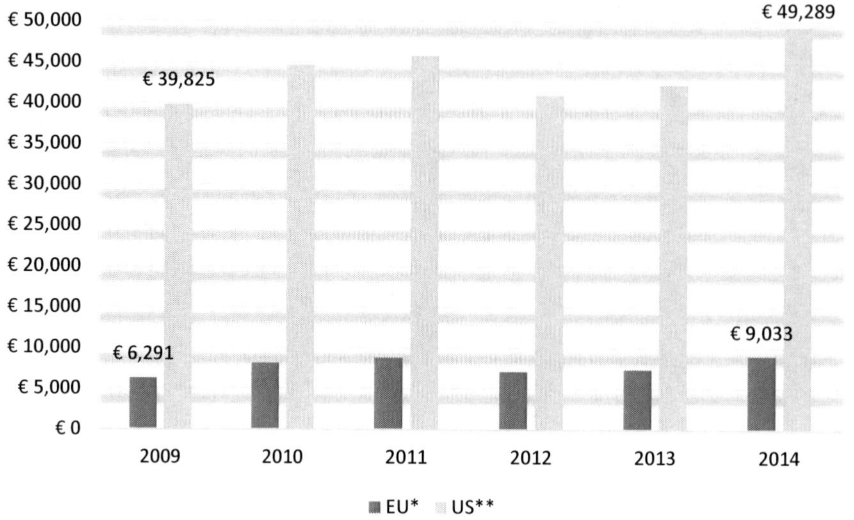

Note: *Includes London, Frankfurt, Paris, Milan, Amsterdam, Madrid, Stockholm, Copenhagen, Brussels, Helsinki, Lisbon, Vienna, Dublin (98% of the market); **includes US NYSE, Nasdaq, BATS (sum of daily data).
Source: BATS Europe, BATS US.

Pan-European venues

With the end of the concentration rule, there is limited evidence of an overall positive increase in market activity, but new trading venues gained market shares in the most liquid European shares. If auctions are excluded, newcomers secured more than one third of the market (see Figure 3.59). As a result, bid-ask spreads have gone down (PWC, 2015), especially in markets where newcomers have managed to gain a high market share. The entry of newcomers did not necessarily push more cross-border consolidation among incumbent exchanges, as their business diversification policies or the national characteristics of the market have limited the erosion of commercial revenues.

Figure 3.59 Turnover of European Exchanges' Groups (% of total; end 2014)

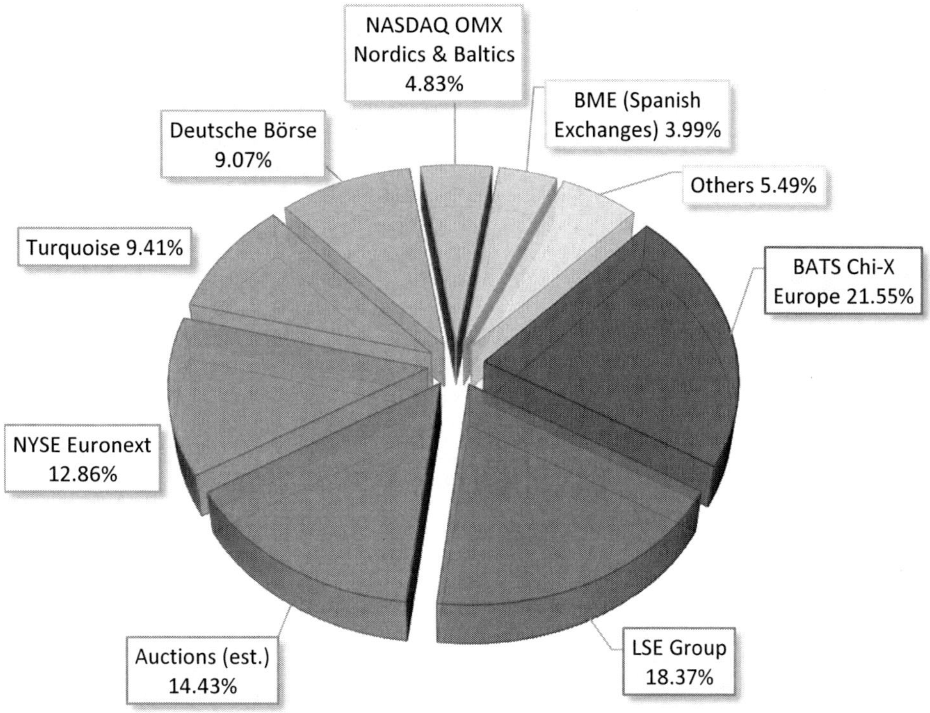

Note: On-order book data (including dark trading). Auctions are removed from local exchanges' turnover data to cover the effective secondary trading activity that is under market competition.

Source: BATS Europe, FESE, individual trading venue.

Small and mid-cap liquidity

Thus cross-border market integration is still poor in secondary trading as well. The quality of the trading flow is also low. Information does not flow easily across markets and some trading venues still keep separate order books, even though some statistics are here aggregated as one trading venue for illustrative purposes, e.g. BATS Chi-X Europe.

The quality of the trading flow is also suggested by the cross-border penetration of newcomers in the indexes of national markets, which are only active at national level. Secondary trading activities of newcomers is still more or less the same until the 50th most liquid share of the different indexes. It then gradually fades away for most markets, except for the UK, where newcomers' trading activities are high also for the 150th most liquid share in the UK market.

Figure 3.60 Newcomers' market share in top 150 most liquid shares by selected national markets (%)

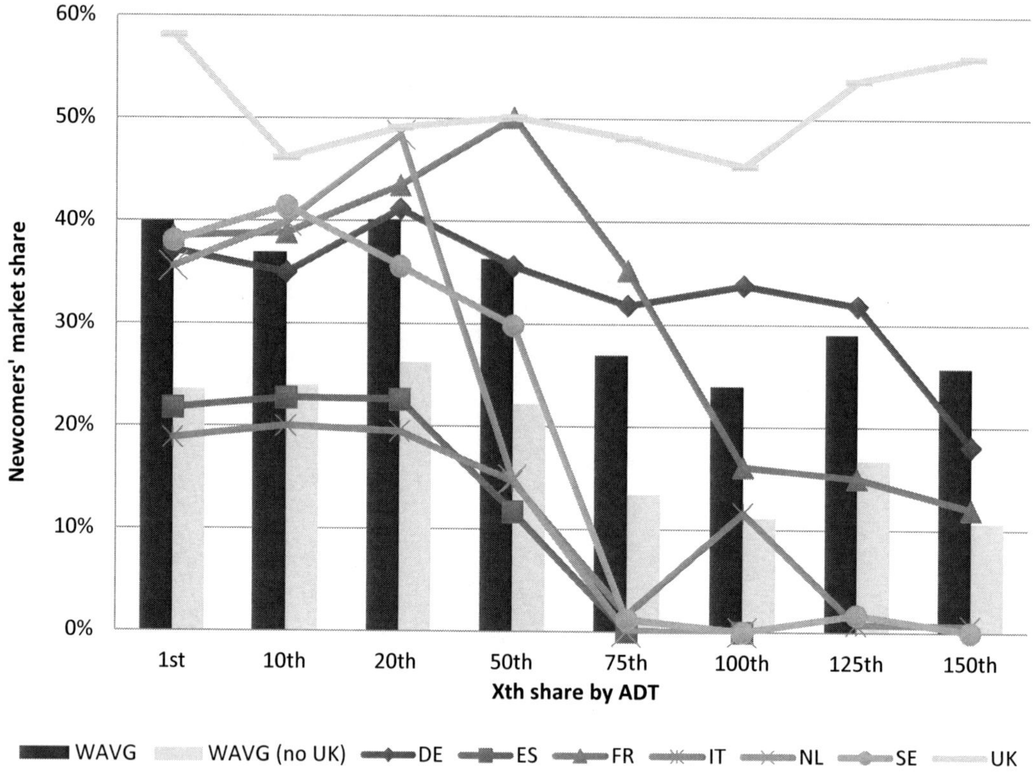

Source: Author's elaboration from ESMA and Fidessa Fragulator. Note: 'WAVG' stands for 'Weighted Average'.

Efficiency

European markets also do not look in such good shape if specific market efficiency indicators are considered. For instance, the value of share traded over market capitalisation puts the European average even behind China and Japan (see Figure 3.61). The level of trading activity is not high enough for the value of companies' net worth.

Figure 3.61 Market efficiency indicator (average 2009-14)

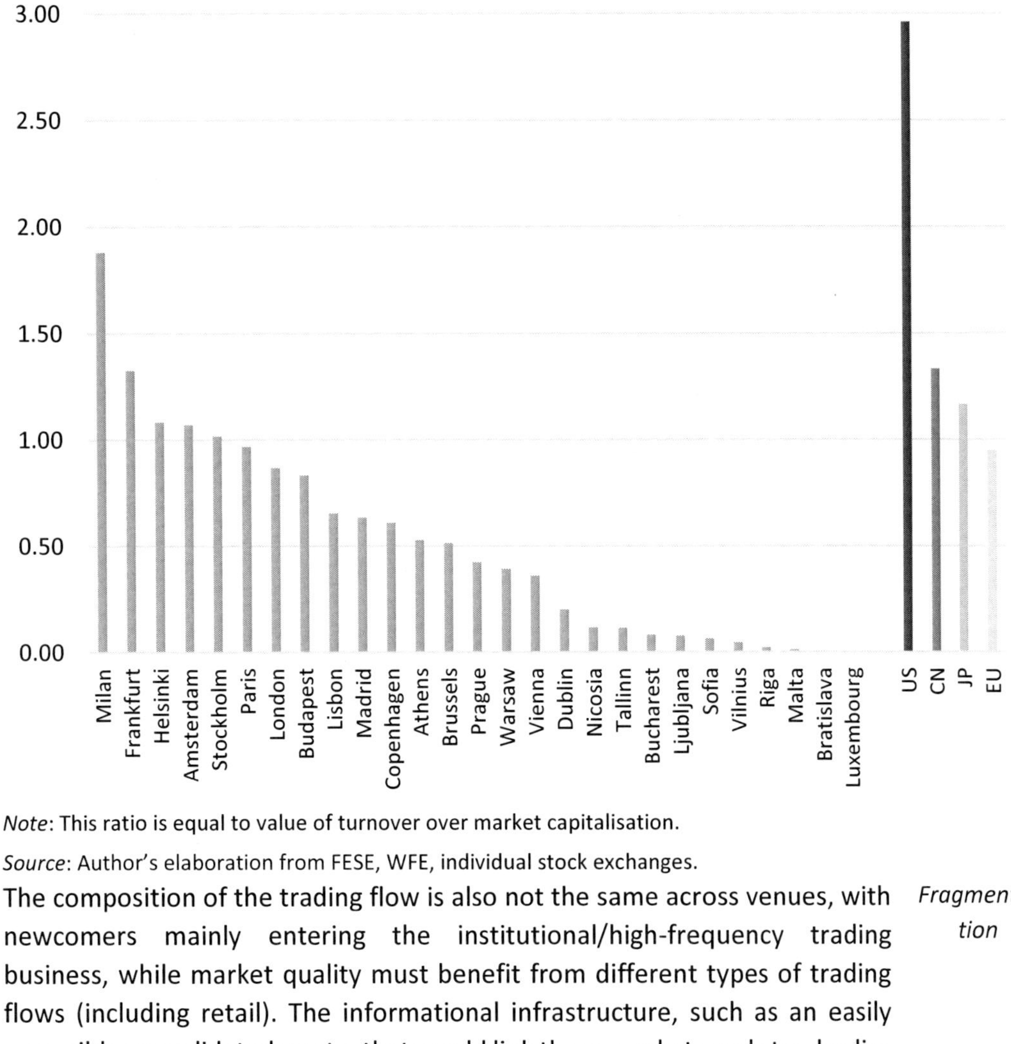

Note: This ratio is equal to value of turnover over market capitalisation.

Source: Author's elaboration from FESE, WFE, individual stock exchanges.

Fragmentation

The composition of the trading flow is also not the same across venues, with newcomers mainly entering the institutional/high-frequency trading business, while market quality must benefit from different types of trading flows (including retail). The informational infrastructure, such as an easily accessible consolidated quote, that would link those markets and standardise even more services is still not there, owing to commercial resistance on the sell-side and a lack of infrastructure (or incentive to invest) to make it happen.

As a consequence, market fragmentation along national borders is stable over time (see Figure 3.62), with movements fairly synchronised across local national markets and with none of them apparently losing market share in favour of other national markets.

Figure 3.62 Electronic order book turnover by local national markets (lit, dark, auction; €bn, 2009-14)

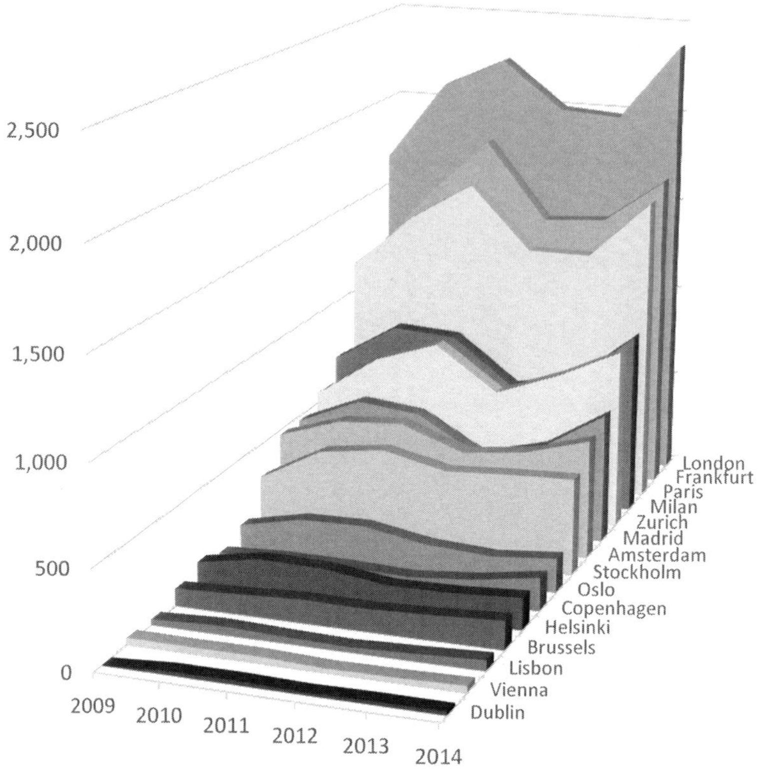

Note: Sum of daily data points.

Data Source: BATS Europe.

The lack of efficiency and the fragmentation along national borders of secondary markets raises legitimate questions about market quality and sustainability of the current market microstructure based on an auction model that provide incentives to push technology to the limits with continuous risks of market disruptions.

Finally, to bring out markets from this dead end of nationally segmented markets, as liquidity sticks around the market where instruments are issued, new bold moves have to be considered to open up the cross-border market for primary issuance of equity instruments, which remains a crucial obstacle to also improving the quality and integration of secondary equity markets. The creation of a solid and common informational infrastructure for price discovery could be a game changer (see section 4.5).

3.4.2 Debt securities markets

Outstanding amounts

Debt securities are historically the most important funding source in Europe that comes from financial markets, especially for governments and financial institutions (including insurance companies). The sector is comparable to that of the US and much larger than those of Japan and China (see Figure 3.63). While debt securities issued by governments and financial institutions have taken up a large part of the financial system, corporate debt securities are still a small fraction, as European NFCs mostly rely on bank lending and unlisted equity capital.

Figure 3.63 Debt securities, amounts outstanding (€bn; end December 2014)

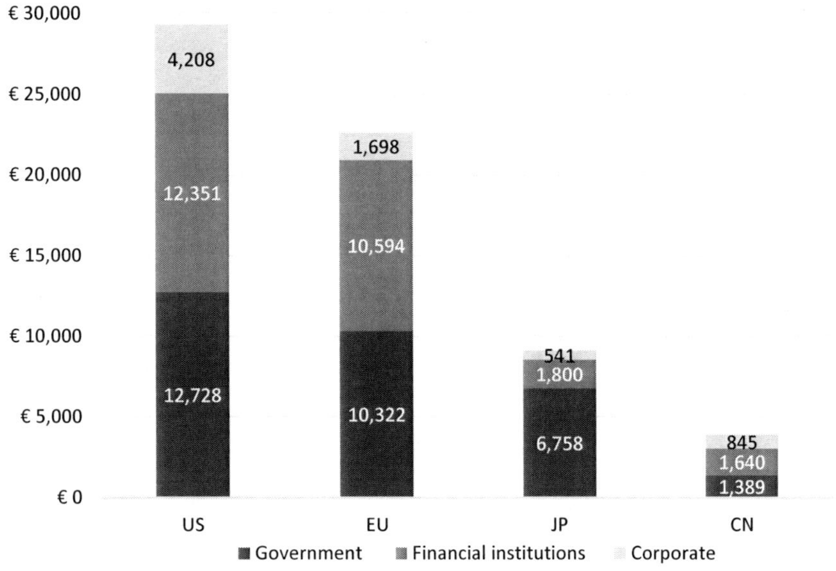

Data Sources: ECB and BIS.

Debt pile-up

The amount of outstanding debt securities in the EU has been constantly growing over the years, with financial institutions providing a big boost before the 2008 financial crisis and governments thereafter (see Figure 3.64). Among other factors, monetary policies that keep interest rates low via asset purchases are a volume-based incentive to issue more covered bonds and (in anticipation) to lengthen the average maturity of government debt securities. In addition, financial institutions in the UK – the main European financial centre and home of many cross-border banks – doubled the amounts of their outstanding debt securities between 2008 and 2009 to face most of the financial issues.

Figure 3.64 EU debt securities outstanding (€bn, 1999-2014)

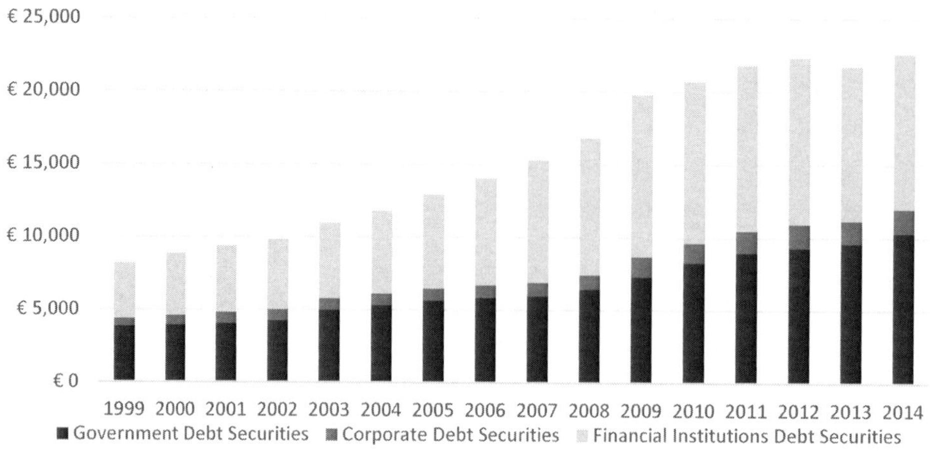

Data Source: ECB.

The breakdown of debt securities holdings suggests a great concentration (almost 50%) of debt securities in the hands of financial institutions (including MFIs), while in the US investment funds, pension funds and insurance companies must be counted to reach that level (see Figure 3.65). *Holdings breakdown*

Figure 3.65 Debt securities holdings by type of entity (€mn; end 2014)

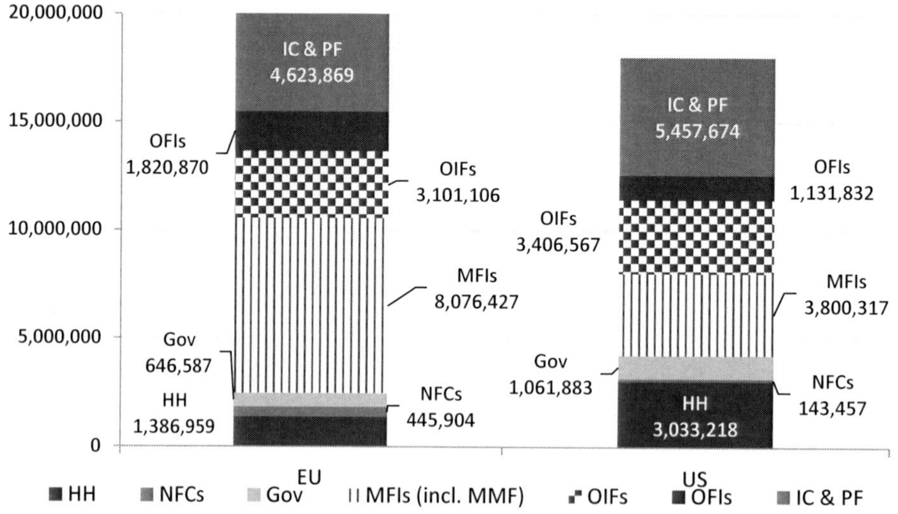

Data Sources: Eurostat and US Fed. Eurostat (exchange rate).

Insurance companies are also important in Europe, while households have a much less important role than in the US. Most notably, EU banks are by far the biggest holder, as a result of multiple factors, such as their capital structure that relies on significant issuance of interbank-held bank debt and high holdings of government bonds (especially in the periphery of the euro area).

Post-EMU integration

For what concerns the euro area, in effect, due to historically liquid debt markets (government and bank debt) and the solid cross-border integration of wholesale banks, the market for debt securities has played a key role in the financial integration process post-EMU. There is some evidence that efficiency and integration in bond markets has improved. In particular, the EMU and the subsequent institutional changes have produced a convergence of yields on public debt, which ultimately has supported the cross-border integration of government bond markets (Pagano & Von Thadden, 2004). Of course, this process reverted with the financial crisis (Lane, 2008) and accelerated later on with the sovereign crisis and the retrenching of government bond holdings within national markets due to the failures in the institutional architecture of the European banking system (Valiante, 2015). This was particularly the case for countries that faced financial problems, as they saw the sudden capital reversal and started to retrench exposure within national borders in order to benefit from the implicit guarantees of local governments (see Figure 3.66 & Figure 3.67). This reversal of integration may only be temporary and shall be minimised (at least for financial institutions) when the common backstop to the resolution of banks will be in place.

Figure 3.66 Euro area MFIs' holdings of debt securities issued by domestic residents – reference country (€bn)

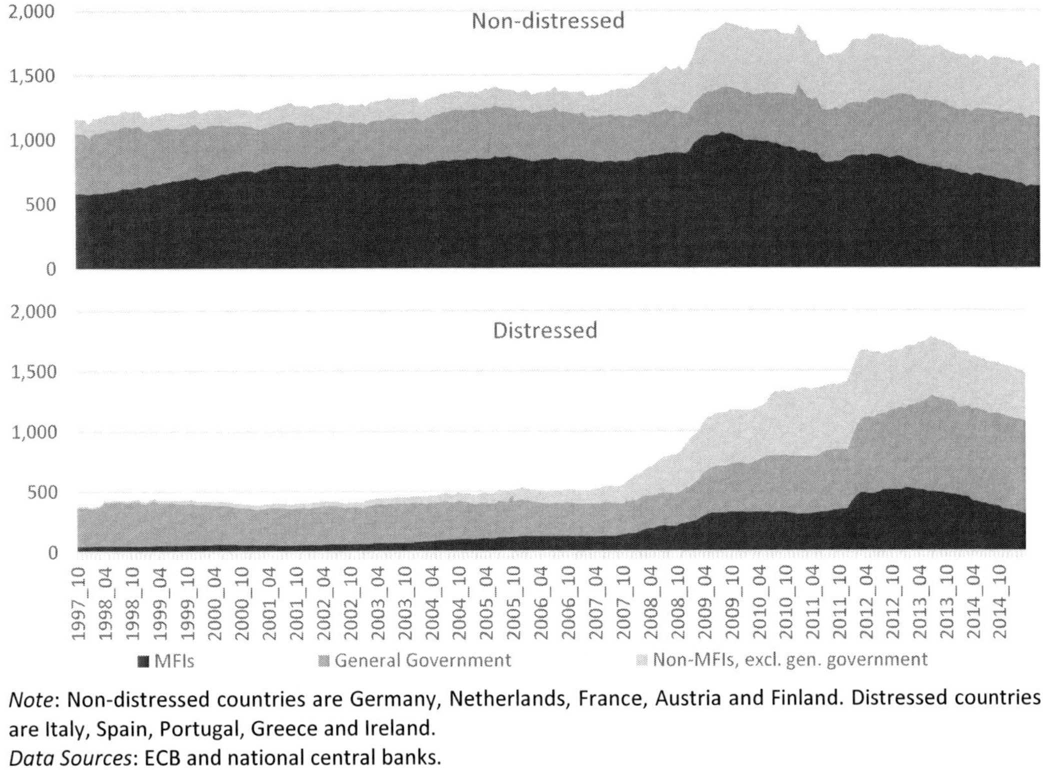

Note: Non-distressed countries are Germany, Netherlands, France, Austria and Finland. Distressed countries are Italy, Spain, Portugal, Greece and Ireland.
Data Sources: ECB and national central banks.

Figure 3.67 Share of MFI cross-border holdings of debt securities issued by euro area and EU corporations and sovereigns (%; 2005-14)

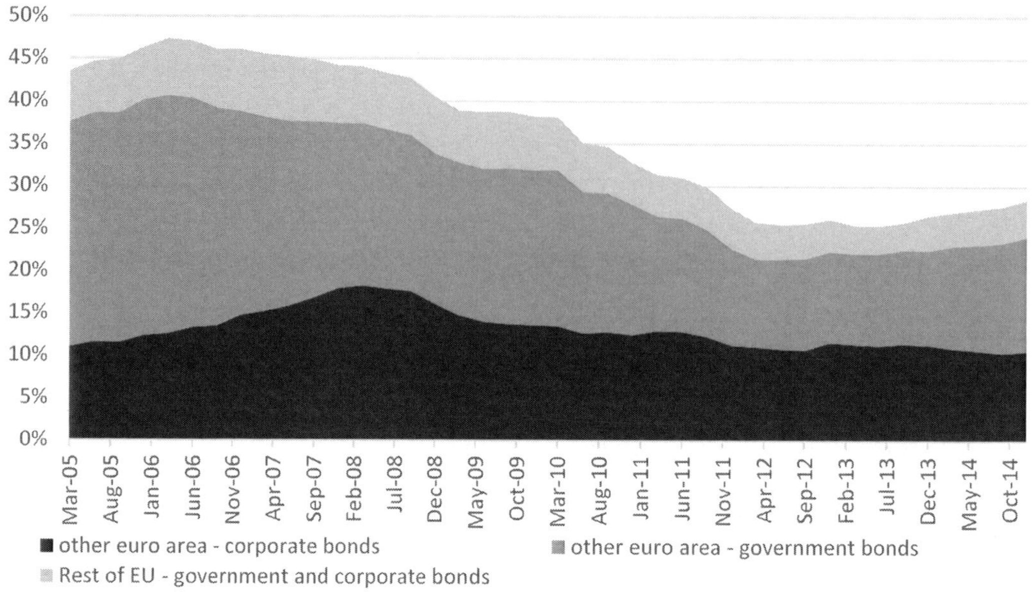

Data Source: ECB.

Nonetheless, market integration is still very much driven by wholesale financial institutions, while accessibility to products by small professional and retail investors is fairly limited or takes place through costly intermediation. Distribution at national level is mainly organised around domestic financial instruments (especially, government bonds). Overall, bond markets are also undergoing more global trends. Bond and stock markets have become increasingly segmented, as a flight-to-quality phenomenon in international financial markets led European and other countries to invest more in bonds, increasing the negative correlation with stock markets (Kim et al., 2006). Evidence shows that the EMU also provided a significant contribution (with the removal of currency risk) to this underlying flight-to-quality process in Europe, which explains the fast and prolonged convergence of yields across the euro area.

Corporate bonds

The corporate bond market also achieved a good level of yields convergence, as they are increasingly driven by common factors rather than those related to the country of issuance (Baele et al., 2004). Also for corporate bonds, the introduction of the euro was an important aspect to boosting at least convergence in yields (Biais et al., 2006). Three factors could have played a key role (Pagano & Von Thadden, 2004; Lane, 2008):

- A greater number of dealership services due to easier access to liquidity decreased trade size and reduced bid-ask spreads (PWC, 2015).

- Prolonged low interest rates on government bonds may have created portfolio rebalancing effects onto riskier assets.
- Increased competition among underwriters may have led to a reduction in issuance costs and improved access for smaller and higher risk firms.

Despite these developments and compared to the past, corporate bond markets are still small compared to the potential of NFC funding and bank lending activities (see section 3.1.1).

3.4.2.1 Primary markets

Shrinking times?

Until the recent financial crisis, primary market issuance of debt securities grew continuously, to almost €18 trillion in 2009. Since then, due to bank deleveraging and financial difficulties, gross debt issuance has dropped below €12 trillion, mainly driven by the drop in debt issuance of financial institutions.

Figure 3.68 European gross issuance of debt securities (€bn; 2005-14)

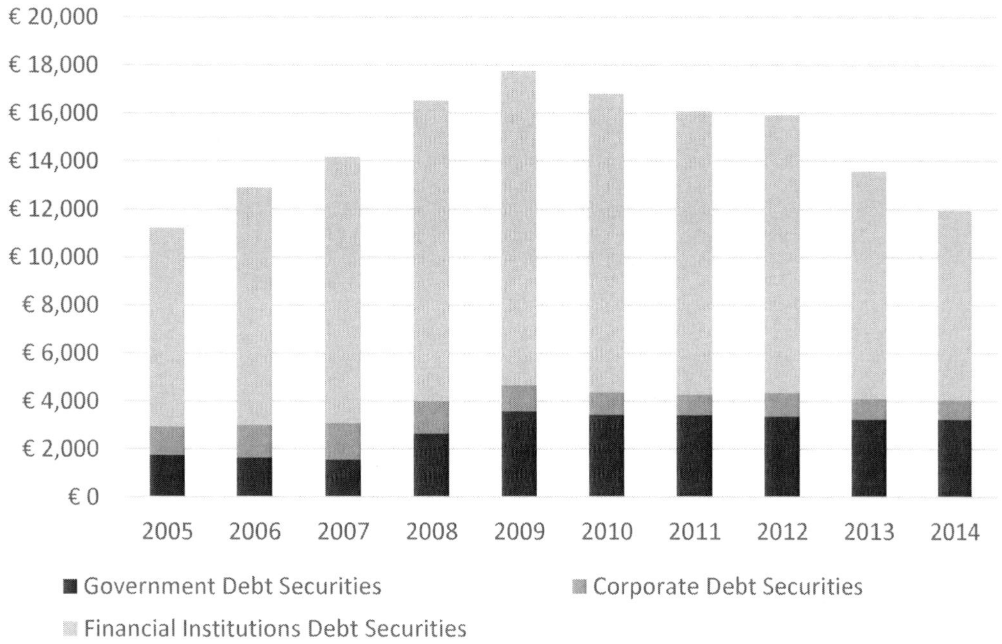

Note: No data available for Luxembourg.

Data Source: ECB.

Euro area vs the rest

The relative weight of non-euro area members is also increasing, as the euro area restructures its banks and government debts (see Figure 3.69).

Figure 3.69 Euro area vs non-euro area gross issuance (% total, €bn; 2005-14)

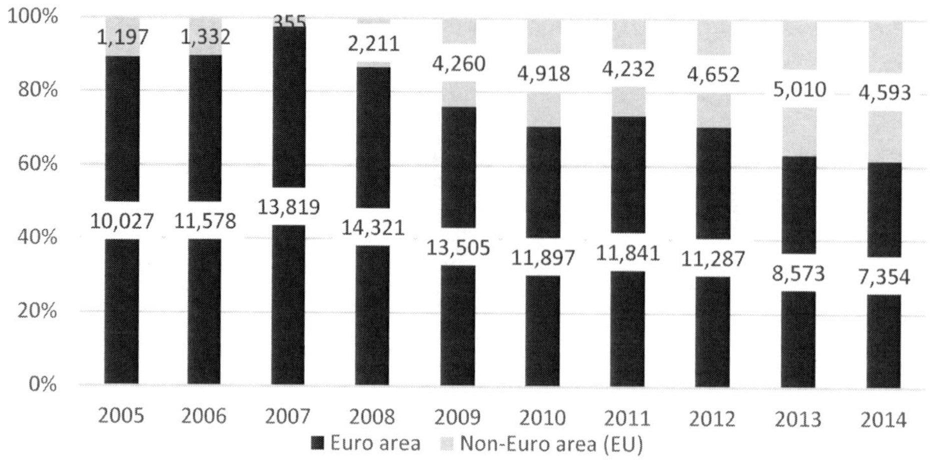

Note: No data available for Luxembourg.

Data Source: ECB.

Cross-country issuance

Gross issuance over GDP shows a major ongoing issuance by financial institutions in Denmark, Hungary, France, Poland and Ireland (see Figure 3.70). Portuguese corporations, however, issue more debt compared to other European countries.

Figure 3.70 EU gross issuance by country (% of GDP; average 2007-14)

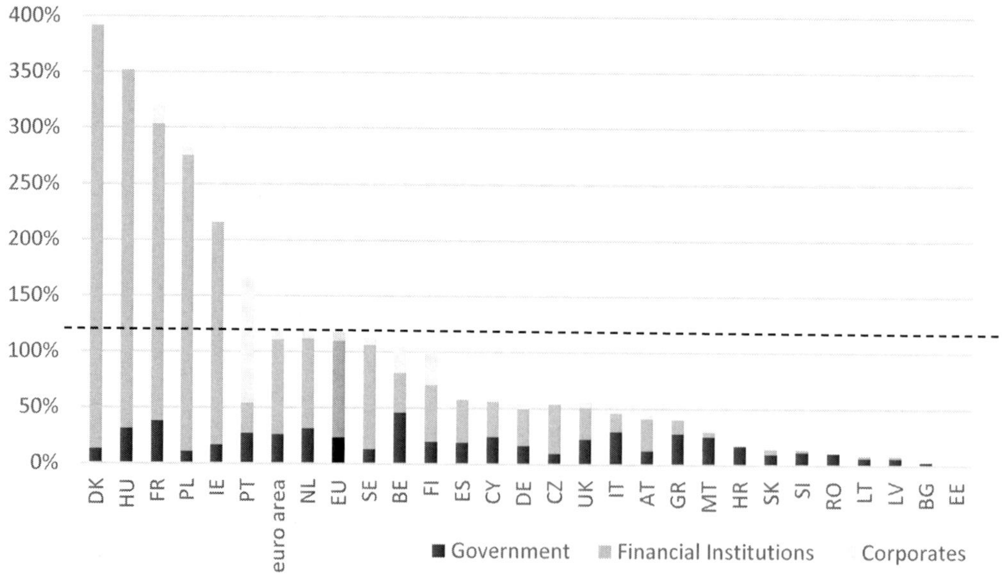

Note: No data available for Luxembourg, but an estimate is included for the EU average.

Source: Author's elaboration from ECB and Ameco.

The net issuance nonetheless paints a different picture for the euro area. Financial institutions are reducing their debt exposure at net, with government and corporate issuance partially offsetting that process (see Figure 3.71). For now, the adjustment in debt exposure is only taking place in countries facing financial difficulties, e.g. Greece, Ireland, Italy, Portugal and Spain, and only partially in Germany and Austria.

Net issuance

Figure 3.71 Euro area net issuance of debt securities (€bn)

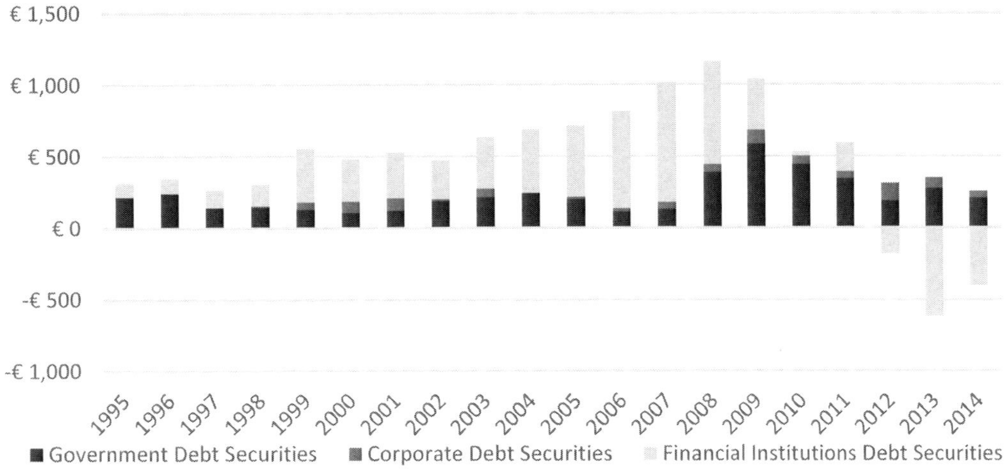

Data Source: ECB.

Figure 3.72 Net issuance by country (% of GDP, end of 2014)

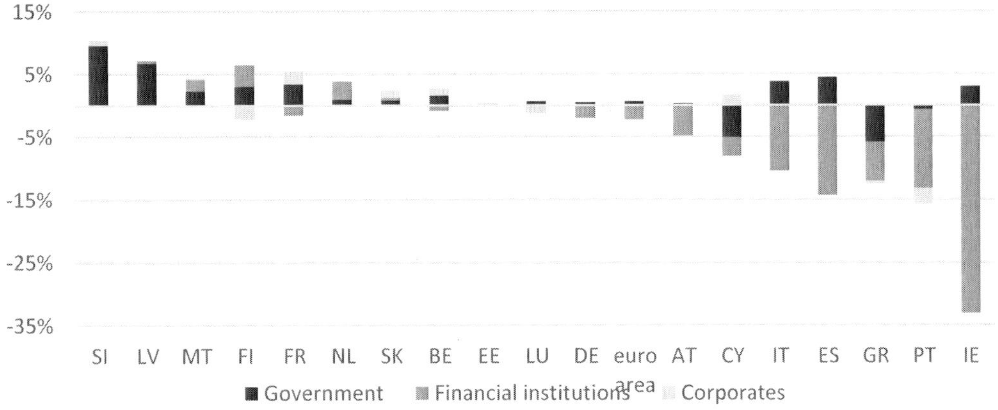

Note: For illustrative purposes, data on financial institutions' issuance in Luxembourg is not included (roughly 200% of local GDP).

Data Sources: ECB and Ameco.

As a consequence, the market for primary issuance is still fairly fragmented, as country risk leads to deleveraging in the financial and public sectors. Issuance takes place mainly via dealer banks that place securities with financial intermediaries or asset management companies. Access for other types of investors, e.g. retail, is fairly limited, but there is growing interest in expanding the distribution channel. Some governments, e.g. Italy, frequently issue debt that is placed directly with retail investors via local trading platforms. There is, in effect, a growing number of trading venues that are also offering primary debt issuance on electronic order books, but the cross-border reach is still limited (see section 3.4.2.2).

Private placement

European private placement

Issuance of debt securities can also take place in a closed environment with selected investors, including investment funds and dealer banks. Debt securities are usually issued in this environment by mid-size or large firms that are typically not rated and looking for opportunities to issue small quantities to one or a few investors without the legal and economic implications of a public listing.

There are two main private placement markets in Europe. The German Schuldschein is by far the biggest private placement market, with the French EuroPP market a distant second. The combined volume of these primary markets in Europe was about €16 billion in 2014, which is a small amount compared to the €822 billion of corporate debt issuance in the EU (almost half of which is issued in France and Germany). Activity is gradually recovering after the financial and sovereign crises, in particular in numbers of trades taking place via this marketplace (see Figure 3.73).

Figure 3.73 Volume (€bn) and number of transactions in Schuldschein and EuroPP markets

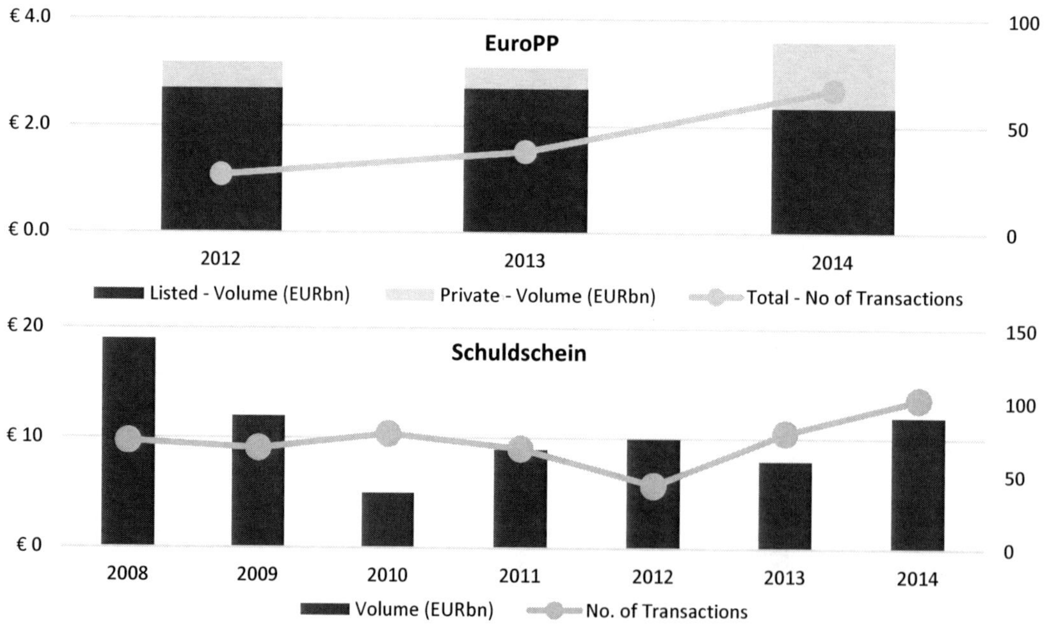

Data Source: HSBC.

EU vs US

Overall, private placement is also still fairly small compared to that of the US in terms of issuance volumes, while the number of transactions is more or less the same (see Figure 3.74). The average size of transactions is thus smaller but still relatively high for most of the European small and medium-sized enterprises (€92 million). According to the European Commission (2015e), the cost of financial due diligence for intermediaries to distribute these instruments only starts to pay for itself at the issue size of around €20 million.

Figure 3.74 USPP vs European private placement (end of 2014)

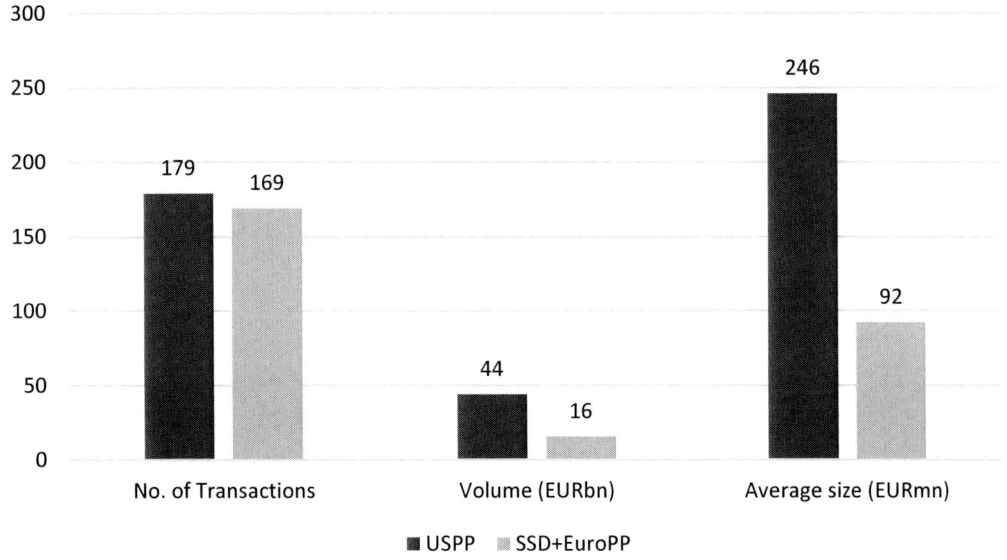

Data Source: HSBC.

Geographical participation

The geographical participation in these markets is also interesting. The European markets are mainly national or regional. The EuroPP is mostly a domestic market for French companies and investors. Non-German firms active in the region comprise only one-third of the German market. Nonetheless, investor participation is more international, with two-thirds of investors being non-Germans and one-fourth from Asia. The institutional nature of these investors helps to achieve more international diversification.

In the US, almost half of the issuers come from countries that are not in the same region (such as the UK or Australia), while the investor base is pretty much national (see Figure 3.75). It is the key private placement market for UK firms.

Figure 3.75 Issuers and investors by country

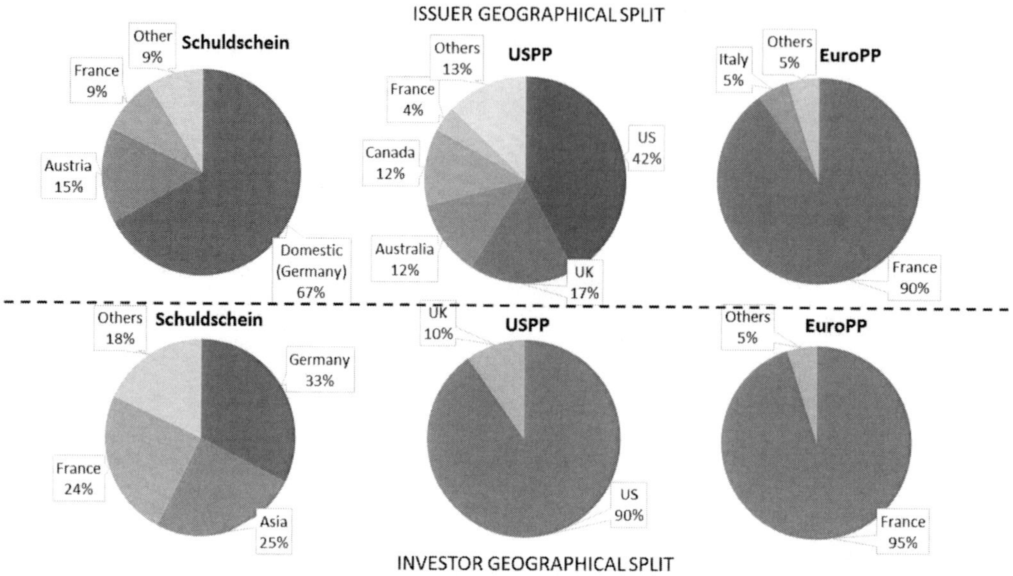

Source: HSBC.

Overall, however, these markets remain fairly local and concentrated around countries with a strong wholesale financial industry, as the composition of investor types may suggest (see Figure 3.76). The German market is primarily driven by banks, while the French and US markets are targets for investments from insurance and asset management companies (and pension funds).

Figure 3.76 Investor type and maturity split (end of 2014)

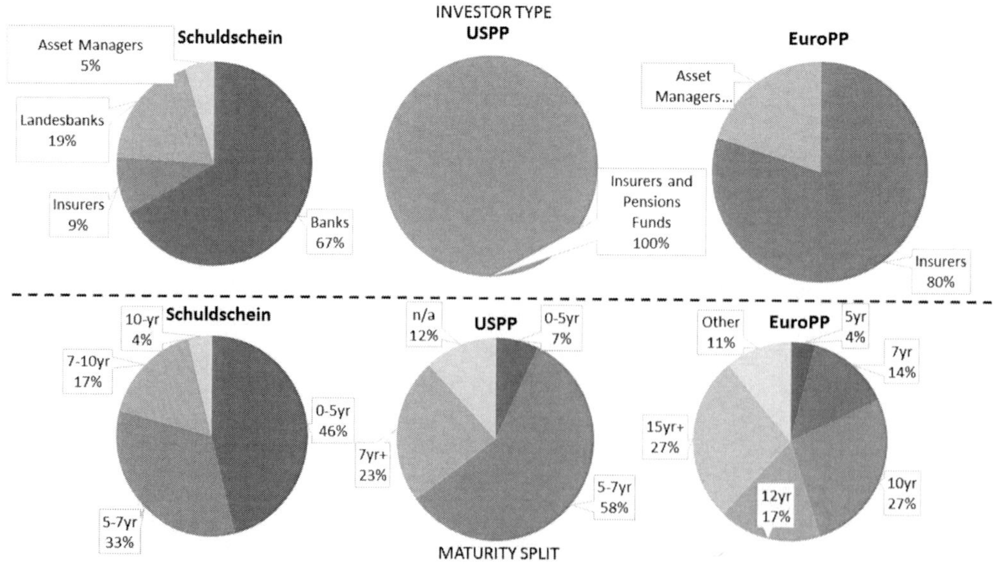

Source: HSBC.

The market mainly serves unrated companies, but it can also provide funding for those that have a rating and find it more expensive to go to public markets for smaller issuances. Greater standardisation of market practices and legal and contractual requirements may increase the size of the markets. Nonetheless, the structural lack of information flow between issuers and investors will keep this market a niche compared to public listing of debt or bank lending.

3.4.2.2 Secondary markets

Secondary trading

To build up a significant amount of debt, an active secondary trading activity is crucial. Bond trading can take place mainly in two ways: on an open limit order book with riskless intermediation, or in a bilateral setting, in which counterparties agree on a market price, usually via an intermediary or platform with non-binding quotes that can also take own risk via interposing itself with own capital between the two counterparties. Open electronic order books (EOBs) are typically pre-trade and post-trade transparent auction systems matching binding buying and selling quotes. They are publicly open to all qualifying investors. This system mainly differs from request-for-quote (RFQ) models, which are auction systems based on non-binding quotes and limited pre-trade transparency (post-trade transparency is typically available on these markets). The execution can be either electronic or by voice. Due to high wholesale activities among financial institutions, there is a big inter-dealer business, which can be estimated at around €9 trillion in annual volume.

Trading on exchanges

Stock exchanges provide aggregate statistics about both their open electronic order books and negotiated deals ('over-the-counter', OTC) for bonds that take place through their electronic platforms or voice systems. Other electronic platforms providing trading functionality similar to negotiated deals on exchange still do not provide any aggregate statistics about their markets for free, leaving only a partial picture of the market and the total market size can only be estimated (see Figure 3.82).

Open electronic order book activity is high in terms of trades but relatively low in terms of turnover (around €700 billion). This is typically a market that mainly gives access to retail and small professional investors in a pre-trade transparent auction system. Moreover, exchanges also run wholesale platforms with access only to specific counterparties, which typically agree on a price in a system that is often not based on an order book auction but on a request-for-quote (RFQ) or voice-based execution model.

Figure 3.77 EOB vs negotiated deals – number of trades and turnover (€mn)

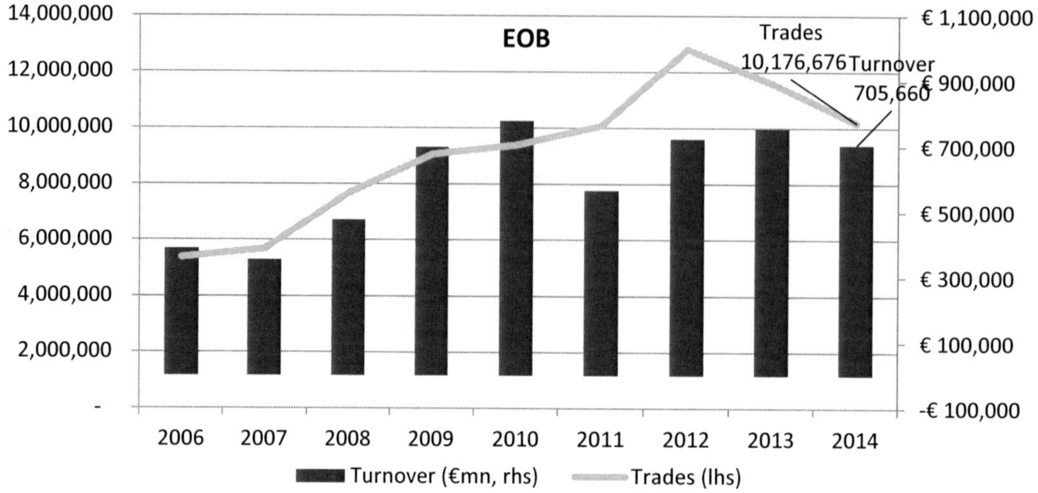

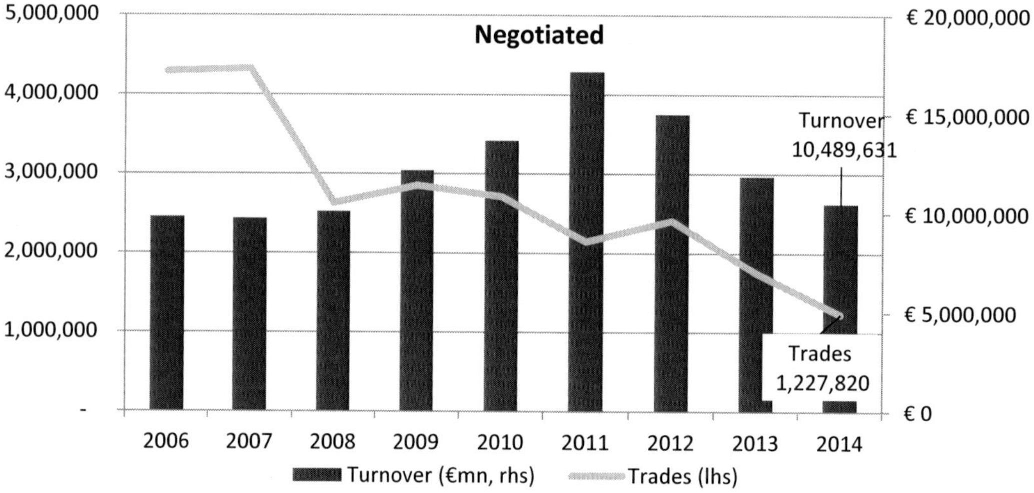

Data Sources: WFE, FESE, individual exchanges.

EOB vs negotiated deals

The market for negotiated deals (OTC) is much bigger in size, but much smaller in number of trades, which hints at a very high average size of transactions in bonds (see Figure 3.78). As a result, the average size of trades in an EOB environment is roughly €70,000, which is closer to retail size than a few years ago. Size quickly goes up to almost €8.5 million in a negotiated deal setting, which is much higher than previous years. This trend may suggest a segmentation of the two markets, with EOB becoming even more retail-driven, while wholesale participants operate much more frequently on alternative electronic platforms. The number of negotiated deals thus collapsed from more than four million in 2006 to less than two million in 2014.

Figure 3.78 Average size of bond trades (estimates)

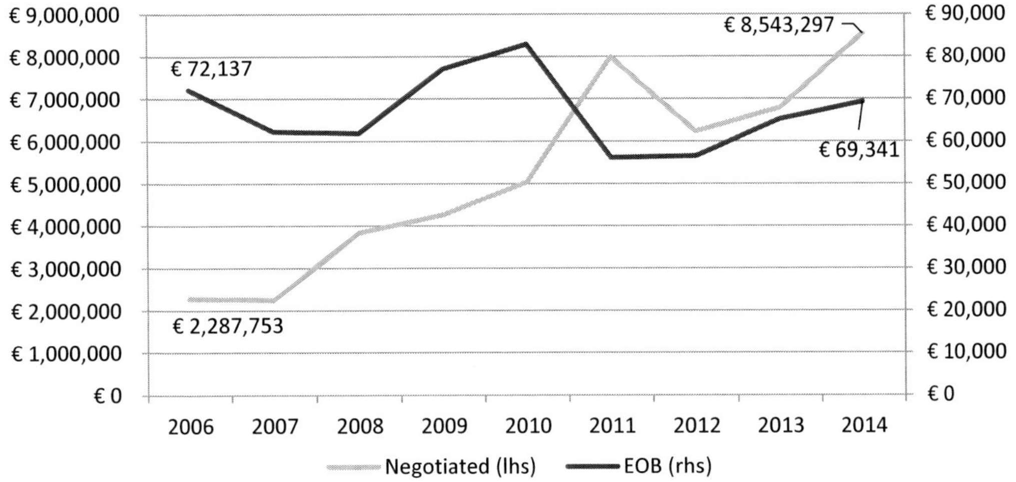

Source: Author's elaboration from WFE, FESE, individual exchanges.

Cross-border dimension

Nonetheless, EOB bond markets are still very fragmented along national lines and dominated by Italian trading venues, which are very active markets for both EOB and OTC. The cross-border component (bonds issued by non-resident firms) is currently very limited in terms of total size of activity, reflecting the poor level of integration of retail markets in Europe, but there is growing activity regarding international bonds on exchanges across Europe (see Figure 3.79).

Figure 3.79 On-exchange bond trades by type of issuance

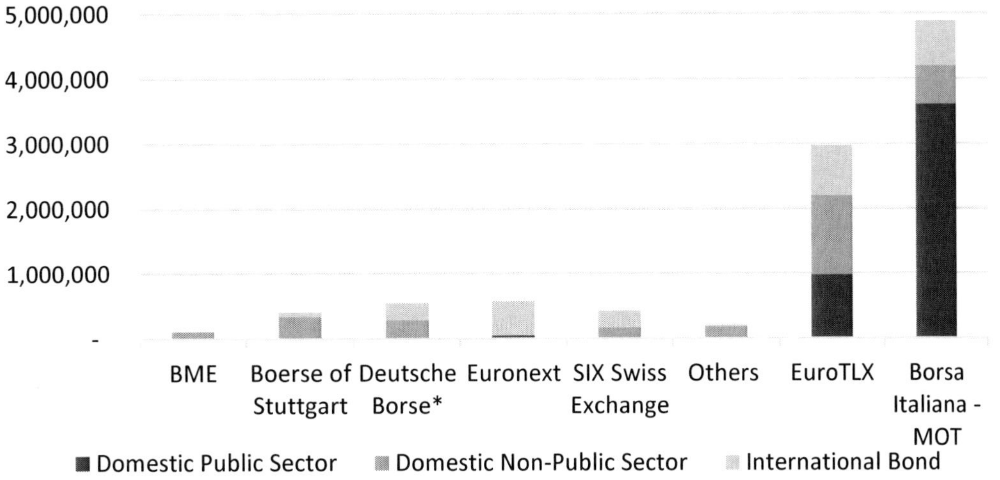

Note: 'Others' include Warsaw SE, Oslo Bors, Hi-MTF, Irish SE, Nasdaq OMX Nordics & Baltics, Athens Exchanges, Budapest SE, Cyprus SE, Ljubljana SE, Luxembourg SE, Malta SE, Wiener Boerse. *Xetra, Frankfurt and TradeGate Ex.

Data Sources: WFE, FESE, individual exchanges.

Also, turnover activity on exchanges has increased, from €400 billion in 2006 to €705 billion in 2014 (see Figure 3.80).

Figure 3.80 On-exchange bond turnover (€bn)

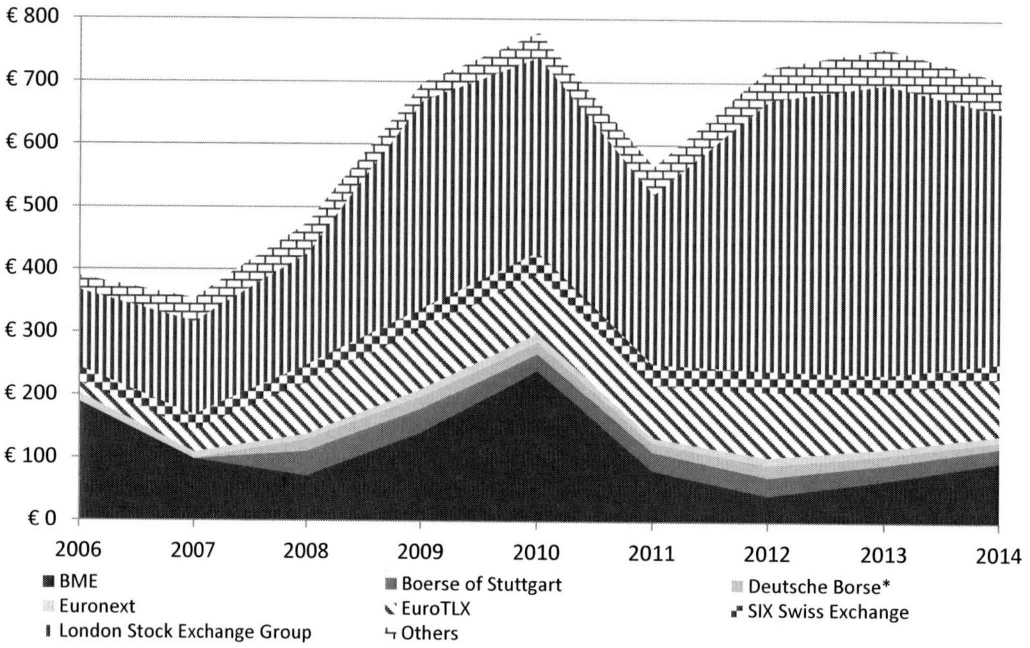

Note: No data for the Irish Stock Exchange. 'Others' include Warsaw SE, Oslo Bors, Hi-MTF, Nasdaq OMX Nordics & Baltics, Athens Exchanges, Budapest SE, Cyprus SE, Ljubljana SE, Luxembourg SE, Malta SE, Wiener Boerse. *Xetra, Frankfurt and TradeGate Ex.

Data Sources: WFE, FESE, Individual exchanges.

Nonetheless, as trading activity is still driven by RFQ and voice-based systems that provide OTC execution, trading is organised around a bunch of electronic platforms that mainly offer RFQ execution, plus a list of big dealer banks that execute on their own or on their clients' behalf big trades via these electronic platforms or voice-based systems. *Market organisation*

Figure 3.81 Main electronic bond trading platforms

Inter-Dealer		Dealer-to-Client	
Government	**Non-Government**	**Government**	**Non Government**
MTS *BrokerTec (ICAP)* *BGC* *Eurex Bonds* *Senaf (BME)* *Other exchanges* *HDAT*	*GFI* *Dealerweb Sweep (Tradeweb)* *BGC* *MTS*	*Tradeweb* *Bloomberg FIT* *BondVision - MTS* *MarketAxess* *Exchanges* *Single-dealer*	*Bloomberg* *Exchanges* *MarketAxess* *Tradeweb* *BondVision - MTS* *Single-dealer*

Source: Company websites.

Total market size

Total size of secondary bond trading activity is €21.3 trillion, i.e. more than double the value of equity trading (€9 trillion). Trade execution based on voice has gone down in recent years and now can be estimated at 35% of the market. Most of it is concentrated in the inter-dealer (IDB) government bond and the dealer-to-client (D2C) non-government bond markets (Celent, 2014). Electronic trading, which is the dominant mean of execution (65%), can be split into open electronic order books and RFQ models (as explained above). EOBs on exchanges comprise only 3.3% of bond trading (mostly the Italian market and a few other smaller venues), while execution takes place mainly on RFQ systems. This suggests that retail or small professional investors have limited direct access. Intermediaries, such as brokers or investment funds, are often the only channel to deal in these instruments for those investors.

Figure 3.82 Annual turnover by trading type (€bn; estimate for 2014)

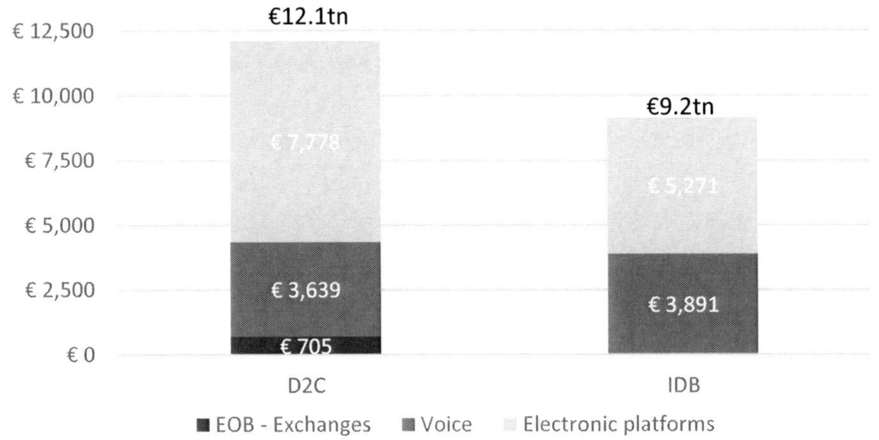

Note: Negotiated deals from exchanges have not been allocated to IDB or D2C business. Total voice activity on exchanges has been estimated at 33% of the total. 'EOB', Electronic Order Book.

Source: Author's elaboration from Celent (2014), WFE and FESE.

As a consequence, bond market trading is less frequent but in relative terms is greater than equity trading, if comparing activity ratios, i.e. volumes/turnover over market capitalisation (for equity) and outstanding amounts (for debt securities). Both equity and bond markets have similar levels of activity ratio (around one to one), despite the OTC nature of bond trading. The same ratio for equity markets is two (turnover) to one (market capitalisation) in the US.

3.4.3 *Derivatives markets and securitisation*

Intro

The markets for derivatives and securitised products are wholesale in nature. Their growth pre-crisis was significant and has contributed to increasing the development and sophistication of the financial system. They rely on easy access to funding and financial guarantees, and offer an excellent tool to redistribute risk in the system. There are three main segments: OTC derivatives, listed derivatives and securitised products. While derivatives have become an indispensable tool for risk management, securitised products have suffered from the recent crisis because of their distorted volume-based incentives, which creates information asymmetries and freezes the market. They are, nonetheless, an important tool for reallocating risk more efficiently and thus finding more funding sources. The European integration of these markets is thus fairly great because of its wholesale nature, so national differences play a limited role.

OTC derivatives

OTC derivatives markets are essentially global in nature. In effect, they rely on a small network of dealer banks and a sound legal framework, but contracts can actually be signed anywhere in the world because there is no financial instrument in custody. As a consequence, European integration already exists in these markets, as the legal framework is mostly based on the same contract terms set by the International Swaps and Derivatives Association (ISDA) master agreement.

The nominal value of these contracts continued to grow in recent years, including during the financial crisis, as they have been widely used for risk management purposes. Gross market value, however, spiked during the different crises as market conditions shifted away from the conditions in which these contracts are negotiated in normal times (see Figure 3.83).

Figure 3.83 Nominal, gross market value and gross credit exposure of OTC derivatives (€tn; 1998-2014)

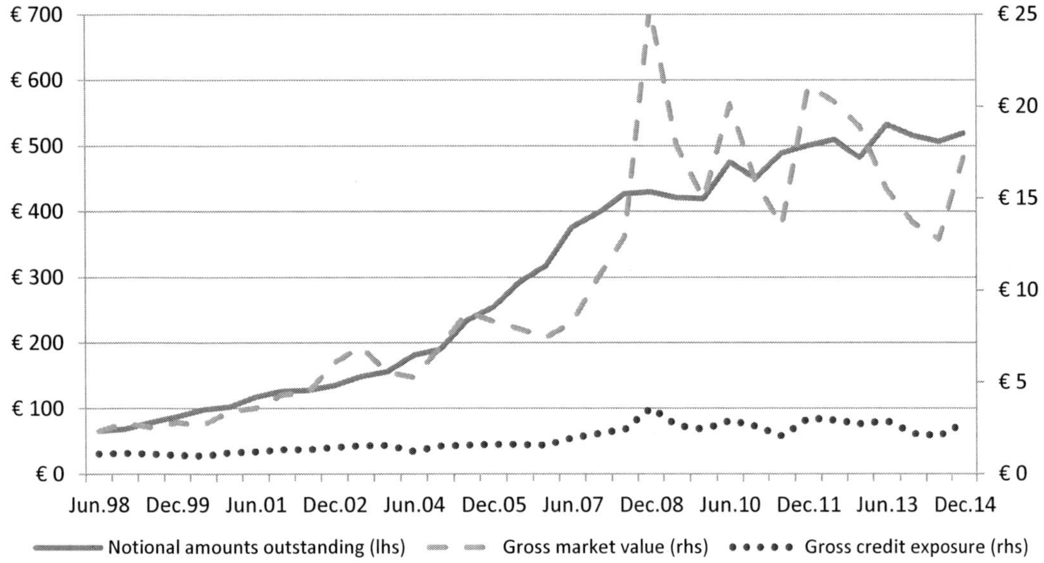

Data Source: BIS.

Figure 3.84 Estimation of uncollateralised exposure for OTC derivatives (€bn)

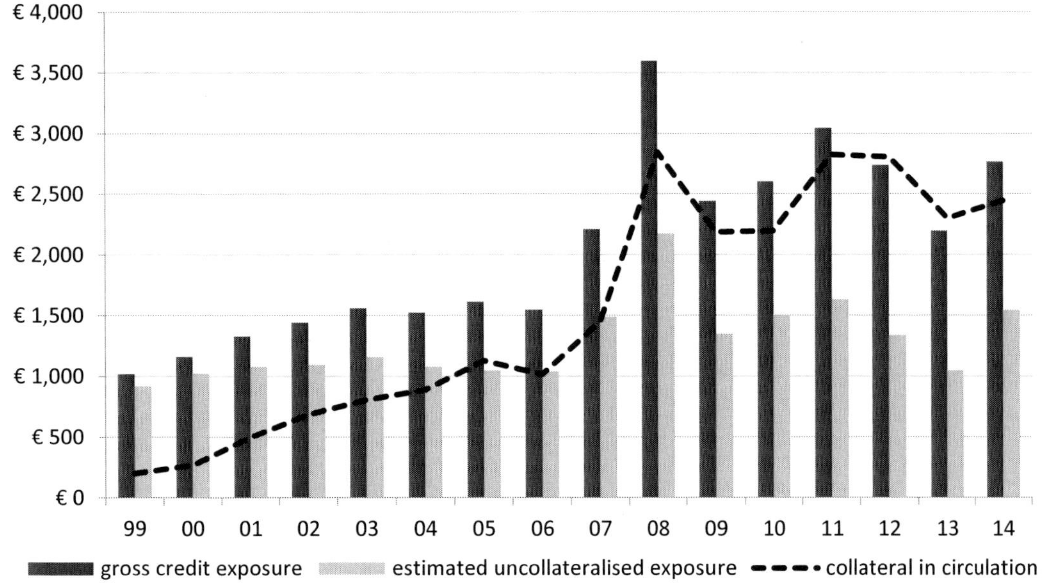

Note: To estimate the level of under-collateralisation, 50% of the collateral in circulation (as estimated in the ISDA Margin Survey) is subtracted from the gross credit exposure (as reported in the BIS semi-annual surveys).[50]

Source: Author's elaboration from 2015 ISDA Margin Survey and BIS.

Therefore, the volatility of the gross credit exposure also affects the quantity of collateral needed in the market, which is now structurally higher than it was pre-crisis. The regulatory reforms to strengthen safeguards and collateral arrangements particularly in less supervised areas, such as OTC derivatives, created a structural upward shift independently of market conditions. Nonetheless, compared to last year, the increase in volatility and worsening of market conditions have increased both gross credit exposure and the estimated uncollateralised exposure, which now stands at above €1.5 trillion (see Figure 3.84).

The market is dominated by derivative contracts on interest rates (75%) and, as currency volatility increases, contracts on currencies are also playing an important role (14%). The client base has also changed in recent years. Dealer banks are gradually reducing their activities in these markets, while asset management and insurance companies are the main counterparties (see Figure 3.85).

Figure 3.85 Distribution of OTC derivatives by counterparty (% of notional amounts outstanding)

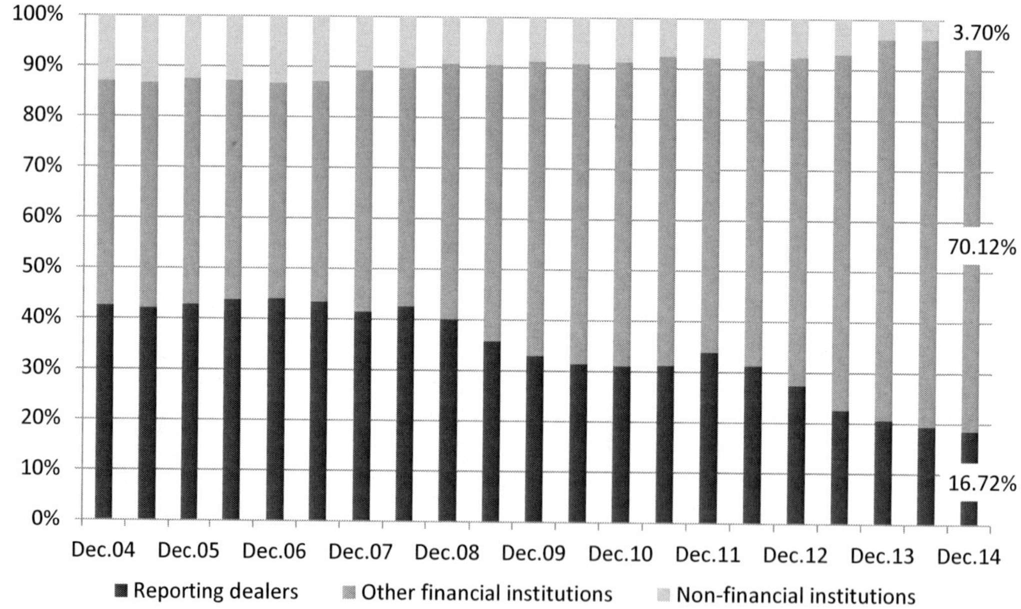

Data Source: BIS.

[50] Total reported collateral for centrally cleared derivatives transactions received and delivered for house and client cleared trades (amount received/delivered to meet Initial/variation margins) was €213 billion in 2013 and €375 billion in 2014. Central clearing of OTC derivatives remains most well-established for interest rate and credit derivatives, while limited progress has been made in other asset classes.

Regarding the trading execution of derivatives contracts, OTC derivatives cover almost the totality of the market (over 90%). Listed derivatives, however, are just less than 10%, but the absolute nominal value of outstanding contracts reached a new historical peak in 2014, estimated at €56.2 trillion (see Figure 3.86).

Figure 3.86 Notional value of outstanding OTC and listed derivatives contracts (€bn)

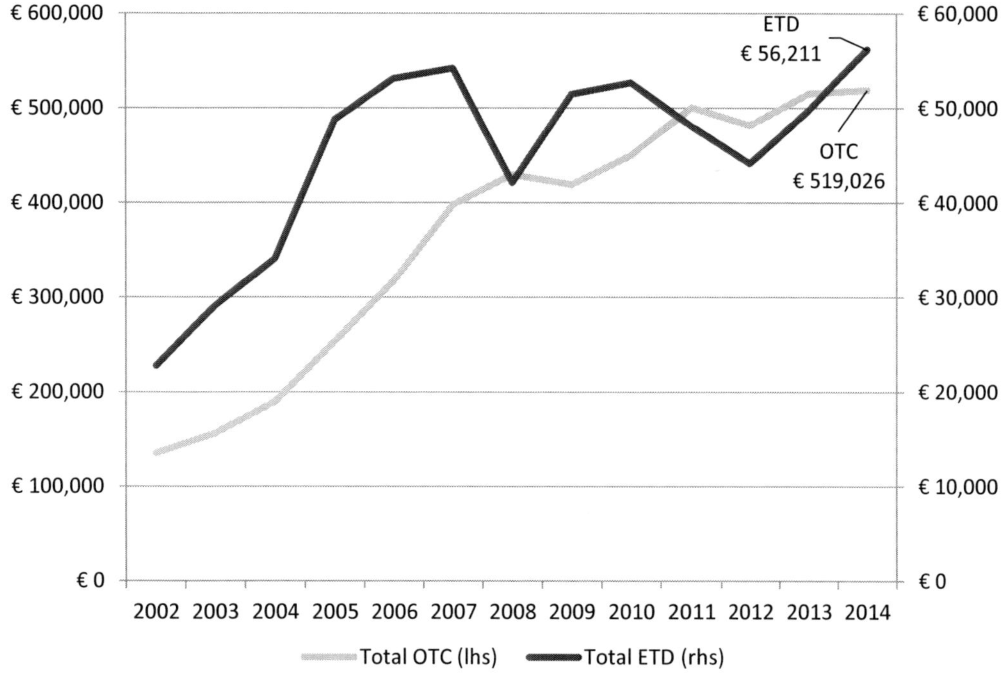

Note: The notional amount outstanding of commodities derivatives were estimated by discounting the total end-year notional turnover value of commodities options and futures (WFEX) by a 'compressing factor' equal to 0.0338977 (see Valiante, 2013, p. 32-33).

Source: Author's elaboration from BIS.

Listed derivatives

Compared to the US, listed derivative markets in Europe are almost three times smaller, with options and futures on stocks the main source of trading activity (see Figure 3.87). Interest rate, stock indexes, and commodities listed derivatives are also important markets in both regions.

Figure 3.87 Open interest of main listed derivatives markets by region (millions of contracts)

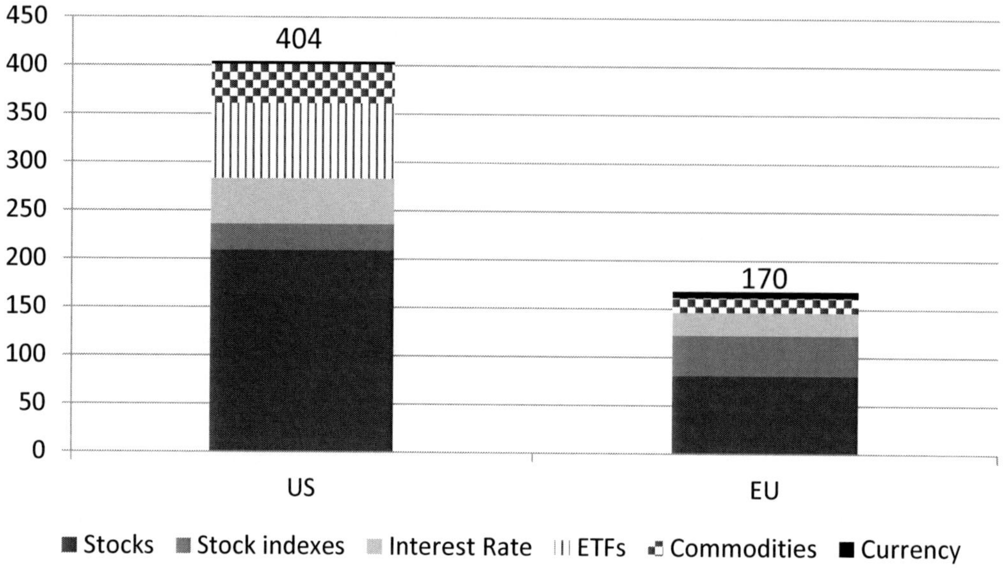

Note: No data on currency options and futures.

Source: Author's elaboration from WFE.

Nonetheless, the structure of the two markets is different. Listed derivatives markets in the US are much more concentrated, with one dominant trading venue in every market. The Chicago Mercantile Exchange is the main venue for interest rate, currency and commodities derivatives, while the Chicago Board Options Exchange is dominant in single stocks, stock indexes and ETFs derivatives. In Europe, there is a bit more competition among a handful of trading platforms in every market (see Figure 3.88). Network effects of liquidity for derivative contracts mainly drive concentration in these markets. Location, at least on a regional level, might thus be irrelevant, in particular if mainly professional investors access these markets. The European listed derivative markets are thus mostly regional, with limited global reach.

Figure 3.88 Open interest of main EU listed derivatives markets (millions of contracts; end 2014)

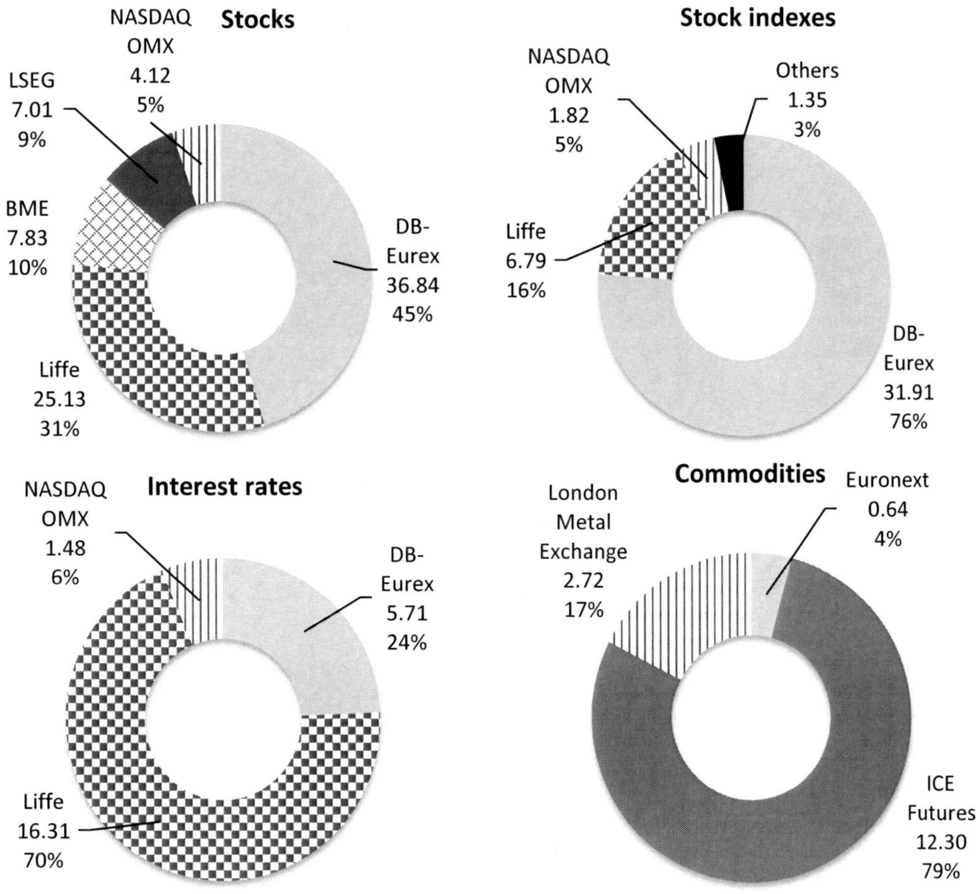

Note: No market split for currency options and futures.

Source: Author's elaboration from WFE.

ICE Futures has recently expanded its market share in the European market for interest rate, stocks and commodities derivatives with the acquisition of the London International Financial Futures and Options Exchange (LIFFE). As a result, the commodity derivatives exchange business is globally dominated by American and Asian exchanges, with CME Group by far the biggest exchange (see Figure 3.89).

Figure 3.89 Open interest of global commodities markets (millions of contracts; 2009-14)

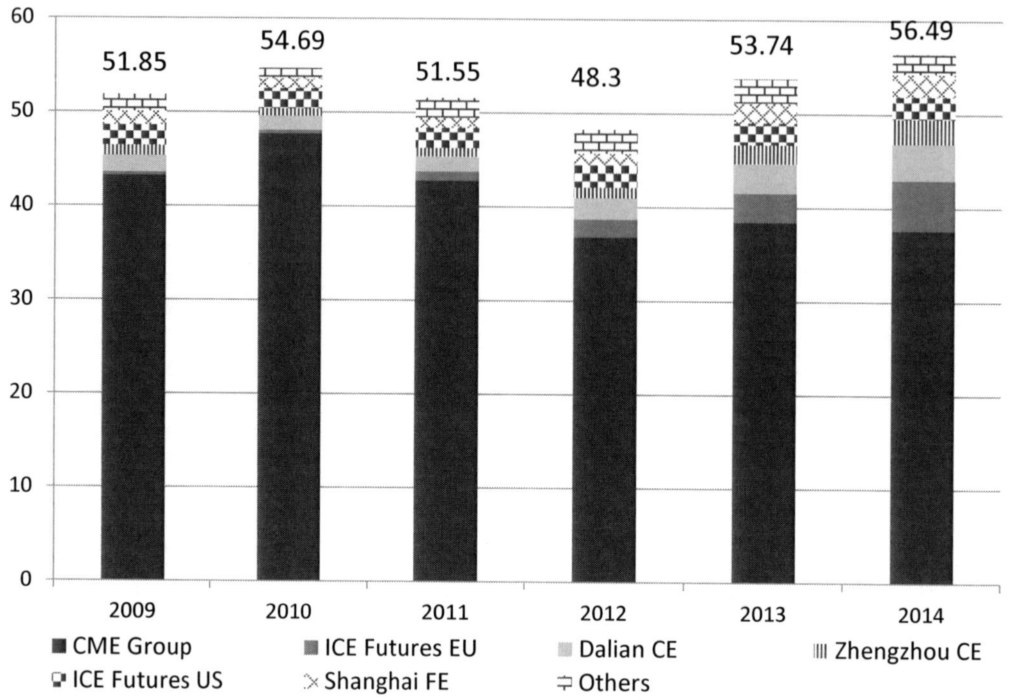

Source: Author's elaboration from WFE.

Finally, the market for securitised products was an important driver of funding for financial institutions before the financial crisis. However, the financial design of many of these products created strong information asymmetries between investors and ultimately the issuer of the underlying asset (volume-based incentives), which caused the market a major adverse selection problem. As a result, issuance froze in 2008 and never really recovered. The issuance (almost €1 trillion in the US and €215 billion in Europe) is mainly retained by financial institutions, which use it for collateral management or liquidity with central banks. The retained share went up to almost 95% in 2009, but it is now close to 65%, as the market is gradually recovering.

Securitisation

The issuance is mainly related to repackaging of residential mortgages and other loans/securities sitting on banks' balance sheets. Repackaging of SME loans is limited (€33 billion) compared to the past but higher in relative terms.

Figure 3.90 European securitisation issuance by collateral (€bn)

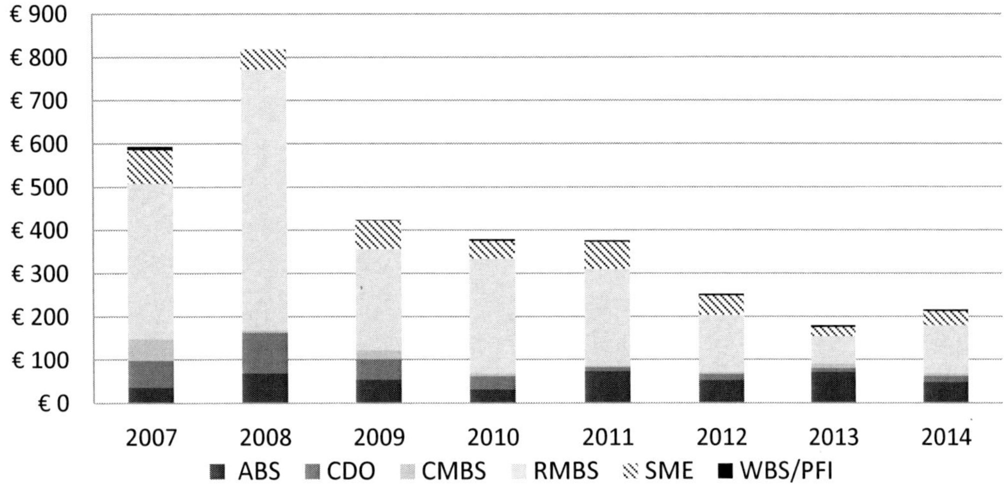

Data Source: AFME.

Moreover, the outstanding amount of securitised products decreased in Europe compared to the past (€2.3 trillion was the peak in 2009) and vis-à-vis the US (€7.8 trillion). It is now around €1.5 trillion. Issued instruments on a cross-border basis (pan-European and multinational) is only a fraction of the total outstanding (around 9%; see Figure 3.91).

Figure 3.91 Outstanding securitised products by country of issuance (€bn)

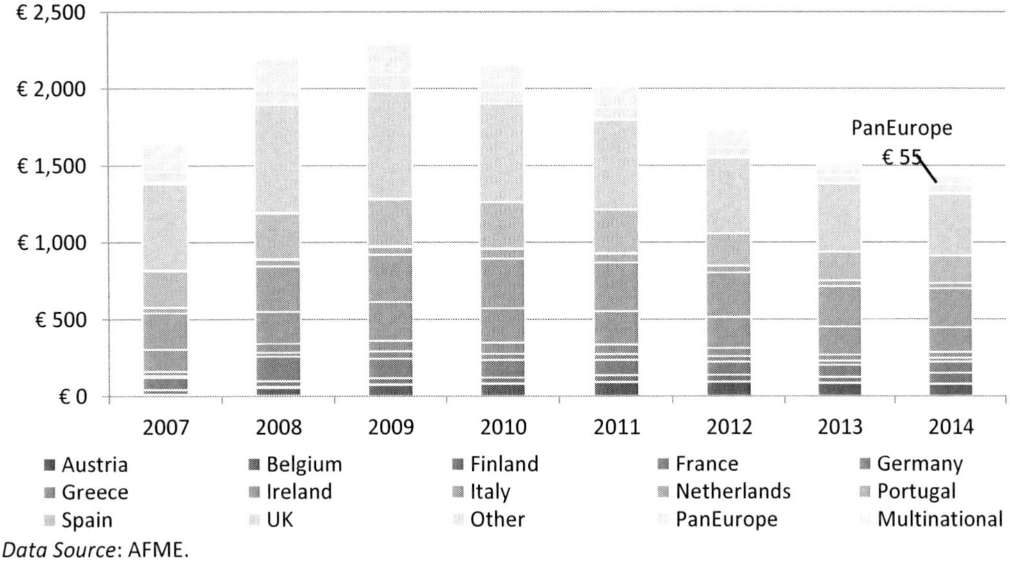

Data Source: AFME.

The biggest European markets are the UK, the Netherlands, Italy and Spain, and cross-country market share has been fairly stable over time.

3.4.4 *Exchange-traded products*

Exchange-traded products (ETPs) are mainly standardised fund structures that trade their units on a trading venue (exchange-traded funds, ETFs), in the same way as equities. Whether tracking an index or a specific underlying asset (such as commodities), the tracking takes place either via the purchase of a portfolio of assets that replicate returns or an underlying total return swap[51] that provides no tracking error but underlying counterparty exposure to the counterparty of the derivative contract. The history of these markets is very recent, as they developed in the early 2000s, mainly to benefit from aggregate movements in equity indexes. Assets under management have currently reached €377 billion, with a growing share of fixed income ETPs.

Figure 3.92 European ETPs AuM by asset class (€bn)

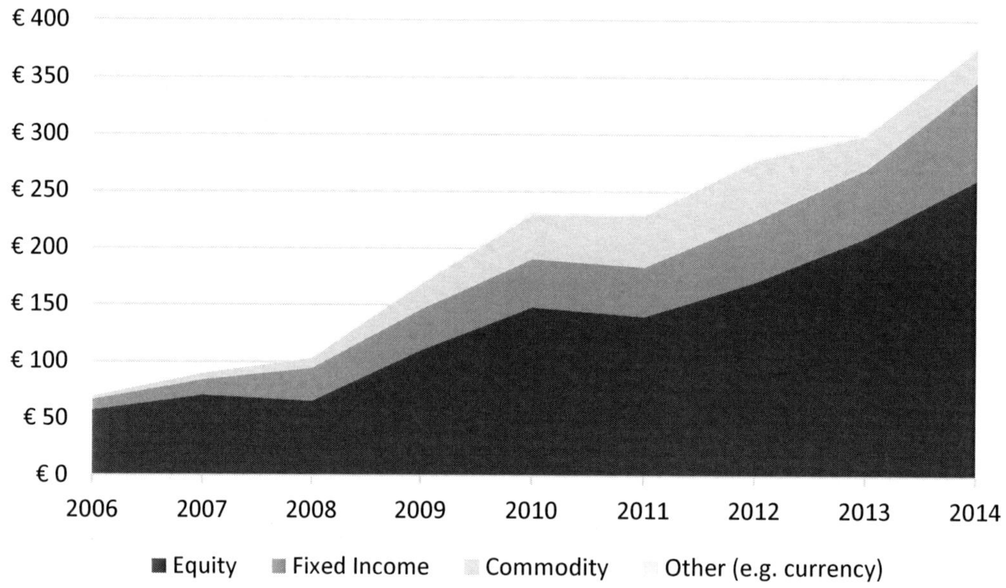

Source: Deutsche Bank.

The size of the market is still fairly small compared to that of the US, but similar in number of transactions (see Figure 3.93). In effect trading is spread across the different venues in Europe, replicating somehow the fragmentation of equity markets (see section 3.4.1).

[51] A collateralised special purpose vehicle often backs the issues of units to fund the return replication via a total return swap or holdings of futures contracts.

Figure 3.93 Total AuM & number of products by regions (€bn)

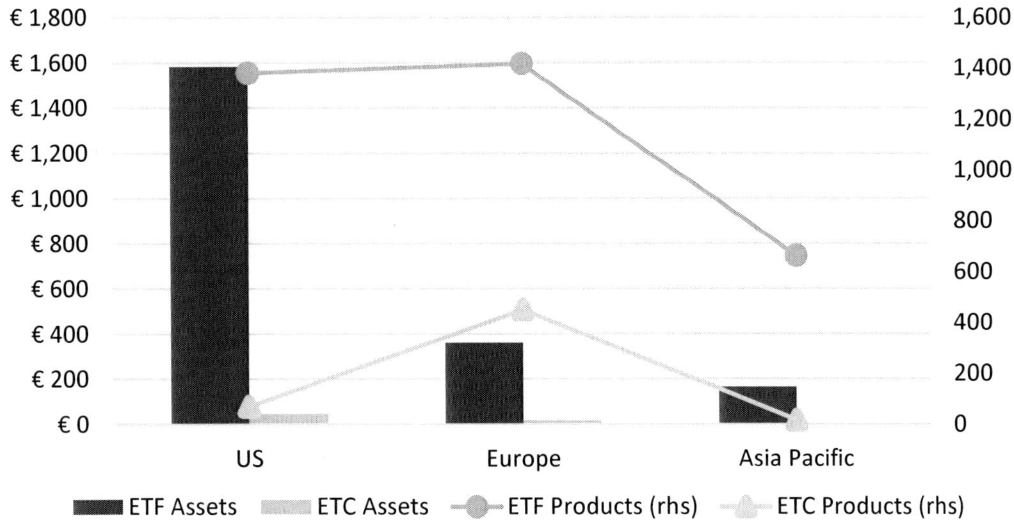

Source: Deutsche Bank.

The vast majority of the investments go into equity products (around 69%), while a 22% goes into fixed income (mainly bonds). In terms of regional investments, the share of investments going into non-EU equity (mostly US equities) has increasingly gone up in the last couple of years, to reach almost 50% of total turnover in these instruments (see Figure 3.94).

Figure 3.94 Turnover equity ETF by investment region (€bn)

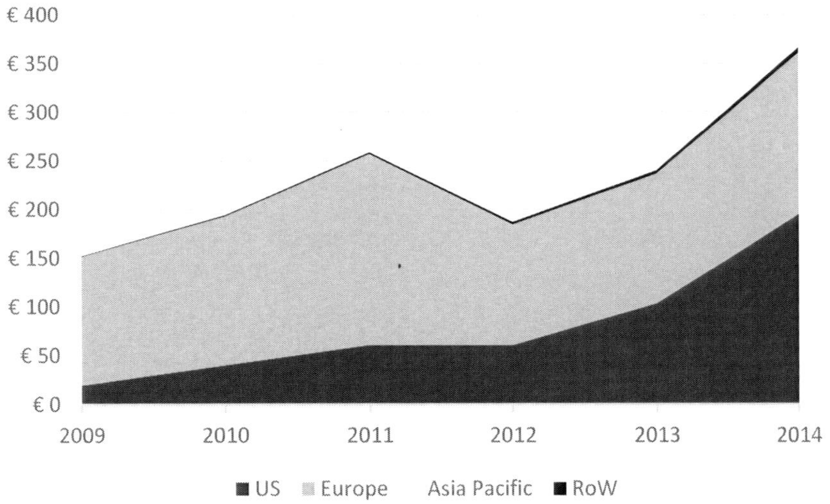

Source: Author's elaboration from Deutsche Bank.

As net inflows continue to grow in Europe (€46 billion in 2014, compared to roughly €13 billion in 2013), these markets could benefit from a less fragmented environment, as they could provide a standardised, liquid and 'easy-to-understand' product for investors and improve the liquidity support for public equity markets.

Key findings #8.

- There is some evidence that the monetary union led to a convergence in equity premia across euro area countries. However, while the euro increased equity markets' global integration, the evidence is mixed about the impact on regional integration and efficiency of equity markets. A static view of the market shows an increase in cross-border equity holdings, reaching a new peak in 2012, but there is no evidence that the euro was the cause of this market development.
- Primary and secondary markets trading, however, provide more mixed evidence. IPO activity in Europe is not far from that of the largest market (US), but 73% of newly raised money went to fund already listed companies in 2014. Secondary markets have experienced increased competition among trading venues with the abolition of the national concentration rules, resulting in a structural drop in bid-ask spreads. However, competition is limited to the most liquid listed shares and the quality of the trading flow is still very low. The process of cross-border integration among trading venues thus slowed down and markets still remain fragmented among member states rather than among specialised segments, e.g. SMEs or high-tech listings.
- Debt securities markets have showed greater integration over the years, driven by wholesale dealer banks integration after the monetary union and EU financial reforms, e.g. FSAP. This is particularly true for bonds issued by governments and financial institutions. However, the impact of the financial crisis on wholesale banks produced a reversal in capital flows that is somehow reverting that process, which nonetheless should be temporary until a common backstop to the banking system is in place.
- Debt markets are also subject to more global trends. Bond and stock markets have become increasingly segmented, as a flight-to-quality phenomenon in international financial markets led to investing more in bonds, increasing the negative correlation with stock markets. This process was even more significant in euro area countries, with the removal of currency risk and freer circulation of capital.
- For government and financial institutions, the market for primary issuance is still fairly fragmented, as country risk (adjustment) leads to deleveraging in the financial and public sector.

- For corporations, primary issuance of debt securities is developed only in a few countries, such as Portugal, France and Germany. Most notably, issuance of debt securities can also take place in a closed environment (so-called private placement), which today amounts to roughly €16 billion compared to €822 billion of corporate debt gross issuance in Europe.
- Private placement markets in Europe are fairly local with limited international participation of issuers and investors. The market structure lacks information flow between issuers (mostly unrated companies) and investors may naturally keep this market to a niche compared to public listings or bank lending.
- The high level of outstanding debt securities in Europe creates the conditions for active secondary markets in the region. Trading activities today take place mainly over-the-counter via electronic platforms (RFQ**Error! Bookmark not defined.**) or voice-matching systems. The average size of debt transactions is €70,000 for order books and €8.5 million for negotiated deals matched by exchanges over-the-counter.
- Participation is mainly offered to institutional investors or banks, which interpose themselves directly or on behalf of a client. Retail investors' participation only occurs on limit order books available in a few markets, such as Italy's. They only represent 3.3% of all secondary bond trading. Matching systems based on voice are mainly used for government bonds trading and represent almost one-third of the total. Electronic platforms are mostly based on a request-for-quote model.
- Overall, by considering outstanding value of shares (market capitalisation) and outstanding value of debt securities over the related trading turnover, bond and equity markets in Europe show similar levels of activity (one to one), despite their OTC nature. Once again, this points to the poor functioning and competitiveness of Europe's equity markets compared to the US, where this ratio is almost two (turnover) to one (market capitalisation) based on a five-year average.
- OTC derivative markets and securitised products are wholesale and international in nature, thus European market integration is less of a concern. Wholesale banks or institutional investors can typically access these markets from anywhere.
- Listed derivatives markets are also accessed by small professional or even retail investors through local brokers. Market concentration is much lower than in the US, where there is mainly one dominant platform in every segment of the market.
- Finally, exchange-traded products trade similarly to equity instruments and often replicate a stock index return. As a consequence, their trading is spread across many venues, with the same fragmented organisation of equity markets and their limited cross-border integration.

4. A single market for capital in Europe: Designing an action plan

Previous sections have provided ample evidence of the need for a more balanced financial integration across Europe and the role of cross-sectional risk sharing offered by financial markets. A single European market for capital has been a long awaited outcome of European policies, to ensure greater financial stability and sufficient funding for EU firms competing in a global economy. Financial integration stimulates further financial development, which can ultimately advance economic development and thus fuel growth and create jobs.

This chapter aims at providing a methodology for the identification and removal of cross-border barriers to capital market integration, as well as a selected list of legal and economic barriers that are standing in the way. The first two sections set the scope of the action and the meaning of Capital Markets Union (CMU), as proposed by Jean-Claude Juncker in 2014. The third and fourth sections offer a methodology to identify barriers and prioritise policy intervention, using a financial contracting approach. Sections 5 to 7 provide a concrete list of barriers in three key areas of capital markets: price discovery, execution and enforcement. Finally, section 8 offers some summary conclusions.

4.1 Defining Capital Markets Union (CMU)

Redefining CMU?

Since it was first announced, the term Capital Markets Union (CMU) has been interpreted several ways, which have finally left the meaning of the word 'Union' largely undefined and mostly secondary to a list of proposals to revive investment in the European Union. The European action plan released by the European Commission (EU COM 2015b; see also Chapter 1) extends the scope of CMU beyond the borders of the single market to include investment policies in the area of long-term finance, such as the recalibration of capital charges in Solvency II and in the Capital Requirements Directive (CRD) IV for infrastructure investment, as well as adjustments to the prospectus requirements to facilitate access of SMEs to financial markets. Notwithstanding their commendable objectives, investment policies apply whether or not a single European market for financial products exists and do not necessarily promote integration but may rather dilute it. For instance, by relaxing capital requirements for a specific sector, the investment policy might perhaps strengthen that sector, which may be strong in a specific country because of national policies subsidising its growth and the entrenchment within domestic boundaries. As a consequence, this sector may be unable to promote cross-border integration and, at the same time, be an obstacle for cross-border providers to enter the domestic market. The final result might be a further widening of divergences among member states and an impediment to the development of a pan-European industry that may not then emerge as a result of cross-border competition. This chapter reorganises the discussion on CMU, emphasising the single market and integration policies to foster financial development and so further economic development and growth. The ultimate objective is in the end similar to investment policies, but the tools to achieve it are different.

EU financial integration 2.0

Evidence discussed in Chapter 2 and 3 shows how the insufficient quality of financial integration in Europe was a major contributor to financial instability in the region during the crisis, but it can also be a great opportunity to be catalyst of more financial diversification to fund growth and jobs.

Since the introduction of the single currency, the financial integration process has been dominated by senior interbank loans (until 2010-11), which entered some domestic banking systems too quickly and inflated asset bubbles. A more balanced financial integration process, with more market-based funding (in particular, equity) that provides cross-sectional risk sharing can improve the stability of the financial system and ultimately minimise risks of capital flights (and local bank runs) with a prolonged credit crunch (see section 2.1). Within the region, moreover, the problem was particularly aggravated in the eurozone because the fiscal capacity of the local government was unable to offer a credible backstop to avoid capital flights, whose negative effects then spilled over to non-eurozone countries in terms of a large drop in financial transactions. As a result, the lack of diversification in the financial system increased risk concentration in member states even further, led by financial institutions retrenching within their national borders, irrespective of whether the individual country was within or outside the monetary union.[52] Hence, in the aftermath of the financial and sovereign crises, the design of the financial integration process has emerged as a crucial challenge for the future of the European Union (Juncker, 2014; European Commission, 2015c, p. 12).

"Over time, I believe we should complement the new European rules for banks with a Capital Markets Union. To improve financing of our economy, we should further develop and integrate capital markets" (Juncker, 2014).

---

[52] While it is true that risk sharing in the euro area is lower compared to the rest of the European Union, the evidence discussed in Chapter 2 shows how the financial diversification is very low within and outside the monetary union.

Limited cross-sectional risk sharing in Europe is a potential source of financial instability and a primary cause of the growing funding gap for companies at an early stage of development, when they need prompt liquidity injections that are rarely offered by traditional banking tools, and for mid-sized companies that are looking for market (equity or debt) funding opportunities to expand their business activity. In effect, section 2.3 shows how markets can offer a better funding mechanism (price signalling) for advancing technological developments that are not easy to assess, as there is no stable cash flow or assets to pledge. If new technologies were predictable and provided a stable cash flow, or if entrepreneurs had personal assets to pledge, banks would be best placed to provide the needed funding stability.

Most notably, market funding provides greater risk dispersion and absorption in case of permanent shocks, e.g. a structural drop in asset prices. The absorption capacity then increases if integration favours greater cross-border holdings of equities. Market-based funding, moreover, provides a transparent and standardised pricing process and is conducive to financial innovation that satisfies the needs of a multitude of agents (investors and issuers; see Table 4.1). Nonetheless, market-based price mechanisms should be balanced with more private information-based ones (such as bank-based finance), as markets provide a form of funding that is pro-cyclical and can produce market impact because of the multitude of agents that will behave strategically when operating in a market with high monitoring costs (dispersion). The balance in Europe nowadays is still in favour of private information-based funding mechanisms, with banks playing a dominant role (see section 3.1).

Table 4.1 Market-based funding mechanisms (cross-sectional risk sharing)

Advantages	Disadvantages
Risk dispersion	Pro-cyclical
Open, transparent & standardised	Market impact
Funding tools diversification	

Source: Author.

The single market dimension

However, more market-based funding can hardly come from a fragmented European environment with small and disconnected liquidity pools. The "U" of "Union" in the acronym "CMU" thus plays a fundamental role in ensuring a more sustainable integration process that can develop efficient and stable capital markets in Europe. Most notably, the integration process can increase the capacity to sustain new investments by building viable links between liquidity pools, which are currently locked in national markets mainly in the form of households' deposits (as suggested by Chapter 0). The plan to enhance market-based funding sources and to increase financial diversification would fix the pipeline through which capital flows move across Europe so as to unlock new funding opportunities for companies with limited risk of leakage (capital flights). A more integrated market infrastructure and disclosure rules to make data about firms more comparable are only some of the measures that are needed to fix the pipeline and avoid imbalances of capital flows. The removal of legal and economic barriers to integration can stimulate the single market for capital flows, thus increasing competition among service providers and reducing the wedge between cost of capital for issuers and returns for investors, which would increase funding availability and stimulate a more efficient financial industry, with greater investments in innovation and ultimately more financial development. Furthermore, the expansion of capital markets may not necessarily come at the expense of the traditional bank-lending channel, but it can rather lead banking systems to integrate further cross-border. In effect, cross-border banking in Europe is still very limited and scarcely developed.

Furthermore, the creation of an integrated market can actually increase the size of the available liquidity by making Europe more competitive in the global financial system. This possibility would reduce the need to reduce excessively the size of the banking system to develop capital markets, with perhaps lower temporary negative effects on funding availability for the EU economy.

A measurable objective

Without a single market dimension, it is also hard to measure the achievement of the key objectives, as European institutions have been created with exclusive competences on single market matters. Measurability of objectives is indeed an important component for the accountability and success of a financial integration plan. With no accountability, the political support for all the necessary measures that a project like CMU would need over time will easily fade away. Therefore, in the attempt to develop capital markets in Europe, it is the term "union" that will ultimately provide the capacity (scale) and measurability of its success for institutions, like the European Commission, that have been created and exist to develop the single market. Chapter 3 has provided sufficient evidence of a widespread lack of integration across the various financial markets in Europe: from closed distribution channels for financial instruments to fragmented equity markets that are unable to provide liquidity for companies with high growth potential.

CMU is not banking union

Finally, the CMU's cross-sectional private risk sharing is strongly complementary to banking union's (BU) intertemporal private risk sharing. However, CMU somehow differs on many important grounds. The CMU applies to the whole European Union and not to a subset of countries, like the

BU. Second, it does not necessarily require the creation of a new institutional architecture (top-down approach) and a public risk sharing mechanism (such as the common fiscal backstop for bank deposits), but it rather relies on a set of actions to strengthen the institutional framework around current institutions and to address the shortfalls of the regulatory and supervisory system emerging in the actual cross-border trading (bottom-up approach). Third, despite its importance to advance the design of EU integration policies, the CMU does not have to face an ongoing crisis, so it can be carefully designed to deal with major differences among legal systems through a phased-in approach over the next four or five years at least.

Key findings #9.

- The lack of cross-sectional risk sharing in Europe is a potential source of financial instability (retrenchment of capital flows) and an important contributor to the growing funding gap for companies at an early stage of development, in need of prompt liquidity injections, and for mid-sized fast-growing companies that are looking for cheap and stable (equity or debt) funding opportunities to expand their business activity.
- Improving the quality of the financial integration process should be at the core of the Capital Markets Union project.
- Measurability plays an important role in the success of a financial integration plan, as it provides accountability. With no accountability, the political support for all the necessary measures that a project like this would need over time would easily fade away.
- CMU also differs from the Banking Union project because it applies to the whole European Union and relies on a set of policy actions to strengthen the current regulatory framework and leverage the current institutional architecture for cross-border trading (bottom-up approach). Banking Union instead lies on a completely new institutional architecture (top-down approach) and needs mechanisms of public risk sharing.

4.2 A diversified financial ecosystem

Financial system organisation

The organisation of the financial system is a complex interaction of legal norms and economic incentives that shape behaviours of institutions and investors (see Chapter 2). Both relationship- and market-based finance are subject to instability and growing evidence shows that the financial system is an ecosystem in which both market and relationship-based mechanisms are required to avoid concentration of capital flows that may result in asset bubbles and permanent loss of productivity. Financial integration has thus the objective of fostering development without making the system more unbalanced towards one intermediation channel. This is particularly true since the recent evidence on economic growth and financial development points to the risk of seeing credit abnormally prevailing over equity markets when the financial system grows and becomes more interconnected. At the core of this dispute there is the problem of excessive debt and risk concentration, mostly via bank credit. Financial markets are a form of intermediation that can help to rebalance the system towards more dispersed risk sharing.

Two fundamental trade-offs

Ultimately, the nature of financial contracting revolves around the ability to manage risk and therefore the structure of the financial system is built on two important trade-offs:

i. Risk dispersion versus risk concentration (space trade-off).
ii. Risk customisation versus risk standardisation (time trade-off).

The ability to spread risk in space (contracting) and time (renegotiation) fits different types of economic activities. Risk dispersion defines the boundaries of financial contracting. Capital-intensive activities certainly require more stable funding and therefore rely on risk concentration to ensure that both parties have enough resources and commitment to bring their financial relationship forward over time, as is necessary to earn the returns that a capital-intensive activity generates in the long term. Relationship or highly collateralised lending would provide a sufficiently stable source of funding over time, while access to private placement for long-term debt issuance could be a support to the long-term growth of the firm. As suggested by the literature reviewed in Chapter 2, high-tech companies usually invest in projects with limited fixed capital but more intensive human capital. Due to limited use of physical capital and the required speed of technological developments, these high-risk/high-return projects make these companies look more for cheap liquidity rather than a costly funding relationship. If the project succeeds, the high return will provide enough to go on with limited use of external resources and will usually offer an excellent exit option via financial markets to the original entrepreneurs. Equity crowdfunding or open markets would be the most suitable funding options for these types of investments, with private equity being a suitable alternative if the entrepreneur needs more guidance during the implementation of the project.

The second trade-off shaping the organisation of the financial system is the ability to offer funding customised around the risk profile of the entity or individual. The level of risk standardisation defines the ability to renegotiate and thus deal with risk over time. A customised funding mean is more difficult to liquidate before maturity. Risk standardisation instead does not offer customisation, but it allows an easier liquidation (exit option) before maturity. This may just reduce the funding cost in the short term. A large wheat farm is exposed to a predictable seasonality pattern in deliverable supply, which is similar to other producers. Wheat is effectively produced simultaneously by thousands of farmers within a given geographical area. Access to standardised futures contracts that settle at a specific date for these producers would be cheaper than a customised derivative product. Hence, the producer would exploit the standardised nature of its risk profile. An airline company, on the other hand, faces multiple (unpredictable) risks that can affect the cost of fuel or other important cost factors and therefore put a strain on the company's cash flow. A customised derivative contract provided by a financial institution (and involving even flat fees) is required by the quasi-unique risk profile of the company, which may be difficult to match with a standardised futures contract.

Of course, the economy is much more complex and diversified than these two extreme examples, but the financial system can reasonably offer a balance between these two trade-offs. On the one hand, if combined with risk dispersion, risk standardisation is able to withstand a structural (permanent) shock (aggregate risk). On the other hand, if combined with risk concentration, risk customisation is able to withstand an idiosyncratic (temporary) shock (individual risk).

As Figure 4.1 suggests, funding in the financial system lies on four cornerstones: secured and unsecured lending, crowd finance and open markets. On the one hand, secured and unsecured lending provide more funding stability (via risk concentration), while open markets and crowdfunding offer lower cost of capital (via risk dispersion). On the other hand, unsecured lending and crowd finance funding are designed around the needs of the company or entity (customisation), while secured lending (such as a repo operation for a firm or a standard home mortgage for a household) and open markets offer more standardisation and easier liquidation on secondary markets (exit option). It is worth noting that market mechanisms do not necessarily provide the cheapest funding option, but they provide a superior option for investors seeking an early exit, which may turn a penalising market evaluation into the best available funding option at a given point in time.

Figure 4.1 Financial system organisation

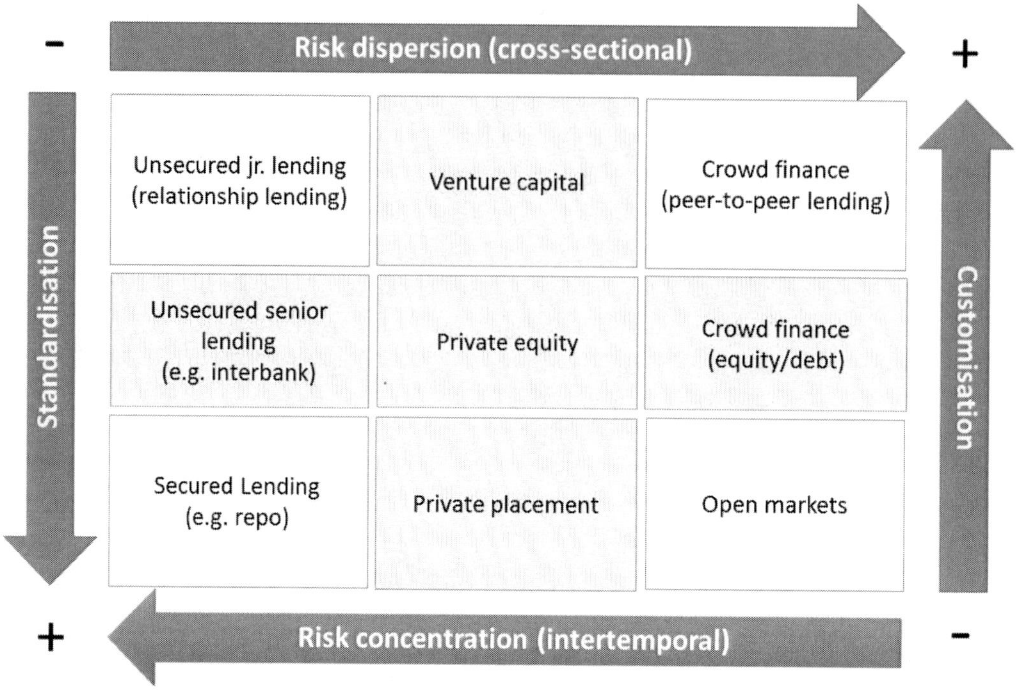

Source: Author.

There are also some forms of hybrid funding, which are less extreme in risk concentration/dispersion and risk customisation/standardisation. These forms of funding include: unsecured senior lending (such as short-term interbank loans), private placement (such as high-yield debt placement to selected investors), crowd finance (in the form of more standard equity stakes or notes to the broader public), and private equity or venture capital. Private equity would be closer to funding in a dispersed environment, but it is typically less customised (based on a sound business plan) than a venture capital investment (often based on an idea to be developed).

This theoretical paradigm describing the organisation of the financial system is ideal. Market frictions, such as the inability to write contracts covering all future contingencies or barriers to the enforcement of a financial claim, are an important source of instability that keeps markets away from the ideal balance. Nonetheless, policy interventions shall attempt to create a financial ecosystem to balance contracting and renegotiation in a way that risk is spread widely across space and time. Chapters 2 and 3 showed how risk in the European financial system is not spread widely in space and only domestically in time.

4.3 Financial contracting in market-based systems

Financial contracting

There is an inner tension in the financial system when it comes to spreading risk in space (contracting) and time (renegotiation). To identify future areas of action, it is necessary to understand the key elements of a financial transaction and then introduce them in a cross-border setting. As discussed in section 4.3, financial contracting faces two major sources of information asymmetry: specification and monitoring costs. The sources of these costs are either contract incompleteness, i.e. counterparties' inability to foresee all (potentially infinite) future scenarios related to a financial contract,[53] or moral hazard, i.e. the strategic behaviour of the counterparty that owns an informational advantage and is used to a free ride at the expense of the less informed one. As a result, there are two important phases in a financial contract that minimise the impact of contract incompleteness and moral hazard: contracting and renegotiation. Contracting is the process leading the investor to enter a financial transaction after using all the information available to price the product and the credit risk of the counterparty (pre-investment). Renegotiation is the process of redefining the terms of a financial contract (via contract) or exiting a financial transaction (via a sale in the secondary market) before the end of the contract (post-investment). When market conditions change, renegotiation might be the most efficient decision due to the incomplete nature of the financial contract, which may lead to a suboptimal outcome. Financial contracting in market-based systems requires a smooth contracting and renegotiation phase.

Market-based financial contracting

Due to the 'dispersed' nature of market-based systems, counterparties are unable to fill the informational gap via private information, and so they need to rely on public information collected and disclosed by third parties. As a result, financial contracting in market-based systems works in a fundamentally different way than financial contracting in relationship-based systems (such as traditional banking). The distribution channel of information is thus different from institution-based systems, e.g. relationship lending. While relationship-based (or institution-based) mechanisms rely on private information and bilateral contracts, market-based mechanisms (due to a multitude of agents) require a different informational infrastructure with public information (mainly reflected into prices), which allows ex ante pricing (contracting) and ex post renegotiation (exit from secondary markets or private enforcement mechanisms) with the signalling of all relevant information to price risk and to equalise information between counterparties.

---

53 This inability is also enhanced by the 'credence' nature of financial services and products (see footnote 31).

Moreover, this system would also rely on the role of third parties, both in the contracting phase, to signal risk and to reduce specification costs, e.g. a credit rating agency, and in the renegotiation phase, to minimise specification and monitoring costs driven by moral hazard and contract incompleteness, e.g. insolvency proceedings. Since a market-based system relies on a flow of public information, third (more independent) parties ensure the quality of the information flow with their reputational capital.

Investor protection

Most notably, while both counterparties of a financial transaction incur costs generated by information asymmetry, smaller counterparties (for instance, 'retail investors' or 'minority shareholders') are usually less informed, when dealing for instance with financial institutions, and more exposed to the strategic behaviour of the counterparty, who will try to extract as much as possible from this asymmetry (moral hazard). As a result, there is usually additional attention paid by policy-makers to investor protection, which is the backbone of the legal architecture (including supervision) that supports capital markets. A well-functioning open market needs participation as wide as possible, thus retail investors (either as a creditor or a shareholder) are crucial for the diversification of the trading flow and to balance informed and uninformed traders, thereby creating additional liquidity (see section 2.2).

Figure 4.2 Stylised view of financial contracting in market-based mechanisms

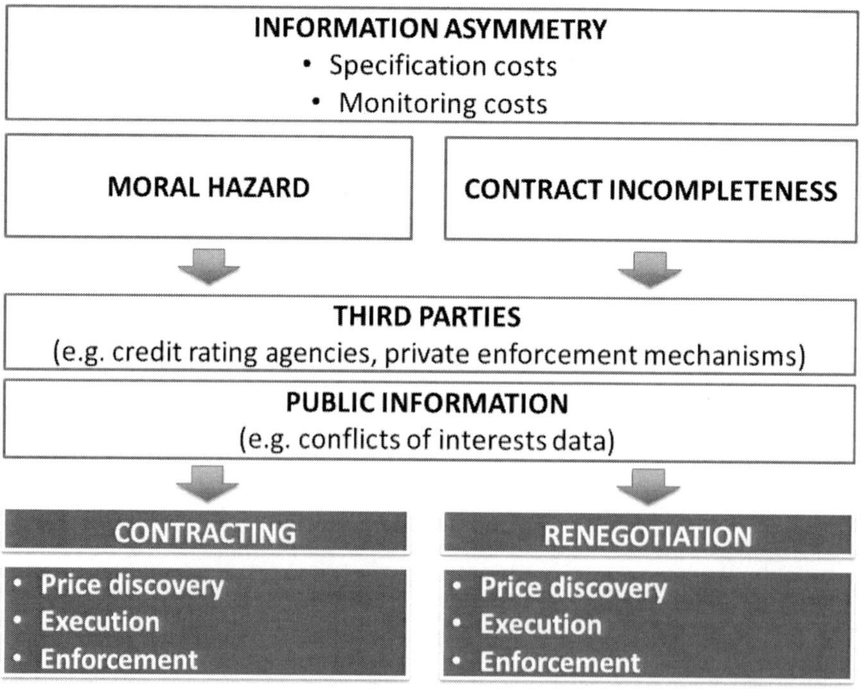

Source: Author.

Three pillars

Both in the contracting and renegotiation phase, a financial transaction relies upon three pillars:

- Price discovery.
- Execution.
- Enforcement.

Price discovery includes the collection of sufficient public and private information for pricing of risk to minimise costs deriving from moral hazard and contract incompleteness, in order to make contracting and renegotiation, in an environment with dispersed agents, more convenient. Key third parties for price discovery services would be mainly information providers, such as credit rating agencies or trading platforms. Execution allows filling informational gaps in the execution of the contracting and renegotiation (or liquidation) of a financial transaction, i.e. to minimise the costs of execution that would not be incurred in a bilateral relationship-based system, e.g. distribution costs for investment products. This also includes costs generated by market structure, such as insufficient competition among market infrastructures. Key third parties would be execution providers, such as asset managers, brokers or dealer banks. Enforcement services include relevant rules, procedures and practices related to the enforcement of private contracts, including minority shareholders and retail creditors' rights. Key third parties are, among others, courts, financial authorities, law firms and so on (see Figure 4.3).

Figure 4.3 Financial transaction, third parties and public information

<table>
<tr><th>PHASES</th><th>THIRD PARTIES</th><th>INFORMATION</th></tr>
<tr><td>PRICE DISCOVERY</td><td>• Credit Rating Agencies (CRAs)
• Trading platforms
• Financial press/data providers
• Analysts
• Auditors
• Self-regulatory bodies (e.g. standard setters)</td><td rowspan="3">• Underlying financial & non-financial info (e.g. company data)
• Conflicts of interest
• Securities prices</td></tr>
<tr><td>EXECUTION</td><td>• Asset managers (incl. pension funds and insurance firms)
• Trading platforms
• Brokers/dealer banks</td></tr>
<tr><td>ENFORCEMENT</td><td>• State (laws; incl. insolvency)
• Competent authorities (regulation and supervision)
• Courts (judicial review)
• Law firms (private settlement)</td></tr>
</table>

Source: Author.

Informational gap

In all three phases, third parties ensure that there is a sufficient flow of information to fill the asymmetry between counterparties and allow the financial transaction to take place. Informational frictions are the main factor shaping geographical distribution of investments, especially for equity transactions (Portes et al., 2001; Portes & Rey, 2005). The type of public information includes financial, e.g. financial statements, and non-financial, e.g. conflict of interests, information about the company or the underlying asset that is the object of the financial transaction. This public information can be used to price risk in order to enter (contracting) or to exit (renegotiating) a financial transaction, either on a market or in an insolvency procedure. Information is at the core of it. This is particularly the case when one of the two counterparties is structurally weaker, because it is a retail bondholder or minority shareholder or a small investor in investment fund units. In this case, investor protection rules have the role of rebalancing the informational gap with stronger rights for the weaker part.

Key findings #10.

- Financial contracting in market-based systems requires public information collected and re-elaborated by third parties, on top of private information, to deal with information asymmetry that creates moral hazard and contract incompleteness. As a result of these market failures, a financial transaction develops in two phases: contracting and renegotiation.
- Due to a multitude of agents and information asymmetry, market-based mechanisms require information, which is reflected in prices and partially disclosed by third parties. Information disclosure allows ex ante pricing (contracting) and ex post renegotiation (exit on secondary markets or via private enforcement mechanisms) by signalling the relevant information to price risk and fill the informational gap between counterparties.
- If there is insufficient information flow, there will be no market price, while in relationship-based mechanisms, such as traditional banking, transactions take place because the counterparty with informational advantage has sufficient contractual power to overcome information asymmetries and offer liquidity in the market.
- A well-functioning market needs participation as wide as possible, thus retail investors (either as a creditor or a shareholder) are crucial for the diversification of the trading flow and to balance informed and uninformed trading activities, which is important for market liquidity. Investor protection (including also minority shareholders) is thus a fundamental objective when monitoring the quality of the information flow.

- Both in contracting and renegotiation phases there are three important sub-phases: price discovery, execution and enforcement.
  - Price discovery (PD) is the process of 'discovering' the market price that is the closest approximation to the reserve value of the investor, considering his/her assessment of counterparty risk or of the value of the underlying asset at that moment in time.
  - Execution (EXE) is the set of procedures that are involved in the execution of financial transactions in the contracting or renegotiation phase. This includes market entry and exit requirements.
  - Enforcement (ENF) is the process of ensuring the smooth performance or renegotiation of a financial contract, i.e. the enforcement of private contracts, including minority shareholders, retail investors and creditors' rights.
- Collection of public information for these three phases is performed by multiple third parties, including credit rating agencies, broker analysts and courts.

4.4 A barriers removal test

Legal determinants

Capital moves from providers to seekers of capital via several channels, which rely on a pricing mechanism driven either by relationship, e.g. traditional relationship banking, or by markets, i.e. a multitude of agents that take on part of the risk, e.g. public equity issuance. A single currency is not a sufficient condition for the emergence of a single market for capital, which relies on the removal of other important frictions, such as laws, tax treatments, etc. (Giovannini Group, 2002, 2003; Jappelli & Pagano, 2008, 2013). Flexibility of the judicial system, creditor rights, shareholders rights and retail investor protection (at-the-point-of-sale) are among the factors that produce a given organisation of investors, banks and intermediaries, i.e. a given structure of relationship- and market-based funding sources. While methodology faces some hurdles, the prevailing stream of literature (reviewed in Chapter 00) points to the fact that legal factors are very important to making banks and markets grow in size and degree of interaction, and thus determine further financial development. The reversed causal link, i.e. financial development causing a change in legal requirements, also exists but becomes weaker as the financial system develops. The development of the single market for goods and services suggests that economic conditions in Europe are already mostly favourable for further financial development. Recent literature also shows that capital markets tend to develop in regions with higher levels of income (Beck et al., 2007), as a sign that private savings are important for capital flows. Europe is one of the wealthiest regions in the world, with large private savings pools. Hence, underlying economic conditions for market mechanisms to develop are already mostly assured. Favourable legal conditions for a market-based system (capital markets) at European level should thus promote further financial development.

A market-based system relies on sound enforcement of private contracts via public information, which distinguishes it from a relationship-based system, mainly relying on private information and bilateral contractual power (Rajan & Zingales, 1998b). As a result, relationship-based systems develop despite weaker legal protections and enforcement, while market-based systems develop in regions with stronger protection of creditor and shareholder rights, including enforcement of private contracts (see section 2.2 for a review of the literature). Relaunching the post-crisis financial integration process means creating the conditions, and most importantly the legal environment, for the deepening of the single market to boost market-based funding channels in Europe. An increase of diversification and consolidation of the financial ecosystem would ultimately provide greater and cheaper access to finance for large, medium and small firms, with more investment opportunities to spur growth and jobs across Europe.

Harmonisation vs regulatory competition

As discussed in Chapter 1, since the 1980s, the European Union has introduced several laws to complement the mutual recognition of national regulations. However, these rules have not been uniformly implemented by all 28 member states and there are areas that have not been dealt with yet at European level. To address this coordination failure, for instance in company law, EU institutions have repeatedly tried to win consensus on a maximum harmonisation and repeatedly failed. It is indeed questionable whether a full harmonisation approach, which de facto replaces national regimes with a '29th regime', will be able to create more favourable conditions for a common capital market to flourish. Compared to the United States, where capital markets initially developed in a legislative (but not judicial) *vacuum* and mainly around commercial centres (thus with limited fragmentation from the outset), Europe has to build its integrated financial market by bringing together 28 different markets and sovereign states, which have developed so far via local financial regulations and legal systems. A maximum harmonisation attempt would be theoretically the easiest way, but in practice it would not get political support, nor would it be a feasible approach to addressing the complexities of often very different legal systems that are entrenched in local legal and cultural customs and cannot be changed at the stroke of a pen without generating negative spillover effects. Nonetheless, regulatory competition can produce beneficial effects if it is left to areas where the law needs to adapt to local conditions in order to deal with potential market failures. As a result, regulatory competition among member states does not necessarily create a 'race-to-the-bottom' or a 'race-to-the-top', but it is complementary to harmonisation in Europe (Sun & Pelkmans, 1995; Radaelli, 2004). An EU-wide plan to develop capital markets could combine harmonisation where economic and legal factors are barriers to cross-border movement of capital, while the rest would be left to national laws (regulatory competition).

Barrier definition

A 'barrier' can be defined as any domestic or European rule (law), (market and supervisory) practice or procedure that is an impediment to data comparability (price discovery), fairness of procedures (execution) and legal certainty (enforcement) in the contracting or renegotiation phase of a financial transaction. A barrier to capital flow can be cross-border or national. It would be 'cross-border' if those laws, practices or procedures increase the costs for a foreign legal entity (headquartered in the EU or authorised to provide services in the EU) of price discovery, execution and enforcement in the contracting and renegotiation phases compared to the costs that are incurred by domestically headquartered legal entities. This foreign legal entity can be either the counterparty of a financial transaction or a third party providing support to these functions.

A barrier can also be artificial or structural. A barrier is artificial if an entity or a process that is exogenous to the financial transaction imposes this additional cost. This barrier can be a rule or a supervisory practice of the local competent authority, as well as a market practice imposed by a dominant firm, e.g. auditing company. A structural barrier is an idiosyncratic barrier that emerges naturally in the contracting or renegotiating phase of a financial transaction, such as language barriers (also cross-border) or the structural lack of information in SMEs' lending operations (in this case, both national and cross-border). Structural barriers, such as the lack of incentives for SMEs to disclose more information, would be there whether or not the transaction (or the services involved) is cross-border, i.e. it involves a foreign counterparty.

Ultimately, a barrier may be harmful for capital markets integration if it affects the cost predictability of a financial transaction. Data comparability, fairness of treatment and certainty of rules and procedures are key sources of cost predictability respectively for price discovery, execution and enforcement functions (see Table 4.2).

Table 4.2 Cost predictability in cross-border market-based financial contracting

Functions	Output	Cost predictability
Price discovery	Data	Comparability
Execution	Entry/exit requirements	Fairness
Enforcement	Rules & procedures	Certainty

Source: Author.

The barriers removal test

The selection of those economic and legal barriers that are an impediment to an integrated capital market, and thus to the interconnection between national liquidity pools and a more efficient asset allocation, requires a test to define when the barrier is harmful and should be removed by a top-down EU intervention. This test should weigh the impact of the different barriers on financial contracting (and renegotiation) and implicitly on the development of an integrated capital market. Furthermore, looking at the different components of a financial transaction reduces the space for discretional action and increases the measurability of its success.

Guiding principle

A guiding principle, in setting priorities for action in the area of capital markets, might come from other experiences. For instance, US case law has strictly enforced the principle of certainty about which state law shall apply to a financial transaction. In particular, the harmonisation tool could definitely be employed where artificial barriers create uncertainty about which member state law applies to the transaction. In effect, legal uncertainty cannot be discounted ex ante by the counterparties and thus priced in a cross-border financial transaction, thereby creating uncertainty about the cost of the transaction. A barriers removal plan, in this way, would distinguish areas where a top-down harmonisation approach is necessary (if generating cost uncertainty) from areas where regulatory competition among member states would not harm the common capital market but rather create competitive pressures that are beneficial for investors and capital seekers. As a consequence, when an artificial (legal or economic) barrier with cross-border impact creates uncertainty about the costs of a financial transaction, thereby impeding the pricing of the rule, practice or procedure in the financial transaction, an immediate action to remove the barrier should be taken (see Figure 4.4).

Figure 4.4 Barriers removal test

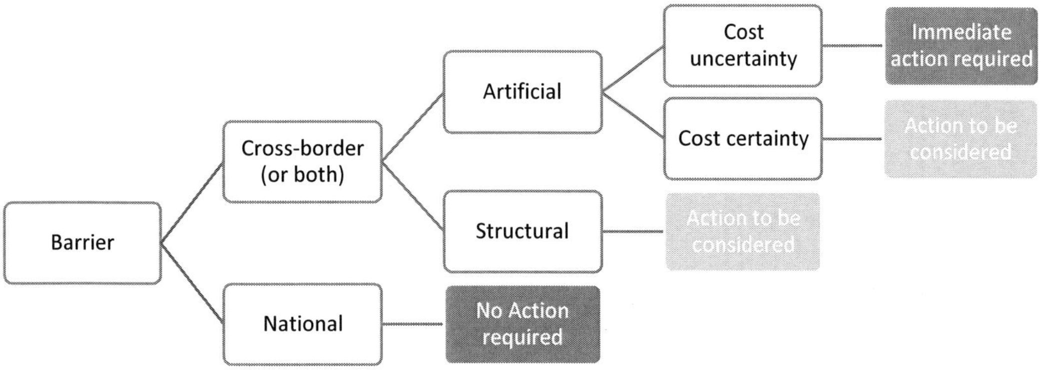

Source: Author.

Cost predictability

Higher transaction costs, due to divergent requirements, are not a problem per se, unless they are incurred because of uncertainty that cannot be somehow discounted in the pricing of a financial transaction. The greater the cost unpredictability, the greater the need for policy intervention. Cases of barriers that create cost unpredictability are, for instance, enforcement procedures. Cross-border insolvency proceedings involve procedures and legal costs that can be hardly estimated ex ante, due to the procedural uncertainties, such as the misuse of secondary proceedings or the discretional use of valuation methodologies that affect the ability to evaluate risk for foreign investors (see following sections). In enforcement, there will always a minimum level of unpredictability, but we review in the following sections ample evidence that some of these barriers create a sizable ex ante disincentive to cross-border financial contracting, which cannot be quantified and discounted in a financial transaction.

There are also barriers that create additional (unnecessary) costs to cross-border financial transactions, but these costs can be fully discounted ex ante. For instance, differences in data formats or accounting reclassification about company data require hiring a local accountant to make this data fit in internal valuation models of the foreign EU investor. The procedure adopted by member states to collect and refund the withholding tax may require hiring a local law or accounting firm just to deal with unnecessarily cumbersome forms and procedures that create local rents. In both cases, there is limited cost uncertainty, as the cost is capped respectively by the cost of the service offered by the accountant and the value of the tax to be reclaimed that will be set as a cap for the service provider. Actions might be considered to lower the unnecessary cross-border cost, but there is no urgency determined by the uncertain cost of the barrier, which would have a high probability to preclude cross-border financial contracting in the first place. Regulatory competition, i.e. lower costs offered by competing member states, may gradually draw away capital from the more costly country, with beneficial disciplining effects that may determine a convergence of those procedures towards the most beneficial outcome for investors. As a result, where costs of the artificial barrier are predictable, EU institutions could apply a 'case-by-case' approach when considering a policy intervention.

Key findings #11.

- A single currency is not a sufficient condition for the emergence of a single market for capital, which relies on the removal of other important frictions, such as differences in investor rights, tax treatment, quality of the judicial system and supervisory practices.
- A maximum harmonisation attempt would be theoretically the easiest way to eliminate these frictions to cross-border trading, but in practice it will not be a feasible approach to address the complexities of often very different legal systems that are entrenched in local legal and cultural customs.
- The financial contracting approach is used to identify and classify barriers on the basis of their harm to cross-border trading. This approach reduces discretional actions and increases measurability against well-defined objectives. It also allows drawing a line between measures that require harmonisation and areas that can be left to regulatory competition among member states.
- The barriers identified are a selection of the most harmful ones and should not be considered an exhaustive list.
- A 'barrier' can be defined as any domestic or European rule (law), (market and supervisory) practice or procedure that is an impediment to data comparability (price discovery), fairness of procedures (execution) and legal certainty (enforcement) in the contracting or renegotiation phase of a financial transaction. Barriers can be artificial (exogenous to the transaction) or structural (embedded in the transaction), as well as domestic or cross-border (or both).
- Barriers are most harmful when they make the costs of a financial transaction unpredictable. The more unpredictable costs become, the more negative the impact these barriers will have on financial contracting.
- At the core of every market-based financial transaction is the potential to discount future cash flows. The less information about direct and indirect costs of the

transaction that may affect future cash flows, the lower the potential to discount future scenarios. Once discounting is impaired, the financial transaction will most likely not take place.

- In a cross-border environment, both economic and legal barriers, identified in the following sections, affect cost predictability.

4.5 Price discovery

Financial and non-financial information

To the extent investors and/or intermediaries can distinguish good from bad projects, funds will go to projects that match the risk/return profile of the investor. Price discovery is the process of 'discovering' the market price that is the closest approximation to the reserve value of the investor, considering his/her assessment of counterparty risk or of the underlying asset at that moment in time. Price discovery is thus crucial to significantly reducing specification and monitoring costs in the contracting and renegotiation phase. Lower costs of discovering prices would thus allow better matching between savings and investment opportunities. Price discovery relies on the ability of investors to assess risk via access to both financial and non-financial information about the underlying asset (whether a company or commodity). While non-financial information is often readily available because of commercial needs, e.g. sales, turnover, etc., financial information is less readily available and often lacks comparability. This makes price discovery rather complex, especially on a cross-border level.

Contracting and renegotiation

Price discovery is important both in the pre-investment (contracting) and in the post-investment phase (renegotiation). In the contracting phase, which involves the process of negotiation before the investment takes place, price discovery helps to signal the actual risk of the investment to a wide set of investors, who may be willing to invest once they have enough information to set their reserve price for the risk they are taking. In the renegotiation phase, which happens after the investment occurs, price discovery helps the investor to benchmark the performance and to check whether the conditions that made the investment profitable are verified over time.

Financial information

Financial information includes all the information related to the financial and accounting position of individual companies, as well as information about the financial instrument at individual and aggregate (primary and secondary market) level. As a result, on top of non-financial information, price discovery in market-based financial contracting and renegotiation depends on:

a. Information about the underlying asset (including counterparty risk, if a derivative contract, e.g. company financial and non-financial data or creditor information).
b. Information about the financial instrument, e.g. market price.

Evidence shows that financial information does reveal the value/risk of the underlying asset, especially if combined with non-financial information (Amir & Lev, 1996; Healy & Palepu, 2001; Flöstrand & Ström, 2006). It is thus the combination of different pieces of information to support price discovery, which is one of the three pillars for a well-functioning capital market. At the European level, there is the additional problem of making this data comparable across borders. Ultimately, this information will also be relevant for the execution and enforcement functions (see following sections).

4.5.1 *Information on the underlying asset*

Underlying asset & conflicts of interest

Information on the underlying asset includes all the data available about a company, a commodity or other assets in which the investor is channelling funds. Most of the capital markets activity is concentrated in financial and non-financial corporations, but data on other underlying assets, such as physical commodities, or on more aggregate macroeconomic indicators (for interest and exchange rates) are also important for capital markets. Company (financial) data and disclosure of conflicts of interest are currently by far the scarcest piece of information to evaluate risks of underlying assets in Europe. For instance, accounting information can significantly improve cost of capital and thus liquidity, especially in systems where levels of disclosure are relatively low (Leuz & Verrecchia, 2000; Lambert et al., 2007). Disclosure of conflicts of interest can reduce the costs imposed on minority shareholders by the separation between ownership and control, such as self-dealing and tunnelling (Djankov et al., 2008; Johnson et al., 2000).

Financial information on listed companies

For what concerns company data, a first distinction should be made between private and publicly listed companies. Publicly listed companies have reported financial information for consolidated accounts via common accounting standards since 2005 (International Financial Reporting Standards, or IFRS, with EC Regulation n. 1606/2002). Evidence about the effects of this harmonisation is weak, due to the design of the legislation with many optionalities, which makes it hard to take into account the dynamic non-monetary effects that accounting rules may generate due to changes in market conditions. In effect, harmonisation across the board has indeed produced common disclosure rules but has increased transparency and improved market liquidity only in some countries (European Commission,

2015d; ICAEW, 2015). These rules produced a positive impact mainly in those countries that, together with the formal implementation of these rules, have tightened their enforcement mechanisms, and even more so for those firms that have voluntarily switched to IFRS reporting before its mandatory implementation (Daske et al., 2008; Christensen et al., 2013). This shows the importance of uniform enforcement of accounting practices at EU level. In effect, even if differences among member states are lessening after the introduction of the IFRS regulation, divergences (national patterns) remain, where the law allowed member states to enforce national accounting practices, which limited cross-border comparability (Kvaal & Nobes, 2010, 2012; European Commission, 2015d; ICAEW, 2015). There is indeed strong path dependence in accounting standards, due to high switching costs (most of them are 'one-off costs') and benefits that only accrue later on in time, i.e. time inconsistent, e.g. increased trade in goods and services or reduced risk of insiders' expropriation (ICAEW, 2015). For instance, despite the US Jobs Act having offered Emerging Growth Companies (EGCs)[54] to move from a full-fledged US GAAP system to scaled disclosure requirements, only 16% of these firms opted in (Ernst & Young, 2015), as they saw this change as damaging the information flow that ensures them sufficient market funding.[55] This suggests strong path dependence, even if firms would receive a high one-off benefit. Optional requirements do not eliminate the problem that costs are one-off, while benefits are diluted over time. As a result, it may not be preferable to shift the decision about a public good (availability of comparable accounting data across Europe) to a system of harmonised but optional (at firm level) requirements. Furthermore, it would be a reasonable step to align accounting standards for consolidated accounts with individual companies' national accounts.

Accounting rules optionalities

Whether fully harmonised or not, the design of accounting rules is complex. More specifically, barriers to data comparability in the area of accounting practices for listed companies emerge from either optionality in the principle-based approach or lack of enforcement of accounting rules (the latter is discussed in section 4.7.1). The optionality is often decided either at a company or country level and it necessarily involves some level of discretion

[54] An ECG is a company with total annual gross value (in US GAAP) of less than $1 billion in its most recent fiscal year, which has issued less then $1 billion in non-convertible debt securities (in registered and unregistered offers) over a rolling 36-month period and a public float of less than $700 million. See JOBS Act, available at www.gpo.gov/fdsys/pkg/BILLS-112hr3606enr/pdf/BILLS-112hr3606enr.pdf.

[55] Most ECGs only opted to reduce executive compensation disclosure and to reduce audited financial statements to two years.

by the management of the firm in the implementation process, as a way to extract as much private information as possible to inform investors. However, excessive optionality and too much complacency with local accounting practices may actually do the reverse and result in hiding information that should be made public. The result of the current framework is, in effect, a low level of comparability across Europe of important balance sheet items, which hampers the ability to evaluate risk among companies at a reasonably low cost *vis-à-vis* comparing financials of firms within the same country. This may require a stricter interpretation of IFRS principles by supervisors, within a harmonised approach.

For instance, asset retirement obligations in IAS 37, i.e. the legal obligation associated with the retirement of tangible assets, whose timing of settlement is conditional on a future event that may not depend on the company's will, include vague guidelines on the actual measurement, such as the discount rate to calculate the net present value of future cash flows, which is left to the management's discretion. Anecdotal evidence shows that German firms tend to be more conservative in this evaluation compared to other European firms, but there is no disclosure on how this evaluation takes place. As it emerged from the 2014 ECB Asset Quality Review (AQR), another example is the loan impairments reporting by banks under IAS 39. IAS 39.59 generally defines a loan impairment as an item recognised in a 'loss event', without further specifying the meaning, which is also left to the management's discretion. In the new IFRS 9, the loan impairment requirement, dealing with the recognition of lifetime losses on loans in case of a "significant increase in credit risk" since initial recognition, leaves the key terminology undefined, and thus at the discretion of the company's management or under uncoordinated guidance of member states' regulators. This is a source of uncertainty regarding the ability to assess counterparty risk and thus the cost of a transaction. Greater transparency of the internal methodology used and the criteria applied in case of discretion are crucial to improving accounting data quality, as ESMA also confirmed after the review of accounting practices for Greek government bonds (ESMA, 2012).

Accounting & taxation

Less uncertainty is required in IFRS optionalities in the evaluation of an asset. It should not leave or limit discretion to detailed items. More discretion can be given on the reclassification, as this optionality still allows the investor to replicate the reclassification of the items according to established methodologies available to the public. In this case, there is a fair level of cost certainty. However, if too loose, this optionality would also increase costs of cross-border capital markets activity. For instance, it creates conflicts with local fiscal authorities over the reclassification to be used for tax purposes. It may be important for local fiscal authorities to clarify ex ante the classifications under the uniform accounting rules to be used for fiscal purposes and allow bilateral case-by-case examination when alternatives can be used (under those rules). Currently, in several countries, firms are obliged to issue a balance sheet under the recognised accounting standards and a different one for tax purposes. This is not an explicit barrier to cross-border transactions, as it applies to domestic and foreign entities alike, but it is nonetheless a significant source of cost and uncertainty for firms (when it comes to conflicting interpretations of the accounting rules by the supervisor and the national fiscal agency) and a way for local governments to increase cross-border switching costs. EU institutions should work more closely with member states to streamline this process. The proposal of the European Commission on the creation of a Common Consolidated Corporate Tax Base (CCCTB)[56] can actually help to align accounting practices for regular and tax reporting.

Alternative performance measures

Furthermore, there is also the practice in some countries of allowing alternative performance measures, which 'adjust' IFRS figures according to internal models for publication purposes. This creates uncertainty or even misleading communication. For instance, 21 companies of the FTSE 100 treated restructuring costs as "exceptional" (for their own adjusted profits), even though they were reported for four consecutive years (Standard & Poor's, 2014). Tighter supervision of practices and greater transparency with an explanatory note on how and why the firms use it might be an improvement for data comparability. The inclusion in the financial statements, under audit assurance, might be an option (Standard & Poor's, 2014).

Off-balance sheet items

Finally, there are 'off-balance sheet' items, such as contingent liabilities or guarantees, that are not captured on the balance sheet, unless the likelihood of an outflow is "probable", i.e. probability above 50%. Here again, the management has full discretion on the definition of this probability, with no disclosure of underpinning criteria. In countries where the regulatory system is stronger and voluntary disclosure higher, there is a general trend to provide more information about these items. In effect, while discretion in some cases might be necessary to extract private information from managers, they may have different incentives according to the reporting behaviour of similar firms in the country, as well as the legal and the enforcement frameworks (Hail et al., 2010).

[56] For more details, please see the European Commission's website available at http://ec.europa.eu/taxation_customs/taxation/company_tax/common_tax_base/index_en.htm.

Disclosure procedures

Another important set of potential barriers to capital markets activities emerges from disclosure procedures. The Transparency Directive (n. 2013/50/EU) set out principles for the development of national rules for listed companies in the area of periodical disclosure. Most notably, due to the directive's nature, it nonetheless left space for listed companies in local markets to adopt different timing and thresholds, with the risk of impairing cross-border data comparability, which is the cornerstone of price discovery mechanisms. For instance, the directive requires the disclosure of the accumulation of different thresholds of voting shares or instruments with economic effects similar to those of holdings of shares and entitlements. It also allows the individual country to set a threshold lower than the minimum, set at 5%. These discretions create additional divergences and cross-border costs. Nonetheless, these costs are known ex ante and can be discounted accordingly. Potential actions should also consider the benefits of regulatory competition to ensure flexibility of legal systems to different governance models. There are also other rules, such as rules on when dividends can be disclosed, which further complicate cross-border operations (especially corporate actions in post-trading) and dilute the benefits of governance model flexibility.

Furthermore, all the filings are collected by local authorities and often are not easily accessible. The potential legal risks of erroneous national filings leads firms to overinvest in legal support in order to be shielded from expensive sanctions and litigations. The US SEC, however, collects all the filings in one repository, the Electronic Data Gathering, Analysis, and Retrieval system (EDGAR), with one standardised filing procedure (and not one for every US state). It may take time and more harmonisation efforts to achieve a similar outcome in Europe, but, in parallel with improving data comparability issues with actions on IFRS optionalities, ESMA could also be given the role of collecting and disclosing the relevant filings to the public via a common centralised European data repository reconciling all the national filing repositories. ESMA would also coordinate with member states if there is additional information requested by national laws and try to act to limit this additional flow or to standardise formats and report timing as much as possible.

An EU business registry

Furthermore, there is no European infrastructure to disseminate basic information about corporations. Europe does not have a common business registry and relies on 28 national registers, which are often very costly and opaque and charge firms when depositing information and data users when collecting it. General information about a company should be easily accessible to the public at a reasonable cost or even for free.

National repositories are not linked to each other with common search tools and data standards, increasing problems with data comparability. As a result, the creation of a European business register should be further encouraged and supported at European level. In particular, the combined centralisation, under the binding supervision of a central body, of official company filings for listed companies and information collected by national business registries about all private companies could provide a significant boost to the adoption of common practices of data disclosure and improve cross-border data comparability (see also section 4.7.1). The benefits of this simplification would trickle down to investors and in particular companies, both domestic and international, which will deal with one entity only under a transparent and fair procedural framework.

Private companies

Private listed companies, unlike unlisted ones, have no incentive and limited legal obligation to disclose financial information to the public. They produce financial information mainly for internal (risk management) and taxation purposes. This information is disclosed through domestic accounting standards, which are different across countries. As a result of the fragmented environment in the reporting of financial information, there are currently few databases of financial information of private (unlisted) companies across Europe, and none of them can offer a complete and fully reliable picture of the financial information of European private companies.

Nonetheless, while private firms might not have economic incentives to access equity markets, data about their financials may be necessary for debt securities issuance, e.g. high-yield bond market, speculative grade liquidity (SGL) ratings or simply to develop sectorial metrics that can be used to better price the risk of underlying assets for related listed financial instruments. Common accounting standards for private (unlisted) companies, including SMEs or subsidiaries of multinational companies, would provide high data comparability and a common set of information to compare firms and sectors across borders. As discussed above, there is high path dependence in accounting standards, due to one-off switching costs and benefits diluted over time, but they are ultimately a pre-condition for the development of a pan-European capital market. The cross-border provision of services will hardly break down into domestic markets to the level of SMEs and retail without a set of information that is comparable and accessible to service providers.

While allowing private companies to opt in to the IFRS regime for listed companies, these companies do not need the same detailed financial information used for listed companies, such as earnings per share or interim financial reporting. A simplified regime harmonised across Europe, with less complex disclosure requirements and limited optionalities, would be a crucial step forward, starting from the work of the IFRS foundation, via the International Accounting Standards Board (IASB), for SMEs accounting standards.[57] The introduction of the Directive 2013/34 aligns rules for consolidated and annual accounts, but leaves most of the options for member states still there. It introduces new definitions of micro and small companies, to which the directive applies a lighter regime.[58] The Directive does not align rules with the IFRS standards for SMEs, but leave the option for firms to use the regime. More should be done to reduce options and align the regime to the IFRS regime for SMEs.

Creditor information

Creditor information also plays an important role in pricing counterparty risk and thus improving price discovery in financial markets. Scoring and access to information are key aspects of credit risk evaluation. As of today, there are no common guidelines for credit scoring (including the definition of 'defaulted exposure') and credit risk information is stored in national credit bureaus that are not linked to each other. The European Commission should continue its effort to promote convergence. An initial step could connect the national credit bureaux within a European network that would facilitate cross-border access to credit scores. This first step could benefit from ongoing initiatives, such as the one run by the ECB.[59] A second step would promote a gradual convergence of credit score methodology under the direction of a common body, such as the European Banking Authority.

Non-financial information

Non-financial information is also another piece of basic information, which (combined with financial information) can help improve information flows and thus price discovery, as explained in previous paragraphs. The most relevant non-financial information includes environmental or social goals, which shall now be included in a non-financial report published by large companies (non-SMEs) as part of a 2014 Directive (2014/95/EU) amending the Accounting Directive (2013/34/EU).[60] Monitoring the implementation of the directive is very important.

---

[57] For more details see materials available at www.ifrs.org/IFRS-for-SMEs/Pages/IFRS-for-SMEs.aspx.

[58] For an overview, see the factsheet prepared by the Federation of European Accountants (FEE) and available at www.fee.be/index.php?option=com_content&view=article&id=1379:factsheet-on-the-new-june-2013-accounting-directive&catid=50:corporate-reporting&Itemid=106

[59] For more details, please see https://www.ecb.europa.eu/explainers/tell-me-more/html/anacredit.en.html.

[60] "Where undertakings are required to prepare a non-financial statement, that statement should contain, as regards environmental matters, details of the current and foreseeable impacts of the undertaking's operations on the environment, and, as appropriate, on health and safety, the use of

Conflicts of interest data

Data on conflicts of interest is as important as the company's financial information for the effective functioning of the market. It includes data on ownership, compensation and related party transactions. Data are often controversial and may enter in the personal sphere of individuals, but they are crucial to ensuring adequate investor protection and surveillance of management against 'tunnelling' resources for self-dealing (Johnson et al., 2000) and to limiting the risk of mispricing (see section 2.2). More specifically, this data disclosure may protect minority shareholders by minimising monitoring costs and thus chances of moral hazard. Evidence suggests that there is an incentive for managers to hide information in countries where there are more private benefits of control and related-party transaction issues (Leuz et al., 2003). Conflicts of interest have thus an impact on reporting quality.

Cross-ownership of firms that are linked by commercial activities may generate important conflicts of interest, which may lead the firm's activity away from its original commercial target, thus affecting its fundamental value and investors' ability to price risk. There is limited data disclosure on cross-ownership of companies in Europe. There is also limited data disclosure and comparability regarding managers' compensation, since this is largely influenced by national regulation and local listing requirements (such as the Corporate Governance Code in the UK). As a result, the regulatory environment for identifying and managing conflicts of interest in Europe is currently worse than in other advanced regions, such as the US and Japan, with great variance across EU member states (see Figure 4.5).[61]

---

renewable and/or non-renewable energy, greenhouse gas emissions, water use and air pollution. As regards social and employee-related matters, the information provided in the statement may concern the actions taken to ensure gender equality, implementation of fundamental conventions of the International Labour Organisation, working conditions, social dialogue, respect for the right of workers to be informed and consulted, respect for trade union rights, health and safety at work and the dialogue with local communities, and/or the actions taken to ensure the protection and the development of those communities. With regard to human rights, anti-corruption and bribery, the non-financial statement could include information on the prevention of human rights abuses and/or on instruments in place to fight corruption and bribery." Recital 7, Directive 2013/34/EU.

[61] Most recently, the European Commission is attempting to introduce more transparency over key information for the governance of a company and its internal conflicts of interest (e.g. related-party transactions), also putting pressure on shareholders to use their rights more actively, with a legislative proposal amending Directive 2007/36/EC as regards the encouragement of long-term shareholder engagement and Directive 2013/34/EU as regards certain elements of the corporate governance statement.

Figure 4.5 Extent of conflict of interest regulation index (0-10)

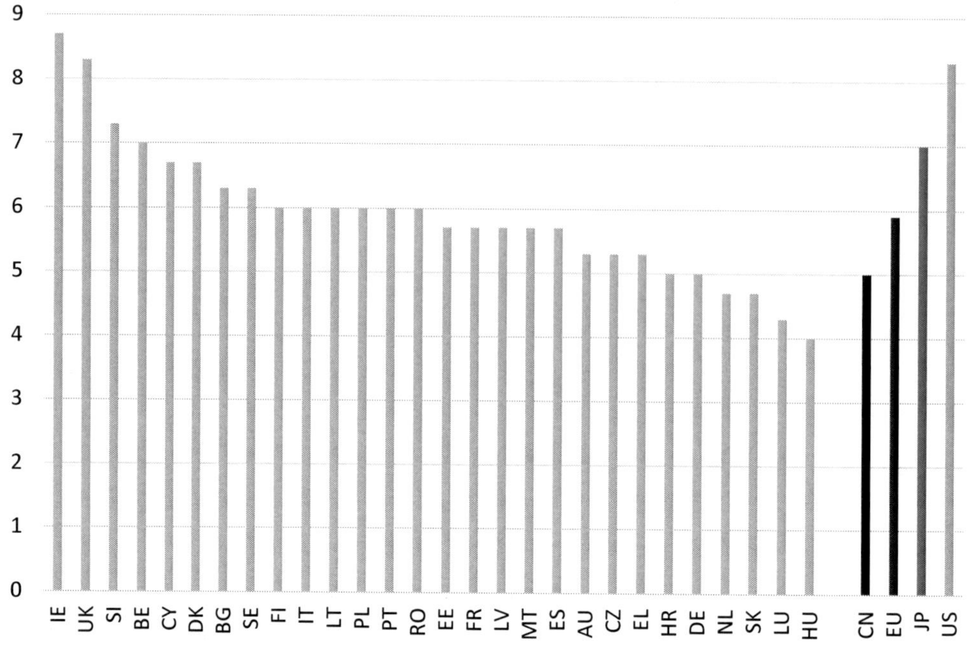

Note: This index is a simple average of three indices: the extent of disclosure index (incl. review and approval requirements for related-party transactions; internal, immediate and periodic disclosure requirements for related-party transactions); the extent of director liability index (incl. minorities' ability to sue and to hold directors accountable for prejudicial related-party transactions and availability of legal remedies); and the ease of shareholder suits index (incl. access to internal corporate documents, evidence obtainable during trial, allocation of legal expenses). For more details, see www.doingbusiness.org/methodology/protecting-minority-investors. "EU" is a simple average of all 28 scores.

Source: 2016 Doing Business Report (World Bank).

Rules on related party transactions (included in IAS 24) are, moreover, particularly complex and designed to allow significant flexibility. They apply to all IFRS reporters (listed companies). As a consequence, they leave several definitions to the local regulator, such as the definition of "control" or of the person that can have a significant influence on the company. Comparability of this information is limited and therefore costly at cross-border level, but further assessment shall be made on whether flexibility of key definitions is necessary to account for different governance models at national level. Should the benefits of flexibility (either at company or national level) outweigh its costs, the disclosure of the methodology and the reasons why it was adopted could increase cost predictability and improve conditions for cross-border investment.

Table 4.3 Selected examples of outstanding cross-border barriers

Cross-border barrier	Nature	Cost predictability	Outcome
1. IFRS optionalities with discretionary evaluation models, e.g. asset retirement obligations, loan provisions, etc.	Artificial	No	Immediate action
2. Domestic accounting standards for non-listed companies	Artificial	No	Immediate action
3. Reporting formats, e.g. half-yearly reports, etc.	Artificial	Yes	Action needed
4. IFRS optionalities for alternative calculation methodologies or definitions, e.g. classification problems, such as pension interest in income statement as interest or operating expense or calculation of debt at amortised cost or fair value	Artificial	Yes	Action needed
5. Alternative performance measures	Artificial	Yes	Action needed
6. Off-balance sheet items	Structural	No	Action needed
7. Voting share disclosure threshold	Artificial	Yes	Action needed
8. Domestic business registries	Artificial	Yes	Action needed
9. Credit risk scoring and national credit bureaus	Artificial	Yes	Action needed
10. Rules on related-party transactions (definitions)	Artificial	Yes	Action needed
11. Compensation disclosure (methodology)	Artificial	Yes	Action needed

Note: This is not an exhaustive list of artificial and structural barriers to cross-border financial transactions.

Outstanding barriers

Two out of 11 selected barriers may require immediate action at EU level.[62] These barriers can be a potential obstacle for cross-border price discovery (risk evaluation) and thus further capital markets integration (see Table 4.3). Remaining barriers, in the area of accounting and other important company and individual data, require an EU intervention that takes into account the differences of local corporate governance systems, as long as the flexibility provided by regulatory competition does not complicate the ability to identify and price costs ex ante.

[62] This is by no means an exhaustive list.

4.5.2 *Financial instrument information*

Definition

The second set of information that is necessary for a financial transaction to take place includes market information about the financial instrument that is part of the sale/purchase or lending/borrowing operation.[63] Information can be organised in two groups: pre-contractual and ongoing (ex post) information.

Pre-contractual information

Pre-contractual information has received a lot of attention in post-crisis financial reforms, both for primary issuance and secondary market activity. For what concerns primary issuance, the revision of the prospectus directive and the obligation to issue the Key Information Document (KID) (per EU Regulation n. 1286/2014), when issuing new UCITS units or other packaged retail and insurance-based investment products (PRIIPs),[64] should make pre-contractual disclosure more readable to retail investors. The KID does not necessarily address an issue that affects capital markets integration, as the problems regarding retail investors' ability to process financial information exist irrespective of whether the transaction is domestic or cross-border. Nonetheless, it may become an issue to be tackled by CMU if the implementation creates barriers to data comparability between UCITS issued in different countries or UCITS and non-UCITS PRIIPs (for instance). Different KIDs for different types of PRIIPs may worsen comparability among PRIIPs. In addition, KID requirements could be extended to all types of retail investment products (especially long-term ones) offered by pension funds, insurance companies and banks, in order to level up different disclosure requirements that are applied by domestic authorities (often rather opaquely).

In relation to the prospectus, which describes the issuance and the characteristics of the newly issued financial instruments, lowering listing costs by reducing disclosure for SMEs might reduce the typically high costs of issuance and push SMEs to issue more. For instance, the implementation of the Jobs Act, which reduced IPO burdens for Emerging Growth Companies (ECGs), may have triggered more IPOs, as roughly 83% of total IPOs in 2014 were ECGs (E&Y, 2015). Nonetheless, while disclosure requirements should ensure that the data disclosed in the revised prospectus are fully comparable across markets, this is not necessarily a barrier to cross-border dealing and an

---

[63] We consider "financial instrument" to cover all financial products (including investment products), which is largely in line with the definition included in the Markets in Financial Instruments Directive (MiFID) II, n. 2014/65/EU, Annex I, Section C.

[64] PRIIPs can be categorised in investment funds, insurance-based investment products, retail structured securities and structured term deposits, as defined by a Memo of the European Commission available at http://europa.eu/rapid/press-release_MEMO-14-299_en.htm?locale=en.

integration problem for CMU, but rather a structural problem classifiable under investment policies, which does not necessarily involve cross-border capital markets activities.

Market data and fragmentation

In addition, pre-contractual information includes secondary market information. For financial instruments other than equity, there is no formal obligation to disclose the prices at which individual transactions are executed in a venue or bilaterally. MiFID II will extend the pre-trade transparency requirement to these instruments, thus creating a harmonised European regime, which ultimately may create better conditions for pan-European trading platforms.

For equities, market prices are already available and should be in theory easy-to-compare information. However, market fragmentation and different data formats make the aggregation of information across trading venues expensive, especially if this data cannot be immediately used to execute orders cross-border. The limited cross-border brokerage activity is mainly driven by the high costs of market infrastructure for cross-border trades. In effect, due to the legal and infrastructural environment surrounding primary issuance, listing of financial instruments is still primarily a 'national thing'. As a result, fragmentation of issuance and trading of financial instruments along national borders in Europe increases the costs of getting a license for the use of the data because every platform charges a monopolistic rent as the only venue where most of the quotes are generated and prices are discovered by a diversified trading flow (combining both informed and uniformed investors, such as retail flows). Moreover, on top of the classic issue of the monopolistic rent, national fragmentation inhibits market liquidity because it increases the informational rent of informed investors, who have access to multiple exchanges, and prevents investors from benefitting from the positive network effects (market externalities) brought about by each additional market participant in a 'thicker market' (Pagano, 1989; Foucault, Pagano & Roell, 2013).

This situation will hardly be overcome if there is no common framework for the cross-border listing of financial instruments and a more integrated financial infrastructure (see also section 4.6.1). In addition, information is often disclosed with different data formats, which increases the costs of reconciling information in cross-border trading and impairing pricing at market microstructural level (O'Hara & Yang, 2013; Cespa & Foucault, 2013). Search costs to collect multiple quotes from multiple venues simultaneously are fairly high. MiFID II should overcome the formats issue via the direct licensing requirements for data providers (including trading venues), but the consolidation of the financial infrastructure depends on multiple factors, including competition policies. Meanwhile, more thinking should go behind the possibility for ESMA to become the listing authority of the European blue chips, using the network of national supervisors and ensuring that its binding supervision ensures greater convergence of practices. More should be done as well to identify and remove the bias in national laws towards the nationality of the regulated market where listing of the security takes place, which should be extended to any member state of the European Union where the venue has received the EU passport. This also means that depository services should accessible on a cross-border basis. The direct supervision of ESMA over international central securities depositories, the harmonisation of some key areas of securities laws (see following sections) may provide fertile ground for greater consolidation among European securities markets and more choice for investors.

EBBO

Linking up trading venues by frictionless information flows can reconcile fragmentation with liquidity and create positive market externalities. Greater venue consolidation may also reduce costs due to market fragmentation, which are impeding the development of a truly consolidated pre-trade European Best and Bid Offer (EBBO). The combined effect of market fragmentation (due to national bias in primary listing) and data formats (due to market practices) make it overly expensive to reconcile information on most liquid European shares, which are spread across dozens of trading venues. Offering consolidated (pre-trade) data solutions at a price that is affordable for everyone (in particular, for retail and small professional investors) is thus limited and so is the possibility of real-time cross-border execution on the basis of this information. The MiFID II proposal for a consolidated tape (post-trade transparency) may hardly see the light, as commercial interest in this solution, for both data providers and investors, is very limited. Post-trade consolidated (not actionable) data solutions have limited commercial value, as they can only be used for sophisticated post-trade analysis and the top of the book data can already be retrieved for free from the venue 15 minutes after the trade is executed. To facilitate the creation of an EBBO, supervisors could give more attention to the sale practices regarding data for the most liquid European share, so as to facilitate reconciliation across venues.

Table 4.4 Selected examples of outstanding cross-border barriers

Cross-border barrier	Nature	Cost predictability	Outcome
1. Ongoing performance disclosure (domestic market practices)	Artificial	No	Immediate action
2. Exit conditions disclosure (domestic market practices)	Artificial	No	Immediate action
3. Prospectus disclosure requirements	Artificial	Yes	Action needed
4. Calculation methodologies for PRIIPs costs (in KID)	Artificial	Yes	Action needed
5. Market data formats/costs & national bias in securities listing	Artificial	Yes	Action needed

Note: This is not an exhaustive list of artificial and structural barriers to cross-border financial transactions.

Ongoing (ex post) contractual information

Ongoing contractual information is not typically in the spotlight of policy-makers. Nonetheless, it plays a fundamental role in the renegotiation phase of financial transactions, as it allows most notably benchmarking of performance and potentially an early exit. It has indeed two main functions (De Manuel & Valiante, 2014):

i. To keep the investor informed of changes in returns and charges, helping *inter alia* to spur competition among providers and reduce switching costs.
ii. To inform the investor of material changes to the product, e.g. changes to the investment policy, providing the knowledge and the opportunity to exit.

Ongoing performance disclosure might help to create sectorial performance indicators. For instance, underlying loan level data can be a good performance indicator on which to rebuild trust for the securitisation market. Similarly, periodic disclosure of performance for investment funds, benchmarking it with the sector, can be of great incentive for investing in cross-border investment products. Current proposals, developed under the KID Regulation for PRIIPs (EU Regulation n. 1286/2014), only deal with pre-contractual disclosure and with the use of historical data. It introduces the concept of 'performance scenarios', which are descriptions of potential performance scenarios via hypotheses that are defined and disclosed in the pre-contractual phase. In addition, UCITS and AIFMD also fail to provide meaningful ongoing performance disclosure (during the life of the investment product), but they rather provide changes to general policies or the fund structure, which are more relevant for policy purposes than for investor protection (De Manuel & Valiante, 2014, p. 19).

EU institutions, together with national competent authorities, should consider action to produce a framework for a standardised template about ongoing performance disclosure during the lifetime of the investment product and disclosure requirements for exit conditions. Ongoing contractual information is currently very fragmented, which increases costs of cross-border investments due to limited comparability. The extension of the regulatory action beyond PRIIPS to create a standardised ongoing performance disclosure and disclosure of exit conditions should be considered. As this area has hardly been scrutinised by regulators in the past, there are no major regulatory barriers to capital markets integration, but there is a lot of market practice diversity. Any policy action in this area should focus on investment products irrespective of the financial sector, e.g. insurance, banking, etc., rather than promote isolated interventions that create further fragmentation. Policy action should also include all products performing similar functions. For instance, collective funding schemes wrapped inside insurance products, such as life insurance products, that perform the same function of an investment product.

Aggregate statistics

Finally, capital markets integration also benefits from the availability of aggregate market statistics, either for analysts to monitor market and macroeconomic trends that can impact different sectors or for policy-makers to monitor the aggregate impact of financial reforms and to ensure the accuracy of legal rules.[65] Aggregate statistics are also important for developing metrics in sectors that are currently emerging, such as crowdfunding for small technological start-ups. Metrics may help investors identify better risks in an area where information is typically scarce.

Key findings #12.

- Price discovery relies on both financial and non-financial information about the underlying asset (whether a company or a commodity) and information about the financial instrument, e.g. post-trade transparency.
- Price discovery is important in both the pre-investment (contracting) and post-investment (renegotiation) phases.

---

[65] There are several regulatory requirements, mainly in MiFID II (Directive n. 2014/65/EU and EU Regulation n. 600/2014) and MAR (EU Regulation n. 596/2014 and Directive n. 2014/57/EU), that rely on statistics on the size of trading activities in the European Union. These aggregate statistics will have to be released by an official public body to ensure legal certainty and smooth implementation.

Information about the underlying asset

- Company (financial) data and disclosure of conflicts of interest are among the scarcest information for assessing the risk of underlying assets in capital market transactions. Lack of comparability and limited cross-border financial research availability are indicators of the need for more harmonised information disclosure.
- Accounting rules play a key role in information disclosure. In particular, IFRS optionalities need to be reviewed, in particular if they create discretional internal calculation methodologies.
- Oversight of IFRS rules enforcement is weak and may require a central EU authority, such as ESMA, with strong powers.
- A simplified but harmonised accounting regime for unlisted companies might be an important improvement for data comparability, but path dependence requires a top-down approach. Disclosure of off-balance sheet items should also be improved.
- Accessibility to general information for both listed and unlisted companies is also very limited. A European business registry would be a key improvement for data accessibility and would offer a single point of entry for coordinating a network of local business registries and ensuring that reporting standards are the same. A centralised infrastructure at European level could also collect listed company filings and promote harmonisation of formats and timing of publications, which would reduce cross-border transaction costs.
- Common credit scoring guidelines and cross-border credit risk information sharing are crucial to counterparty risk assessment on a cross-border level.
- Conflicts of interest disclosure is crucial to market-based systems, as it reduces monitoring costs and at the same time improves quality of financial information. Data (cross-ownership, related-party transactions, compensation disclosure, etc.) are either absent or insufficiently implemented cross-border. For instance, IAS 24 rules leave too much flexibility at national level for what concerns definitions.

Information about the financial instrument

- Pre-contractual disclosure in primary markets can be further simplified for small and medium-sized enterprises, e.g. simplified prospectus. For secondary markets, besides the important ongoing work to expand pre-trade transparency requirements to all relevant asset classes, more work is needed to link up trading venues via frictionless information flows that can help to reconcile market fragmentation.
- Ongoing contractual disclosure is as important as pre-contractual disclosure. However, more needs to be done to improve performance disclosure, support the creation of sectorial benchmarks and increase the disclosure of exit conditions, in particular for investment products. The creation of a standardised template for ongoing performance disclosure might facilitate this process.

4.6 Execution

Market entry & exit

Execution (EXE) is the set of procedures that are involved in completing the contracting or renegotiation of a financial transaction. This includes market entry and exit requirements. Cross-border barriers for the accessibility to financial contracting and renegotiation are difficult to spot and often entrenched in the domestic legal system or market/supervisory practices. Barriers are sometimes raised by regular practices of local authorities or incumbent market participants (such as the static implementation of execution policies). Financial contracting in market-based mechanisms also depend on the role of third parties to overcome information asymmetries, in the form of barriers to direct market entry and exit, as well as in the form of obstacles to a smooth execution of a financial transaction via a third-party mechanism (indirect access). Investors, especially smaller ones, rely on easy accessibility (low transaction costs) to enter and exit financial contracting with dispersed multiple agents (markets). A well-functioning market ensures at all times that entities and financial instruments can access or be admitted to markets based on fair and objective criteria. This should create the conditions for contracting or renegotiation of a financial transaction at the lowest cost. The fairness of the procedures through which contracting and renegotiation take place ensures cost predictability and is a guiding principle for identifying and ultimately managing barriers to the execution process. For instance, fair accessibility, which includes non-discriminatory and non-discretionary rules and procedures, to trading of the same share across different equity markets creates the pre-condition for easier accessibility to the instrument and potentially more cross-border financial contracting. For instance, cost predictability of cross-border procedures for the determination of the tax on capital gains would reduce the transaction costs of renegotiation taking place via a sale of the financial instrument on a secondary market.

Discretion & discrimination

Discretionary procedures to entry or exit a financial transaction, whether directly or via a third-party mechanism (intermediary), can be an impediment to cross-border dealing, as it dramatically reduces cost predictability. As a result, it is crucial that procedures to contract or to renegotiate a financial claim can be discounted ex ante. Nonetheless, barriers may also emerge when there is a clear discrimination between cross-border and domestic financial contracting. While cost uncertainty is more damaging for financial contracting, the discrimination based on nationality of the counterparties or of the instrument can similarly hamper cross-border capital market integration. However, compared to discretionary procedures that are always damaging, discrimination based on nationality may be damaging only if the cost of the discrimination offsets the net spillover effects created by cross-border capital market activity. This is compatible with the barrier removal test above, which suggests resorting to immediate policy action only when there is cost unpredictability in the execution process (discretionary processes).

Market fragmentation

As demonstrated in Chapter 0, there is substantial market fragmentation in Europe in almost all asset classes, which makes cross-border contracting and renegotiation very costly, compared to other financial markets worldwide. Market fragmentation along national borders is mainly created by artificial (legal and economic) barriers and only in part by structural barriers, such as language or different levels of financial education. In effect, linking up markets can maximise information sharing and minimise transaction costs, with a greater amount of securities increasingly sold at the best available price across competing trading or other services (such as advice) platforms. Increasing connection (accessibility) among different national markets, however, may not necessarily result in greater consolidation and may also generate monopolistic rents (Foucault & Menkveld, 2008). As a result, this process should be guided by a sound combination of rules and supervisory practices.

Competition policies

To ensure the development of ideal conditions for a smooth execution, regulatory actions are insufficient if there is no constant oversight of their implementation. This joint action also includes competition policies, which should adapt to a changing market structure. The relevant market for a growing set of financial activities is now pan-European.

4.6.1 Entry procedures

Definition

Accessibility to markets, whether for new contracting or renegotiation of financial terms, requires fairness. Entry procedures are all those rules or market practices that are (directly or indirectly) involved when entering a financial transaction to provide/receive a service or to sell/buy an investment product or to list a financial instrument on a trading platform. The objective of these procedures is to lower the transaction costs involved in financial contracting. Such requirements may include *inter alia* authorisation or listing rules, open access requirements, tax incentives, execution policies or corporate actions.

Authorisation and listing rules

These entry requirements are naturally a barrier to enter markets. However, more generally, they can actually facilitate financial contracting because, by meeting some minimum requirements, they signal the good quality of the counterparty, e.g. a financial service provider, reducing the transaction costs of the counterparty that has to verify the provider's ability to deliver the services. This is particularly true for market-based systems, where information asymmetries are particularly high and the system relies on third parties to bridge the gap. However, authorisation or listing requirements may also create barriers if they (directly or indirectly) discriminate between domestic and foreign investments and entities. This is often the case for local marketing rules of investment products. More specifically, there are requirements in EU Directives, such as UCITS (Art. 92), that are interpreted by most of the financial authorities as the basis to mandate local facilities (customer service) and paying agents in the authorisation process for foreign entities. These local agents are often not even used because nowadays cross-border payments and information flow are much easier and cheaper than in the past, when these rules were originally put into place. This also ties investment fund providers to the local market structure for banking services, which might be very expensive in some European countries and increase uncertainty of transaction costs. As a result, this situation is an additional cost for non-domestic companies wishing to offer investment products on a pan-European level. In addition, there are also national differences in the filing process for UCITS, including registration fees, which make procedures more burdensome for cross-border service providers. These aspects could be left to regulatory competition in the presence of a regulatory environment for the marketing of investment products that does not leave pockets of uncertainty over costs. A review of procedures, nonetheless, may be necessary to understand whether different quality standards for supervision hide behind some of them. ESMA or the European Commission might be best placed to do that.

Furthermore, the fragmentation of rules and procedures for the marketing of investment products keeps distribution channels fairly different across member states. A review of marketing rules to ensure no discrimination between foreign and local distributors, together with rules to improve transparency of products (as discussed above), would provide a tool to open up distribution channels and increase choice and returns for end investors.

Private placement

Issuance requirements are also important aspects for the development of private placement markets, which currently rely on local contractual arrangements. The development of harmonised standards by market initiatives shall provide sufficient tools to further develop this funding source. Since there is no clear domestic framework, there are no relevant barriers to the accessibility to those markets that may require a policy intervention. Market initiatives should be able to achieve an efficient result under the monitoring of supervisory authorities.

Open access

The creation of a common market for capital requires greater integration of the market infrastructure. As markets are still fragmented, there have been instances in the past of incumbent market infrastructures attempting to increase barriers for competitors trying to access the local market and compete on service provision. As a result, the new MiFID rules introduce open access requirements that will address the potential obstructing behaviours of incumbent infrastructures,[66] but there should be constant monitoring of the procedures set up by domestic financial authorities to resolve disputes and provide access to non-domestic market infrastructures. ESMA might need more binding powers in the mediation of the implementation of open access requirements locally, if the national authority does not sufficiently justify the decision concerning an access request. In particular, different interpretations may emerge regarding the requirements that may entitle the local incumbent to forbid access in case, for instance, access would create 'undue risk' to the stability of the infrastructure.

Execution policies

For several investors, access to financial markets and instruments depends on the intermediation of brokers and other intermediaries because they provide the infrastructure to cut the high costs of a direct connection with a marketplace. In this type of contractual relationship, execution policies provide the terms of access for investors and for competition among intermediaries, as investors (at least professional and institutional ones) would compare different policies. Execution policies also define the strength of the intermediary's efforts to make the execution of a financial transaction as successful as possible, considering the investors' preferences. However, the implementation of execution policies diverges across countries. This is particularly true for retail investors, whose protection depends on the quality of execution policies. Execution policies are difficult to implement especially for retail investors, while institutional ones have the contractual power to negotiate terms with their intermediary. As a consequence, implementation of execution policies for retail investors has thus far relied on a static approach (a 'box-ticking' exercise), which for instance does not require a constant update of competing trading venues to source quotes for execution. This static implementation also produces an impact on market structure, as the lack of harmonised practices places new trading venues and intermediaries at a disadvantage when trying to enter a local market. It thus leaves too much discretion at the intermediary level, as conditions related to costs remain vaguely defined (De Manuel & Valiante, 2014).[67] MiFID II

---

[66] See "Open access requirements for CCPs and trading venues" in the MiFID II RTS submitted by ESMA to the European Commission, available at www.esma.europa.eu/system/files/2015-esma-1464_-_final_report_-_draft_rts_and_its_on_mifid_ii_and_mifir.pdf, p. 275.

[67] For instance, under the current MiFID framework, the best execution for retail investors is determined by 'price and cost' (Art. 44, Impl. Dir. MiFID I), but "where there is more than one

attempts to improve the quality of execution policies, but a more uniform cross-country implementation is even more important for building a pan-European market architecture. A weak framework for the implementation of execution policies leaves potential newcomers (such as trading venues) unable to predict the costs of the different execution policies applied locally to their ability to access the (retail) trading flow, which is so important to gain a stable market share and compete fairly. This space for discretionary action potentially increases the expected negative impact and probability of discrimination based on nationality. Conditions for the provisions of execution policies to retail investors should be more dynamic, with a binding annual revision, more specific conditions for the identification of a 'material change' that triggers the revision and possibility for investors to easily compare policies with the use of a standard format.

Corporate actions

A security is a bundle of property rights and, in particular when it comes to equity shares, can involve different ongoing corporate actions, such as voting, share splits, dividend distribution and so on. Entry of a non-domestic market infrastructure can be impaired by local rules concerning the execution of corporate actions. As this problem concerns different company laws, market initiatives have recently looked at harmonising the standards used to implement corporate actions, rather than making corporate actions uniform across the European Union. In this way, the infrastructure should be able to cope with different regimes without facing the additional costs of changing all the procedures and increasing predictability of cross-border costs. Nonetheless, this harmonisation process is not yet complete, but implementation is ongoing and expected to be completed by end 2016. Authorities need to monitor this process very closely, but additional results, for instance, may come from the policy intervention on reporting formats for company filings, as discussed in previous sections.

---

competing venue" the "firm's own commissions and costs for executing the order on each of the eligible execution venues shall be taken into account" (Art. 44.3, Impl. Dir. MiFID I). This general and unspecified clause on costs makes it hard for authorities to assess whether the whole best execution framework has been effectively implemented at all. New MiFID II rules do not address the broad scope of this clause, which may be ineffective in addressing the issue.

Table 4.5 Selected examples of outstanding cross-border barriers

Cross-border barrier	Nature	Cost predictability	Outcome
1. **Execution policies**	Artificial	No	Immediate action
2. **Tax discrimination**	Artificial	Yes	Action needed
3. **Local facilities, paying agents & other marketing rules**	Artificial	Yes	Action needed
4. **Corporate action standards**	Artificial	Yes	Action needed
5. **UCITS filing process**	Artificial	Yes	Action needed
6. **Passport processing fees**	Artificial	Yes	Action needed

Note: This is not an exhaustive list of artificial and structural barriers to cross-border financial transactions.

Tax discrimination

Tax treatment plays a role in financial contracting (entry). In some countries, such as Denmark, a lower withholding tax rate is charged on Danish domiciled investment funds (KPMG, 2014). Most notably, those Danish investment funds that have the status of 'IMB' may receive total exemption at fund level from dividends distributed to them. As a result, similar investment funds may be treated differently according to their nationality. This example is not the first in the recent history of capital markets in Europe and perhaps will not be the last. An action plan at European level should review all current taxation arrangements at national level and monitor their development over time. The following section discusses further tax discrimination cases in exit procedures.

4.6.2 Exit procedures

Definition

Accessibility to markets also depends on fair exit requirements, in particular when financial contracting requires an exit as part of the renegotiation process. Exit procedures are all those rules or actions that are (directly or indirectly) involved in exiting a financial transaction. The objective of these procedures is to lower the transaction costs involved in the renegotiation of a financial contract. Such procedures may include collection or refund of withholding taxes on dividends, exit rights for investors (investment products) or exit charges, among others.

Exit rights

Investors may enter a financial transaction for several reasons. However, over time, these reasons may evolve and the conditions that were favourable when entering the contract may change. Contractual conditions usually set the procedures for exiting a financial transaction, especially in the case of more intermediated financial instruments, such as investment products. For plain vanilla products, the ability to exit is defined by the liquidity in the market and thus might just require the immediate execution of a sale transaction at market price. Investment products, however, might consist of multiple investments and thus exit procedures might be burdensome. Transparency of exit conditions and charges are overly important to shape incentives, especially in a cross-border setting, where investors might have to deal with a different language or multiple exit conditions in different countries that are often left to multiple national legislations. Transparency and simplification should be the guiding principle to ensure that exit procedures are fair and do not add unnecessary costs to cross-border transactions. The extent of application of these principles should also depend on the investors to whom these products are potentially addressed. As for the disclosure requirements for entry purposes, the fair implementation of exit rights would also be one of the defining aspects of a good quality distribution channel for investment products.

Withholding tax procedures

Taxation also plays a role in the renegotiation (exit) of a financial transaction. In the contracting phase, the ex ante incentives that taxation may create are very important, especially if they provide a bias towards specific instruments (debt versus equity, for instance). Nonetheless, taxation might become a source of concern for cross-border transaction in particular when it comes to collection and refund procedures of the withholding tax. In particular, the concern is with the different procedures adopted by member states, which can be rather costly and lead to substantial costs. The European Commission (2009, 2015e) reports three major costs generated by the complexity of the withholding tax reclaim procedures: an opportunity cost due to delayed claims and payments estimated at €1.84 billion per year; €5.47 billion per year of tax relief that is not reclaimed; and administration costs related to the reclaim procedures of about €1.09 billion per year. This complex and fragmented procedure thus costs in total roughly €8.4 billion per year. This is a significant cost that is passed onto investors, plus the negative incentives for those investors that refrain from entering a cross-border transaction due to the additional or uncertain cost of going through burdensome local procedures to reclaim the tax. This kind of barrier provides cost predictability, as it puts a cap on pursuing the procedure that is equal to the value of the tax reclaim, but it is nonetheless expensive.

As a consequence of these additional cross-border costs, both the European Commission and the OECD have set up groups that have produced two reports with recommendations (OECD, 2013; T-Bag, 2013). In particular, among the areas identified by the two reports, regulators should prioritise the harmonisation of the following areas across the EU:

- The use of electronic processing (including online access, if possible).
- The standardisation of tax reclaim formats (even including the possibility to submit the form in English).

- The recognition of authorised intermediaries (AI)[68] that can collect taxes or claim exemptions or reductions on behalf of their clients periodically, e.g. annually, on a pooled basis (using the Power of Attorney, PoA, tool).
- The acceptance of self-declaration of residence (instead of producing a certificate for every transaction).
- The creation of memoranda of understanding (MoUs) among national agencies to share information about fiscal residence and withholding tax reporting for the specific transaction, using a common identification system (also called Taxpayer Identification Number, or TIN).

These changes should promote the widespread use of relief-at-source mechanisms (ex ante), allowing also the possibility to look into case-by-case tax reclaims if a relief-at-source cannot be applied (but limiting it to well-defined exceptions).

Table 4.6 Selected examples of outstanding cross-border barriers

Cross-border barrier	Nature	Cost predictability	Outcome
1. Withholding tax refund and collection procedure	Artificial	Yes	Action needed
2. Full disclosure of exit charges and conditions	Structural	-	Action needed

Note: This is not an exhaustive list of artificial and structural barriers to cross-border financial transactions.

Outstanding barriers

The set of exit procedures that may affect the costs of a financial transaction and (directly or indirectly) the incentives of an investor to enter a cross-border transaction is typically an area where policy-makers have not focused much in the past. Nonetheless, potential barriers in this area are highly damaging for cross-border trading, especially if there is no disclosure and they operate under conflicting national legislation. More work should be done to monitor and map market and supervisory practices in this area.

[68] The TRACE Implementation Package (OECD, 2013) suggests that the AI would need to be compliant with a list of requirements and apply different sets of regulation to their own clients, such as know-your-customer rules, anti-money laundering rules, and so on. It would also be subject to independent reviews of its compliance by the source country (which can of course be different from the country where the intermediary has been authorised). Most important, the AI would have to set up different agreements with the various source countries where the AI operates.

Key findings #13.

- A well-functioning market ensures at all times that entities and financial instruments (admission procedure) can access markets based on fair and objective criteria, allowing contracting or renegotiation of a financial transaction at the lowest transaction cost.

Market entry

- Local supervisory authorities, in some instances, still apply discriminatory requirements based on nationality of the service provider, e.g. the use of local payment agents. For instance, more attention should be paid to supervisory practices in implementing open access requirements for market infrastructure. There are also examples of practices that may result in tax discrimination, which should be further investigated.
- Stricter oversight of execution policies is important not just for the quality of execution, but also to reduce barriers to entry for competing market infrastructure and brokerage services.
- Different formats and procedures also affect the integration of post-trading infrastructures, which are still imposing additional costs to cross-border versus domestic financial transactions. Corporate actions, among other factors, are a key source of such high costs.

Market exit

- Local tax procedures regarding the collection and refund of withholding taxes is a source of cost on cross-border transactions, which is estimated to top €8 billion per year. Bolder action is required to push member states to adopt harmonised and electronic collection and refund procedures.
- Availability of exit rights and transparency of exit conditions are important aspects of a financial transaction, especially for investment products. There is currently no harmonised regime concerning the disclosure of such information, which is usually left to patchy national requirements.

4.7 Enforcement

Legal certainty & ex ante incentives

Enforcement includes all public and private measures to ensure the smooth performance or renegotiation of a financial contract. It plays a fundamental role both in the contracting and renegotiation phase because it provides certainty to the counterparties on how their claim will be treated, even in a situation in which one of the counterparties is unable to perform. The ex-ante incentives, which a good enforcement mechanism provides, are crucial for contracting in a cross-border setting with multiple jurisdictions and legal systems. The effect of trust on contracting is strongest when companies are located in countries with better legal enforcement (Bottazzi et al., 2011). European rules do not necessarily need to provide a fully harmonised environment, but rather ensure the legal certainty of the procedures and leave it to counterparties to discount as much as possible the costs of the different legal systems in the pricing of the financial transaction. Certainty over the enforcement and accountability for misconduct is an important aspect for financial contracting. Uncertainty of enforcement proceedings, in effect, may produce a lack of enforcement and impact the cost predictability of a cross-border financial transaction, reducing ex ante incentives to enter into a contract in the first place. Unclear obligations for the counterparties may signal weak enforcement and can also lead to more misconduct.

Public & private enforcement

Chapter 2 reviews the empirical literature on how financial markets are typically more developed in countries with better enforcement regimes. An effective enforcement mechanism consists of both private and public mechanisms, which not only include sanctioning powers by centralised authorities, but also an efficient judicial system that stimulates private settlements and other private enforcement mechanisms (decentralised enforcement). The unmatched ability in the United States to pursue securities law violations with both public and private enforcement tools provides companies with a market-based system with lower cost of capital to access market funding and so control contestability (Doidge et al., 2004, 2009; Hail & Leuz, 2006; Coffee, 2007). Enforcement would therefore play the role of limiting the negative effects on financial contracting of both moral hazard (via the ex-ante threat of sanctions and ex post public/private monitoring) and contract incompleteness (via allowing the orderly management of a financial claim if a counterparty fails or is likely to fail to meet his/her obligation).

Credible deterrence

Both private and public enforcement, therefore, jointly provide the conditions for a credible deterrence, i.e. the minimisation of the net expected profits from wrongdoing. These expectations have two components: the probability of succeeding in the wrongdoing and the size of the profits generated by the wrongdoing. These profits would have to be compared with the expected costs of the wrongdoing, i.e. the probability of getting caught multiplied by the size of the sanction (monetary and/or criminal). In a dispersed market environment, the probability of getting caught is naturally fairly low, while the reward from the misconduct is fairly high, as the source of funding is potentially the whole market for financial instruments. As a consequence, enforcement is a crucial tool to ensuring market confidence that financial contracting in a market-based system will not result in exploitation by a more informed counterparty. Both public and private enforcement, by public authorities and private investors that monitor trading activities (misconduct deterrence), influences the probability of getting caught. Moreover, public enforcement authorities typically set the legal sanction via regulation, but private enforcers can actually impose significant direct sanctions via the judicial system, e.g. class litigations, and indirect ones by barring from the wrongdoer the possibility of raising funds in the future (reputational mechanisms). This points to the importance of two key components: a punitive system of sanctions and a well-functioning judicial system. Ex ante requirements, such as authorisation procedures to engage in financial services provision, are also monitoring tools that would be able to support deterrence of misconduct.

4.7.1 *Public enforcement*

Public enforcement & cost of capital

Public enforcement mainly focuses on the implementation of the rules, via ongoing monitoring of their actual application by member states and their policing actions to ensure that market participants are compliant, e.g. sanctions. A growing body of literature shows the negative impact of weak public enforcement mechanisms on the cost of capital and the effective functioning of capital markets (among others, Hail & Leuz, 2006, and Christensen et al., 2015). Public enforcement improves financial depth and is as important as disclosure requirements and private enforcement mechanisms (Jackson & Roe, 2009).

Public enforcement includes multiple areas that can help to minimise the net benefits of the wrongdoing in a market-based system (see, among others, IOSCO, 2015): the supervisory architecture (including powers of intervention, governance, information sharing and other regulatory practices), the sanctioning regime and the architecture of the legal system, e.g. securities law and judicial system.

The European

The enforcement of financial markets regulations typically depends on a solid architecture of supervising institutions with sufficient legal powers to offer immediate and effective action for enforcing rules in the market. In recent years, the European supervisory architecture has dramatically changed. The de Larosière report (de Larosière Group, 2009) upgraded the old committees under the Lamfalussy procedures into European agencies, with the legal basis that these new agencies would provide a better approximation of the law in member states than national authorities in achieving the single market objective (Article 114 TFEU). The recent decision of the European Court of Justice on short selling (case C-270/12) has reinterpreted the past doctrines in *Meroni* and *Romano* to confirm the soundness of the legal basis,[69] and clarified that the Commission can delegate discretionary powers to European agencies, as long as this does not involve policy choices.[70] Despite the simplification that a single supervisory authority could bring to European markets, it is unlikely that the ECJ decision will anyway lead to the creation of a full-fledged European financial markets authority without a Treaty change. There is, however, further space to strengthen the role of ESMA within the network of European securities regulators. In effect, ESMA's role could actually be very important to overcoming uncertainty in the enforcement proceedings that may affect the cost predictability of a cross-border financial transaction and are an impediment to capital markets integration.

supervisory architecture

ESMA currently coordinates the work of the authorities under a peer review model and, together with the sister agencies in banking and insurance sectors, has obtained delegated powers under Articles 17 and 18 of the ESA Regulations (EC Regulation n. 1095/2010, in the case of ESMA). Article 17 empowers ESMA to review the supervisory practices of national authorities and issue a recommendation. Then the European Commission can issue a formal opinion to the national supervisor, which (if the national authority does not comply) allows ESMA to issue a compliance decision directly

ESMA's key powers

[69] With the Meroni case (Case 9/56 Meroni v High Authority [1957 and 1958] ECR 133), the ECJ ruling confirmed that the delegation of powers to EU agencies is possible, if these powers are already in the remit of the European Commission. Most notably, these agencies cannot be granted powers to adopt general regulatory measures (thus conditions for their intervention shall be clearly specified) and they cannot not exercise political discretion. The recent Short Selling case (Case C-270/12, United Kingdom v Council and European Parliament) updated the Meroni doctrine by ruling that there can be conferral of discretionary powers to EU agencies in the following situations: the body is a European Union entity, and the conditions for the use of delegated powers and their scope are specified in detail. These powers cover individual decisions, as well as acts of general application, such as the emergency powers in the Short Selling Regulation (Art. 28).

[70] The ECJ ruling on short selling also implies that Article 114 TFEU could be a sound basis for the creation of a full-fledged European supervisory authority enjoying discretionary powers, provided that no policy choices are regulated and the conditions for the use of those powers are clearly defined ex ante. There might not even be the need for the formal endorsement of ESMA's decision by the European Commission.

applicable to market participants. Article 18 gives ESMA direct powers to take specific actions immediately applicable to the national authority or to the market when the Council detects an emergency situation, e.g. halting trading on all markets. ESMA has also gained exclusive competence in some areas, such as the licensing and supervision of credit rating agencies and trade repositories. Interestingly, ESMA has also acquired the role of settling disagreements among competent authorities, whenever an authority of a member state requests ESMA to assist the authorities in reaching an agreement (Article 19). In particular, the authority can set time limits for the negotiation and take a binding decision on whether the authorities should take an action if they fail to agree within the given limit (Article 19.3).

Breach of EU law (Art. 17)

There are several areas, such as the enforcement of accounting rules (as described in section 4.5.1), where implementation of EU rules and supervisory practices greatly diverge, increasing uncertainty about the general enforcement of the rules and thus the predictability of costs for existing regulations and their impact on financial transactions. Whether or not ESMA could have an exclusive competence in some of these areas (for listed companies, for instance), ESMA's top management has so far made little use of powers under Article 17, which are key to dealing with uncertainty generated by different applications of EU rules by national competent authorities (NCAs). Most of the actions brought to the Board of Appeal explicitly mention the lack of initiative by ESMA in this area, which may significantly weaken the credibility of the institution and keep the institution far away from the market practice.

The procedure to begin investigations under Article 17 was defined by a 2012 Decision of the Board of Supervisors.[71] The procedure is cumbersome and shifts the responsibility of the proceedings entirely onto the Chairperson, who can decide to proceed either without formal request (ex officio) or on a request by an EU institution, competent national authority or stakeholder group. The Chairperson operates with very limited resources and runs the risk of being held accountable for a wrong decision by the Management Board first (if there is disagreement with the Vice Chairperson) and the Board of Supervisors later on, as the Board will have to take the final decision to issue the recommendation (which may then become a binding decision) based on the information collected by the Chairperson.[72]

---

[71] See Decision n. ESMA/2012/BS/87rev, available at www.esma.europa.eu/system/files/2012-bs-87rev_rules_of_procedure_on_breach_of_union_law_investigations.pdf.

[72] On top of this, the General Court (Third Chamber), 9 September 2015, SV Capital OÜ v European Banking Authority (EBA), Case T-660/14, ruled on the lack of jurisdiction of the Board of Appeal of

The recommendation issued by ESMA would apply to those competent authorities that are taking the very same decision in the Board of Supervisors. In addition, this is the same Board that decides on the extension of the office of ESMA Chairperson and Vice-Chairperson, which is then proposed to the European Parliament for approval. As a result of this cumbersome procedure for launching an investigation into a breach of European Union law (Article 17) and the conflicting roles in its governance, ESMA management has instead resorted to the Article 16 'soft' peer review mechanism, which allows ESMA to issue a (non-binding) recommendation to the national competent authority, in case it finds the local authority's supervisory practice diverging significantly from the uniform EU interpretation. In this case, the national competent authority is not bound to implement the changes, but it can comply or explain why it is using a different supervisory approach. Thus far this procedure has not often succeeded.

In the end, the peculiar proceedings of Article 17 affect ESMA's ability to credibly tackle national decisions and promote supervisory convergence in a cross-border setting with national gold-plating of EU laws. The procedure under Article 17 would thus benefit from a more independent action of ESMA's top management, perhaps shifting either the approval to issue the recommendation under Article 17 or the appointment of the top management (or both) to either the European Commission, the European Parliament or another body that does not have such internal conflicts. The European Parliament could indeed directly nominate, approve and review ESMA's top management directly. Overall, there is a need to strengthen the EU-wide interests in ESMA's decision-making process (Demarigny, 2015).

It would also help to beef up the management board with additional independent components (nominated by the Commission), and to give them voting rights in the Board of Supervisors, which would ensure that the EU-wide interest leads the decision-making process. Moreover, there is strong incompatibility between the extensive role given to ESMA in achieving supervisory convergence and the limited resources currently allocated to the execution of these tasks, and there is a limit to the number of tasks that can be delegated to NCAs without affecting convergence.

Shared competences

As discussed in the section on price discovery, there are areas where national practices jeopardise the implementation of common EU rules and thus the convergence of supervisory and market practices. For instance, the design of accounting rules may require the support of an agency with legal powers to

EBA in relation to a decision under Article 17 of Regulation 1093/2010. This creates additional uncertainty about the effectiveness of this entire procedure.

uniformly enforce some accounting practices. The Securities and Exchange Commission (SEC) in the United States, for example, is directly responsible for the enforcement of accounting rules in listed companies. Currently, ESMA coordinates a network of European supervisors, called the European Enforcers Coordination Sessions (EECS), which produces periodically a list of decisions taken by local supervisors that facilitates analysis of emerging issues related to supervision of IFRS for over 6,400 listed companies across Europe. These analyses are intended to be merely informative, in the hope that this will stimulate a common approach among supervisors to IFRS enforcement. Evidence discussed above suggests otherwise.

In this respect, strengthening ESMA's direct supervisory role in well-defined areas to support regulatory and supervisory convergence can be done in different ways. One of the following three options, to be implemented with a 'phase-in' timeline, could be considered:

a. to give ESMA direct supervision of all the EU listed companies;
b. to give ESMA direct supervision of all the firms that will be classified as 'cross-border' (either listed-only or both listed and unlisted companies);[73] and
c. to give the possibility to an entity, when applying for an EU passport, to opt in to ESMA supervision.

The areas where ESMA will exercise its direct supervision will be in reality part of a joint supervisory framework, through colleges of supervisors, with ESMA (acting with voting rights) issuing binding decisions for NCAs as part of the ESMA network. The structure of the legal mechanism could follow the Single Supervisory Mechanism setting for the banking union. The areas in which ESMA could already take up the role of direct supervisor could be:

- Accounting rules and practices (for listed companies and for unlisted companies if common EU principles will be law).
- Supervision (with harmonisation of timing and formats) and collection of listed company filings.
- Coordination of the national business registries.
- Listing authority of firms that want to list in an EU country different from where their legal headquarters is located (and for those listed companies that want to opt-in).
- Licensing and ongoing supervision of UCITS and AIFs.
- Prospectus issuance approval and monitoring.

---

[73] A 'cross-border' firm could be any legal entity with legal headquarters and operations in a different EU country.

- Supervision over the licensing procedures of the EU passport granted by NCAs, and the power to revoke the license.

ESMA's decision in these areas would become binding for NCAs and be enforced directly by them, so the new supervisory architecture would still rely on the current network and resources of national authorities, rather than requiring a new parallel infrastructure. The decision-making structure of bodies like the SSM or the new European Deposit Insurance Scheme could offer a good benchmark to start discussions. Nonetheless, ESMA's resources would need to be beefed up substantially to keep up with the new tasks. Costs would be most likely offset by benefits stemming from the simplification of supervisory practices in capital markets transactions for investors and other market participants.

Exclusive competencies

For what concerns exclusive competences for specific entities, on top of credit rating agencies and trade repositories, the exclusive competence of ESMA should be extended to all the entities that are the backbone of a pan-European market architecture. This list would include data providers (under MiFID II), benchmark providers, auditors (via more binding powers over the committee of national auditing oversight bodies), trading venues, central counterparties (CCPs) and International Central Securities Depositories (ICSDs).

Due process

Furthermore, recent cases, such as SV Capital versus EBA (see footnote 72) and Grande Stevens and others versus Italy,[74] have emphasised the importance of ensuring an adequate judicial review of the ESAs' decisions in order to strengthen their decision-making power and credibility, and to protect human rights (D'Ambrosio, 2013; Lamandini et al., 2013; Ventoruzzo, 2014). In particular, the courts highlighted the importance of a due process, with a fair trial run by an independent tribunal that has full jurisdiction over the case (and not an internal body of the authority or a body that can only review the legality of the action). It would also require a public hearing for the defendant to exercise his right to be heard. As a consequence, the possibility to challenge the decision in court should provide enough due process. Cooperation between ESMA and national courts that may review the decision formally adopted by NCAs may support this process. In particular, a cooperation arrangement with the possibility to transmit information and submit observations, as well as training a programme for national judges, could be set up in a way similar to what was done for competition rules under vertical agreements (Regulation 1/2003).

---

[74] Grande Stevens et autres c. Italie, No. 18640/10, 18647/10, 18663/10, 18668/10, European Court of Human Rights (ECHR), 4 March 2014.

Retail investor protection

The ESMA Regulation (Article 9, Reg. 1095/2010) introduced another important power for the authority, i.e. the possibility to ban a financial product that could harm consumers. However, the lack of resources to monitor markets at sale level makes the use of this tool very difficult. In effect, the absence of a pan-European agency that provides unified supervision in matters of consumer protection is indeed the missing building block of the European institutional architecture. There is no real pan-European capital market without greater retail markets integration, and national consumer laws protect the current fragmentation of retail service providers. A dedicated agency would provide support for a more coherent implementation of national consumer laws and limit the proliferation of local supervisory approaches, and offer more tools for investor protection with stronger monitoring and easier access to private enforcement tools against harmful practices. In conjunction with Article 17 on the breach of EU law, the expansion of Article 9 to create a common European consumer agency (for retail investors) within ESMA could be an important institutional innovation that finally fosters greater retail markets integration. It would reduce NCAs' role in retail investor protection matters and be a single point of entry for reporting widespread harmful practices. Nonetheless, a pan-European consumer agency can only achieve meaningful results if it is provided with sufficient resources to deal with the cross-border nature and the dimension of its potential regulatory and supervisory activities.

Sanctions

As discussed above, in a dispersed environment with high net expected profits from wrongdoing, (punitive) sanctions deter misconduct and thus are an important ex ante incentive for financial contracting in market-based systems. European Commission (2010) and IOSCO (2015) suggest that sanctions should be effective, proportionate and dissuasive. As a result, sanctions should at least require the restitution of the amount of all the profits made by the wrongdoing (IOSCO, 2015). However, in order to be more dissuasive, punitive damages, i.e. multiples of the illicit profits, and criminal charges might be considered.

Europe's landscape today is fairly fragmented; some NCAs do not have proper sanctioning powers (such as authorisation withdrawal) or can impose only administrative sanctions (European Commission, 2010). Also, the efficiency of the judicial system (courts) plays an important role in supporting sanctioning powers, which is also scattered across Europe (see following section). High variance across Europe might be a source of distrust among supervisors and hence a source of fragmentation. Further convergence can result in greater trust among supervisors, service providers and investors; providers might be more willing to offer, and investors to enter into, a cross-border financial transaction if common safeguards against misconduct are in place. Sanctioning powers do not only include the absolute level of the sanction, but also the type (administrative or criminal, monetary sanctions or remedial action). In particular, 'double jeopardy' legal risk, i.e. the risk of having to undergo a second procedure for the same conducts, requires an accurate separation between criminal and administrative charges, e.g. respectively with the intention to harm or in case of negligence (Ventoruzzo, 2014). This distinction should be taken into account when further harmonising sanctioning powers. Moreover, the disclosure of past enforcement actions and sanctions, together with transparent proceedings and objectives pursued by enforcement agencies, are also important for building metrics and measuring the effectiveness of regulatory actions.

Finally, self-regulatory organisations (SROs), such as standard setters or professional bodies, help raise awareness of best practices and illicit market practices – awareness that may have existed domestically before common EU rules were implemented.

Table 4.7 Selected examples of outstanding cross-border barriers

Cross-border barrier	Nature	Cost predictability	Outcome
1. Accounting rules enforcement mechanism (role of ESMA)	Artificial	No	Immediate action
2. 'Good faith' acquisitions	Artificial	No	Immediate action
3. Acquisition and disposition of securities	Artificial	No	Immediate action
4. Conflict-of-laws regime	Artificial	No	Immediate action
5. Art. 17 Breach of EU law proceedings (ESMA)	Structural	n/a	Action needed
6. Art. 9 consumer protection powers (ESMA)	Structural	n/a	Action needed
7. Sanctioning regimes (illicit profits restitution)	Artificial	Yes	Action needed

Note: This is not an exhaustive list of artificial and structural barriers to cross-border financial transactions.

Securities law

Securities law provides the essential toolkit for public enforcement of a financial contract. It embodies the necessary legal architecture to recognise and apply contractual terms in financial transactions. Uncertainty over the legal terms of a financial transaction creates significant entry barriers in a cross-border setting, which can increase the cost of financial contracting for non-domestic investors that have to interact with different legal systems. Over the years, the European Union has introduced important safeguards to ensure legal certainty in the application of securities laws across Europe. The

Settlement Finality Directive (SFD; 98/26/EC) and the Financial Collateral Directive (FCD; 2002/47/EC, amended in 2009 with Directive 2009/44/EC) have, among other actions, propped up financial infrastructures with 'safe harbouring clauses' in case of default of a participant; extended collateral use to credit claims; and ensured enforceability of close-out netting arrangements. The derogation to the principle of equal treatment of insolvency creditors, by providing a safeguard for close-out netting if one of the counterparties fails, has been widely implemented across the European Union with the FCD. However, more should be done to verify whether the implementation has gone smoothly and has not created major inconsistencies.

Yet there are no clear rules to protect collateral use, which can go from hand to hand without the final counterparty's knowledge of the legal conditions of the security used as collateral before he/she bought it. As a result, the lack of a widespread recognition of 'good faith' acquisition can produce cross-border barriers and additional costs for investors trying to enter into a cross-border transaction with the risk that the acquisition can later be voided (AFME, 2015). Without such protection in a cross-border context, collateral may lose its fungibility, reducing incentives to enter into a financial transaction in the first place. There is currently no common framework in Europe in this area. However, this should not result in inflating the number of securities by recognising them twice (for the last acquirer and for the parties involved in the voided transaction). This mechanism should therefore establish which party must suffer the loss of the securities, which would then be compensated with alternative securities or financially.

Furthermore, the problem with 'good faith' acquisitions also raises the question of whether EU securities laws recognise the acquisition or disposition, i.e. respectively, the transfer of the legal title or the acquisition of limited rights, of a security at the same point in time. In a cross-border setting, lack of harmonisation can increase downside risks because of the inability to predict potential costs ex ante, thus inhibiting cross-border financial contracting. There should be perhaps a clear recognition that the registration of the security in the account of the CSD is the decisive moment when the legal transfer takes place.

Finally, when disposing or acquiring a security, a conflict of laws may emerge, especially in a cross-border setting. The conflict-of-laws regime in the Financial Collateral Directive (Article 9, FCD) states that the law where the relevant account is maintained should govern the matters related to the book entry of securities. The possibility to extend this regime to the Settlement Finality Directive (SFD) and in general to all other acquisition or disposition of securities, as suggested by AFME (2015), or to establish a new harmonised regime for other transactions than collateral arrangements, should be considered.

4.7.2 Private enforcement

Private enforcement mechanisms

As discussed in Chapter 2, the law and finance literature suggests that private enforcement is a key driver of financial markets development (see, among others, La Porta et al., 2006; Djankov et al., 2008). While a relationship-based system (like traditional banking) can live with low quality rules and legal environment, because of the superior information that the bank has, the prompt and unbiased enforcement of contracts by courts is a pre-condition for the viability of a market-based system (Rajan & Zingales, 1998b). Private enforcement is a solid protection against the negative effects of contract incompleteness, i.e. the inability to write a contract that anticipates all future scenarios. Private enforcement of contracts is also crucial to protecting investors (venture capitalists), in the early stage of financing a small firm, against the free riding of the entrepreneur (Balcarcel et al., 2010). Doidge et al. (2004, 2009) show that companies tend to cross-list in markets where there is a reduced risk of expropriation by controlling shareholders, mostly to complement private control with external monitoring, in line with the literature on law and finance. This is also consistent with earlier findings by Pagano et al. (1998), which suggest that, in a large database of Italian firms, IPOs are usually followed by higher turnover of control, as markets keep higher pressure on controlling shareholders and managers than unlisted environments.

In a market-based system, however, this threat is credible if there is a well-functioning private enforcement mechanism. Private enforcement mechanisms include:

a. Gatekeepers' supervision (including liability).
b. Insolvency proceedings.
c. Private settlements.
d. Functioning of courts, e.g. choice-of-law regime.
e. Whistle-blower programmes and other redress procedures, e.g. class actions, minority shareholders rights.

The role of gatekeepers

As extensively discussed in Chapter 2, market-based mechanisms rely on public information produced by third parties, which make their living by selling this information to a large set of investors. In a dispersed environment, the role of third parties is also crucial to the selection and aggregation of information used in the enforcement of financial claims and to securities markets as a whole. This information is also complementary to disclosure rules and it facilitates the work of supervisors in many instances. This has led over the years to an established framework for gatekeepers' liability when they fail to support the enforcement of rules (Kraakman, 1986; Choi, 1998). The gatekeepers' function (and their liability) emerged as a fundamental aspect for market-based economies, especially in the aftermath of scandals like Enron and WorldCom in the United States, or Parmalat, Cirio and Vivendi in Europe. Gatekeepers can be defined as:

"[...] reputational intermediaries who provide verification and certification services to investors. These services can consist of verifying a company's financial statements (as the independent auditor does), evaluating the creditworthiness of the company (as the debt rating agency does), assessing the company's business and financial prospects vis-a-vis its rivals (as the securities analyst does), or appraising the fairness of a specific transaction (as the investment banker does in delivering a fairness opinion)" (Coffee, 2002, p. 1405).

This definition can also include lawyers when they provide their reputation to validate the legality of a financial transaction (Partnoy, 2001; Fisch & Rosen, 2003; Coffee, 2002, 2003).

In providing signals to the market about the riskiness of a company and its financial products, gatekeepers mostly rely on their reputational capital. However, the corporate scandals of important listed companies in early 2000s and the more recent issues with ratings of subprime collateralised securities suggest that the reputational capital is not sufficient to ensure the quality of the gatekeepers' activity at all times. As a result, in a cross-border setting, divergence of supervisory practices in relation to gatekeepers (entry and ongoing requirements) might result in distrust among supervisors relating to the quality of their information and action, and thus may raise costs for end investors. In this respect, the decision to assign exclusive competence to ESMA for what concerns credit rating agencies would be an important precedent for extending the competence to other gatekeepers. Among these, auditors are very important for the harmonisation of accounting practices, and the industry is naturally becoming more integrated at European level. Industry concentration at national level can also put gatekeepers in a position of dominance versus national firms and supervisors, undermining the effectiveness of supervisory practices. Moreover, there is no harmonised framework concerning gatekeepers' liability, leaving different tiers of quality of supervisory enforcement across member states and creating market perceptions of the quality of the service, often offered cross-border. The centralisation of supervision may also help deal with a common legally recognised framework for gatekeepers' misconduct.

Insolvency proceedings

There are particular situations in which enforcing exit or renegotiation of a financial contract is harder, due to the financial conditions of one of the two counterparties. In these cases, it indeed may occur that the counterparty is unable to fulfil his/her financial obligation, due either to a temporary liquidity issue (he/she has enough assets that could cover the value of the financial obligation) or to a more fundamental mismatch between assets and liabilities (insolvency), which may not be solved by a sale of assets or a temporary liquidity facility. In the latter case, an insolvency proceeding may begin. These proceedings would impose losses on equity holders and only in part (depending on seniority) on all the different classes of creditors, including bondholders. Some operations, such as netting of derivatives contracts, would be shielded from bankruptcy procedures due to safe-harbour clauses. In a cross-border setting, the inability to know what would happen if the counterparty (located in another country) does not perform is a major source of uncertainty concerning the total expected costs of the financial transaction. As a result, this lack of information about the procedures that are involved in the renegotiation phase of a financial contract and their expected costs create a big ex ante disincentive to enter into a cross-border capital market transaction. This is particularly the case for market-based systems, as the transaction often takes place in an environment with dispersed agents and limited knowledge about the credit risk of the counterparty. In addition, there might be no long-term relationship between the two counterparties to shape incentives, as for a relationship-based system, e.g. traditional banking.

Insolvency proceedings deal with the attempt to recover the viability of a business from bankruptcy. These proceedings may affect several stakeholders, whether debtors or creditors. In effect, since they directly touch material interests of certain groups of individuals, there is always a strong conservative pressure when it comes to modifying these rules or updating them to the most recent developments. It took almost a century for the United States to develop a full-fledged federal system of bankruptcy norms and courts (from 1898 to 1973; Tabb, 1995). Even though the clause giving power to introduce a common federal legislative framework was already enshrined in the US Constitution (Art. I, §8, cl. 4), it was only exercised almost a century later (1898) and fully implemented almost two centuries after that (1973). That clause was introduced precisely because of the harm that fragmented bankruptcy laws could inflict on creditors resident in other states and thus on interstate commerce.

Therefore, it is reasonable to expect that a full-fledged EU bankruptcy regime would not emerge soon, but a fragmented system of bankruptcy laws can be damaging for cross-border financial transactions. In this respect, there are important areas in which harmonisation can be achieved without putting into question the different legal systems currently coexisting in Europe, leaving the counterparties of a cross-border financial transaction to price these differences (measurable ex ante) in the final price. There are two important areas *vis-à-vis* insolvency proceedings that deserve more attention: the regulatory framework and the judicial review by dedicated courts.

For what concerns rules, the European Commission already started to look into it in the early 2000s, with Regulation n. 1346/2000, which established for the first time a conflict-of-law regime and cooperation obligations. Most recently, with the entry into force of a recast of Regulation n. 1346/2000 (Regulation n. 2015/848), the European Commission, among other things, extended the scope of the EU bankruptcy rules to the pre-insolvency stage, improved the conflict-of-law regime and revised the regime for secondary proceedings.

Nonetheless, the recast still leaves grey areas when it comes to the implications for cross-border financial contracting. The complexity and political intricacies of the matter may require a step-by-step approach. Following the methodology developed in this report, some areas may still have a significant impact on cross-border capital market activity, as they are sources of cost unpredictability. These areas, already partially included in the Commission's proposal, are:

- Conflict-of-law (jurisdiction).
- Secondary proceedings.
- Stays.
- Company evaluation methods.

Conflict-of-law regime

For what concerns the identification of the jurisdiction that will apply to the insolvency proceeding, Regulation 2015/848 establishes the framework for a conflict-of-law system in cross-border insolvency matters, except for the wind-up of insurance, credit institutions and investment undertakings, which are dealt with by separate legislation. The standard conflict of law system relies on the principle that the proceeding will be opened in the Centre of Main Interest (COMI) of the debtor (*lex concursus,* Article 3). The proceeding will also cover related actions (mainly under civil and commercial laws). For companies, this is presumed to be the registered office, unless there is proof of the contrary (Art. 3.1). For individuals, the regulation refers to the 'habitual residence' of the individual without further specifying how 'habitual residence' shall be defined. The uncertainty about the COMI presumption for individuals can still be a source of cross-border litigation in insolvency proceedings (in line with Wessels, 2003), after the new rules enter into force in 2017. In addition, the decision on where a proceeding should be opened can be challenged in any court in Europe, while it may be preferable to have a centralised European court where such decisions can be subject to appeal. Alternatively, the law could provide for the possibility of European courts to resolve matters of where to open proceedings, with a contractual clause signed ex ante.

Secondary proceedings

Another important matter for cross-border capital market transactions is the possibility to open secondary proceedings in one of the European countries where the debtor has an establishment in order to protect local creditors. This is a great source of concern for cross-border activities, as it affects the predictability of the costs that a counterparty may incur in a cross-border insolvency proceeding. With the recast, on the one hand, the possibility to open a secondary proceeding is expanded from merely winding-up proceedings to potentially any proceeding (including restructuring) in any place of operation where *"the debtor carries out an economic activity with human means and assets"* (Recital 24; Article 2 n. 10). On the other hand, though, the new rules allow the court of establishment (not the court where proceedings are opened), upon request of the main liquidator (who can also be heard), to refuse the opening if not necessary to protecting the interest of local creditors. In addition, the main liquidator can offer to treat the local creditors in the same way as they would have been treated if a secondary insolvency proceeding had opened in that country. While this was an improvement compared to the previous rules, it is still a cumbersome procedure, which leaves a great deal of ex ante uncertainty about the applicable law to the cross-border litigation. The court of the country of establishment may tend to be excessively conservative in its attempt to protect local creditors under local laws (as history tells us). Perhaps, as requested for the conflict-of-law in the opening of the main insolvency proceeding, a more neutral venue, such as a European court, may be a more appropriate judge of the need to open a secondary proceeding in the country of establishment. In addition, the situations in which the interests of the local creditor may be affected could be further specified in a positive list (whatever is not in the list shall not be considered a justification for opening the secondary proceeding). Most notably, this uncertain procedure can be a great disincentive if we consider the high variance among European countries for what concerns the quality of the insolvency framework (see Figure 4.6, Figure 4.7 and Figure 4.8). For instance, the UK insolvency framework is very efficient in terms of time needed to complete the proceedings, recovery rates and period required to commence proceedings. However, it is less so for what concerns the creditors' involvement in the process and the reorganisation proceedings. There is perhaps a trade-off among these features and the insolvency framework has to strike the right balance among all of them. It also depends on the availability of other enforcement mechanisms and of a solid legal basis for the contractual claims (securities law).

Figure 4.6 Insolvency framework index (0-16)

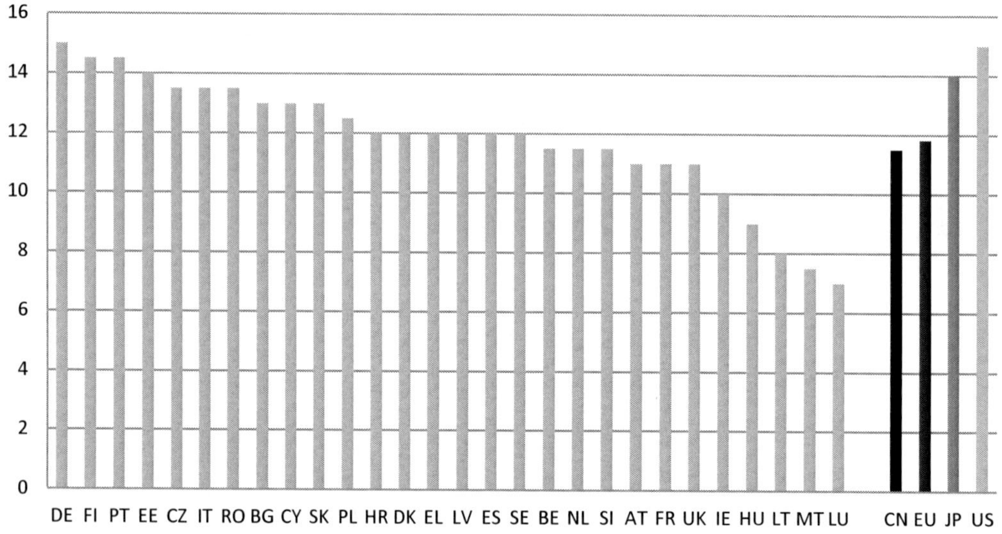

Note: It is an average of four indexes (commencement of proceedings, management of debtor's assets, creditor participation, reorganisation proceedings). For more information on the methodology, see www.doingbusiness.org/methodology/resolving-insolvency.

Source: 2016 Doing Business Report (World Bank).

Figure 4.7 Recovery rates (% of assets)

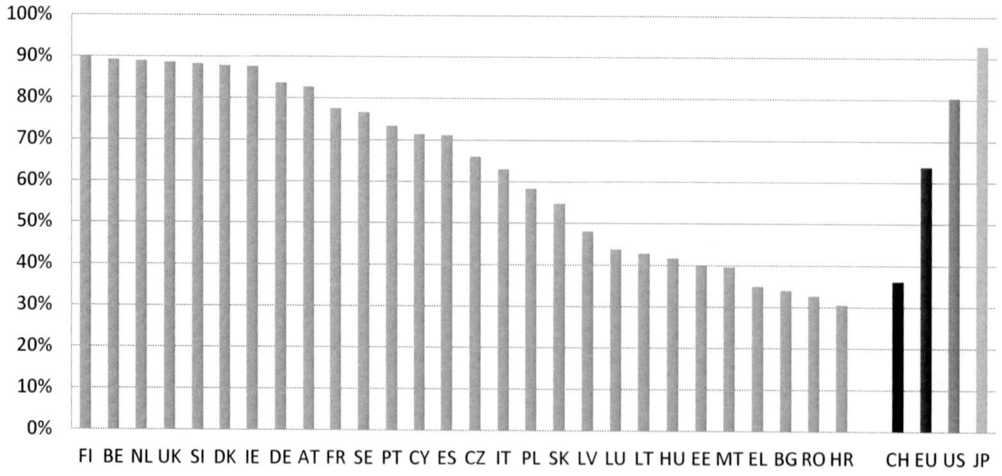

Source: 2016 Doing Business Report (World Bank).

Figure 4.8 Number of years required to resolve an insolvency

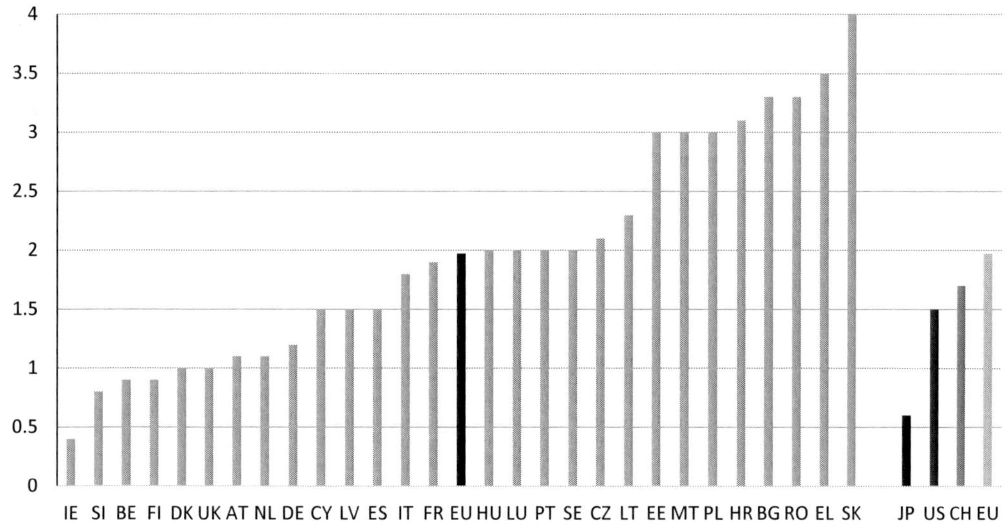

Source: 2016 Doing Business Report (World Bank).

On average, however, Europe lags well behind Japan and United States in all the key quality indicators of insolvency proceedings and scores even below China for what concerns the average time to resolve an insolvency proceeding. As a result, there is an important need for the EU to improve the general insolvency framework. EU rules could set the general framework in the areas here identified and then leave market forces to direct their financial transactions towards those systems that provide better judicial protection in case of insolvency. This approach could also promote competition among member states to improve their insolvency framework and bring it up to international standards. The risk of forum shopping is tempered by the current clause that does not allow openings in the current country of incorporation if the change took place in the previous three months; it is also in the interest of the creditor that the other counterparty is in a country where his/her claim can be dealt with as well as possible in case of insolvency.

Stays

Another source of potential uncertainty for cross-border financial transactions comes from the use of stays, i.e. court injunctions to temporarily halt creditor actions on debtor assets. There is currently no common regime on when and under what conditions stays can apply. Therefore, it would be preferable to consider an automatic stay when the proceedings begin, rather than the current patchy framework across Europe. Stays on request could be more clearly regulated with criteria as objective as possible.

Company valuation

According to the type of insolvency proceeding, for instance in the case of restructuring, the use of a specific methodology to assess the value of a company can improve certainty. For instance, the use of a methodology assuming the 'going concern' or the liquidation of the company can lead to very different actions and company valuations. A liquidation approach would yield a lower value, which will be close to market value at that point in time. In a cross-border setting, there is a risk that multiple methodologies would apply, especially if a secondary proceeding takes place and the evaluation is done in accordance with local laws, which may be different from laws in the country of the main proceeding. Some general guidance about which methodology could be used in the different circumstances could be of great help to increase the certainty of procedures and cost predictability. For instance, in restructuring proceedings, a going concern approach should always be used.

The role of courts & 29th regime

Notwithstanding the importance of rules and common principles at EU level, private enforcement heavily relies on the quality of the judicial system. The functioning of courts is a key determinant of the choice of legal system in which the cross-border transaction could take place. The credibility of the threat to resort to the judicial review is crucial to the functioning of alternative dispute resolution (ADR) mechanisms. Private enforcement might thus involve multiple judicial systems across Europe. As they currently stand, there is a lot of variability among member states in the quality of the judicial process (see Figure 4.9). Even countries where the efficacy of public institutions is above average, such as the Netherlands, the quality of the judicial process might be fairly low.

Figure 4.9 Quality of judicial processes index (0-18)

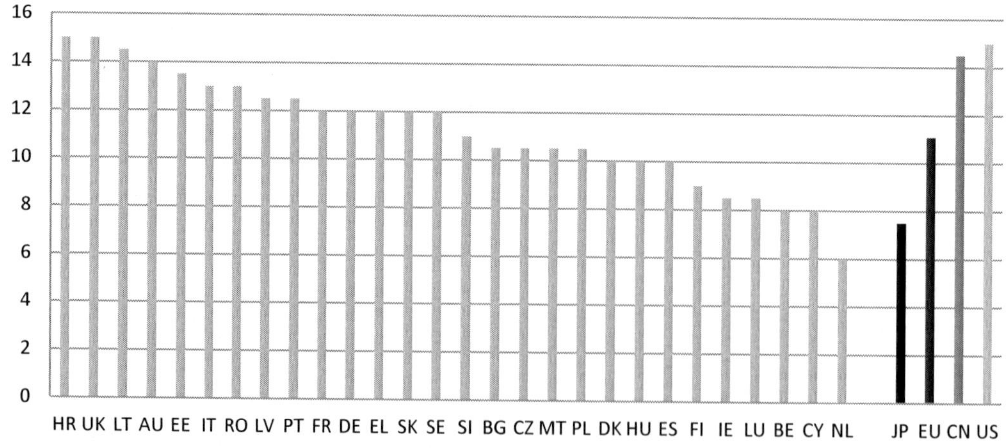

Note: It is the sum of four indexes (court structure and proceedings, case management, court automation, alternative dispute resolution). For more information about the methodology, see www.doingbusiness.org/methodology/enforcing-contracts.

Source: 2016 Doing Business Report (World Bank).

With regard to the time required to enforce a contract through courts, the variance among EU countries is even higher and the average puts the EU well ahead of the US, China and Japan (see Figure 4.10). The EU average is an important indicator because the EU adopts a passport for the provision of financial services and every country's judicial system has the same weight. For instance, the judicial system where the insolvency proceeding would take place, under the COMI presumption, is the country of incorporation, which can be any EU member state (according to the EU passport approach).

Figure 4.10 Time required to enforce a contract through the courts (calendar days)

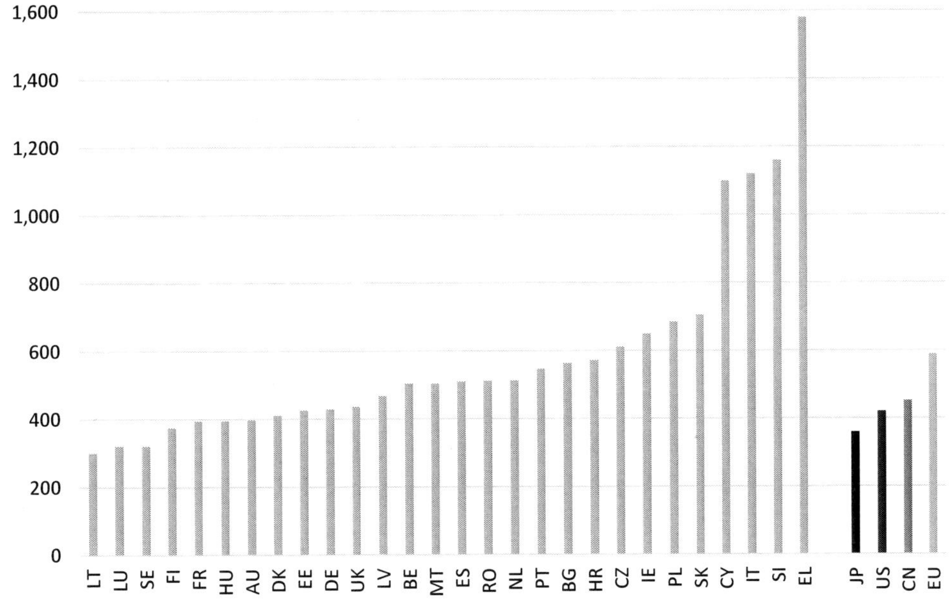

Source: 2016 Doing Business Report (World Bank).

As a result, in the long run it may prove very difficult to bring the judicial systems in all EU member states up to the same level. Hence, it may be better to consider the gradual introduction of a 29th regime for cross-border financial transactions (for insolvency to begin with) under the judicial review of dedicated EU courts with branches in every member state. Domestic financial transactions would still be run under local proceedings, with the possibility to opt in to the EU proceedings.

Redress procedures

Private enforcement also relies on the possibility to resort to alternative redress procedures, especially for retail investors, who cannot leverage their contractual power to push the counterparty to agree to a private settlement. In 2013, the European Commission published a Communication (European Commission, 2013) and a list of recommendations to member states

(Recommendation n. 2013/396/EU) in order to improve the domestic frameworks for collective redress procedures, both for monetary and injunctive actions. The current landscape is fairly fragmented and mainly focused on domestic cases with, on average, high litigation costs, long proceedings and limited enforcement of rulings (European Commission, 2012). Nonetheless, retail banking and investment services are among the top areas where private enforcement activities can be more effective, as there is usually a gap in contractual power between the service provider and the investor. Redress procedures can take the form of either a judicial proceeding or an alternative dispute resolution (ADR). While the judicial solution is expensive for both parties, the ADR schemes are certainly easier to handle and most of the complaints typically end with a non-judicial solution. In 2001, the European Commission introduced the Financial Dispute Resolution Network (FIN-NET), which was set up to deal with cross-border disputes in financial services.[75] Due to the small central infrastructure and the reliance on a burdensome procedure run by local members, as well as the limited awareness of the wider public of its existence, FIN-NET never really took off, with only 3,000 cases reviewed in 2014 (European Commission, 2015f). In the UK, the Financial Ombudsman Service (FOS) was also created in 2001 but only in 2013-14 did it process complaints: more than 2 million in total, solving over 230,000 of those complaints below £150,000 (for a recent overview of the ADR schemes across Europe, see CFA Institute, 2014). While the guidance of EU-wide principles could be beneficial for local ADRs, in a cross-border setting, it is highly unlikely that a local authority (on behalf of FIN-NET) will properly consider the complaint and hold discussions with foreign financial authorities without the real mediation of a neutral institution to facilitate the cross-border interaction. Even if there would be more awareness about the existence of FIN-NET, the uncertainty of the procedure represents a barrier to cross-border retail financial services provision, as local authorities run it. In particular, clients may not trust a cumbersome procedure that provides no certainty of the time required and the procedure to get to a resolution of the complaint if the service provider is located in another country.

As a consequence, on the one hand, it may be beneficial to strengthen the quality of ADR procedures across member states, which were first introduced by the Directive 2013/11. On the other hand, a bolder action is required to create an EU-wide 'Financial Ombudsman Service', which could be run by a dedicated infrastructure under the current European Ombudsman Service and Network, acting as a single point of contact for users of financial services. This body of the European Ombudsman, through the use of the Ombudsman

---

[75] For more information, see http://ec.europa.eu/finance/fin-net/index_en.htm.

network, would collect and run a first screening of the complaints regarding the cross-border provision of financial services, which may involve a local broker and a foreign service provider (FSP). Once the validity of the complaint is confirmed, the EU body would connect the national ombudsmen that are involved and offer mediation in defining which of the two national authorities shall take the initiative first, in relation to whether action will be taken against the local broker or the FSP. The FSP may also provide services directly in the country, in which case the EU 'ombudsman' will directly contact the home authority and make sure that the procedure begins and the results or request for information are communicated to the user.

Table 4.8 Selected examples of outstanding cross-border barriers

Cross-border barrier	Nature	Cost predictability	Outcome
1. **Automatic stays**	Artificial	No	Immediate action
2. **Company's valuation in insolvency (principles)**	Artificial	No	Immediate action
3. **Secondary proceedings (conditions & deciding court)**	Artificial	No	Immediate action
4. **COMI for legal persons (uncertain presumption) & decentralised appeal**	Artificial	No	Immediate Action
5. **Gatekeepers' supervision and liability**	Structural	n/a	Action needed
6. **Quality of judicial systems**	Structural	n/a	Action needed
7. **Cross-border alternative dispute resolution (ADR) mechanism (EU-wide)**	Structural	n/a	Action needed

Note: This is not an exhaustive list of artificial and structural barriers to cross-border financial transactions.

Safety valves

Another important element, which cannot be easily expressed in an actionable policy action, regards the role of legal 'safety valves' to allow the rigid legal infrastructure of the financial system (necessary for creating liquidity in good times) to bend in case of major systemic events (Pistor, 2013). In practice, for the effective functioning of safeguards for European capital markets, this implies an overall EU strategy in ensuring that legal safeguards, such as bail-in requirements, collective action clauses and so on, are fully actionable all across the EU. The solid mechanisms of private enforcement thus need to be fine-tuned in such a way that they are able to bend in case of a systemic event via embedded mechanisms of private risk sharing, rather than disorderly bail-outs or unlimited monetary policy interventions. The academic literature in this field is still developing, but attention at European level to map the presence and effectiveness of these 'valves' across member states would be a good prudential exercise.

Key findings #14.

- Enforcement is about legal certainty of procedures to enforce a legitimate financial claim or deter the market from misconduct.
- Credible deterrence in market-based systems requires punitive sanctions and a well-functioning judicial system.

Public enforcement

- Europe's institutional architecture is still in the making, but recent cases (such as the ECJ Short Selling case) confirm that much can be achieved without reforming the EU Treaties. In particular, more attention should go towards the Article 17 breach of EU law procedure, to make it more effective and easy to use, removing the internal conflicts in its governance mechanism. ESMA's lack of independence from national supervisory authorities is an inner conflict that does not allow this procedure to work. Shifting the approval procedure of the investigation and the designation for approval of ESMA's top management to the Commission and/or the European Parliament might ensure greater use of this indispensable tool for regulatory and supervisory convergence.
- ESMA should also receive exclusive support for additional entities, such as benchmark providers and CCPs, and for specific areas, such as accounting rules. The authority would still rely on the network of national authorities, but its decisions would be binding in the identified areas via a college of supervisors. The supervisory architecture should also be reinforced with institutional changes that ensure the defendant's due process and the right to be heard.
- Investor protection is a crucial aspect of financial market oversight. Building on the powers of Article 9 of ESA Regulations, an agency dedicated to ensuring investor protection across the many regulatory areas and supervisory actions across Europe might be more effective than current loose national supervisory actions.
- Sanctions are also another area of divergence across member states. Combined with passporting of financial services, high variance of sanctioning regimes (going from administrative sanctions to criminal charges) among member states is a source of significant regulatory and supervisory arbitrage that can discourage cross-border trading activities and service provision.
- The lack of an EU conflict-of-law regime and other securities law safeguards (such as 'good faith' acquisition) can undermine enforcement of contractual claims and increase cost unpredictability.

Private enforcement

- Private enforcement relies on three key elements: the quality of the judicial system, the quality of gatekeepers, and the accessibility of alternative dispute resolutions (ADRs).
- The quality of the judicial system is on average very low, compared to other advanced economies, such as Japan and the United States. Investment might be necessary to improve the functioning of courts across Europe. The difficulty of bringing all 28 judicial systems to the same level may require a gradual introduction of a European system of courts, which will be dedicated to cross-border financial transactions in specific areas such as insolvency proceedings and/or enforcement of private contracts.
- Nonetheless, the market can on its own improve the judicial system by removing other sources of costs to cross-border competition. The selection that service providers will make on the basis of the quality of the judicial system shall produce incentives for member states to converge.
- Current insolvency proceedings, even after the recent reform, are still inadequate to ensure sufficient cost predictability. COMI presumption for legal persons, (automatic) stays, secondary proceedings, and standards for companies' valuation are important areas that should be further harmonised. Bolder EU action is required to remove strong national resistance.
- Gatekeepers (such as auditors, rating agencies and law firms when performing some functions) are key users of public information, which they re-elaborate and aggregate in a way that exerts an impact on capital market pricing; they are an important mechanism for stimulating private enforcement. Their crucial role in managing information cannot be controlled by divergent supervisory practices. In line with what has been done for credit rating agencies, it may be appropriate to shift the competence for some of them (such as auditors) at European level, perhaps under ESMA, in order to strengthen the joint supervision of accounting rules via mandatory oversight of the committee of national auditing oversight bodies (CEAOB).
- Access to ADRs is still very cumbersome for some national ones and certainly for counterparties to cross-border financial transactions. This may require the establishment of an EU institution working as a mediator between financial authorities. The current FIN-NET solution is inadequate for the proportions and complexity of cross-border capital markets activities.

4.8 Integration barriers: a quick recap

Uncertainty

There are multiple barriers to cross-border market-based financial contracting and to a better quality of financial integration in Europe. Data comparability issues for price discovery processes, discriminatory actions in market entry or exit and legal uncertainty in the enforcement of financial claims and in the application of rules defining the financial environment are key sources of both artificial and structural barriers against the deepening of Europe's capital markets. The objective of an action plan should be the gradual removal of these barriers and the creation of better conditions for the diversification of the financial ecosystem and in order to favour cross-sectional (cross-country) risk sharing via capital markets.

Methodology

This chapter is not an exhaustive list of barriers but rather offers a selection of them and a methodology for their identification and to prioritise intervention, on the basis of their impact on the cost predictability of a financial transaction. In this way, policy actions can be promptly directed to reduce cost uncertainty and improve the information flow in order to stimulate more cross-border dealing (for more details, see sections 4.2 and 4.4). Working groups of experts at European and domestic level should work in all the identified areas to investigate those barriers and directly drive policy actions within the CMU action plan, exposing the outstanding practices by individual member states that are most damaging to the single market for capital. The proposed methodology also helps identify areas in which an immediate 'top-down' policy response is necessary, complementing the 'bottom-up approach' proposed by the European Commission. In effect, immediate actions needed to reduce cost unpredictability have to be taken in an environment where there are already 28 pre-existing legal systems, laws, supervisory institutions, local vested interests, etc. The proposed approach tries to strike a balance between harmonisation (top-down) and regulatory competition (bottom-up). As a result, this methodology sets three key measurable objectives:

- Improving data comparability of underlying assets and financial instruments.
- Reducing discrimination in market entry and exit.
- Increasing legal certainty and accessibility of public and private enforcement mechanisms.

*Table 4.9 Summary table: selected barriers**

Cross-border barrier	Nature	Cost predictability	Policy outcome
	PRICE DISCOVERY		
C. INFORMATION ON THE UNDERLYING ASSET			
1. IFRS optionality for discretionary evaluation models, e.g. asset retirement obligations, loan provisions, etc.	Artificial	No	Immediate action
2. Domestic accounting standards for non-listed companies	Artificial	No	Immediate action
3. Reporting formats, e.g. half-yearly reports, etc.	Artificial	Yes	Action needed
4. IFRS optionality for alternative calculation methodologies or definitions, e.g. classification problems, such as pension interest in income statement as interest or operating expense or calculation of debt at amortised cost or fair value	Artificial	Yes	Action needed
5. Alternative performance measures	Artificial	Yes	Action needed
6. Voting share disclosure threshold	Artificial	Yes	Action needed
7. Domestic business registries	Artificial	Yes	Action needed
8. Credit risk scoring and national credit bureaux	Artificial	Yes	Action needed
9. Rules on related-party transactions (definitions)	Artificial	Yes	Action needed
10. Compensation disclosure (methodology)	Artificial	Yes	Action needed
11. Off-balance sheet items	Structural	No	Action needed
D. FINANCIAL INSTRUMENT INFORMATION			
12. Ongoing performance disclosure (domestic market practices)	Artificial	No	Immediate action
13. Exit conditions disclosure (domestic market practices)	Artificial	No	Immediate action
14. Prospectus disclosure requirements	Artificial	Yes	Action needed
15. Calculation methodologies for PRIIPs costs (in KID)	Artificial	Yes	Action needed
16. Market data formats/costs & national bias in securities listing	Artificial	Yes	Action needed

	EXECUTION		
D. ENTRY PROCEDURES			
17. Execution policies	Artificial	No	Immediate action
18. Tax discrimination	Artificial	Yes	Action needed
19. Local facilities, paying agents & other marketing rules	Artificial	Yes	Action needed
20. Corporate action standards	Artificial	Yes	Action needed
21. UCITS filing process	Artificial	Yes	Action needed
22. Passport processing fees	Artificial	Yes	Action needed
E. EXIT PROCEDURES			
23. Withholding tax refund and collection procedure	Artificial	Yes	Action needed
24. Full disclosure of exit charges and conditions	Structural	n/a	Action needed
	ENFORCEMENT		
C. PUBLIC ENFORCEMENT			
25. 'Good faith' acquisitions	Artificial	No	Immediate action
26. Acquisition and disposition of securities	Artificial	No	Immediate action
27. Conflict-of-laws regime	Artificial	No	Immediate action
28. Art. 17 Breach of EU law proceedings (ESMA)	Structural	n/a	Action needed
29. Art. 9 consumer protection powers (ESMA)	Structural	n/a	Action needed
30. Sanctioning regimes (illicit profits restitution)	Artificial	Yes	Action needed
D. PRIVATE ENFORCEMENT			
31. Automatic stays	Artificial	No	Immediate action
32. Company's valuation in insolvency (principles)	Artificial	No	Immediate action
33. Secondary proceedings (conditions & deciding court)	Artificial	No	Immediate action
34. COMI for legal persons (uncertain presumption) & decentralised appeal	Artificial	No	Immediate Action
35. Gatekeepers' supervision	Structural	n/a	Action needed
36. Cross-border alternative dispute resolution (ADR) mechanism (EU-wide)	Structural	n/a	Action needed

Note: *This list contains a selection of the most harmful barriers and should not be considered exhaustive.

Investor protection

In tackling all these barriers, policy responses should be calibrated as a function of their ultimate beneficiaries. In particular, specific actions may be needed to fill the informational gap and promote greater cross-border activity of smaller counterparties (for instance, 'retail investors' or 'minority shareholders') that are usually less informed and more exposed to the strategic behaviour of the counterparty, who will try to gain as much as possible from this asymmetry (moral hazard). As a result, there is usually additional attention by policy-makers to investor protection. Laws to protect retail investors are mainly national, leading to divergent supervisory practices. Action at EU level to protect retail investors via a common supervisory umbrella, led by ESMA or another European agency, could offer a true level playing field for investors and service providers alike. A well-functioning market needs participation as wide as possible and retail investors (either as creditors or shareholders) are crucial to the diversification of the trading flow and to balancing informed and uninformed traders, which are very important for market liquidity.

References

Abiad, A., D. Leigh, and A. Mody (2007), "International Finance and Income Convergence: Europe is Different", IMF Working Paper No, WP/07/64, March.

Acemoglu, D. and F. Zilibotti (1997), "Was Prometheus Unbound by Chance? Risk, Diversification, and Growth", *Journal of Political Economy*, Vol. 105, No. 4, August, pp. 709-751.

Acemoglu, D. and F. Zilibotti (1998), "Information Accumulation in development", IEES Seminar Paper, No. 652, Stockholm University, Stockholm.

Adjaouté, K., and J.P. Danthine (2004), "Equity returns and integration: is Europe changing?", *Oxford Review of Economic Policy*, Vol. 20, No. 4, pp. 555-570.

Admati, A. R. and P. Pfleiderer (1988), "A Theory of Intraday Patterns: Volume and Price Variability", *Review of Financial Studies*, Vol. 1, No. 1, pp. 3-40.

Adrian, T., M. Fleming, O. Shachar and E. Vogt (2015), "Has U.S. Corporate Bond Market Liquidity Deteriorated?", Blog post on Liberty Street Economics, Federal Reserve Bank of New York, October 5th, available at http://libertystreeteconomics.newyorkfed.org/2015/10/has-us-corporate-bond-market-liquidity-deteriorated.html#.VpYjKlKkHSF.

AFME (2015), "Note on securities law reform", May (www.afme.eu/WorkArea/DownloadAsset.aspx?id=12769).

Aggarwal, R., and S. Dahiya (2006), "Demutualization and public offerings of financial exchanges", *Journal of Applied Corporate Finance*, Vol. 18, No. 3, pp. 96-106.

Aggarwal, R., B. Lucey and C. Muckley (2010), "Dynamics of Equity Market Integration in Europe: Impact of Political Economy Events", *Journal of Common Market Studies*, Vol. 48, No. 3, pp. 641-660.

Aghion, P. and P. Bolton (1992), "An Incomplete Contracts Approach to Financial Contracting", *Review of Economic Studies*, Vol. 59, No. 3, July, pp. 473-494.

Akerlof, G.A. (1970), "The market for 'lemons': qualitative uncertainty and the market mechanism", *Quarterly Journal of Economics*, Vol. 84, pp. 488-500, August.

Albuquerque, R. (2003), "The composition of international capital flows: risk sharing through foreign direct investments", *Journal of International Economics*, Vol. 61, pp. 353-383.

Alcidi, C. and D. Gros (2013), "Country adjustment to a 'sudden stop': does the euro make a difference?", Economic Papers, No. 492, European Commission, April.

Allen, C., M. Gasiorek and A. Smith (1998), "The competition effects of the Single Market in Europe", *Economic Policy*, Special Issue, October.

Allen, F. and D. Gale (1995), "A welfare comparison of intermediaries and financial markets in Germany and the US", *European Economic Review*, Vol. 39, pp. 179-209.

Allen, F. and D. Gale (2000a), Comparing Financial Systems, Cambridge, MA: MIT Press.

Allen, F. and D. Gale (2000b), "Financial Contagion", *Journal of Political Economy*, Vol. 108, No. 11.

Allen, F. and D. Gale (2004), "Financial Intermediaries and Markets", *Econometrica,* Vol. 72, No. 4, pp. 1023-1061, July.

Allen, F. and W-L. Song (2005), "Financial Integration and EMU", *European Financial Management*, Vol. 11, No. 1, pp. 7-24.

Allen, F. and D. Gale (1998), "Optimal Financial Crises", *Journal of Finance*, Vol. 53, No. 4, August.

Allen, F., and Gale, D. (1994), "Limited market participation and volatility of asset prices", The *American Economic Review*, Vol. 84, No. 4, September, pp. 933-955.

Allen, F., and Gale, D. (1997), "Financial markets, intermediaries, and intertemporal smoothing", *Journal of Political Economy*, Vol. 105, No. 3, pp. 523-546.

Allen, F., E. Carletti and D. Gale (2009), "Interbank market liquidity and central bank intervention", *Journal of Monetary Economics*, Vol. 56, pp. 639-652.

Allen, F., L. Bartiloro and O. Kowalewski (2006), "Does Economic Structure Determine Financial Structure", AFA 2007 Chicago Meetings Paper (http://ssrn.com/abstract=891313 or http://dx.doi.org/10.2139/ssrn.891313).

Allen, Franklin and Douglas Gale (1999). "Diversity of opinion and the financing of new technologies", *Journal of Financial Intermediation*, 8: 68-89.

Amir, E. and B. Lev (1996), "Value-relevance of nonfinancial information: The wireless communication industry", *Journal of Accounting and Economics*, Vol. 22, pp. 3-30.

Armour, J. (2005), "Who Should Make Corporate Law? EC Legislation Versus Regulatory Competition", Working Paper Series, No. 41, Institute for Law and Finance, Goethe University Frankfurt

Asdrubali, P., B. E. Sorensen and O. Yosha (1996), "Channels of Interstate Risk Sharing: United States 1963-1990", *Quarterly Journal of Economics*, Vol. 111, No. 4, pp. 1081-1110, November.

Assi, B. and D. Valiante (2011), "MiFID Implementation in the midst of the Financial Crisis", Research Report, European Capital Markets Institute (ECMI).

Ayadi, R. (2011). Integrating Retail Financial Markets in Europe: Between Uncertainties and Challenges. Centre for European Policy Studies (CEPS) Paperbacks.

Baele, L., and Inghelbrecht, K. (2008), "Time-varying integration, the euro and international diversification strategies", *European Economy Economic Papers*, European Commission, July.

Balcarcel, A., M. Hertzel and L. Lindsey (2010), "Contracting Frictions and Cross-Border Capital Flows: Evidence from Venture Capital", SSRN Working Paper, January (http://papers.ssrn.com/sol3/papers.cfm?abstract_id=1571928).

Balli, F., Kalemli-Ozcan, S., and Sørensen, B. E. (2012), "Risk sharing through capital gains", Canadian *Journal of Economics/Revue canadienne d'économique*, Vol. 45, No. 2, pp. 472-492.

Balta, N., and Delgado, J. (2009), "Home bias and market integration in the EU", *CESifo Economic Studies*, Vol. 55, No. 1, pp. 110-144.

Baltzer, M., L. Cappiello, R. A. De Santis and S. Manganelli (2008), "Measuring financial integration in new EU member states", ECB Occasional Paper Series, No. 81, March.

Bebchuk, L. A. (1999), "A rent-protection theory of corporate ownership and control", NBER Working Paper No. 7203. July.

Beck, T. and R. Levine (2002), "Industry growth and capital allocation: does having a market- or bank-based system matter?", *Journal of Financial Economics*, 64, pp. 147-180.

Beck, T., Demirgüç-Kunt, A., and Levine, R. (2007), "Finance, inequality and the poor", *Journal of economic growth*, Vol. 12, No. 1, pp. 27-49.

Beck, T., Demirguc-Kunt, A., Laeven, L., and Levine, R. (2008), "Finance, firm size, and growth", *Journal of Money, Credit and Banking*, Vol. 40, No. 7, pp. 1379-1405.

Beck, T., R. Levine, N. Loayza (2000), "Finance and the sources of growth", *Journal of Financial Economics*, Vol. 58, No. 12, pp. 261-300

Bekaert, G., C. R. Harvey, C. T. Lundblad and S. Siegel (2013), "The European Union, the Euro, and equity market integration", *Journal of Financial Economics*, Vol. 109, pp. 583-603.

Berger, A. N. (2003), "The efficiency effects of a single market for financial services", *European Journal of Operational Research*, 2003, Vol. 150.

Berger, A. N., and G. F. Udell (1990), "Collateral, loan quality and bank risk", *Journal of Monetary Economics*, Vol. 25, No. 1, pp. 21-42.

Bester, H. (1987), "The role of collateral in credit markets with imperfect information", *European Economic Review*, Vol. 31, pp. 887-899.

Bloomfield, M. J., Brüggemann, U., Christensen, H. B., and Leuz, C. (2015), "The Effect of Regulatory Harmonization on Cross-border Labor Migration: Evidence from the Accounting Profession", National Bureau of Economic Research (NBER) Working Paper, No. 20888 (http://www.nber.org/papers/w20888).

Bonfiglioli, A. (2008), "Financial integration, productivity and capital accumulation", *Journal of International Economics*, Vol. 76, No. 2, pp. 337–355.

Boot W. A. A. and A. Thakor (1997), "Financial System Architecture", *Review of Financial Studies*, Vol. 10, No. 3, pp. 693-733.

Boot, A. W. (2000), "Relationship banking: What do we know?", *Journal of Financial Intermediation*, Vol. 9, No. 1, pp. 7-25.

Bos, J.W.B. and H. Schmiedel (2007), "Is there a single frontier in a single European banking market?", *Journal of Banking and Finance*, Vol. 31, pp. 2081–2102.

Bottazzi, L., M. Da Rin, T. F. Hellmann (2011), "The importance of trust for investment: evidence from venture capital", NBER Working Paper, No. 16923, April.

Boyd, J. H. and B. D. Smith (1998), "The evolution of debt and equity markets in economic development", *Economic Theory*, Vol. 12, pp. 519-560.

Brunnermeier, M. K. and L. H. Pedersen (2009), "Market Liquidity and Funding Liquidity", *Review of Financial Studies*, Vol. 22, No. 6, pp. 2201-2238.

Cajueiro, D.O., P. Gogas, B. M. Tabak (2009), "Does financial market liberalization increase the degree of market efficiency? The case of the Athens stock exchange", *International Review of Financial Analysis*, Vol. 18, pp. 50-57.

Calomiris, C. W. and R. E. Litan (2000), "Financial Regulation in a Global Marketplace", Brookings-Wharton Papers on Financial Services.

Casu, B. and C. Girardone (2006), "Bank competition, concentration and efficiency in the single European market", *The Manchester School*, Vol. 74, No. 4, pp. 441-468.

Cecchetti, S. G. and E. Kharroubi (2012), "Reassessing the impact of finance on growth", BIS Working Papers, No. 381, July.

Cecchetti, S. G. and E. Kharroubi (2015), "Why does financial sector growth crowd out real economic growth?", BIS Working Paper, No. 490, February.

Cespa, G., and Foucault, T. (2013), "Sale of price information by exchanges: does it promote price discovery?", *Management Science*, Vol. 60, No. 1, pp. 148-165.

CFA Institute (2014), "Redress in Retail Investment Markets*", International Perspectives and Best Practices*, August.

Choi, S. (1998), "Market Lessons for Gatekeepers", *Northwestern University Law Review*, Vol. 92, No. 916, pp. 934-49.

Christensen, H. B., L. Hail and C. Leuz (2013), "Mandatory IFRS reporting and changes in enforcement", *Journal of Accounting and Economics*, Vol. 56, pp. 147-177.

Christensen, H. B., L. Hail, and C. Leuz (2015), "Capital-market effects of securities regulation: The role of implementation and enforcement", National Bureau of Economic Research (NBER) Working Document, forthcoming Review of Financial Studies (http://citeseerx.ist.psu.edu/viewdoc/download?doi=10.1.1.469.2688&rep=rep1&type=pdf).

Claessens, S. (2009), "Competition in the Financial Sector: Overview of Competition Policies", *World Bank Research Observer*, Vol. 24, No. 1 February.

Coase, R. (1937), "The Nature of the Firm", *Economica*, Vol. 4, p. 386.

Coffee, J. C. Jr. (2007), "Law and the Market: The Impact of Enforcement", *University of Pennsylvania Law Review*, Vol. 156, No. 2, pp. 229-311.

Coffee, J. C. Jr. (1994), "Competition Versus Consolidation: The Significance of Organizational Structure in Financial and Securities Regulation", *The Business Lawyer*, Vol. 50, p. 447.

Coffee, J. C. Jr. (2003), "The Attorney As Gatekeeper: An Agenda for the Sec", Columbia University School of Law, W.P. No. 221, April.

Commission of the European Economic Community (CEEC) (1966), "The development of a European capital market", Report of a Group of Experts chaired by Claudio Segre, November.

D'Ambrosio, R. (2013), "Due process and safeguards of the persons subject to SSM supervisory and sanctioning proceedings", *Quaderni di Ricerca Giuridica*, No. 74, Bank of Italy, December.

Darby, M.R. and E. Karni (1973), "Free Competition and the Optimal Amount of Fraud", *Journal of Law and Economics*, Vol. 16, No. 1, pp. 67-88.

Daske, H., L. Hail, C. Leuz and R. Verdi (2008), "Mandatory IFRS Reporting around the World: Early Evidence on the Economic Consequences", *Journal of Accounting Research*, Vol. 46, No. 5, December.

Daude, C. and M. Fratzscher (2008), "The pecking order of cross-border investment", *Journal of International Economics*, Vol. 74, pp. 94-119.

De Bruijn, R., H. Kox and A. Lejour (2008), "Economic benefits of an Integrated European Market for Services", *Journal of Policy Modelling*, Vol. 30, pp. 301-319.

De Manuel, M. and D. Valiante (2014), "A life-cycle approach to investor protection", ECMI Working Paper, No. 1, September.

Deakin, S. (2000), "Two types of regulatory competition: competitive federalism versus reflexive harmonisation. A law and economics perspective on Centros", *Cambridge Yearbook of European Legal Studies*, Vol. 2, p. 231.

Demarigny, F. (2015), "Investing and Financing Recommendations for the forthcoming Capital Markets Union", Report for the French Minister of Finance and Public Accounts (www.economie.gouv.fr/files/rapport_demarigny_en.pdf).

Demigurc-Kunt A., E. Feyen and R. Levine (2011), "Optimal s and Development: The evolving importance of banks and markets", World Bank, June.

Di Noia, C. (1999), "The Stock-Exchange Industry: Network Effects, Implicit Mergers, and Corporate Governance", *Quaderni CONSOB*, No. 33, March.

Diamond, D. W. and R. G. Rajan (2001), "Banks, short-term debt and financial crises: theory, policy implications and applications", Carnegie-Rochester Conference Series on Public Policy, Vol. 54, pp. 37-71.

Diamond, D. W. (1984), "Financial Intermediation and Delegated Monitoring", *Review of Economic Studies*, Vol. 51, No.3, pp. 393-414.

Diamond, D. W., and Dybvig, P. H. (1983), "Bank runs, deposit insurance, and liquidity", *Journal of Political Economy*, pp. 401-419.

Djankov, S., La Porta, R., Lopez-de-Silanes, F., and Shleifer, A. (2008), "The law and economics of self-dealing", *Journal of Financial Economics*, Vol. *88,* No. 3, pp. 430-465.

Doidge C., G. Andrew Karolyi, René M. Stulz (2015), "The U.S. Listing Gap", NBER Working Paper, No. 21181, May.

Doidge, C., G. A. Karolyi and R. M. Stulz (2004), "Why are foreign firms listed in the U.S. worth more?", *Journal of Financial Economics*, Vol. 71, pp. 205-238.

Doidge, C., G. A. Karolyi and R. M. Stulz (2009), "Private benefits of control, ownership, and the cross-listing decision", *Journal of Finance*, Vol. 64, No. 1, pp. 425-466.

Dorodnykh, E. (2011), "What Drives Stock Exchange Integration", *International Journal of Economic Sciences and Applied Research,* Vol. 6, No. 2, pp. 47-79.

Draghi, M. (2015), "Speech by the President at SZ Finance Day 2015", Frankfurt, March 16th

Easley, D., O'Hara, M., and Yang, L. (2013), "Differential access to price information in financial markets", Working paper (http://papers.ssrn.com/sol3/papers.cfm?abstract_id=1787029).

ECB (2015), "Financial Integration in Europe", April (www.ecb.europa.eu/pub/pdf/other/financialintegrationineurope201504.en.pdf).

Economides, N. (1993), "Network Economics with Application to Finance", *Financial Markets, Institutions and Instruments*, Vol. 2, No. 5, December, pp. 89-97.

Eichengreen, B., R. Gullapalli and U. Panizza (2011), "Capital account liberalization, financial development and industry growth: A synthetic view", *Journal of International Money and Finance*, Vol. 30, No. 6, October.

Eiling, E., Gerard, B., and De Roon, F. A. (2012), "Euro-zone equity returns: country versus industry effects", *Review of Finance*, Vol. 16, No. 3, pp. 755-798.

Engurgor, E. O. (2008), "Financial system structure and economic growth: structure matters", *International Review of Economics and Finance*, 17, pp. 292-305.

Enriques, L. (2004), "EC Company Law and the Fears of a European Delaware", *European Business Law Review*, No. 15, p. 1259.

Enriques, L. (2006), "EC Company Law Directives and Regulations: How Trivial They Are", *Journal of International Law*, Vol. 27, No. 1, Article 1.

Ergungor, O.E., (2004), "Market- vs. bank-based financial systems: Do rights and regulations really matter?", *Journal of Banking and Finance*, 28, pp. 2869-2887.

Ernst and Young (2015), "The JOBS Act: 2015 mid-year update. An Overview of implementation and an analysis of merging growth company trends", EY Analysis, September.

European Commission (2007), "European Financial Integration Report", Commission Staff Working Document, SEC(2007) 1696, Brussels.

European Commission (2009), "The Economic Impact of the Commission Recommendation on Withholding Tax Relief Procedures and the FISCO Proposals", Staff working document C(2009)7924.

European Commission (2010), "Reinforcing sanctioning regimes in the financial services sector", Communication from the Commission to the European Parliament, the Council, the European Economic and Social Committee and the Committee of the Regions, COM(2010), No. 716, December 8th.

European Commission (2012), "Report on the application of Directive 2009/22/EC on injunctions for the protection of consumers' interests", COM (2012) 635 final, June 11th.

European Commission (2013), "Towards a European Horizontal Framework for Collective Redress", Communication of the European Commission, COM(2013) 401 final, June 11th

European Commission (2015a), "Building a Capital Markets Union", Green Paper, COM(2015) 63 final, February 18th.

European Commission (2015b), "Action Plan on Building a Capital Markets Union", Communication, COM(2015) 468 final, September 30th.

European Commission (2015c), "Completing Europe's Economic and Monetary Union", The Five Presidents Report, June, available at http://ec.europa.eu/priorities/economic-monetary-union/docs/5-presidents-report_en.pdf.

European Commission (2015d), "Evaluation of Regulation (EC) N° 1606/2002 on the application of International Accounting Standards", Report from the Commission to the European Parliament and the Council, COM(2015) 301 final, available at http://eur-lex.europa.eu/legal-content/EN/TXT/PDF/?uri=CELEX:52015DC0301&from=EN.

European Commission (2015e), "Economic Analysis accompanying the Action Plan on Building a Capital Markets Union", Commission Staff Working Document, SWD(2015), 183 final, September 30th.

European Commission (2015f), "Better products, more choice, and greater opportunities for consumers and businesses", Green Paper on retail financial services, COM(2015) 630 final, December.

European IPO Task Force (2015), "Rebuilding IPOs in Europe Creating jobs and growth in European capital markets", Final Report of the EU IPO Task Force run by European Issuers, EVCA and FESE, March.

European Securities and Markets Authorities (ESMA) (2012), "Review of Greek Government Bonds accounting practices in the IFRS Financial Statements for the year ended 31 December 2011", ESMA Report, No. ESMA/2012/482, July 26th available at https://www.esma.europa.eu/sites/default/files/library/2015/11/2012-482.pdf.

Faria, A., P. R. Lane, P. Mauro, and G. M. Milesi-Ferretti (2007), "The shifting composition of external liabilities", *Journal of the European Economic Association*, Vol. 5 (2-3), April-May, pp. 480-490.

Fisch, J. E. and K. M. Rosen (2003) "Is There a Role for Lawyers in Preventing Future Enrons?", *Villanova Law Review*, Vol. 48, No. 4, p. 1097.

Flöstrand P. and N. Ström (2006), "The valuation relevance of non-financial information", *Management Research News,* Vol. 29, No. 9, pp. 580-597.

Foucault, T., M. Pagano, E. Roell (2013), *Market Liquidity: Theory, Evidence, and Policy,* Oxford University Press.

Freixas, X., B. Parigi and J-C. Rochet (2000), "Systemic Risk, Interbank Relations, and Liquidity Provision by the Central Bank", *Journal of Money, Credit and Banking*, Vol. 32, No. 3, August.

Freixas, X., P. Hartmann and C. Mayer (2004), "The Assessment: European Financial Integration", Oxford Review of Economic Policy, Vol. 20, No. 4.

Furceri, D. and A. Zdzienicka (2013), "The Euro Area Crisis: Need for a Supranational Fiscal Risk Sharing Mechanism?", IMF Working Paper, No. WP/13/198, September.

Gai, P. and S. Kapadia (2010), "Contagion in financial networks", Proceedings of the Royal Society A, doi:10.1098/rspa.2009.0410.

Garcia de Andoain, C., P. Hoffmann, S. Manganelli (2014), "Fragmentation in the Euro overnight unsecured money market", *Economics Letters*, Vol. 125, No. 2, November, pp. 298–302.

Gilson, R. J. and R. Kraakman (1983), "The Mechanisms of Market Efficiency", *Virginia Law Review*, Vol. 70, pp. 549-644.

Gilson, R. J. and R. Kraakman (2003), "The Mechanisms of Market Efficiency Twenty Years Later: The Hindsight Bias", *Journal of Corporation Law*, Vol. 28, p. 715.

Giordano, L. and C. Guagliano (2014), "Financial architecture and the source of growth", CONSOB Working Papers, No. 78, July.

Giovannini Group (The) (2002), "Cross-border clearing and settlement arrangements in the European Union", *Economic Papers*, No. 163, Brussels, February.

Giovannini Group (The) (2003), "Second Report on EU Clearing and Settlement Arrangements", Brussels, April.

Goldsmith, R. W. (1969), *Financial structure and development*, New Haven, CT: Yale University Press.

Gorton, G. (1988), "Banking Panics and Business Cycles", *Oxford Economic Papers*, New Series, Vol. 40, No. 4, December, pp. 751-781.

Grossman, E., and Leblond, P. (2011), "European Financial Integration: Finally the Great Leap Forward?", *Journal of Common Market Studies*, Vol. 49, No. 2, pp. 413-435.

Grossman, S. J., and Hart, O. D. (1986), "The costs and benefits of ownership: A theory of vertical and lateral integration", *Journal of Political Economy*, Vol. 94, No. 4, pp. 691-719.

Grossman, S. J., and O. D. Hart (1980), "Takeover bids, the free-rider problem, and the theory of the corporation", *Bell Journal of Economics*, Vol. 11, No. 1, pp. 42-64.

Hail, L., and Leuz, C. (2006), "International differences in the cost of equity capital: Do legal institutions and securities regulation matter?", *Journal of Accounting Research*, Vol. 44, No. 3, pp. 485-531.

Hail, L., Leuz, C., and Wysocki, P. (2010), "Global accounting convergence and the potential adoption of IFRS by the US (Part I): Conceptual underpinnings and economic analysis", *Accounting Horizons*, Vol. 24, No. 3, pp. 355-394.

Hardouvelis, G. A., D. Malliaropulos, R. Priestley (2006), "EMU and European Stock Market Integration", *Journal of Business*, Vol. 79, No. 1, pp. 365-392.

Hart, O. (2001), "Financial Contracting", Harvard John M. Olin Discussion Paper Series, No. 327, May.

Hartmann, P., A. Maddaloni and S. Manganelli (2003), "The Euro-Area Financial System: Structure, Integration and Policy Initiatives", *Oxford Review of Economic Policy*, Vol. 19, No. 1.

Hasan, I., H. Schmiedel and L. Song (2012), "Growth Strategies and Value Creation: What Works Best for Stock Exchanges?", *Financial Review*, Vol. 47, pp. 469-499.

Healy, P. M. and K. G. Palepu (2001), "Information asymmetry, corporate disclosure, and the capital markets: A review of the empirical disclosure literature", *Journal of Accounting and Economics*, Vol. 31, pp. 405-440.

Heine, K. and W. Kerber (2002), "European Corporate Laws, Regulatory Competition and Path Dependence",

Heine, K. and W. Kerber (2002), "European Corporate Laws, Regulatory Competition, and Path Dependence", *European Journal of Law and Economics*, Vol. 13, pp. 47-71.

Hermalin, B. E., A. Katz and R. Craswell (2007), "Contract Law", in *Handbook of Law and Economics*, Vol. 1, edited by A. M. Polinsky and S. Shavell, Elsevier.

Hertig, G. and J. A. McCahery (2003), "Company and Takeover Law Reforms in Europe: Misguided Harmonization Efforts or Regulatory Competition?", ECGI Law Working Paper, n. 12/2003, August.

Hertig, G. (1994), "Imperfect Mutual Recognition for EC Financial Services", *International Review of Law and Economics*, Vol. 14, pp. 177-186.

Holmstrom, B. (1979), "Moral Hazard and Observability", *Bell Journal of Economics*, Vol. 10, No. 1, pp. 74-91, Spring.

Holmström, B. and J. Tirole, "Market Liquidity and Performance Monitoring", *Journal of Political Economy*, Vol. 101, No. 4, pp. 678-709.

ICMA (2015), "European Repo Market Survey", No. 29.

IMF (2012), "The liberalization and management of capital flows: an institutional view", Staff Document, Washington, DC, November 14th.

International Monetary Fund (2013), "Towards A Fiscal Union for the Euro Area: Technical Background Notes", Washington DC, September.

International Organization of Securities Commissions - IOSCO (2015), "Credible Deterrence In The Enforcement Of Securities Regulation", Report of IOSCO's Committee 4 on Enforcement and the Exchange of Information, June.

IODS (2014), "Study on the Performance and Efficiency of the EU Asset Management Industry", A study for the European Commission (Internal Market and Services DG) and the Financial Services User Group (FSUG), August (http://ec.europa.eu/finance/finservices-retail/docs/fsug/papers/1410-eu-asset-management-industry_en.pdf).

Jackson, H. E. and M. J. Roe (2009), "Public and private enforcement of securities laws: Resource-based evidence", *Journal of Financial Economics*, Vol. 93, pp. 207-238.

Jappelli, T. and L. Pistaferri (2011), "Financial integration and consumption smoothing", *Economic Journal*, Vol. 121, June, pp. 678–706.

Jappelli, T. and M. Pagano (2008), "Financial Market integration under EMU", CFS Working Paper, No. 2008/33, Goethe University Frankfurt

Jappelli, T. and M. Pagano (2013), "Financial Integration in Europe", in G. Caprio (ed.), *The Evidence and Impact of Financial Globalization*, Vol. 3, pp. 367-378, Oxford, Elsevier.

Jappelli, T., A. M. C. Menichini, M. Padula, M. Pagano (2002), "Analyse, Compare, and Apply Alternative Indicators and Monitoring Methodologies to Measure the Evolution of Capital Market Integration in the European Union", CSEF Working Paper, University of Salerno.

Johnson, S., R. La Porta, F. Lopez-de-Silanes, and A. Shleifer (2000), "Tunneling," *American Economic Review Papers and Proceedings* 90, No. 2, pp. 22-27.

Kalemli-Ozcan, S., B. E. Sorensen and O. Yosha (2004), "Asymmetric shocks and risk sharing in a monetary union: Updated evidence and policy implications for Europe", CEPR Discussion Paper, No. 4463, CEPR London, June.

Kalemli-Ozcan, S., Luttini, E., and Sørensen, B. (2014), "Debt Crises and Risk-Sharing: The Role of Markets versus Sovereigns", *Scandinavian Journal of Economics*, Vol. 116, No. 1, pp. 253-276.

Kalemli-Ozcan, S., Papaioannou, E., and Peydró, J. L. (2010), "What lies beneath the euro's effect on financial integration? Currency risk, legal harmonization, or trade*?", Journal of International Economics*, Vol. 81, No. 1, pp. 75-88.

Karlsson, A. and L. Norden (2007), "Home sweet home: Home bias and international diversification among individual investors", Journal of Banking and Finance, Vol. 31, pp. 317–333.

Katz M. L., and Shapiro C. (1985), "Network Externalities, Competition, and Compatibility," *American Economic Review*, Vol. 75, No. 3, pp. 424-440.

Katz, M. L. and C. Shapiro (1986), "Technology Adoption in the Presence of Network Externalities", *Journal of Political Economy*, Vol. 94, No. 4, August, pp. 822-841.

Kim, S. J., F. Moshirian and E. Wu (2006), "Evolution of international stock and bond market integration: Influence of the European Monetary Union", *Journal of Banking and Finance*, Vol. 30, No. 5, pp. 1507-1534.

King, R. G. and R. Levine (1993), "Finance and Growth: Schumpeter Might be Right", The Quarterly *Journal of Economics,* Vol. 108, No. 3, pp. 717-737.

Klein, B. and K. B. Leffler (1981), "The Role of Market Forces in Assuring Contractual Performance", *Journal of Political Economy*, Vol. 89, No. 4, pp. 615-641.

Kose, A. M., E. S. Prasad, M. E. Terrones (2009), "Does financial globalisation promote risk sharing?", *Journal of Development Economics*, Vol. 89, pp. 258-270.

Kose, M. A., Prasad, E., Rogoff, K. S., and Wei, S. J. (2006), "Financial globalization: a reappraisal", National Bureau of Economic Research Working Paper, No. w12484, August.

Kose, M.A., Prasad, E.S., Terrones, M.E. (2004), "Volatility and co-movement in a globalized world economy: an empirical exploration", in Siebert, H. (ed.), *Macroeconomic Policies in the World Economy*, Springer, Berlin.

KPMG (2014), "Denmark discriminates foreign investment funds", *Alert*, No. 11, November.

Kraakman, R. (1986), "Gatekeepers: The Anatomy of a Third-Party Enforcement Strategy", *Journal of Law, Economics, and Organization*, Vol. 2, No. 1, Spring, pp. 53-104.

Kumar, K. B., R. G., Rajan, and L. Zingales (1999), "What determines firm size?", National Bureau of Economic Research (NBER) Working Paper, No. w7208, July.

Kvaal, E. and C., Nobes (2010), "International differences in IFRS policy choice: a research note", *Accounting and Business Research*, Vol. 40, No. 2, pp. 173-187.

Kvaal, E. and C., Nobes (2012), "IFRS Policy Changes and the Continuation of National Patterns of IFRS Practice", *European Accounting Review*, Vol. 21, No. 2, pp. 343-371.

La Porta, R., F. Lopez-de-Silanes and A. Shleifer (2006), "What works in securities law?", *Journal of Finance*, Vol. 61, No. 1, February.

La Porta, R., F. Lopez-de-Silanes, A. Shleifer, R. Vishny (1996), "Law and Finance", NBER Working Paper, 5661, July.

La Porta, R., F. Lopez-de-Silanes, A. Shleifer and R. Vishny (1997), "Legal Determinants of External Finance", *Journal of Finance*, Vol. 52, No. 3, July, pp. 1131-1150.

La Porta, R., F. Lopez-de-Silanes, A. Shleifer and R. Vishny (1999), "The Quality of Government", The Journal of Law, Economics, and Organisation, Vol. 15, No. 1.

La Porta, R., F. Lopez-de-Silanes, A. Shleifer and R. Vishny (2000), "Investor protection and corporate governance", *Journal of Financial Economics,* Vol. 58, pp. 3-27.

Lamandini, M., D. Ramos Muños and J. Solana Álvarez (2015), "Depicting the limits to the SSM's supervisory powers: The Role of Constitutional Mandates and of Fundamental Rights' Protection", *Quaderni di Ricerca Giuridica*, No. 79, Bank of Italy, October.

Lambert, R., C. Leuz and R. Verrecchia (2007), "Accounting Information, Disclosure and the Cost of Capital", *Journal of Accounting Research*, Vol. 45, No. 2, May.

Lane, P. (2013), "Capital flows in the Euro area", CEPR Discussion Paper, No. 9493, London, May.

Lane, P. R. (2008), "EMU and Financial Integration", IIIS Discussion Paper, No. 272, December.

Lane, P. R. and G. M. Milesi-Ferretti (2007), "The International Equity Holdings of Euro Area Investors," in *The Importance of the External Dimension for the Euro Area: Trade, Capital*

Flows, and International Macroeconomic Linkages (Robert Anderton and Filippo di Mauro, eds), Cambridge University Press, 2007.

Langfield, S. and M. Pagano (2015), "Bank bias in Europe: Effects on systemic risk and growth", *Economic Policy*, 61st Panel meeting, Bank of Latvia, March.

Lannoo, K. (2014), "ECB Banking Supervision and Beyond", CEPS Task Force Report, Centre for European Policy Studies, Brussels, December.

de Larosière Group (2009), "The high-level group on financial supervision in the EU", Brussels, 25 February (http://ec.europa.eu/finance/general-policy/docs/de_larosiere_report_en.pdf).

Leuz, C. and R. Verrecchia (2000), "The Economic Consequences of Increased Disclosure", *Journal of Accounting Research*, Vol. 38, Supplement.

Leuz, C. (2010), "Different approaches to corporate reporting regulation: how jurisdictions differ and why", *Accounting and Business Research*, Vol. 40, No. 3, pp. 229-256.

Leuz, C., Nanda, D., and Wysocki, P. D. (2003), "Earnings management and investor protection: an international comparison", *Journal of Financial Economics*, Vol. 69, No. 3, pp. 505-527.

Levine, R. and S. Zervos (1998), "Stock Markets, Banks, and Economic Growth", *American Economic Review*, Vol. 88, No. 3, pp. 537-558.

Levine, R. (1997), "Financial Development and Economic Growth: Views and Agenda", *Journal of Economic Literature,* Vol. 35, No. 2, pp. 688-726.

Levine, R. (2002), "Bank-based or market-based financial systems: which is better?", *Journal of Financial Intermediation*, 11, pp. 398-428.

London Economics (2002), "Quantification of the Macro-Economic Impact of Integration of EU Financial Markets", Final Report to the European Commission, Directorate General for the Internal Market, November.

Lozano-Vivas, A., S. C. Kumbhakar, M. D. Fethi, and M. Shaban (2011), "Consolidation in the European banking industry: how effective is it?", *Journal of Productivity Analysis*, Vol. 36, No. 3, pp. 247-261.

Luintel K. B., K. Mosahid, P. Arestis, K. Theodoridis (2008), "Financial structure and economic growth", Journal of Development Economics, 86, pp.181-200.

Maes, I. (2008), "A Single European Financial Market: A Progress Report After Half a Century", Speech US Fed of St. Louis, 14-16 May 2008.

Manganelli, S., and A. Popov, A. (2013), "Financial dependence, global growth opportunities, and growth revisited", *Economics Letters*, Vol. 120, No. 1, pp. 123-125.

Massolution (2015), "2015CF – Crowdfunding Industry Report" (http://reports.crowdsourcing.org/index.php?route=product/product&product_id=54#oid=1001_23_banner_38).

Mattei, U. 2000, Comparative Law and Economics, Ann Arbor, MI: University of Michigan Press.

McKinnon, R. I. (1973), *Money and capital in economic development*, Brookings Institution Press.

Mendoza, E. G., V. Quadrini, J.-V. Rios-Rull (2007), "Financial integration, financial deepness, and global imbalances", NBER Working Paper Series, No. 12909, February.

Merler, S. and J. Pisani-Ferry (2012), "Sudden stops in the Euro area", Bruegel Policy Contribution, No. 2012/06, March.

Mersch, Y. (2015), "Advancing Monetary Union", speech given at the Euro Exhibition, Osnabruck, January 25th.

Michael M., A. J. Padilla and M. Pagano (2001), "Collateral versus Project Screening: A Model of Lazy Banks", *RAND Journal of Economics*, Vol. 32, No. 4, pp. 726-744.

Miles, D. (1996), "The Future of Savings and Wealth Accumulation: Differences Within the Developed Economies," London: Global Securities Research and Economics Group, Merrill Lynch.

Milesi-Ferretti, G. M., & Tille, C. (2011), "The great retrenchment: international capital flows during the global financial crisis", *Economic Policy*, Vol. 26, No. 66, pp. 285-342.

Milgrom, P. and J. Roberts (1992), *Economics, Organization and Management,* Prentice Hall Inc., New Jersey.

Morduch, J. (1995), "Income Smoothing and Consumption Smoothing", *Journal of Economic Perspectives*, Vol. 9, No. 3, pp. 103-114.

OECD (2013), "TRACE Implementation Package for the adoption of the authorised intermediary system", Committee of Fiscal Affairs and the Business and Industry Advisory Committee, Final Report (www.oecd.org/ctp/exchange-of-tax-information/TRACE_Implementation_Package_Website.pdf).

Oliver Wyman (2014), "Towards better capital markets solutions for SME financing", Financial Service (www.oliverwyman.com/content/dam/oliver-wyman/global/en/files/insights/financial-services/2014/July/FINAL3_BetterCapitalMarketMechanismsSMEs.pdf).

Oliver, P. and J-P. Baché (1989), "Free movement of capital between the member states: recent developments", *Common Market Law Review*, Vol. 26, pp. 61-81.

Pagano, M. (1989), "Trading Volume and Asset Liquidity", *Quarterly Journal of Economics*, Vol. 104, No. 2, May, pp. 255-274.

Pagano, M. (1993), "Financial Markets and Growth: An Overview", *European Economic Review*, Vol. 37, pp. 613-622.

Pagano, M. (2012), "Finance: Economic Lifeblood or Toxin?", in *The Social Value of the Financial Sector Too Big to Fail or Just Too Big?, World Scientific Studies in International Economics*, Vol. 29, pp. 109-146.

Pagano, M., S. Langfield, V. Acharya, A. Boot, M. Brunnermeier, C. Buch, M. Hellwig, A. Sapir and I. van den Burg (2014), "Is Europe overbanked?", Report No.4 of the European Systemic Risk Board's Advisory Scientific Committee.

Papaioannou, E. (2007), "Finance and growth: a macroeconomic assessment of the evidence from a European angle", ECB Working Paper Series, No. 787, July.

Partnoy, F. (2001), "Barbarians at the Gatekeepers: a Proposal for a Modified Strict Liability Regime", 79 *Washington University Law Quarterly*.

Petersen, M. A. and R. G. Rajan (1994), "The Benefits of Lending Relationships: Evidence from Small Business Data", *Journal of Finance*, Vol. XLIX, No.1, March.

Petersen, M. A. and R. G. Rajan (1995), "The Effect of Credit Market Competition on Lending Relationship", *Quarterly Journal of Economics*, Vol. 110, No. 2, May.

Pistor, K. (2013), "A legal theory of finance", *Journal of Comparative Economics*, Vol. 41, No. 2, pp. 315-330.

Portes, R. and H. Rey (2005), "The determinants of cross-border equity flows", *Journal of International Economics*, Vol. 65, pp. 269-296.

Portes, R., H. Rey and Y. Oh (2001), "Information and capital flows: The determinants of transactions in financial assets", *European Economic Review*, Vol. 45, pp. 783-796.

Posner, R. (1998), "Creating a Legal Framework for Economic Development", The World Bank Research Observer, Vol. 13, No.1, pp. 1-11

PWC (2012), "UCITS funds distribution 2012" (http://download.pwc.com/ie/pubs/2012_ucits_fund_distribution_exec_summary.pdf).

PWC (2015), "Global financial markets liquidity study", Study commissioned by IIF and GFMA, August (www.iif.com/publication/regulatory-report/pwc-global-financial-markets-liquidity-study).

Quaglia, L. (2010), "Completing the single market in financial services: the politics of competing advocacy coalitions", *Journal of European Public Policy*, Vol. 17, No.7, pp. 1007-1023.

Radaelli, C. (2004), "The Puzzle of Regulatory Competition", *Journal of Public Policy*, Vol. 14, No. 1, pp. 1-23.

Rajan, R. G. and L. Zingales (1998b), "Which Capitalism? Lessons from the East Asian Crisis", *Journal of Applied Corporate Finance*, Vol. 11, No. 3, Fall.

Rajan, R. G. and L. Zingales (2001), "The Influence of the Financial Revolution on the Nature of Firms", *Organizational Economics*, Vol. 91, No. 2, pp. 206-211.

Rajan, R. G. (2012), "Presidential Address: The Corporation in Finance", *Journal of Finance*, Vol. 67, No. 4, August.

Rajan, R. G. (2012), "Presidential Address: The Corporation in Finance", *Journal of Finance*, Vol. 67, No. 4, pp. 1173-1217

Rajan, R.G. and L. Zingales (1998a), "Financial dependence and growth", *American Economic Review*, Vol. 88, No. 3, pp. 559-586.

Ramos, S. B. (2003), "Competition Between Stock Exchanges: A Survey", FAME research Paper, No.77, February.

Rangvid, J., P. Santa-Clara, M. Schmeling (2014), "Capital Market Integration and Consumption Risk Sharing over the Long Run", Working Paper, January, available at ssrn.com.

Reinhart, C. M. and Kenneth S. Rogoff (2010), "Growth in a Time of Debt", The American Economic Review, Vol. 100, No. 2, Papers and proceedings of the 122nd Annual Meeting of the American Economic Association, pp. 573-578.

Rochet, J.-C. and J. Tirole (2003), "Platform Competition in Two-Sided Markets", *Journal of the European Economic Association*, Vol. 1, No. 4, pp. 990-1029.

Ross, S.A. (1973), "The Economic Theory of Agency: The Principal's Problem", *American Economic Review*, Vol. 63, No. 2, pp. 134-139.

Sapir, A. and G. Wolff (2013), "The neglected side of banking union: reshaping Europe's financial system", Note presented at the informal ECOFIN 14 September 2013, Vilnius.

Schmidt R.H. and M. Tyrell (1997), "Financial systems, corporate finance and corporate governance", *European Financial Management*, Vol. 3, No. 3, pp. 333-361.

services in Europe", *European Journal of Operational Research*, Vol. 150, pp. 466–481.

Sharpe, S. A. (1990), "Asymmetric information, bank lending, and implicit contracts: A stylized model of customer relationships", *Journal of Finance*, Vol. 45, No. 4, pp. 1069-1087.

Shevlin, T. (1996), "The value-relevance of nonfinancial information: A discussion", *Journal of Accounting and Economics*, Vol. 22, pp. 31-42.

Shleifer, A. and R. Vishny (2011), "Fire Sales in Finance and Macroeconomics", Journal of Economic Perspectives, Vol. 25, No. 1, pp. 29-48.

Shleifer, A., and R. W. Vishny (1992), "Liquidation Values and Debt Capacity: A Market Equilibrium Approach," *Journal of Finance*, Vol. 47, No.4, pp. 1343–66.

Sorensen, B. E. and O. Yosha (1998), "International risk sharing and European monetary unification", *Journal of International Economics*, Vol. 45, pp. 211-238.

Sorensen, B.E., Y.-T. Wu, O. Yosha, Y. Zhu (2007), "Home bias and international risk sharing: Twin puzzles separated at birth", *Journal of International Money and Finance*, Vol. 26, pp. 587-605.

Spiegel, M. M. (2009), "Monetary and financial integration in the EMU: push or pull?", *Review of International Economics*, Vol. 17, No. 4, pp. 751-776.

Standard & Poor's (2014), "Why Inconsistent Reporting Of Exceptional Items Can Cloud Underlying Profitability At Nonfinancial FTSE 100 Companies", RatingsDirect Analysis, February 18th.

Steil, B. (1999), "Regional financial market integration: learning from the European experience", Tokyo Club Papers, Vol. 12.

Stiglitz, J. E. and A. Weiss (1981), "Credit Rationing in Markets with Imperfect Information", *American Economic Review*, Vol. 71, No. 3, pp. 393-410, June.

Strategic Insight (2011), "Fund fees in Europe: Analyzing investment management fees, distribution fees, and operating expenses", Study prepared for EFAMA, October (www.efama.org/Publications/Statistics/Other%20Reports/EFAMA_Fund%20Fees%20in%20Europe%202011.pdf).

Sun, J.-M. and J. Pelkmans (1995), "Regulatory Competition in the Single Market", *Journal of Common Market Studies*, Vol. 33, No. 1, March.

Tabb, C. J. (1995), "The history of the bankruptcy laws in the United States", *ABI Law Review*, Vol. 3, No. 6.

Tax Barriers Business Advisory Group T-BAG (2013), "Workable solutions for efficient and simplified fiscal compliance procedures related to post-trading within the EU", Final Report (http://ec.europa.eu/internal_market/financial-markets/docs/clearing/tbag/130524_tbag-report-2013_en.pdf).

Thakor, A. V. (1989), "Strategic Issues in Financial Contracting", *Journal of Financial Management Association*, Summer.

Valiante, D. and K. Lannoo (2011), *MiFID 2.0: Casting New Light on Europe's Capital Market,* CEPS Task Force Report, CEPS, Brussels.

Valiante, D. (2013), Commodities Price Formation: Financialisation and Beyond, CEPS-ECMI Task Force Report, CEPS Paperback, CEPS, Brussels.

Ventoruzzo, M. (2014), "Do Market Abuse Rules Violate Human Rights? The Grande Stevens v. Italy Case", ECGI Law Working Paper N° 269/2014, October.

Verdier, P. H. (2011), "Mutual Recognition in International Finance", *Harvard International Law Journal*, 52(1).

Walter, I. (2002), Financial integration across borders and across sectors: implications for regulatory structures", in J. M. Kremers, D. Schoenmaker, P. J. Wierts (2002), *Financial Supervision in Europe,* Edward Eldgar Publishing.

Weill, L. (2009), "Convergence in banking efficiency across European countries", *Journal of International Financial Markets, Institutions and Money*, Vol. 19, pp. 818-833.

Wessels, B. (2003), "International Jurisdiction To Open Insolvency Proceedings in Europe, in Particular Against Groups of Companies", Institute for Law and Finance, Working Paper No.17, Goethe University, Frankfurt.

Williamson, O. E. (1979), "Transaction-cost economics: the governance of contractual relations", *Journal of Law and Economics*, Vol. 22, No. 2, pp. 233-261

Williamson, O. E. (1985), *The Economic Institutions of Capitalism: Firms, Markets, Relational Contracting*, New York, NY: Free Press.

Williamson, S. (1986), "Costly monitoring, financial intermediation, and equilibrium credit rationing", *Journal of Monetary Economics*, 18, pp. 1519-179.

Annex 1. Matching objectives and proposals of the CMU action plan

Key objective	Actions	Purpose
More funding opportunities for European firms (SMEs, in particular)	- *Funds-of-funds in EuVECA* - *EuVECA & EuSEF option for large fund managers* - Best practices on tax incentives for EuVECAs & SEFs - Harmonised feedback for SME bank loans - Pan-European credit information system (SMEs) - EU advisory hub for SMEs - Regime for loan-originating funds - Best practices for private placement	- Open access to institutional investors - Promote availability of start-up equity capital - Increase information flows from SMEs to banks and vice versa - Fostering new funding models (loans & debt securities)
Improving the listing environment	- A European advisory structures for issuers - *Higher threshold for prospectus (>€500k)* - *More lenient listing requirements in SME growth markets* - Monitor liquidity in corporate bond secondary markets - Support for voluntary & tailor-made accounting standards for SMEs - Proposal on common corporate tax base & opening discussion on debt/equity bias	- Streamline information and reduce one-off and ongoing costs for SMEs equity listing - Reduce tax bias between equity and debt instruments
Boosting long-term finance	- *Amendments to Solvency II to favour investments in infrastructure and ELTIFs* - *Amendments to CRR to favour investments in infrastructure* - Assessment of cumulative impact of reforms on the investment environment - Attention to environment, social & governance (ESG)	- Facilitate channelling of investments from institutional investors and banks in project finance
Fostering EU-wide distribution of financial instruments for retail and institutional investors	- *Green Paper on retail financial services and insurance* - Comprehensive assessment of distribution & advice channels of investment products for retail investors to define potential policy actions - Evaluation of a European personal pension product	- Improve cross-border choice and access to investment products for retail investors (for investment and retirement) - Promote access for investments of institutional

	- Assessment of potential amendments to Solvency II for private equity and privately placed debt	investors (e.g. insurance) and remove barriers to cross-border distribution
Increasing bank funding capacity	- Promoting credit unions across Europe - *Amendments to Solvency II and CRR for Simple, Transparent & Standardised (STS) Securitisation* - *Consultation on a pan-European regime for covered bonds*	- Provide additional funding sources for SMEs - Restart capital market-based funding for banks to improve access to finance for SMEs
Eliminating infrastructure barriers to cross-border investing	- Proposal for uniform rules to ensure certainty surrounding security ownership - Review of the progress on the removal of the Giovannini barriers for post-trading and cross-border clearing and settlement - Map and remove barriers to free movement of capital, using a 'collaborative approach' with national authorities (with a report at the end of 2016) - Legislative proposal on business insolvency to remove barriers to capital flow - Withholding tax relief principles and investigation on tax obstacles for life insurers and pension funds - Macroprudential review of market-based finance	- Uniform application of the single rulebook and updated macroprudential framework - Removal of barriers to free movement of capital for market infrastructure and selected areas (e.g. insolvency) - Limit double taxation in cross-border financial transactions

Notes: Actions appearing in italics will be immediately implemented as a result of this plan. ELTIFs, EuVECAs and EuSEFs stand for European Long-Term Investment Funds, European Venture Capital Funds and European Social Entrepreneurship Funds. More information is available at http://ec.europa.eu/finance/investment/index_en.htm. They are a sub-category of alternative funds investing in specific assets, according to European legislation, and can use the European passport granted to alternative investment fund managers.

Source: Author from European Commission (2015a & 2015b).

Annex 2. Task Force Members and Observers

TASK FORCE

Sandra Anderson, Junior Policy Assistant, FESE

Javier Arias, Head Representative to the EU, BBVA

Sara Baldi, Senior Policy Adviser, Federation of European Securities Exchanges (FESE)

Mathias Bauer, Advisor to the Board, Raiffeisen Zentralbank Österreich AG

Mark van Binsbergen, Managing Director, Debt Capital Markets, Rabobank

Nick Collier, Global Head of Government & Regulatory Affairs, Thomson Reuters

Daniele De Gennaro, Policy Adviser, Financial Markets, European Banking Federation

Godfried De Vidts, Director of European Affairs, ICAP

Bernard Delbecque, Director, Economics and Research, EFAMA

Alexandra Dimitrijevic, Head of Corporate Research, Standard & Poor's

Jan Eger, Manager, Head of Financial Services, Government and Regulatory Affairs, Thomson Reuters

Carey Evans, Director, Government Relations & Public Policy, BlackRock

Annalaura Gallo, Consultant, Afore Consulting

Judith Hardt, Managing Director, Swiss Finance Council

Priyanka Harkness, Government and Regulatory Affairs, Deutsche Bank AG

Georg J. Huber, Deputy Head of the EU Representative Office, Head of EU-Policies, Association of German Savings Banks (DSGV)

Peter Jayaswal, Deputy Director, Association of Danish Mortgage Banks (Realkreditrådet)

Elisabeth Ottawa, Head of RZB EU Liaison Office, Raiffeisen Zentralbank Österreich AG

Carlos Pardo, Chief Economist, AFG (French Asset Management Association)

Ilse Peeters, Director, Corporate Strategy and Public Affairs, Euroclear S.A.

Pedro Pinto, Director of Advocacy, AFME

Ben Pott, Head of European Affairs, ICAP

Victoria Powell, Policy Director, Capital Markets, British Bankers' Association

David Reed, Partner, Head of Financial Services, Kreab Gavin Anderson

Nickolas Reinhardt, Director, Afore Consulting

Rainer Riess, Director General, FESE

Benoit Sauvage, Senior Adviser Financial Market Regulations, ABBL - Luxembourg Bankers' Association

Sander Schol, Vice President, Government Relations, JP Morgan & Chase

Sally Scutt, Deputy Chief Executive, British Bankers' Association and Member of Executive Committee, European Banking Federation

Daniel Trinder, Managing Director, Global Head of Regulatory Policy Deutsche Bank

Geert Vanderbeke, Executive Director, Global Sales & Sales Support, ABN AMRO Clearing

Rick Watson, Managing Director and Head of Capital Markets

Paul Watters, Senior Director, Standard & Poor's/

Ed Wells, Head of Global Markets Policy, HSBC

DISCUSSANTS

Luca Bagato, Sales and Business Development, EuroTLX

John Barrass, Deputy Chief Executive, Wealth Management Association

Leonie Bell, DG FISMA, Financial Market Analyst

Paul A. Bodart, T2S Board Member, European Central Bank

Carsten Borring, Head of Listings and Capital Market, NASDAQ Denmark

Evelyn Bunn, Director, Head of Banking Accounting Advisory, KMPG UK

Luigi Campa, Managing Director, Strategy, Business Development & Administration, EuroTLX

Giusy Chesini, Professor of Economics of Financial Intermediaries, University of Verona, Department of Business Administration

Stuart Corrigall, Director (Solicitor), Head of Product Structuring, Blackrock

Miguel de la Mano, Executive Vice President, Compass Lexecon, former Head of Unit, Economic Analysis of Financial Markets, European Commission

Bernard Delbecque, Director, Economics and Research, EFAMA

Alexandra Dimitrijevic, Head of Corporate Research, Standard & Poor's

Françoise Flores, Chairwomen, European Financial Reporting Advisory Group

Werner Frey, Managing Director. Post, Trade, AFME

Mauro Grande, Director of Strategy and Policy Coordination, Single Resolution Board, former Adviser to the ECB Executive Board

Ali Kazimi, Partner-Financial Services, Mazars

Philipp Paech, International financial markets law and regulation, London School of Economics

Raj S. Panasar, Partner, Cleary Gottlieb Steen & Hamilton LLP

Markus Schaber, CEO, European Datawarehouse

Caro van den Broeck, Institute for Commercial and Insolvency Law, KU Leuven

Juan Manuel Viver, Policy Officer, Better Finance

Rick Watson, Managing Director and Head of Capital Markets, AFME

Bob Wessels, Professor of International Insolvency Law, University of Leiden

ACADEMIC OBSERVERS

James Barr, Visiting Fellow, The Policy Institute, King's College London

Oronzo Daloiso, EU Account Manager, Paragon Europe

Nicholas Dorn, Associate Research Fellow, Institute of Advanced Legal Studies, School of Advanced Study University of London

Guillaume Hingel, Head of Research, The Banker, Financial Times Limited

Tamar Joulia-Paris, Lecturer at Facultés Universitaires Saint-Louis and Risk Senior, TJ Capital

Josué Mathieu, FNRS Researcher, Université Libre de Bruxelles

Caroline Metz, PhD, Politics, School of Social Sciences, University of Manchester

Anthony S. Theuma, President of Paragon Europe, Professor of Research and Innovation, University of Malta

Gerda Zigiene, Associate Professor, Vilnius University, CEO, Lithuanian Financial Markets Institute

POLICY OBSERVERS

Leonie Bell, DG FISMA, Financial Market Analyst

Wouter Coussens, Head of ECB Representative Office in Brussels

Marit de Vrijer, Policy Expert, Autoriteit Financiele Markten (AFM)

Angelos Delivorias, European Parliamentary Research Service

Johanne Evrard, Economist, Directorate General EU Institutions & Fora, European Central Bank

Jean-Luc Filippini, Principal Administrator, General Secretariat of the Council

Luc Goupil, Economist, Analysis, Strategy and Risk Division, Autorité des Marchés Financiers (AMF)

Mauro Grande, Director of Strategy and Policy Coordination, Single Resolution Board, former Adviser to the ECB Executive Board

Steffen Kern, Head of Economics and Financial Stability at the European Securities and Markets Authority (ESMA)

Kimmo Koskinen, Senior Economist, Bank of Finland

Sven Langedijk, Researcher, Joint Research Center, Ispra, European Commission

Gert Luiting, Manager, Public & International Affairs, Netherlands Authority for the Financial Markets (AFM)

Gundars Ostrovskis, Senior Economist, Economic Analysis and Evaluation Unit, DG FISMA, European Commission

Eric Perée, Deputy Director, Institutional Strategy Department, European Investment Bank

Michaela Posch, DG Macro-Prudential Policy & Financial Stability, European Central Bank

George Zavvos, Legal Adviser, European Commission

RESEARCH SUPPORT

Cosmina Amariei, Research Assistant, European Capital Markets Institute

Jan-Martie Frie, Policy Analyst, Economics Team, European Political Strategy Centre (EPSC), former Research Assistant, European Capital Markets Institute

Annex 3. List of Abbreviations

ADR	Alternative Dispute Resolution
AFME	Association for Financial Markets in Europe
AI	Authorised Intermediaries
AIFMD	Alternative Investment Fund Managers Directive
AIFs	Alternative Investment Funds
AQR	Asset Quality Review
AuM	Assets under Management
BIS	Bank for International Settlements
BoJ	Bank of Japan
BoS	Board of Supervisors
BU	Banking Union
CCCTB	Common Consolidated Corporate Tax Base
CCPs	Central Counterparties
CDO/CLO	Collateralised Debt Obligation /Collateralised Loan Obligations
CEAOB	Committee of National Auditing Oversight Bodies
CEEC	Commission of the European Economic Community
CEPS	Centre for European Policy Studies
CICC	Collective Investments in Transferable Securities
CMBS	Commercial Mortgage-backed Security
CMU	Capital Markets Union
COMI	Centre of Main Interest
CPIS-IMF	Coordinated Portfolio Investment Survey-International Monetary Fund
CRA	Credit Rating Agency
CRD	Capital Requirements Directive
CRR	Capital Requirements Regulation
CSD	Central Securities Depository
EBA	European Banking Authority
EBBO	European Best and Bid Offer
ECB	European Central Bank
ECJ	European Court of Justice
ECMEG	European Capital Markets Expert Group
ECMI	European Capital Markets Institute
ECU	European Currency Unit
EDGAR	Electronic Data Gathering, Analysis, and Retrieval system
EEC	European Economic Community
EECS	European Enforcers Coordination Sessions

EFAMA	European Fund and Asset Management Association
EGCs	Emerging Growth Companies
EMEA	Europe, the Middle East and Africa
EMS	European Monetary System
EMU	European Economic and Monetary Union
ENF	Enforcement
EOBs	Electronic Order Books
ERM	Exchange Rate Mechanism
ESAs	European Supervisory Agencies
ESCB	European System of Central Banks
ESG	Environment, Social & Governance
ESMA	European Securities and Markets Authority
ESRB	European Systemic Risk Board
EU	European Union
EuroPP	Euro Private Placement
EuSEF	European Social Entrepreneurship Funds
EuVECA	European Venture Capital Funds
EVCA	European Private Equity & Venture Capital Association
EXE	Execution
FCD	Financial Collateral Directive
FDI	Foreign Direct Investment
Fed or FED	Federal Reserve
FESE	Federation Of European Securities Exchanges
FIN-NET	Financial Dispute Resolution Network
FINTEC	Financial Technologies
FOS	Financial Ombudsman Service
FSAP	Financial Services Action Plan
FSP	Foreign Service Provider
GDP	Gross Domestic Product
GNP	Gross National Product
HH	Households
MTF	Multilateral Trading Facility
IAS	International Accounting Standards
IASB	International Accounting Standards Board
IC & PF	Insurance Companies & Pension Funds
ICAEW	Institute of Chartered Accountants in England and Wales
ICMA	International Capital Market Association
ICSDs	International Central Securities Depositories
IDB	Inter-Dealer Business

IFRS	International Financial Reporting Standards
IMF	International Monetary Fund
IOSCO	International Organization of Securities Commissions
IPO	Initial Public Offerings
ISD	Investment Services Directive
ISDA	International Swaps and Derivatives Association
KID	Key Information Document
LIFFE	London International Financial Futures and Options Exchange
LoP	Law of one Price
LSEG	London Stock Exchange Group
MAD	Market Abuse Directive
MFIs	Monetary financial institutions
MiFID	Markets in Financial Instruments Directive
MMF	Money Market Funds
MoUs	Memoranda of Understanding
NCAs	National Competent Authorities
NFCs	Non-financial Corporations
NI	Net Income
NPI	Net Portfolio Investments
NYSE	New York Stock Exchange
OECD	Organisation for Economic Co-operation and Development
OFIs	Other Financial Institutions
OIFs	Other Investment Funds;
OTC	Over-the-counter
PBoC	People's Bank of China
PCS	Prime Collateralised Securities
PD	Price Discovery
PoA	Power of Attorney
PRIIPs	Packaged Retail and Insurance-based Investment Products
PWC	PricewaterhouseCoopers
RBS	Royal Bank of Scotland
RFQ	Request-for-quote
RRP	Repo and Reverse Repo
SBD	Second Banking Directive
SE	Stock Exchange
SEC	Securities and Exchange Commission
SEFs	Social Entrepreneurship Funds
SEIS	Seed Enterprise Investment Scheme
SFD	Settlement Finality Directive

SIFMA	Securities Industry and Financial Markets Association
SMEs	Small and Medium-sized Enterprises
SMP	Single Market Programme
SRM	Single Resolution Mechanism
SSM	Single Supervisory Mechanism
STS	Simple, Transparent & Standardised
TARGET	Trans-European Automated Real-time Gross Settlement Express Transfer
TER	Total Expense Ratio
TFEU	Treaty on the Functioning of the European Union
UCITS	Undertakings for Collective Investments in Transferable Securities
UK	United Kingdom
UNCTAD	United Nations Conference on Trade and Development
US	United States
US GAAP	United States Generally Accepted Accounting Principles
US SEC	United States Securities and Exchange Commission
WFE	World Federation of Exchanges

Index